Harvard University
Graduate School of Design

BARCELONA
the urban evolution of a compact city

Joan Busquets

Nicolodi

Author
Joan Busquets

Graphic design
Giancarlo Stefanati
BAU S.L.

Printed in Italy by
Litografia Stella,
Rovereto (Tn) Italia

©2005 Nicolodi editore
via dell'Artigiano, 30
38068 Rovereto (Tn) Italia
tel. 0039 0464 430330
fax 0039 0464 423808
info@nicolodieditore.it
1^ ristampa: maggio 2006

ISBN 88-8447-204-0

The Harvard University Graduate School
of Design is a leading center for education,
information, and technical expertise
on the built environment. Its departments
of Architecture, Landscape Architecture,
and Urban Planning and Design offer
masters and doctoral degree programs
and provide the foundation for its
Advanced Studies and Executive
Education programs.

Summary

Index of illustrations

Introduction

Barcelona can be considered as the prototype of a Mediterranean European city with a long urban tradition. Cities in the south of Europe have quite specific formal characteristics and processes of historical formation: the density and compactness of their urban form and their evolution by means of extension rather than remodelling sets them apart from the European cities of the north. Furthermore, their Mediterranean nature gives them very temperate climatic conditions and has involved them in the various cultures to have colonised the shores of this historical sea.

This city, with its over 2000 years of history, has played the role of capital of Catalonia in the second half of this period and in the last two centuries has undergone major growth, coinciding with the development of the modern city and its industrial expansion.

In 2004, Barcelona city had 1,578,500 inhabitants in 100 square kilometres, and its metropolitan area had a population of 2.9 million in 478 square kilometres. Almost half the population of Catalonia lives in this area, which represents just 1.5 % of the territory. In the same year, the metropolitan region, the setting for everyday working and living relations, had a population of 5,100,000 inhabitants, representing 80% of Catalonia.

Barcelona is situated on a plain that slopes gently down towards the sea, delimited by the rivers Llobregat and Besòs and the coastal mountain range of Collserola, with its highest point of Tibidabo (512 metres). The Barcelona Plain is only interrupted by the mountain of Montjuïc beside the sea and the *tres turons*, or three hills, in the north.

The plain is a space of confluence for the inland prelittoral corridor that runs in a north-south direction, and the coastline marks out a geographical system that has governed communication axes and modern urban expansion. As this book explains, today's metropolitan space has overflowed this natural space and its everyday influence exceeds the limits of the province of Barcelona.

This initial description of the city aims to prevent confusing this book of interpretation of the urban construction of a compact city with a book about the city's history. Both the scope of the work and the author's training called for other intentions and a different method.

While urban events are generally narrated according to a time sequence in order to allow a better understanding and comparison of historical episodes, a chronological description is not the main theme here. Various histories of Barcelona are used and quoted in the book as a basis for explanation, but it is above all the interventions and projects, the acts and decrees, the ideas and schemes, the strategies and processes marking the physical evolution of the present-day city that are the main characters of the book.

Exploring and interpreting the city and its associated human phenomena are difficult tasks due to the diachronic study of very different moments, making comparison a complex process. If however we give priority to the physical dimension of the city, its spaces and its architectures, we may make faster progress.

The city is time solidified; it crystallises the old territorial configurations and, at the same time, perpetuates the social practices of preceding generations.

All "histories" are based on an analytical approach and an interpretation of salient facts and events. A history of urban development has to take in the territorial and urban experience, and, despite the existence of cultural, economic, ideological and political interpretations, concentrate particular attention on the city's physical dimensions, which influence and to some extent even determine cultural and economic development. This does not mean that we should place greater value on a city's "stone" than on its social evolution; just as an explanation of the economic development of some cities highlights trade as an innovative factor of change, though it affects only a minority of the population, in other cases the city and its physical form represent a true synthesis of the historical development of a society: the ruins of Pompeii, for example, condense its lifestyles, production and its whole culture.

In the city, houses, workplaces, street networks, public spaces, lifestyles, the technical organisation of production and exchange, forms of entertainment and recreation are always shaped by the past and modified by changing times, though there are on occasion typological changes, or changes in forms of procedure that mark a breakaway from preceding systems.

Studies of genetic morphology tend to seek a logic in the evolution of urban forms: firstly, they state the various thresholds of space and time with regard to both major urban development interventions and the countless urban projects effected in small-scale urban fabrics and their transformations; then they interpret the permanence of the network of streets, more lasting than plot divisions, which are dependent on buildings, with their more variable social function.

The decision to highlight the dimensions of urban development in this "history" will call for a valuation of the specific aspects of this young discipline – this "practical knowledge", to use Foucault's expression – of "urbanism" that sets out to understand the city and the urban phenomenon in all their interdisciplinary analytical variables, but also with a specific application to the designs and proposals of urban construction and transformation. Because the history of civilisation in Europe shows that cities are the place of innovation and change: the big cultural and technological events have taken place in cities; they have also been the setting or the expression of the most important political movements and changes.

It is therefore essential to interpret the content of these projects and their social and economic implantation. As the reader will see, these proposals or patterns of urbanisation have shaped the urban form of cities and materialised as specific conditions for demographic, social and political organisation and the reinterpretation of geographical space.

The approach taken by this book is based on the constitution of Barcelona, picking out the operations to shape or design the city that have been crucial to its development. It therefore refers to very differing sources: from archaeological to historical, from urban planning projects to an interpretation of very recent events, from a key architectural design to a new regional organisation... Of all the different periods, priority is given to the evolution of the modern city. Written and graphic depictions also compete for precedence and provide complementary readings. The changing representations of the city are accompanied by variations in the way projects are drawn up, and plans and strategies are expressed, contributing to an understanding of the cultural evolution of urban development.

The history of Barcelona, like so many European cities, shows us how the city has constantly addressed new issues – we might say that each generation conducts its own revision –, and it is useful to understand both the mechanisms of the social, economic and ideological emergence of these themes and the options and projects to which they give rise, consequently introducing new constituent elements of the city. As regards methodology, priority is given to the regulations governing layout and project that give form to the city and its parts, and their relation to forms of social organisation and power structure.

Some periods are of course more prolific or more innovative, just as there are projects with the strength to survive or adapt for several generations, as in the controversial case of the development of Cerdà's Eixample, which therefore became the paradigm of the symbolic identification of the city. This would be the case of great projects such as Haussmann's remodelling of the centre of Paris in the 19th century, leading to the consolidation, though not without great difficulties, of the charismatic image of that great capital.

The histories of cities reveal overlapping processes, and their projects and proposed changes cannot be seen simply from the point of view of the plan or the finished work; it is also important to include their genesis and the mechanisms of change and adaptation that tend to accompany them.

Overlaying the values of innovation and mutation that take place in the city is its symbolic, representative component. A great urban project or a monumental building symbolises forms of coexistence as well as the form of government of the time. Its compositional and figurative content defines the ideology behind it, to some extent idealised by the status accorded socially to any work of art.

Each urban project in the city can be seen as an expression of the power, wealth or even the poverty of the people responsible for its construction and their contemporaries. This is, ultimately, the authentic content of the city and its projects: not the simple satisfaction of functional needs, but the added connotation that extends or changes the balance of power and representativeness of the different social classes. The bourgeois house in the Barcelona of the second half of the 19th century was based on the ideas of order, cleanness, rationalisation and social stratification of an emerging class, which thereby acquired greater social substance. In other cases, the urban project in the city is the result of a conflictive process between what the plan intended and what the city actually constructed: the metropolitan development of the post-war years is an obvious example.

As part of this approach, it is important to point out that while each city has its own origins and civic history, the various geographical areas are marked by broad-based schemes and projects for urban evolution that many cities follow or share in: hence the need for cross references with the processes adopted by other cities.

In turn, the relative brevity of this text requires concentration on the most dynamic or outstanding periods of the city's general history and a summary of studies of urban history, mainly concerning Modern Barcelona, which appear in the footnotes for closer consultation.

The long period that the book aspires to cover suggested presenting the role of Barcelona in the context of Catalonia, especially as the city in itself proved to be a fundamental element in the creation of national identity.

It is hard to look at the past and the present and think about the future, yet this is an exercise that can also offer new fields for reflection on the city. It is also hard to detach oneself from the present-day meaning of the city and its parts, which necessarily requires us to understand that books "belong" to the specific time at when they were written. Because today, we have to see Barcelona as one of the few European cities of the two thousand of a considerable size that existed in the Middle Ages that has been capable of becoming a metropolis. This warrants a study to explain the situation, with all the processes and projects leading to it.

The reader will see that the urban formation process is full of great "historical" contradictions: the great capital of the Mediterranean without a port, the factory of Spain on a site with no energy resources or prime materials...

In the history of Catalonia, the city may have been the civil catalyst of a strong identity, the *cap i casal de Catalunya*; first as a solid fortified town, then as a "hinge" between Old Catalonia, built of stone in the north, and New Catalonia, of rammed earth walls in the south. But it is also the urban system to have suffered most in its fabric from the country's political setbacks, such as those of 1714 or 1936, when it emerged as the "loser".

All of this illustrates the great interest and variety of its urban construction, despite never having had the involvement of great royal or aristocratic projects in its historical development that produced the avenues and parks of European capital cities. The local scale of its projects contrasts with the ambitious, cosmopolitan determination – to produce what the cities in the vanguard produce – that has made many of its schemes so innovative and gives it a special dimension.

Perhaps this is why the rate of urban development has varied so greatly between the long-term projects or plans that have developed fragmentarily and the short-term schemes, such as the big events that have produced singular programmes every half century.

Altogether, this work sets out to offer an interpretation of the evolution and formation of Barcelona on the basis of significant elements of urban development that may be shared by other European cities.

There are excellent works of city interpretation by ages (the medieval, Gothic, baroque, modern city, etc.), geographical location (hill cities, river cities, etc.) or economic importance (market cities, port cities, etc.), but there are few that take as their basis the morphological logic of the city, aspiring to produce a more general interpretation based on urban development. Fortunately, Barcelona has a good bibliography by themes or periods of the development of the city, without which this work would not have been possible; this book owes much to these publications which are duly referred to in the footnotes and throughout the text itself.

This book is divided into ten chapters that interpret the stages of its morphological constitution. The first two guide us through the formation of the medieval city on its Roman origins, which we can identify as a traditional city with its streets, squares and neighbourhoods. While the old town had these elements, their form and content were redefined. Others, such as the town walls and main streets are continually reinterpreted. In this first part, the diachronic description of events is borrowed from "histories" of the city and, alongside the archaeological research, a series of invariables is formulated as to the urban form that takes into account the continuance of street layouts, elements of infrastructure and systems of control that help us to understand what the pre-industrial city was like. The forms of representation of the city are very diverse, and interventions in its construction have as yet been little studied.

As Maurice Halbwachs comments in relation to the evolution of Paris: "The past cannot be conserved and is not represented just as it is. At each stage, society reworks its own memories to adapt them to its present conditions of functioning. By means of a constant process of reconstruction, memory wrings an interpretation of the past out of the present: in the form of collective memory, it strengthens the cohesion of the group in question, it is an integral part of its essence, it is transformed as the group evolves. The same thing happens with space..."

It was with the arrival of the industrial city that urban development schemes became more document-based with the creation of a series of urban planning guidelines that throw some light on the construction of present-day Barcelona.

The role of infrastructure in colonising the territory and its various phases, the different scale of urban development projects, the city as an instrument of social progress and political development, the influence of the urbanism of political defeats, the major dynamics of the population and its habitual demands, movements of cultural and urban innovation, and the strategies behind the great events of 1888, 1929 and 1992 – these are just some of the themes developed in the central chapters.

The 19th-century city marked the entrance of industrialisation into the city with the definition of new urban forms: new types of buildings (stations, markets, restaurants, etc.) and urban planning schemes involving the construction of new streets and the introduction of new services (gas, drainage, etc.). This may seem like the construction of "yesterday's city", with images we know from the cinema and literature, but it existed alongside aspects of the modern city. This was the time of the great new town project, the Eixample; of suburban development and the demolition of the Citadel.

The great urban explosion probably took place in the 20th century, when industrialisation organised the city in accordance with its strong technological development. This was also the period of consolidation of urban development as a technical and social practice. The city was laid out like the big European cities and new morphological proposals took shape. The new county scale developed in the grey post-war period, and the major shortcomings in services in the peripheral city have carried on until our time.

The recovery of Barcelona beginning in the 1980s took the form of an appreciation of existing urban spaces and structures, leading to a rebirth of the city. The urban planning instruments used were many and varied, and quite innovative.

The changes undergone by Barcelona in the last 25 years cannot be explained merely in terms of the designs put forward by an individual or group of people, or a singular, personal determination; they required a broader-based, collective trend or demand that involved the public initiative of the council and its members, but also of architects, groups of local residents, private operators, etc., who clearly defined an awareness of change from what had gone before and formed the basis of a new conception. There has been a breakthrough and a thoroughgoing modernisation of the city and its spaces, but this was a process that extended to the economic context, to collective ambition, civic pride and the affirmation of identity.

Now, in the new century, fresh prospects are opening up due to the European institutional framework and, above all, changes in the economic system that is moving towards a post-industrial phase, marked by different means of communication and a growing feeling that the city we are constructing is not sustainable – it consumes non-renewable energies and produces a great deal that cannot be recycled. The repercussions for urban development are difficult to evaluate, but we can trust to the force with which Barcelona has already overcome major "contradictions" in relation to its port, raw materials and energy sources.

The broad overview presented by this book allows us to avoid the simplistic pitfalls of the catastrophists. But nor is it an end to discussion, as the city will continue to undergo major transformations as it has in the past. However, we will see the force of continuity and morphological transformation. The city continues and reproduces in the same way that seeds and plants change and adapt to similar structures in a continuity that allows mutation.

In any case, today's challenge is to work at understanding the forms of the past when we know that the future "has no form". It will probably be constructed on the basis of a judicious interpretation of history and the correct application of the creative processes that urban culture successively promotes.

Acknowledgements

This work is presented as an open-ended research process, and its current form is a summary of the reading, work and articles of the last thirty years. However, it also represents new hypotheses that will be put to the test in the mid-term.

Most of the works were carried out in the framework of the Laboratori d'Urbanisme (LUB) of Barcelona School of Architecture (ETSAB), of the Universitat Politècnica de Catalunya, for which I would like to thank the Director, Manuel de Solà-Morales, for his advice and friendship; José Luis Gómez Ordóñez for his help and company in many of the discussions; and Antonio Font, Miquel Domingo, Josep Parcerisa, Joaquim Sabaté, Amador Ferrer and Xabier Eizaguirre, among others, for their miscellaneous contributions.

My involvement in the Urban Planning Department of Barcelona City Council, as Director between 1983 and 1989, also allowed me to add new viewpoints to form a comprehensive overview of the city. I have to express my appreciation of the drive and energy of Oriol Bohigas, the solidarity of José A. Acebillo, the exemplary support of Miquel Corominas, Jaume Sanmartí, Ricard Fayos, José A. Tajadura, among others. Two versions of this book have appeared in Spanish, a shorter one in 1992 (Fundación Mapfre) and an extended version in 2004 (El Serbal) which, duly revised, served as the basis for this book.

Much of the book was put together at the Graduate School of Design of Harvard University, and I should like to thank the Dean, Peter Rowe, for his enthusiasm and his example. The task of publication was carried out with the support of Dean Alan Altshuler and Melissa Vaughn, Director of Publications. The English version of the text was made possible by the patient, meticulous work of Elaine Fradley, the initiative of Claudio Nicolodi and Emanuela Zandonai, and the enthusiasm of Rocco Cerone.

This book is also proof of the invaluable practical support of Maria Mercè Busquets and Rosa Bastías, who typed it out, and of the graphic design work of Antonio Moro and Jaume Barnada, in the first phase, and David Moncusí, Maria Elena de la Torre and Montse Vendrell, in this. But, finally, the book would never have existed without the constant, generous encouragement of Rosalía, to whom I owe the additional energy that an undertaking of this scope requires.

J.B.
Barcelona, July 2005

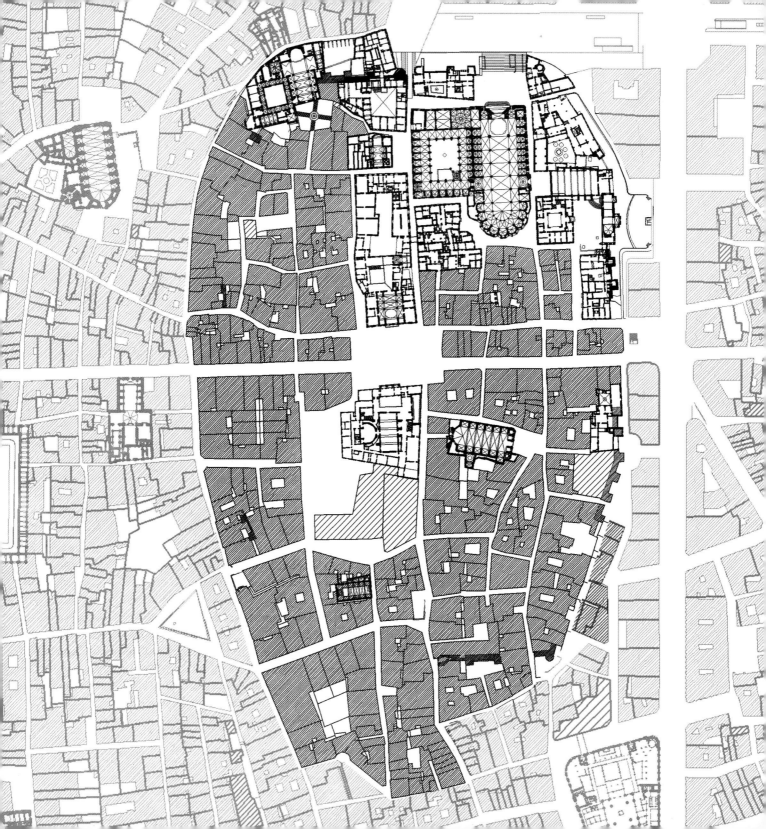

I.

From its origins to capital of the medieval Mediterranean

I.1 The birth of Barcelona. A two thousand year old city

While there are signs of the existence of scattered population in the environs of Barcelona as early as the sixth millennium BC, it was in the late 5th century BC that a series of more or less stable settlements began to appear in the coastal area as the result of an increase in trade. One stands out in particular: the settlement that existed around the harbour situated to the south-west of Montjuïc, next to the river Llobregat delta, exploiting its condition as a natural port to load the farm surplus that was stored there in silos, according to archaeological studies carried out in the 1940s.[1]

But the first Barcelona, the germ of today's city, dates back to the 1st century BC, possibly between the years 15 and 13, under Roman domination. The arrival of the Romans had taken place some time before, coinciding with the founding of Emporion in 218 BC, and the Romanisation of the region was by then well under way.

The colony of Barcino is described in Agrippa's compendium, published by Pliny the Elder during the reign of Augustus. It stands on the site of earlier settlements, like most Catalan Roman settlements.[2] At the same time, various Roman villae in the plain accounted for the farming of crops. Its strategic position is due to its situation on Mons Taber, a small promontory rising to an approximate height of fifteen metres, between two torrents, the Cagalell to the west and the Merdança to the east. Their proximity to the sea meant that their basins to some extent provided a natural port.

However, the alluvium deposited by the torrents and the sand of the coastal currents were to hinder its functioning. This contradiction between good natural conditions for a port and the difficulty of maintaining a working depth was to condition the maritime splendour and the constraints on this infrastructure throughout many centuries of city development.

The colony of Barcino was sited according to the same criteria as the many other colonies of the great Roman Empire established the length and breadth of the Mediterranean region, with the Mare Nostrum as the hub of this widespread colonisation, well communicated both by maritime transport and by the dense network of Roman roads.

Barcino was not founded on the network of main Roman arteries that from Narbonne ran to Tarraco (Tarragona) before continuing to Gades (Cadiz). Yet this second-level colony had potential location and siting conditions that were to favour its subsequent evolution.

1.1
The medieval city
and the first town wall

[1] Oriol Granados: "Los primeros poblados del Pla de Barcelona", El Pla de Barcelona i la seva història. Barcelona, 1984.
[2] M. Taradell: "La romanització", Història de Catalunya. Barcelona, 1978.

1.2
Position of the city
in the coastal system.
Barcelona stands on the plain
where the two north-south
corridors meet.

I.2 The patterns of a Roman colony

The Romans' notion of city was in part taken from Greek civilisation. The very structure of the Roman Empire was organised on the basis of its cities, which were called urbs. Citizens had certain rights and took part in the city's decision-making. Rome delegated to each city a series of powers, making it a centre for administration, legal matters, religion and culture, and so forth.

The original layout of Barcino supposedly follows in the planning tradition of Roman foundings, at an advanced stage of technical development at this time.

The centuriation was designed on the basis of two main axes, the cardo maximus and the decumanus maximus, which crossed at the central point of the colony. Treatises of the time considered the ideal model to be when the centre coincided with the intersection of the two basic axes of the territorial system.

A specific practice existed at the time of the founding of Barcino: that of the "surveyors or gromatici", who were responsible for designing city layout. To do so, they used a device called a groma[3] that was used to trace perpendicular lines; it consisted of four 45-cm-long wooden arms from which four plumb lines were suspended. The column supporting the cross-shaped structure was driven into the ground so that the centre coincided with the intersection of the main axes. The position could be adapted to each specific topography by reference to the "wind

[3] See P. Frigerio: Antichi Instrumenti Technichi. Como, 1933.

1.a Layout and town wall of the Roman city.

1.3, 1.4
Hypothetical Roman layout
and illustration of the groma,
an instrument using
in founding the city

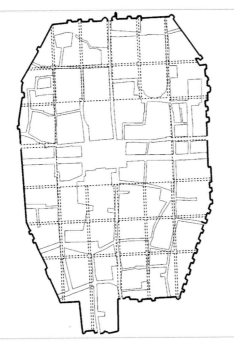

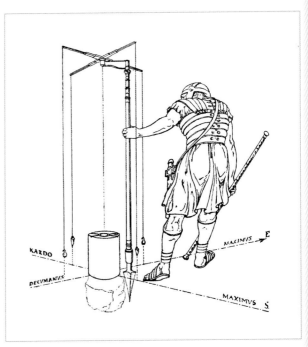

1.5
Adaptation of the Roman
site to the topography

1.6
Archaeological remains
of the Roman city

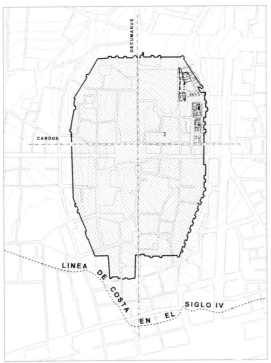

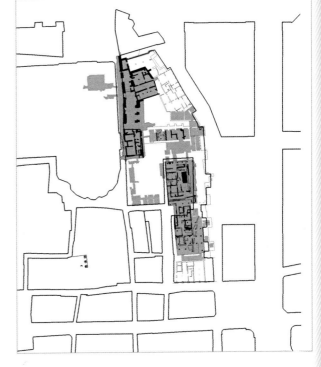

rose", such as the one used by Vitruvius,[4] that divided the circle into sixteen winds related to the Etruscan divinities and the names of Osiris.

The classic Roman city founding therefore involved three well-structured decisions:

1) Observation of the direction of the rising sun on the day of founding, placing the groma on a raised point, in this case Mons Taber, according to which the decumanus was laid out using the Etruscan procedure that had been assimilated by the Romans and made the founding a highly spiritual event, as explained in the sacred books or libri rituales.

2) Determination of the perpendicular that would define the cardus maximus, in this case orthogonal to the line of the coast, and

3) Finally, the course of the parallel streets, which would be laid out in the course of time.[5]

Archaeologists describe the founding settlement as an oppidum fortified by a wall of an average thickness of two metres. This layout with its seventy-eight towers is the most prominent in the Roman period. The wall was reinforced in the 3rd century AD, when a new wall was built up against some stretches of the Augustan wall.[6]

The archaeological hypothesis explains that access to the city was via four gates, situated one at the centre of each side and forming the ends of the two main axes. The initial Roman nucleus was the basis for an urban configuration that despite a series of transformations over the last two thousand years still represents the seminal core of Barcelona.

[4] Of the famous treatises by Pliny, Hyginus and Vitruvius (Diez libros sobre la Arquitectura. Murcia, 1981), it is the work of the latter that was to have the greatest influence. Written in the century before the Christian era, it describes in great detail how the city's site was chosen, the process of constructing buildings, etc. Vitruvius divides the physical construction of the city into two differentiated parts: on the one hand, the town walls and public buildings and spaces, and on the other, private buildings. The use of public buildings responds to three aspects: defensive (defensio), religious (religio) and services to the population (oportunitas). The latter include public spaces (fora), porches, baths, theatres, etc. This text that follows the rich Greek tradition of treatise writing was rediscovered in the Renaissance thanks to the protection of the monasteries' libraries and became the prototype of the new wave of architectural treatise writing. It has been interpreted and reprinted many times.

[5] This traditional interpretation of Roman founding has been challenged by J. Le Gall who, on the basis of archaeological proof, questions the regularity of the Roman city and suggests that the terms decumanus and cardus are taken from the centuriation of the territory and are erroneously applied to a description of cities. See J. L. Gall: Les rites de fondation des villes romaines. Bull. Soc. Antiq. France, 1970. However, I maintain the hypothesis of a relatively regular layout maintained by most historians. One such is Joseph Rykwert, who explains how profoundly the city and the Roman military camp are interwoven when he says that it is the camp that is conceived in the same way as a city. See The Idea of the Town and, more generally, The Seduction of the Place.

[6] See the studies by Francesca Pallarès and Oriol Granados cited by Josep Guitart, "El redescobriment de la Barcelona antiga", Homenatge a Barcelona. Barcelona, 1987.

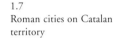

1.7
Roman cities on Catalan
territory

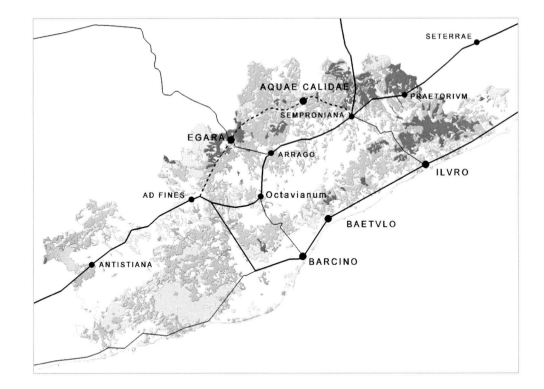

The city was consolidated in Roman times but, more importantly, it incorporated a system of urbanisation and a culture that were latent in its later development.[7]

The original core was, then, 300 metres wide and covered an area of eleven hectares. As we have seen, it was organised on the basis of orthogonal axes that marked out two basic lines (northeast-southwest and southeast-northwest) in the urban development of Barcelona. The surface area of early Barcino was that of an average-sized city on the scale of the Roman Empire, which had large cities easily covering 50 hectares or more. The principal axes crossed at the centre, which was the site of the forum with the main buildings: one religious (the Roman temple), of generous dimensions judging by archaeological evidence, and of which three columns remain today, and another civic, the thermae. This central point is situated in the northernmost corner of present-day Plaça de Sant Jaume, which was remodelled in the 19th century and is still Barcelona's main representative space today.

The orthogonal regularity of square or rectangular street blocks had been used in other cultures such as Egypt, Mesopotamia, Greece, etc. In general, the orthogonal system obeyed criteria of regularity, one of the most illustrated examples being Miletus' grid plan, later theorised by Hipodamus. The Romans were familiar with these experiences, particularly with the Greek cities constructed in the south of the peninsula and in Sicily, and had learned the Etruscan techniques for regular layouts.[8]

[7] See the double volume by William MacDonald, The Architecture of the Roman Empire (New Haven, 1965), which is a very complete interpretation of the forms of urban planning and typologies employed in Roman colonisation, particularly the second volume entitled An Urban Appraisal. Also André Pelletier, L'Urbanisme Romain sous l'Empire. Paris, 1982; and James C. Anderson, Roman Architecture and Society. London, 1997.
[8] R. Martín: L'Urbanisme dans la Grèce antique. Paris, 1974.

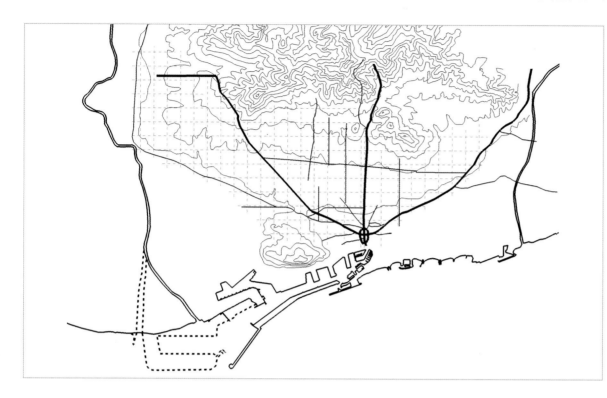

1.8
The centuriation of Barcino and its influence on the organisation of the city's road system

The Roman city identified the city layout with a mesh of streets, established according to very precise territorial axes, as already described. We might say that the Greeks established grids (regular spaces for construction), whereas the Romans chose meshes, layouts of streets into which urban buildings or spaces were later inserted.[9]

This then was the basis for an urban order born of the principles of regularity and Roman city planning techniques, which were to mark the urban development of Barcelona.

The same order of horizontal and vertical axes (north-west/south-east and south-west/north-east) was later subject to a similar interpretation in Cerdà's 19th century plan as the main axes for the colonisation of the Barcelona Plain. The central urban space was actually organised by the rationality of Roman city planning techniques, with aqueducts bringing water from Collserola and Montcada and sanitation systems, until well into the Middle Ages. The regional structure was well established by the Roman system of bridges and roads to ensure the movement of troops but also commercial and administrative traffic. Via Augusta and the Travessera (a horizontal axis across the plain) were the main external axes. The influence of Roman culture on forms of trade, institutional organisation, law that is, Romanisation, also played a vital role in later development.

Although Barcino started out as a small part of the orbis romanus, it went on to become a Mediterranean urban centre of the first order, with a surprising evolution based on the most common guidelines of Roman city founding. The specific nature of this formidable transformation calls for closer attention.

9   I have borrowed this meaning from Manuel de Solà-Morales: Las formas del crecimiento urbano", LUB. UPC, 1988.

1.9
Fragment of a mosaic
showing races in the circus,
c. 4th century, found
in Barcelona.

I.3 Reuse of the Roman city and urban crisis

In the 3rd century, Barcelona acquired Roman citizenship and the former colony became Civitas Julia Augusta Paterna Faventia Barcino. This was the start of a process of reuse of the Roman urban core that has existed until the present day, after a long period of seven centuries of successive adaptation to barbarian invasions and various colonisations and influences. These events followed each upon the last until the terrible catastrophe of the year 985 when the city was sacked and set on fire by the hordes of al-Mansur.

Various historical works about European cities coincide in their telling of the events of a difficult period; although archaeological research is not yet fully developed, it points to both a shrinking or withdrawal of cities and a rapid superposition of cultures over a single space, the city, that was seen as an object of domination.[10]

Hypotheses emerged during this long period as to the cultural difficulties of an ideal model of urban life,[11] and the city (its location, urban structure and monuments) was put to the test by the differing demands of the most varying civilisations and cultures. Generally speaking, the Roman Empire migrated eastwards across this European region due to the pressure of the Germanic invasion of the West. However, the arrival in Barcelona of

[10] P. Sica: La imagen de la ciudad. De Esparta a Las Vegas. Barcelona, 1977.
[11] By way of example, the historian A. García Bellido (La Edad Antigua, "Resumen Histórico del Urbanismo en España"), when addressing the end of the ancient period of Spanish cities, writes, "the collapse of urban life reached its limits with the great Germanic invasions of the 5th century (...) the disorganisation of cities was then absolute" (pp. 63-64).

peoples such as the Visigoths does not seem to have destroyed the urban and territorial structure of the previous Roman period; rather, as Henri Pirenne suggests, they settled there in order to "enjoy" the advantages of that civilisation on the Mediterranean shores.

Pirenne[12] stresses a kind of separation between the Carolingian world and Moorish domination of the Mediterranean. However, the many colonisations and invasions of Barcelona gave rise to a very interesting phenomenon of succession and superposition of civilisations.

Despite the difficulties of historical and archaeological verification, Barcelona was definitively marked out as a capital city by changes in its physical configuration and in the evolution of relations with its immediate hinterland.

Major reinforcement work was done to the Roman wall in the 3rd century to provide protection from possible barbarian invasions. The general overall layout retained the first wall but strengthened it with 76 towers and an enceinte of 1,500 metres. Construction was completed in a short period of time, as stones and elements of demolished city buildings were used.

The consolidation of its wall made Barcelona a fortified town, and the city began to take shape as a compact unit in the region, raised slightly above the Barcelona Plain beside the sea. This fact sublimated the Roman nature of the city and increased its importance with regard to other Roman colonies whose greater vulnerability to external attacks led to defeat.

Within the city, the substitution of monuments began under Roman domination. Christianity was authorised in the early 4th century and a basilica had already been constructed. Later, the church of Sant Just and Sant Pastor was built on the remains of the former Roman temple.

Barcelona began to be regarded as a capital power centre when Ataulf proposed that the main Visigoth court be set up there. However, this idea came to nothing and in the 5th century Barcino was governed from Toulouse. A further attempt took place later under Charlemagne.

The Moorish invasion in 711 marked an intermediate period. The fact that this was a region of transition between Arab and Gallic domains meant that Charlemagne saw control of Barcino as a priority. Control of a fortified town of this magnitude would represent a solid buffer from the Islamic peoples. Louis the Pious conquered Barcelona, which then became the seat of the Governor of the March.

The position of buffer between two opposing blocs was not conducive to trade, however, and city administration was totally subject to the Franks. There was also greater emphasis on colonising the countryside, with the characteristic domination structures of the feudal system.

---

[12] Henri Pirenne: Las ciudades de la Edad Media. Madrid, 1971. Original text, Brussels, 1927.

1.10, 1.11
Church of Sant Pau del Camp,
late 19th century engraving
and detail of the cloister.

In the 9th century, the Frankish governors' continuing poor management led to Guifré being named Count of Barcelona, as well as Urgell, Cerdanya and Conflent. This heralded the start of Barcelona's emergence as a capital in relation to a large sector of Catalunya Vella (Old Catalonia), with what has been referred to as the First Independence of the Counts.[13] Guifré established a succession mechanism by means of his heirs, Borrell I and II, forming an independent countship between the great Moorish and Frankish domains. This increased scope of domination and the situation as intermediary enabled the creation of trading relations, conducted by Jews and religious orders between the two great neighbouring civilisations.

This period saw an incipient suburbanisation or development in the plain, outside the city walls, in the form of early ravals or suburbs and the establishment of convents and churches.

Early sites had already been established and damaged by successive invasions, such as Sant Pau, near Cagalell torrent, and Sant Jeroni de la Murtra on the other side of the river Besòs. Now, in the 9th century, Sant Pau was reconstructed to become a key part of the Catalan Romanesque, while on the other side of the city Sant Pere de les Puelles was constructed, later to spawn a new neighbourhood.

At this time, new parishes were also being built at the main crossroads in the plain, such as Sant Andreu in Palomar, Sant Genís in Agudells, Sant Vicenç in Sarrià and Santa Eulàlia in Vil·lapicina, among others. These

[13] For a fuller description of this period, see Pau Vila and Lluís Casassas, Barcelona i la seva rodalia al llarg dels temps (Barcelona, 1974), from which this information is taken.

parishes were later to form the municipal structure of the Barcelona Plain until it was annexed to the central city in the late 19th century.

The suburbs extended towards the port, giving rise to the later development of the neighbourhood of Santa Maria del Mar, accompanied by the growth of Santa Maria del Pi, beside Collserola torrent to the west of the town walls.

The city's recovery was cut short by al-Mansur, of the Caliphate of Cordova, who in 985 defeated the troops of Borrell II in Penedès, and the city was sacked, burnt and razed.

The Roman structure and wall once again came to the fore in the physical reconstruction of the city in later centuries. As explained above, their use and reinterpretation was the principal support through this period of urban crisis and also gave the city an opportunity to sound out the role of capital of the Catalan Countship.

The protagonism of the Roman city, and particularly of its wall, has been identified and highlighted by historians and restorers of the old town[14]. In his prominent research into Catalan architecture, the architect Josep Puig i Cadafalch based a prime nationalist argument on the country's Roman architecture, particularly from this period of the formation of Barcelona[15].

In the 1920s various attempts were made to enhance old Barcelona, including the efforts of the architect Joan Rubió i Bellver[16] to reconstruct the Roman wall, demolishing the buildings that concealed it and prioritising the maintenance of Gothic buildings. Rubió coined the name of "Gothic quarter" for this walled Roman kernel of the city of Barcelona. This new name became so successful that from then on, both in tourist guides and in everyday use, this urban core is known as the "Gothic city".

---

[14] The systematic study of the ancient city was initially addressed sporadically in the 19th century (Antonio Celles's studies and his topographic map of 1835, commissioned by the Board of Trade) and at the turn of the century with the creation of the History and Archaeology Section of the Institut d'Estudis Catalans in 1907. Later, Carreras Candi, in his Geografía General de Catalunya published in 1916, and Agustí Durán i Sanpere, as director of the Arxiu Històric de la Ciutat after 1920, systematically promoted the process.

[15] J. Rohrew, I. Solà-Morales: J. Puig i Cadafalch. La arquitectura entre la casa y la ciudad. Barcelona, 1989.

[16] J. Rubio i Bellver: Taber Mons Bacinonensis. Barcelona, 1927.

1.b The viles noves in city expansion. Images of old Barcelona.

1.14
The viles noves as non-continuous expansion of the walled town, drawn over the 19th-century city layout, showing the constancy of the medieval layout.

1.15, 1.16
Plaça de la Llana.

1.17 Carrer d'en Carabassa

During the post-war years Barcelona's council offices, in the person of the architect Adolfo Florensa,[17] gave a new impetus to the reconstruction of the Roman wall which then acquired its present-day image, with the complete reconstruction of the north and east façades in the Plaça Nova, Avinguda de la Catedral, Plaça Berenguer and Carrer Sots-tinent Navarro.

I.4 The re-birth of Barcelona

The terrible destruction of the city in the High Middle Ages called for a major effort to reconstruct it, particularly as physical destruction was accompanied by the expense of recovering the surviving population. Much of the populace was held captive by the Emirate of Cordova, who was to sell their freedom at a high price. This critical situation was also marked by serious succession disputes between the various heirs to the Countship of Barcelona.

The medieval city began to experience the expansion of trade and exchange that once again set in motion the consolidated urban nucleuses. The city was a refuge for people who escaped the feudal system in search of personal freedom and a degree of legal autonomy. Their participation in the taxation system might to a large extent be said to have guaranteed works of public utility, particularly protection from invaders.

[17] A. Florensa: Las murallas romanas de la ciudad. Barcelona, 1958. Also La urbanización urbanística del circuito romano. Barcelona, 1964, and M. de Solà-Morales et al.: Adolf Forensa. Barcelona, 1998.

1.20, 1.21
Medieval paintings: the image of the city was associated with the town wall and its gates.

The medieval city may well have been an excellent way for the trader to escape from feudal logic; however, the land he used did not belong to him. The feudal system of landownership and its legal privileges were to continue until Napoleonic times. Power over land lay in military conquest and the relations established between the counts and the nobles. Thus the logic of landownership was not urban in nature and this was a decisive fact that the bourgeois and artisan classes had to live with until they were able to change it. The interests of the nobles and the bourgeoisie were conflicting, though the two parties managed to coexistence to their mutual benefit; the basic conflicts, however, did not disappear.

In the city, the old town wall was consolidated, with the superposition of a castle at each gate to increase defensive capacity and clarify the institutional responsibility and authority they represented. The castles also provided protection from a potentially hostile urban context. Two such examples were Regomir castle, to the south of the current-day square of the same name, under the jurisdiction of the counts, and the castle at the north gate (Porta Nova) which was built and governed by the Church and guaranteed protection for ecclesiastical properties in the vicinity.

The most expressive component in the city's rebirth took the form of the viles noves, new districts or hamlets that sprang up outside the walled town to accommodate the growing population and new economic activities. This was the start of a model of settlement that, despite having its own internal structure, was organised around the old centre, using pre-existing elements of urbanisation. The most dynamic viles noves were situated to the east of the Roman city, a sign of the growing importance that the seaport was once again acquiring. The vila nova of Mercadal, opposite the market at the Portal Mayor, was soon extended by the vila nova of Sant Cugat with its own chapel on the old Roman road to France (the site of the present-day streets

Carders and Llana). Further to the north, the vila nova of Sant Pere appeared beside the monastery of Sant Pere de les Puelles.[18]

The vila nova of Els Arcs grew up to the north of the Porta Bisbal and, to the south of the vila nova of Mercadal, the vila nova of El Mar appeared, the most populous of the various districts outside the walled city. It extended towards the sea, along present-day Carrer Argentería, its boundary being the site for Santa Maria de les Arenes, later Santa Maria del Mar. Finally, near the Jewish quarter, to the west, the vila nova of El Pi developed more slowly around the nucleus that had grown up around the church of the same name. The viles noves each had a radial connexion with the gates in the city wall and were all connected by a track that provided the function of a ring road.

I.5 Social evolution in the Middle Ages leads to the creation of a new urban world

In medieval southern Europe, the population was at least two-thirds rural, though the city was coming into its own as the seat of urban civilisation whose importance has lasted until the present day.

There had been precedents in Europe, particularly under the Roman Empire, of the discovery of urban life, but with a system of social relations imposed by the conquerors; when the conquerors disappeared, there was no social structure to replace them and although some infrastructures remained, the cities generally experienced a crisis.

Medieval urban growth was different, however, and represented an important evolution in the social relations constructed over the centuries; the transformation of rural and agriculture ways of life was essential. Civilisation is associated with the city, and it is easy to overlook the influence of rural processes on its construction and gradual evolution. While it is true that Roman colonisation established important guidelines, the Middle Ages actually reinvented the city.[19]

This was the advent of a time during which man built cities not just as a place to live, but also on the basis of an innovative "idea" that laid the foundations of today's urban civilisation. These bases include institutional and operative structure and also the physical elements on which our historical foundations rest.

[18] The significance of these churches to an understanding of the viles noves could respond to the hypothesis formulated by André Corboz with his idea of "church city" as a pattern of implantation of this period in other European cities such as Utrecht, Milan, Verona, Lyons, etc., and which is worthy of further investigation. See Corboz, "La ville comme temple", Le Territoroire comme palimpseste. Paris, 2001.
[19] Tierry Dutour: La Ville Médiévale. Origines et triomphe de l'Europe urbaine. Paris, 2003.

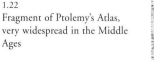

1.22
Fragment of Ptolemy's Atlas, very widespread in the Middle Ages

1.23
Scope of the Consell de Cent according to the description in the White Paper for the city. Interpretation by Joan Maluquer i Villadot.

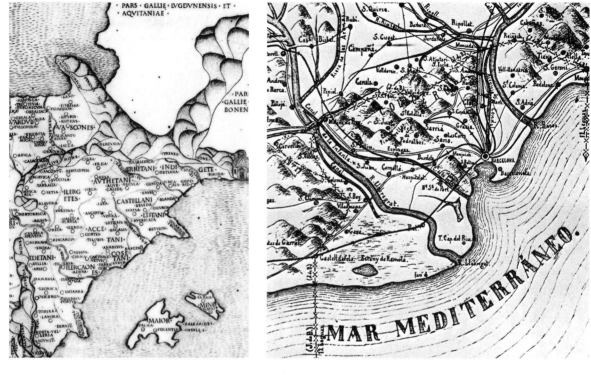

The development of this new idea of city in the Middle Ages was a long process, and its construction both its physical entity and new social and institutional relations was extremely complex.

Historians date the change from the Low to the High Middle Ages in the 10th century, and it is in this latter phase that the most substantial changes took place, before the Middle Ages burst forth in all their splendour in the 13th century.

The city as a new urban entity was associated with the image of the town wall and its gates that was transmitted in paintings and religious documents and on coins. Normally this was an ideal rather than a realistic representation that emphasised the condition of a closed, fortified city.

During the early periods, the city was episcopal, a sacred place reserved for individuals who had contact with God. This led to the biblical explanation according to which the Christian king is a mediator between God and men, and the city becomes the privileged place in which this relation is manifested.

In the Low Middle Ages, however, the organisation of power was more complex. During the reign of Ramon Berenguer I in the 11th century, for example, many important members of society swore oaths of allegiance to the prince. Zimmermann's study refers to the vow of loyalty associated with the person of the Count of Barcelona, who until the late 9th century exerted his authority over three countships: Barcelona, Girona and Vic.[20] Loyalty was related to the city over which the count held authority.

---

[20] M. Zimmermann: Le chateau contre la cité. Les représentations de l'espace politique dans la Catalogne féodale. Rouen, 2002. M. Zimmermann: Entre royaume franc et califat, soudain, la Catalogne. Paris, 1990.

1.24
Map of Catalonia drawn
by Gerardus Mercator
in the 17th century.

In fact, as of the Frankish period, it was the name of the city that became important in the succession of the counts, such as Count Borrell of Barcelona in the 10th century.

A functional transformation in society was to have major implications for the urban form. Thus the city became a place for trade, with people buying and selling; it was also a space for specialised production, with its guilds and trades.

Social organisation also became more complex as it began to address the different roles and attributes of individuals and their trades. This structuring also led to the creation of new forms of government.

The city truly was the seat of social life and it became an autonomous entity within the territory. It was a vital part, and its efficiency and smooth functioning were also responsible for its prestige and reputation. The city was beginning to be recognised as a "centre" that represented its entire hinterland, and this was the logic for the organisation of the modern city.

This was accompanied by a decentralisation of power for more effective running and control of the region. Rural domination was organised by means of rural domains and royal power took the form of territorial seigneuries, normally with castles as their seats.

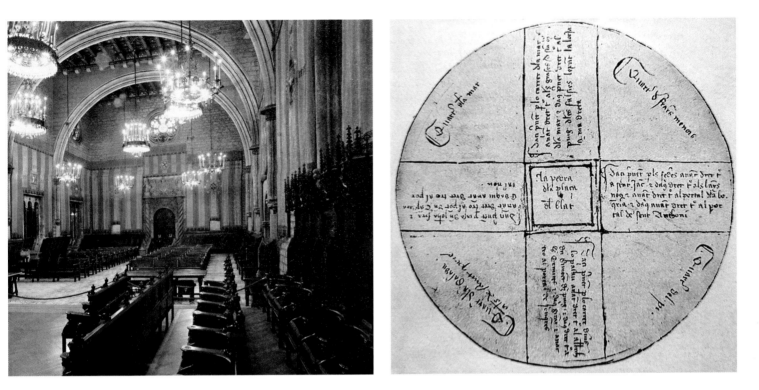

1.25
Hall of the Consell de Cent in City Hall.

1.26
Stone in the Plaça del Blat, late 14th century, marking the division of the city into neighbourhoods to draw up the census.

Population growth and agricultural expansion were the driving force behind the cities, providing a boost that enabled local nobles to take action against central power or territorial seigneurs who were more interested in perpetuating the established situation.

I.6 The formation of Catalonia and the capital of the Counts

This was the context for the construction of Catalan unity during the reigns of Ramon Berenguer the Great and Ramon Berenguer IV, Count of Barcelona and Prince of Aragon. The process culminated under Alfonso I when the countships of Besalú and Cerdanya, and Urgell and Empuries were incorporated to Barcelona.

The formation of Catalonia with its present-day borders took place in the mid-12th century, after Tortosa and Lleida were wrested back from the Moors. Barcelona formed the lower boundary of Catalunya Vella, consolidated centuries previously, and Catalunya Nova was not established until this period.

Thus the geographical position of Barcelona as the capital of Catalonia was reasserted and acquired greater importance. It was also in this period that the terms "Catalonia" and "Catalans" began to be used in the bordering countries to define this new consolidated entity.

However, the borders of Catalonia underwent major changes in this period of the Middle Ages as a result of both the alliance with the Kingdom of Aragon and future conquests in the Mediterranean. In this border creation process, the existence of a well-organised capital was perhaps one of the keys to the existence of today's Catalan hinterland.

1.27
Santa Maria del Mar in the
Born was an active space in
Barcelona's commercial life.

I.7 The Consell de Cent as the government of the City of the Counts

The increase in size of the city and its urban complexity led to the need for a specific system of government for the City of the Counts. The emergence of new issues such as supply, maritime trade and so forth called for clear regulations in keeping with everyday reality.

The Consell de Cent or Council of 100 Jurors was formed, with representatives of all social strata except the military. King Jaume I pronounced decrees in 1249 and 1265 to implement this system of organisation. Each year, of the 100 jurors, five were elected to govern the city with the help of a standing council of thirty members, called the Trentenari.

The city's scope of action extended from Molins de Rei to Montcada and from Castelldefels to Montgat, with the attendant urban problems. This represented in the region of one hundred square kilometres and corresponds approximately to the Metropolitan Corporation of Barcelona, which operated as a metropolitan administrative body between 1974 and 1986.

It was the task of the Consell de Cent to rule on issues such as water, recovering part of the old Roman system; supply, rationalising the consumption of meat and wheat, and the conversion of the latter into flour, among other issues.

It was also responsible for the network of roads leading to the city, the passage of boats along the river Llobregat at Sant Boi and on the river Besòs, on the route to France.

The Consell also laid down early guidelines to regulate urban building and classify common urban practices; these were the Consuetuds de Santacilia, promulgated by Jaume I, which, for centuries, represented

[21] On these customs and their importance up until the Edict of Works (1771), see the doctoral thesis of J. Sabaté: El proyecto de la calle sin nombre. Arquithesis, Barcelona, 1999.

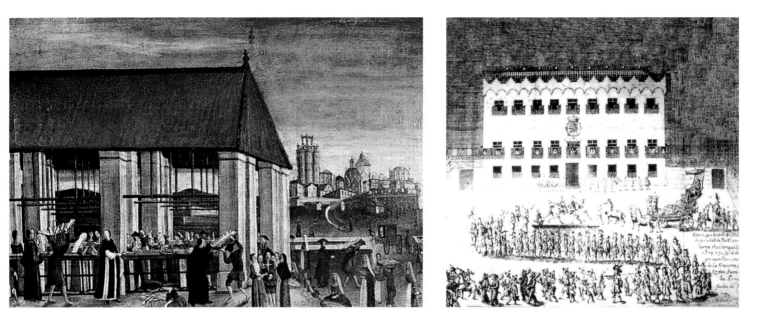

1.28
El Bornet. Anonymous painting, 1775

1.29
Engraving of 1677 reproducing the celebration of the silversmiths on the occasion of the election of Juan of Austria.

the first guidelines to prevent private construction from prejudicing either neighbours or the general public good.[21]

To this end, censuses were drawn up of occupied houses and families, and spatial demarcations were established, such as the "stone in the Plaça del Blat", which delimited four neighbourhoods within the walled town, with its geometric centre in the Plaça del Blat.[22] This diagram dating from 1389, in the form of a regular cross, divided the city into four sectors: Mar, Framenors, Pi and Sant Pere.

At institutional level, an important event in the 13th century for the country as a whole was the creation of the Generalitat. It came into operation in 1287 for the purpose of tax collection, and retained an administrative rather than political role until 1640, when it became the Catalan government body.

I.8 Medieval urban structure

The rebirth of Barcelona was based on the creation of new urban elements that responded to this functionality. It is however difficult to ignore the typical image of the medieval city that 19th century or Renaissance reconstructions have handed down to us.[23] Until archaeological research makes further advances, the spatial distribution of the city at that time is pure guesswork.[24]

---

[22] Sebastià Riera: "El Consell de Cent: creació i desenvolupament del seu règim de govern (1249-1462)", Barcelona gótica. Barcelona, 1999.

[23] H. Saalman (Medieval Cities. London, 1968) reminds us of the Tudor flavour of the medieval city idealised by Pugin in "Contrasts" in 1836.

[24] It is important to appreciate the spatial patterns and behaviour that informed medieval society, which are very far from the irrationality sometimes attributed to them. See J. Heers: La ville au moyen âge. Cher, 1990; Le Goff, La civilisation de l'occident medieval. Manchecourt, 1997; A. de Libera Penser au Moyen Âge. Manchecourt, 1996.

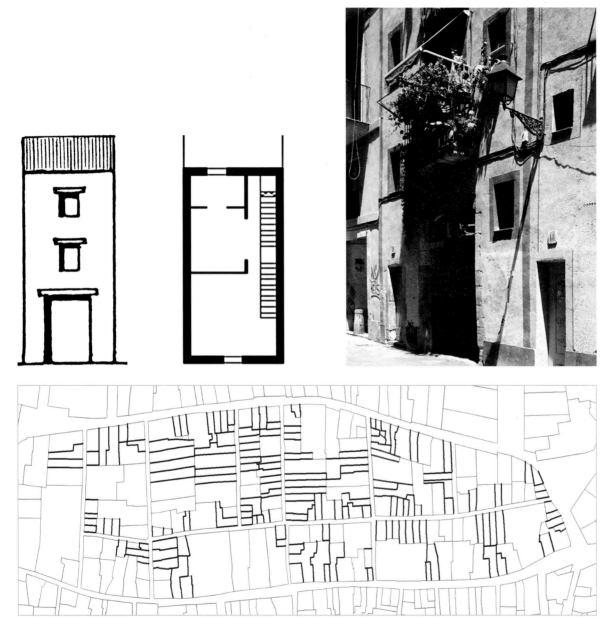

1.30, 1.31
Artisan's house. Façade, layout and floor plan.

1.32
Example of the plot division of original artisan houses.

In order to understand the urban structure of the period, it is important to remember that the streets formed a continuous but weak urban system with a very irregular layout. The streets were all different and the existence of large or public buildings helped orientation. Many were particularly characterised by the dominant trade of their inhabitants.

Squares came into being practically to widen the streets, and public space was complex to master, in that it also reflected the distribution of power between the different parts of the city (diocese, municipal government,

1.c Montcada, a street of townhouses.

1.33, 1.34
Neighbourhood of Santa Maria del Mar and Carrer Montcada.

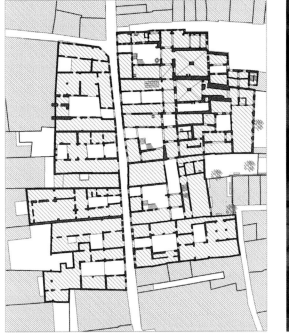

1.35
Fragment of one of the townhouses that makes up today's Picasso Museum.

religious orders, guilds, etc.). However, some small squares were built when houses were demolished in order to create spaces in keeping with the new, thematically-grouped commercial functions: wheat, coal, wool, etc.

In this medieval context, work began on another town wall in 1260, in the reign of Jaume I, to enclose the viles noves described above. It enclosed in the region of 130 hectares of land and coincided with today's layout of the Citadel, Carrer Santa Anna and the Rambla.[25] The wall extended for 5 kilometres with eight gates that provided communication with buildings scattered across the plain. The layout was left open towards the sea to allow the toing and froing of people and goods access. It was a purely defensive construction and only the gateways received any kind of adornment.

The town wall formed part of a defensive system spread across the region, including elements from much earlier epochs, presenting a much stronger protective structure. These included the Port Castle, on the mountain of Montjuïc, important for its elevated position so close to the city; the rest were situated at the entrances to the Barcelona Plain: Martorell castle and the old castle at Rosanes at the river Llobregat entrance, Eramprunyà and Castelldefels castles at the river's delta, and Montcada castle at the river Besòs entrance.

The viles noves were built up around small "artisan's houses", built in rows, which gradually converted the city approach roads into streets. Various descriptions present us with a prototype of a building used mainly by an extended family. It comprised the artisan workshop on the ground floor with the working space required by the trade in question and one or two floors above, where the family lived. The houses sometimes had a mezzanine floor drawn back from the street façade, with ventilation through the workshop. The building could be as wide as four metres, varying in depth between 10 and 12 metres. The building did not occupy the whole parcel, the middle of which was used as a kitchen garden to supply the family with food.

Large institutional buildings were also constructed inside the urban enclosure. Some old churches such as Sant Pere, the cathedral and Sant Miquel were rebuilt, while others were new constructions offering health and welfare services. These initiatives were financed as charitable works by city hierarchs and leaders, and by the various religious orders. As of 1191, the Count ceased to rule over the property of the Church, which became an independent estate like the nobles and, later on, the bourgeoisie. The facilities set up included the church and Saint John's hospital, of the military order of the same name, the canonry with its hospital and canons' residence, and the paupers' hospital, situated beside the city wall.

These buildings were inserted at strategic points and selectively enhanced the most immediate urban spaces: the names of many streets in the old town still recall these sites. They were generally built in the Romanesque style that inspired the singular buildings of this period. One outstanding example is the cloister of Sant Pau del

[25] According to A. Durán i Sanpere (1975), the existence of this wall is historically proven, but its exact layout is still uncertain.

Camp, which combines good Romanesque in the form of its heavy proportioned cloister with double columns and capitals, and Mudejar style, in its trilobe arches with Mudejar details.

The flagship urban operation of this period was the development of Carrer Montcada, in the vila nova of El Mar, which henceforth became the street of seigneurial palaces. The initiative was begun by Guillem Ramon de Montcada, who had taken an active part in the conquest of Tortosa and was granted a privilege by Pere I in 1209. This was an urban development operation on a different scale to the infilling of existing urban fabric with small houses. It represented the decision to construct a singular street running from La Bòria towards the sea. It was laid out in a straight line with a substantial width: it was to be the site for a series of large houses or palaus that, despite their stylistic variety, formed a prestigious urban space outside the walled town. This model of locating the residential areas of the emerging classes outside the town walls includes paradigmatic examples in the cities of Genoa and Rome, which are still very relevant references.[26]

The process of construction of Carrer Montcada began in the 13th century, though it was consolidated and reached the height of its splendour in the following centuries, becoming a civilian space of great representative value in the 14th-17th centuries.[27]

In later centuries, many buildings were subdivided into rented apartments as the ruling classes began to settle in other areas of the city. Carrer Montcada comprises a series of palaus in the Catalan Gothic civilian style; the palau is part house, part castle, separated from adjacent constructions by strong party walls. Of particular architectural note are Palau de Cervelló (15th century), Palau Dalmases,[28] Palau Aguilar, originally built in the 13th century and later modified by successive owners; it now houses the Picasso Museum. Today, the various palaus are generally restored and used as museums.

[26] See, principally in Italy, the strade di palazzi (streets of palaces). These streets were a specific element of urban development that consisted in the spatial grouping of the residences of noble families who decided to live in the same area.
Carrer Montcada may be likened to the districts created by the Medicis in Florence and the Dorias in Genoa. Genoa's famous strada nuova (1550) was for centuries the loveliest street in Europe according to the Flemish painter Rubens, who publicised it in Antwerp by proposing it as a residential form for the rich merchants from the north of our continent. Naples too has its Via Toledo, the loveliest street of the cinquecento, built for the Viceroy Pedro of Toledo. Rome has similar interventions by Bramante on both banks of the Tiber: Via Giulia and Via della Lungara. L. Grossi Bianchi and E. Poleggi (Una città portuale del medioevo Génova nei secoli X-XVI. Genoa, 1987) interpret the case of the Strada Nuova constructed in 1550 as the "alternative city of the nobles".
[27] A. Cirici Pellicer: L'arquitectura catalana. Ed. Moll. Palma, 1950. Barcelona's famous historian cast doubts on the exact date on which the street was constructed (between the 13th and 14th centuries), despite corroborating its innovative value.
[28] According to Victor Balaguer (Las calles de Barcelona. Monterrey, Barcelona, 1866), this is the palace Guillem de Montcada built for his family. It was later occupied by the Cervelló-Giudice family and reconstructed in the17th century after a fire.

1.d Barcelona capital del Mediterráneo.

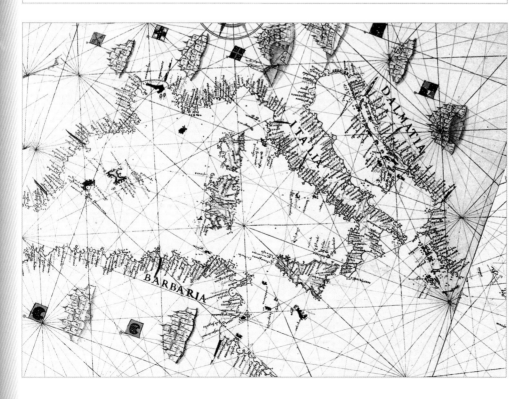

1.36
Catalan-Aragonese domination
and the consulates of
Barcelona.

1.37
Map of the western
Mediterranean taken from Joan
Oliva's Nautical Atlas, 1592.

I.9 Barcelona, capital of the Western Mediterranean

Barcelona's role as capital grew as the scope of government of the house of the Counts and its dynasty continued to expand.[29] In the 12th century, the Counts of Barcelona extended their influence in Occitania and Provence by means of military action, marriage alliances and acts of vassalage. However, some operations were less effective and the advance north was brought to a halt in 1213 by the death of Pere the Catholic at the Battle of Muret.

From then on, influence and efforts turned towards the Western Mediterranean, and during the 13th century and the first thirty years of the 14th, Barcelona was the capital of one of Europe's largest empires. This situation produced a new internal dynamic in its urban organisation, but it also exerted a strong influence on dominated cities and regional systems.

The fusion of the Countship of Barcelona with the Kingdom of Aragon in the person of Jaume I merely served to increase the city's role. It took place at the end of the 13th century when three states were ruled by the house of Aragon: Aragon, Catalonia and Valencia; the Kingdom of Majorca, comprising the Balearic Islands, Roussillon and Sardinia; and the Kingdom of Sicily, to which the Duchy of Athens was added.

The strategic role of the city of Barcelona in the economic and commercial revival of this sector of the Mediterranean, and particularly Catalonia, emerges very clearly in Fernand Braudel's[30] comprehensive study of Mediterranean countries. He stresses the role of the metropolises, pointing out that "Without Barcelona that is, without the combination of its artisan class, its Jewish merchants, its adventurous soldiers and the thousand resources of the neighbourhood of Santa Maria del Mar, it would be difficult to form a full picture of the maritime growth of the Catalan coast (...) which was a port of call not just for sailing ships from the Balearic Islands, but boats from Valencia, whaleboats from Biscay and ships from Marseilles and Italy".

[29] See the book by Antoni Nicolau et al. La Barcelona gótica. Barcelona, 1999. This is the catalogue of an excellent exhibition organised by the Museu d'Història on the occasion of the 750th anniversary of the city privileges granted to Barcelona by King Jaume I. It takes an interesting look at this "Gothic" period, from the 13th to the 15th centuries, during which the city underwent an unprecedented process of economic growth and commercial expansion. Barcelona was one of the most important centres in the Mediterranean and played a similar role to other city-states.

[30] F. Braudel: El Mediterráneo y el mundo mediterráneo en la época de Felipe II. (2 vol.) FCE. México, 1976 (p. 190).

1.38
Mural with an idealised view
of Barcelona. Sant Raimon
de Penyafort, anonymous, early
17th century.

I.10 Maritime activity in the city without a port

This domination of the Western Mediterranean intensified maritime, military and above all commercial activities. However, this nascent capital did not have a large enough port to maintain the network of communications required of it, and this was a source of continual dispute between the city's different social sectors.

The port had no breakwaters like those of other large maritime cities such as Genoa and Venice, which also enjoyed optimum natural conditions. Barcelona had to wait until the 15th century for the start of work on the construction of its artificial harbour, when the Catalan fleet had already reached the peak of its greatness.[31] However, the port had been used since Roman times due to basic conditions of natural shelter provided by the small inlet defined by the Puig de les Falsies, a small promontory opposite today's Llotja or Exchange.

Furthermore, the port only admitted small-scale shipping, and the Ordinacions de la Mar, a body of maritime law, required larger ships to be unloaded by smaller ones, and even the crew and the ship's captain "could not disembark before the merchandise was unloaded", to ensure its safety. There were also other, natural harbours on the Catalan coast, such as Sant Feliu de Guíxols and Salou, among others, which promoted Catalan maritime activity.

[31] J. Vicens Vives: Historia económica de España. Ed. Vicens Vives. Barcelona, 1969. He summarises thus: "The true Catalan navy came into being in the 12th century, developed in the 13th, reached its peak in the 14th and declined in the 15th, though its ruin was not complete until the 16th century."

Despite the infrastructure difficulties of the port, the organisational base of maritime activity relied on two different institutions:[32] 1) the overseas consuls as representatives of the authorities, responsible for safeguarding the general interests of Catalan trade, and who came to number as many as seventy and 2) the Consolat de Mar, an association of Barcelona traders and ship-owners which ensured the conservation and regulation of its port and shores. The latter institution was created by Jaume I in 1257. The Consolat de Mar was present in the main ports of the metropolis.

I.11 The splendour of the Catalan Gothic

The Gothic style was rather late in arriving since the Romanesque was so well established. It made its first incursions in the Cistercian monasteries of Catalunya Nova, in Poblet and Santes Creus.

Catalan Gothic architecture is characterised by simplicity of volumes, sober decoration and the tendency to unify interior spaces. This meant that the aisles were identified with the central nave, as seen in the large churches built during this period. The shearing of the arches is compensated by strong buttresses with space at their bases for chapels. The great monuments of the historic city were built in this style: work began in 1329 on Santa Maria del Mar, in the vila nova of El Mar, on the site of the former church of Santa Maria de les Arenes, and it is the most expressive example of the structural advances of the Catalan Gothic. The nave and the two aisles are all practically the same height, and the distance between pillars is 13 metres. The pillars have orthogonal bases without ribs to increase their slenderness. Construction work was overseen by Berenguer de Montagut, and the result is one of the most perfect elaborations of the Catalan Gothic. Its position in the most dynamic neighbourhood of the time and its bell tower which was clearly visible from the sandbank before the port make this monument a triumphant symbol of Barcelona's maritime empire.[33]

The Banqueting Hall of the Great Royal Palace represents the singularity of a monumental space with the sobriety that characterises the Catalan Gothic. Its great span comprises six semicircular arches forming diaphragms between which the timber ceiling is inserted.

[32] J. Alemany: El port de Barcelona. PAB. Barcelona, 1984.

[33] A metaphorical but eloquent reference is Le Corbusier's comment on Gothic cathedrals in Quand les cathedrales étaint blanches. Paris, 1937. He interprets this period in European cities thus: "The cathedrals were white because they were new (…). In every city and hamlet circumvallated by new town walls, God's skyscraper dominated the landscape (…). It was disproportionate in its setting; but no, it was an act of optimism, a gesture of daring, proof of mastery (…) It had turned its back on the past."

1.e Some key urban works of the Catalan Gothic.

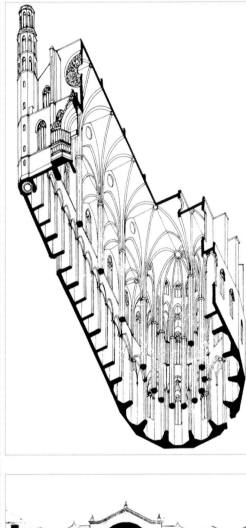

1.39
Santa Maria del Mar, paradigm of the Catalan Gothic, with its tower overlooking the port.

1.40
View of the Plaça del Rei with the Royal Palace, showing King Martí's lookout; left, the Lieutenant's Palace.

1.41, 1.42
The Drassanes (shipyard) in an elevation drawn in the 17th century and an aerial view from 1920.

1.43
Schematic illustration
of the buildings and streets
of the walled town
of Barcelona and of the Sea
Wall, showing the church
of Santa Maria, the Born
and the Exchange. From the
Llibre de Comptes del Plat dels
Pobres de Santa Maria del Mar.

The arches rest on low pilasters that use the wall to counteract the shearing of the arch. Pere the Ceremonious ordered the start of construction in 1359, and the work was directed by Guillem Carbonell and completed in 1370.

Clear exponents of the Catalan maritime apogee of the time are the buildings of the Llotja and the Drassanes.

The Llotja (Exchange), a trading place where merchants effected transactions, is a representative example of the great importance of public civilian architecture. Built by Pere Arvey between 1380 and 1392, it has a rectangular floor plan and a flat roof resting on two rows of three diaphragm-arches, the usual buttresses being replaced by thick side walls. Only the original Trading Hall has been conserved; the rest of the building was restored in the neoclassic style by Joan Soler i Faneca in the 18th century, and it became an emblematic building in the Pla de Palau in the early 19th century.

Other Exchanges were built on similar lines: those in Majorca (1426-1448) and Valencia (1483-1498).

The Drassanes (shipyard) was built by Pere the Great, most of the work being completed in 1381. Constructed by master builder Arnau Ferrer, it comprises a series of parallel naves of varying widths and lengths, the maximums

being 12 and 120 metres. It is one of the most complete examples of a medieval shipyard to exist today. Its dimensions correspond to the magnitude of the maritime activity of the time. The building came under military jurisdiction in the 17th century, when it was remodelled, and was enclosed by the final town wall in 1681.

The cathedral stands on the site of former Barcelona cathedrals, construction of the present-day building beginning in 1298. It comprises three naves and an apse, covered by a pointed vault. The buttresses are inside the building and are used for side chapels. The construction process lasted until 1448. In the 19th century a competition was announced for the main façade, which was built by Oriol Mestres and Augusto Font, and completed in 1898.

Gothic buildings constructed in the Barcelona Plain include the monastery of Pedralbes, attributed to Reinard des Fonoll[34] and built by Jaume II for his wife, Elisenda de Montcada. In addition to the monastery, the original walled enclosure included streets with lay buildings, forming an independent monastic settlement.

The complex is a representative of the High Gothic, with great sobriety in the use of decorative elements and still in an excellent state of conservation.

Meanwhile, inside the town walls, the Consell de Cent built the Hall of the Trentenari as a meeting place within the future city hall. It also carried out a series of reforms geared to increase the number of the city's squares: Plaça de Calderers and Pla d'en Llull in Ribera and the extension of Plaça Nova and Plaça del Blat, all very busy public places. An open piece of land was appointed to the east of Santa Maria del Mar as a place to hold festivals, markets and tournaments in the vicinity of what is now El Born. This was the beginning of the rationalisation of the city's representative and leisure functions.

This great blossoming of Gothic architecture was accompanied by sober sculptural work that concentrated its efforts more on the exterior of buildings. Guillem de Sagrera, Pere Oller, Pere Joan (sculptor of the Saint George in the Gothic façade, 1418, of the Palau de la Generalitat), Antoni Claperós (the Saint George in the cathedral cloister) and Guillem Soldevila were the foremost exponents of this great period.

[34] J. Vives Miret: Reinard des Fonoll. Escultor i arquitecte anglès, renovador de l'Art Gòtic a Catalunya (1321-1362). Barcelona, 1969. Also Anna Castellano, Pedralbes a l'Edat Mitjana. Història d'un monestir femení. Barcelona, 1998; and various authors: Petras Albas. El monestir de Pedralbes i els Montcada. 1326-1673. Barcelona, 2001.

1.46, 1.47
Alghero and its bay
in the 19th century.

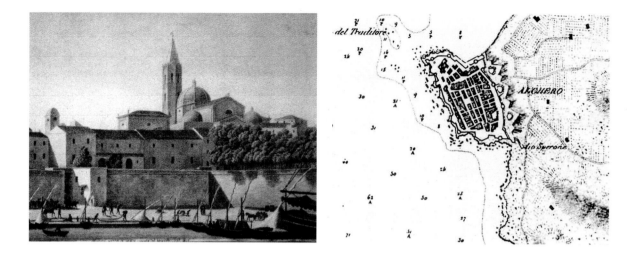

I.12 Cultural expansion and city development

Cultural influence on dominated cities was to a large extent expressed by means of emblematic works of architecture. Guillem de Sagrera[35] made a decisive contribution to the construction of major monuments in other Mediterranean cities dependent on Barcelona: the Exchange in Majorca and Naples's Castel Nuovo. This is just one example of a widespread tendency that was to continue for several centuries in an important process of mutual cultural influence.[36]

On another scale, the case of Alghero, a town on the west coast of Sardinia, is an interesting one. The present-day inhabitants still speak Alguerés, a Catalan dialect, as a living language and a sign of identity. Alghero was founded in 1102 by the Doria family of Genoa as a city fortress, with three sides surrounded by sea and the fourth in contact with terra firma, and duly walled.

In 1354, after a combined Sardinian-Genoese rebellion, Pere III imposed Catalanness on Alghero, expelling the native inhabitants and encouraging the immigration of Catalan colonisers, and passing laws that forbad Sardinians to stay overnight in the city. In this way, the city came to act as a veritable fortress of Catalan colonisation.

Three hundred miles from Barcelona and in the same direction as the maestrale or west wind, Alghero is the "diagonal of the islands", the backbone of the economic and military empire that Barcelona was building in Mediterranean along the spice route (rotta delle spezie)[37].

The town still has a district called Barcelonetta, and Carlos V, on a visit after his second expedition to Africa, pronounced it "beautiful and well settled". The Genovese defences were reinforced by the Catalan towers that still

[35]   See G. Alomar, Guillem Sagrera y la arquitectura gótica del siglo XV. Barcelona, 1970. An excellent compendium of the work of this architect and sculptor.
[36]   M. Rosi, Architettura meridionale del rinascimento. Naples, 1983.
Puig i Cadafalch himself (Les influences lombardes en Catalogne. Congrès Archeologique de France 1960) points out the Lombard influence on the Catalan Romanesque of the 10th and 11th centuries.
[37]   J. Carbonell, F. Manconi: I catalani in Sardegna. A. Pizzi. Milan, 1984. Also: E. González Hurtebise: Guía historica-descriptiva del Archivo de la Corona de Aragón en Barcelona. Madrid, 1920; Francesco Manconi: Libre Vell. 2 libri dei privilegi della città di Alghero (2 vol.). Sassari, 1997; Gianni Mura and Antonello Sanna: La città. Paesi e Città della Sardegna (2 vol.). Cagliari, 2002.

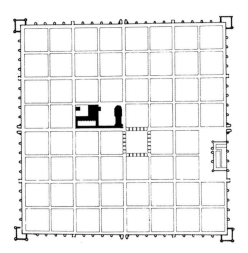

bear the arms of the city that directed colonisation. The sea walls are still standing and the banked earth bastions were only demolished in the mid-19th century when the city opened up towards its agricultural inland. Today, it is a very lovely tourist spot that conserves in its stones the history of that period and in Algherese culture its own identity.

atalan was also a language used as a matter of course in many of those cities for conducting business. Today it is still going strong in the form of Mallorquí, Valencià and other dialectal languages used within the realms of Catalan domination in the Western Mediterranean.

As explained above, the establishment of the population was vital to processes of conquest and expansion with the purpose of ensuring a native productive structure in each territory. One particularly ambitious project was the regional development planned by Jaume II in the Kingdom of Majorca to create a series of 14 pobles, small centres of colonisation and agricultural establishment that would act as veritable poles of growth. Planning took the form of ordinacions, a royal text that stipulated the rights and duties of the settlers and set out the general dimensions for street widths and plot sizes.[38]

Precedents obviously included the ancient Hipodamic and Roman layouts, but another influence was the military bastide[39] of Saint Louis in Languedoc, and the colonisations of his father, Jaume I,[40] advancing across eastern Spanish lands such as Castellón, Almenara, Soneja, Nules, Villarreal and Burriana.[41]

[38] Gabriel Alomar: Urbanismo regional en la Edad Media: Las "ordinacions" de Jaume II (1300) en el Reino de Mallorca. Barcelona, 1976. The construction of each pobla involved the specific application of the grid layout to the geography of the specific site. Roman centuriation had wrought a similar system in other regions, though the scale of the layout corresponded to a different logic.

[39] See F. Divorne, Ph. Panerai et al.: Les bastides. Essai sur la regularité. Brussels, 1985, which describes the importance of this process in France and the principles of composition that governed it.

[40] David Friedman: Florentine New Towns. Urban Design in the late Middle Ages. Cambridge, 1988. A comprehensive work about Florence's "new colonies" in the 14th century and the emergence of the figure of the engineer Nicolosa, originally from the Liguria coast, who, under the orders of Jaume I, produced the design for the central square of Villarreal in 1274. Once more this goes to show the process of mutual cultural influence in this Mediterranean region that was so open at the time.

[41] P. Ramon de Maria: l ripartiment de Burriana y Villarreal. Valencia, 1935.

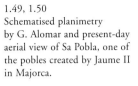

1.49, 1.50
Schematised planimetry
by G. Alomar and present-day
aerial view of Sa Pobla, one of
the pobles created by Jaume II
in Majorca.

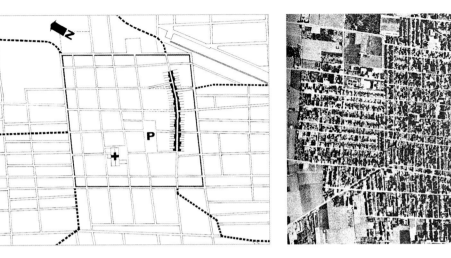

I.13 The ideal city

It was this system of urban development that was theorised in the late 14th century by Francesc Eiximenis, a Franciscan who lived first in Barcelona and then in Valencia, and who in his Regiment de Prínceps e de las Ciutats e de la cosa pública described how to build a city that was "beautiful and well constructed".[42]

The city "must be established in the plain, so that it can extend without obstacles; its ground plan should be square, with sides of one thousand paces; in the middle of each there shall be a main gate, flanked by two smaller doorways, reinforced like those of castles; the spaces too shall be fortified. From gate to gate, two broad streets will divide it into four quarters, each with a spacious and beautiful square. The prince's palace, strongly built and in an elevated position, should rise on one side, with direct access to the exterior. The cathedral will stand in the vicinity of the junction of the two main streets; [...] each district will have monasteries of mendicants and parish churches, butcher's, fishmonger's, corn exchanges and several shops. The hospitals, lepers' colonies, gambling dens, brothels and sewer outlets should be located on the opposite side to the direction from which the prevailing winds blow. People of a same profession shall live grouped together in a single district".[43]

In the context of the strong urban planning dynamic of the time, Eiximenis brought a humanist approach to the ideal city, designing a complex city that took into account geographical and aesthetic aspects and internal structure. His "regular plan" was based on classical Mediterranean culture and aimed to produce the perfect city according to his Christian religious principles. His was a global reflection on the city that represented a real step forwards towards the Renaissance city and away from the apparent irregularity of the medieval conception.[44]

Compared to the difficulty of understanding the aggregated space of the Gothic city, the Renaissance city features space as a system of organisation in itself.

[42] S. Vila: La ciudad de Eiximenis: Un proyecto teórico de urbanismo en el siglo XIV. Valencia, 1984. This book presents Eiximenis' work as an early forerunner of Renaissance city theory. Also: J. Puig i Cadafalch: Idees teòriques sobre urbanisme en el segle XIV. IEC. Barcelona, 1936.
[43] F. Eiximenis: El Crestià, Vol. XII. Els nostres clàssics. Barcelona, 1929.
[44] G. Muratore: La città rinascimentale. Tipi e modelli attraverso i trattati. Milán, 1975.

0   50 100   200   N

II From the urbanisation of the Raval to the start of industrialisation

II.1 The population crisis in Barcelona

After this period of great splendour, Barcelona, like so many European cities, sunk into a major population crisis. A series of plagues (1285, 1291, 1333, 1348) devastated the urban and rural populations and changed the demographic rate of preceding centuries. Pierre Vilar describes this situation most expressively in his masterwork *Catalunya dins l'Espanya Moderna*.[1] As a result, the evolution of the city and the great historical events of this period were marked by the vicissitudes of plague and epidemic. Even the movement between the population residing inside the city walls and the population living in the plain and in nearby rural settlements began to be quantitatively important.

However, comparative studies of cities[2] in the Middle Ages show that there were no large cities in Europe. A dozen principal cities, including Venice, Milan, Ghent, Cologne, Florence and Paris, covered surface areas of between 400 and 600 hectares, with between 100,000 and 150,000 inhabitants.

Barcelona is listed in the first twenty, with an enceinte of 200 hectares in 1350, and an estimated population of 30,000 inhabitants.

II.2 The influence on the city of a change of dynasty

The change from the 14th to the 15th century saw the decadence of the Catalan dynasty, with Joan I and Martí the Humane, leading to a general lack of direction and to succession disputes. The Diputació de les Corts had to take charge of government and seek a compromise between the three kingdoms. It was decided, against the opinion of Barcelona, to use an electoral procedure to choose the monarch. In Caspe, the crown was granted to Fernando of Antequera.

This political change was to have major effects on a capital city that was used to deciding its own strategies and playing an important role in the western Mediterranean[3].

2.01
Interpretation of the layouts
of the walled city.

[1] Pierre Vilar: Catalunya dins l'Espanya moderna. Barcelona, 1966. To explain the dramatic nature of Barcelona's population crisis, he writes: "In 1362-63, the plague reappeared in Barcelona, where the Pope authorised the people to pray not just for the dead, but also for those who would die in the three weeks following the prayer."
[2] L. Benévolo: L'arte e la città medioevale. Latenza. Rome, Bari, 1975.
[3] C. Carrère: Barcelona 1380-1462. Un centre econòmic en època de crisi. (2 vol.) Curiel. Barcelona, 1977.

Fernand Braudel[4] links together a series of negative elements to explain the marked change of pace that became apparent in Barcelona as of the early 15th century.

This notwithstanding, for a long period of time the existing civil structure continued to operate with initiative. In 1401, the Consell set up the *"Taula de Canvi i comuns dipòsits de la ciutat"*, which began to act as the city's bank after the disappearance of the Jews who had played such an important role in the sector.

But the loss of inherent strength affected Barcelona's leadership in its relations with other capital cities around the Mediterranean. The great innovative capacity of Italian cities at this time was manifested in many ways. One, in the field of art, was the development of the Renaissance as a line of reflection and action that failed to take root in a Barcelona still anchored in the Gothic. The capacity for dynamism and drive in this incipient "ideal" city was cut short and, for the moment, the city departed from the forefront that it had occupied on its own scale.

II.3 The consolidation of urban culture

Despite this change of rhythm in Barcelona, the resurgence of cities in the Middle Ages led to the creation of a specific urban culture in southern Europe. Braudel's comment in his work about the second half of the 16th century is very eloquent: "The prevailing human order in the Mediterranean was dictated mainly by the cities and their communications, subordinating the rest to these requirements."[5] Braudel's work pinpoints cultural history as being far more relevant to an understanding the transformation of society than the simple juxtaposition of political organisation or the direct sequence of events.[6]

This hypothesis certainly appears to be valid in explaining the construction of urban culture in Mediterranean cities in the early Modern age and seems to establish a major difference from cities in the north of Europe, where the rural environment was still the dominant scenario.

In fact the urban ideology that establishes the priority of urbanitas (the city) over rusticitas (the country)[7] stems from classical Greece and was disseminated by Aristotle in his defence of man as a "social animal",

---

[4] F. Braudel, op.cit. p. 190. On the impact on Barcelona of these events: "When Barcelona lost its independence, when it succumbed after the long fight against Juan of Aragon, when it lost its liberties and when twenty years later in 1492 it lost its Jewry, no less serious; ultimately, when its capitalists began to give up risky ventures for a regular income from the 'Taula de Canvi', or the purchase of land close to the city; when all of this happened, [it also represented] the decadence of the mercantile city and the Catalan coast that were its lifeblood."

[5] F. Braudel: op. cit. 1976.

[6] A. Cowan: Mediterranean Culture. 1400-1700. Exeter, 2000.

[7] M. Richter: Urbanitas-Rusticitas: Linguistic Aspects of Medieval Dichotomy. Studies in Church History. 1979.

2.02, 2.03
Carrer Ample and Plaça
Nova by Lluís Rigalt, 1867.

insistently proclaiming the ethical, cultural and social advantages of the urban environment over the rural world beyond the town walls.[8]

After the Middle Ages, the image of urban superiority had public and economic effects that also extended to the social environment, as Pierre Vilar reminds us in his work on the 18th century in which he so clear-sightedly refers to the advantages of the urban over the rural, described as boring and lacking in innovation.[9]

This situation of prevalence has been passed down to the present day; only in the Romantic period was there a tendency to value the country and to see the city as an unnatural phenomenon.

However, the difference between the urban environments of northern and southern Europe lay in how cities were created and particularly in the differing uses made of their public communal spaces.

It is important to refer here to both the theoretical formulation of the city's civic discourse, particularly in Florence, a pioneering city in these matters,[10] and the dominant classes' commitment to the city, whereas in the north of Europe the aristocracy remained in their castles and created a totally different system of spatial organisation.

The city was, then, a place of order, progress and social betterment. There were a series of elements that facilitated social interaction: the importance of family relations; the creation of clear hierarchies in trade and the organisation of work; the existence of patronage in the form of persons or institutions who acted as mediators in social relations; the aggregative value of the neighbourhood; and also some almost "theatrical" but well established principles of social interaction, such as honour, vengeance, etc. Altogether, they establish a system of civic values that gave rise to and encouraged urban sociability.

[8] J. Caro Baroja: "The City and the Country: Reflexions on Some Ancient Commonplaces", J. Pitt-Rivers: Mediterranean countrymen. The Hague, 1963.

[9] P. Vilar: Assaigs sobre la Catalunya del S. XVIII. Barcelona, 1973.

[10] Florence is a requisite reference, as the breeding ground for the modernisation of urban culture, ranging from theoretical works such as Alberti's with his new view of the city, or as the object of aesthetic contemplation for an educated elite, such as the urban descriptions by Leornardo Bruni, Laudatio Florentinae, as a model for other cities, to Machiavelli's proposals in his Discourses 1519, in which he refers to the city as the suitable place for political decision-making.

In order to introduce and regulate these values, the authorities established control mechanisms such as the Inquisition, a most regretful chapter, to shape social patterns. The description of these episodes became a fertile practice and in the case of Barcelona, according to J. Amelang, the "histories" written between the 15th and 18th centuries can be counted in their dozens; of particular notes are Jeroni Pau's Barcino in the late 15th century and Miquel Parets' Diarios in the 17th century.[11]

To substantiate this consolidation of urban culture, scholars refer as a source of information to travellers who, as in the case of the Swiss Thomas Platter in 1599, were struck by the personal relations and the intensity of use in public spaces.[12] It seems that streets and squares were also places for production and trading: in working districts, looms and other devices were placed out in the street, and many trades were very obvious from the outside, creating a sensation of vitality that astounded visitors.

However, not all citizens used space in the same way; social stratification was highly complex and the various symbolisms differed greatly according to social class, as well as gender: there was a very marked separation between the roles of men and women.

Space, too, was stratified. There was a clear distinction between the laws for offences or crimes committed inside or near churches, as this space was regarded as sacred. Codes of behaviour in public space were also taught in schools, as J. Amelang[13] reminds us. These were elements that promoted and encouraged sociability in the use of public space, making it a characteristic agglutinant of urban culture, firstly as a place for intensive use, but also as a space for the celebration of religious and/or civil rituals and therefore functionally and symbolically charged even in Mediterranean cities today.

Thus far we have observed the consolidation of this new urban culture; now we should devote a little attention to aspects of transformation of the conception of urban space with the introduction of new forms of representation.[14]

The innovation ushered in by the Renaissance involved a far-reaching cultural change. For Erwin Panofsky,[15] the discovery and advance of "perspective" as a way of drawing space was central to that change and converted the "desire to formalise" into a fundamental component of Western thought, comprising thought, culture and forms of behaviour.

---

[11] J. Amelang: The Myth of the Mediterranean City. Perceptions of Sociability, in A. Cowan, 2000.

[12] R. Alba: Viaje por España y Portugal. Madrid, 1991. Also J. García Mercadel: Viajes de extranjeros por España y Portugal. Madrid, 1952.

[13] J. Amelang, op.cit. He records the instructions given by the Jesuit school, the Col·legi de Cordellers, to its pupils, exhorting them to "behave themselves in the street, not to look into the houses, not to shout", etc., establishing rules of behaviour in public space.

[14] James S. Ackerman: "The Origins of Architectural Drawing in the Middle Ages and Renaissance", Origins, Imitation, Convention. Berkeley, 2002.

[15] E. Panofsky: Perspective as Symbolic Form. New York, 1997 (originally published in Berlin, in 1927).

2.04, 2.05
Views of the old centre in the 19th century according to Dionís Baixeras. It still suggests the specific use of the various streets by different guilds.

Although space was understood and represented in ancient cultures, and even Vitruvius describes the term "scenography" as representation in three dimensions, they produced no drawings with a central vanishing point. It was not until the specific invention of perspective (which, in Latin, means "to look through") that representation and reality were identified as forming a continuous abstract space.

This came with Dürer, Leonardo and Alberti, among others. According to Dürer, this new form of painting represented in one "plane the transparent intersection of all the rays that are directed from the eye to the object in question...", or became a glass wall on which to paint, for Leonardo, or enable "accurate geometric construction" as of the Renaissance.

II.4 Medieval production means and the city streets

In Catalan and Barcelona society, working processes were clearly dominated by the influence of the rural world and the services required by this production system, subsequently with major dependence on the sector now referred to as primary (agriculture and stock-keeping).

Within this rural structure, the typical unit in terms of decision-making and the work force was the family. As necessary, the workforce was completed by the figures of the apprentice or the farmhand who received monetary wages or were paid in kind (accommodation, food and apprenticeship).

In the urban environment, another concern was guaranteeing the availability of foodstuffs (vegetable gardens both within and outside the town walls), but there was also a degree of land use specialisation in the production of manufactured consumer goods.

2.06
View of Barcelona from Montjuïc. Drawing by J. C. Vermeyen in 1535, published in Civitates, Orbis, Terrarum.

Work was normally divided into the trades system in order to maximise each operator's skills. The guilds were of fundamental importance in the Middle Ages, constituting a very active sector in the urban organisation of Barcelona.

Nonetheless, production techniques were basically manual, with extremely rudimentary implements and only minimal investment in fixed capital (buildings, tools, etc.).

The traditional manufacturing sector was textiles, and the fibres used (cotton, hemp, linen and wool) were all locally produced. Spinning and weaving methods were manual and were truly primitive until the 18th century.

As regards production goods, only rural industry and metallurgy presented precedents of any importance to the industrial expansion of the 19th century. Shipbuilding enjoyed the importance that the Catalan economy assigned to overseas relations. Shipping was the principal means of transport, hence the importance of the shipyards that were set up in the vicinity of Barcelona.

Iron production was necessary for the tools of the various trades and also for the construction of ships and buildings. The first pre-industrial iron and steel works were the Catalan fargues (smithies) that used hydraulic energy and gas created from charcoal. Most of them were located outside the city.

The names of the streets in Ciutat Vella still offer a faithful reflection of that production system. Durán i Sanpere[16] lists streets that still bear the name of the dominant or exclusive trades practised in them; for example, Dagueria (cutlers' street), Tapineria (cork cutters' street), Boters (coopers' street), Assaonadors (tanners' street), etc., were all named after the shops and workshops of these trades. He also points out that "the blind could find their way around a medieval city due to the noise and the smell that characterised each trade".

The call or Jewish quarter occupied the western sector of the walled town, between Porta Bisbal (Plaça Nova) and Portal Nou (Carrer de la Boquería). It was Barcelona's most important cultural centre, as until the late 14th century it had its own schools, hospitals, baths and two synagogues. The call functioned as an independent city inside the town walls and had its own gates when Jaume I ordered that the quarter be closed. The Jews enjoyed

[16] A. Durán Sanpere: Els noms dels carrers ens parlen de la història de la ciutat de Barcelona i la seva història. Curial. Barcelona, 1972. p. 426.

2.07
Town wall, monasteries and
convents, and roads.

2.08
Aerial photo of the Raval,
2000.

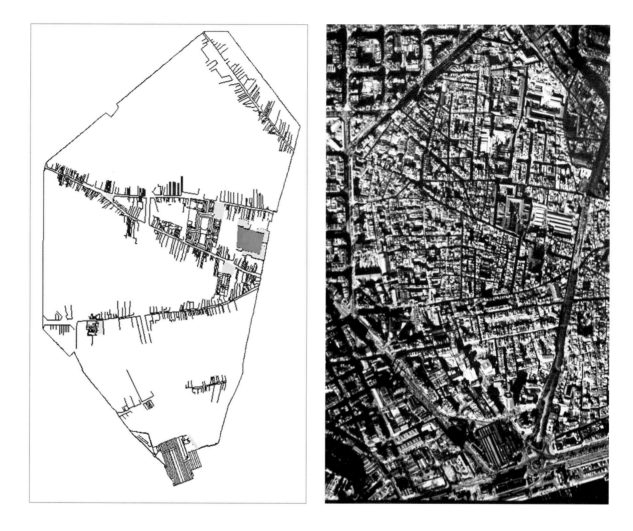

royal protection and wore long capes and hoods. In 1348 they were accused of having introduced the Black
Death, and anti-Semitism gradually grew until, in 1492, the Jews were definitively expelled.

II.5 The third town wall completes Ciutat Vella

The urban form of Barcelona underwent a major change between the 14th and 15th centuries with the
construction of the wall around the Raval (meaning suburb) to surround the western lands, encircling various
religious facilities and institutions which had been gradually moved to locations outside the city wall, along the
roads leading to the city.

This was the pattern followed by the suburbs of European cities: in some cases, they were the destination
of housing and workplaces that could not be situated inside the town walls due to lack of space; in others,
they became the site for larger-scale institutions that would thereby become more independent and which, as

2.09
View of Barcelona from
the sea in 1563 by Antoon
van den Wijngaerde.

monasteries or hospitals, were not afraid to settle outside the city. Barcelona's raval falls into the second category. It became the site for such prestigious city institutions as Sant Pau del Camp, an excellent Romanesque bastion, or later on the Hospital de la Santa Creu, built in 1403 with a rectangular Gothic patio, which was to replace the four earlier medieval hospitals.[17]

The construction of the third wall extended the enclosed city to over 6 kilometres and circumvallated a surface area of 218 hectares, twice the surface area of the central Roman city. It originally had three gates, marking the three westward exits: Santa Madrona in the direction of Montjuïc, Sant Antoni in the direction of the Llobregat delta, and Tallers towards Sarrià.

It is important to remember that at this time, fortifications were often the largest and most costly works to be undertaken by cities. The projects were carried out by specialists who consulted quite specific treatises on architecture. Visitors and travellers to the city were usually impressed by the force and beauty of the walls and by the decoration of their gates.

The evolution of the different walls and their different forms and sections is related to changes in defensive and ballistic techniques. The flat walls with quadrangular towers characterising medieval warfare gave way to the walls built under Pere III, with triangular bastions to preclude blind spots at the base of the walls and produce a perimeter that was more resistant to the impact of enemy canons. Verboom's proposal was paradigmatic in this evolution; it responded to an archetypal layout of late 17th century tendencies and stood out for the severity of the layout of the wall and bastions and the zigzag of the banked earth that formed an impressive landscape.

It is important to realise the value of this major extension of the wall's perimeter. While there were already some established activities in the new enceinte, the city now had vegetable gardens and farming activities in the short term, and a large semi-urbanised, well-defined space for future expansion. This situation came about in a period in which the city, as explained above, was to experience a drastic fall in population as a result of which there was little new building work in the sector for a long time to come. However, it was a great potential reserve for the development of Ciutat Vella when industry and manufacturing became booming sectors.

The wall also enclosed the shipyards that were now at their peak and represented a major incentive to Barcelona's maritime aspirations. However, there was still no port as such, despite two attempts to construct a perpendicular wharf, in 1439 and 1477.

---

[17] Although later added to and extended, the size of this complex makes it extremely interesting, bearing in mind the scale of building in the 15th century.

2.10
Western sector of the city,
drawing by Wijngaerde,
showing the Rambla and
the Church of El Pi, 1563.

The walled enclosure was not completed until the construction of the Sea Wall, which was not built until the reign of Carlos V (1553-1963). When it was constructed, a strip of open land was left on the inside, between the wall and the city, both for defensive purposes and representative functions between the Portal de Mar and the Rambla.

Antoon van den Wijngaerde's drawings from 1563[18] are interesting illustrations of the city seen from Montjuïc and from the sea, the best and most used vantage points from which to view the city's urban evolution. The view from the mountain bears witness to both the compact nature of the walled medieval city and the new Raval, and the contrast between the smallness of the port and the intense maritime activity taking place there. This is one of the first views of Barcelona to be produced with precision and detail.[19]

[18] M. Galera: Anton van den Vijngaerde, pintor de ciutats i de fets d'armes a l'Europa del Cinc-cents. Barcelona, 1998.

At the heart of the old town, the building of the Generalitat, by this time a decisive body in political affairs, was gradually acquiring its definitive form. Land in the former call was turned to other purposes: the Gothic building dating from 1418, directed by Marc Safont, was extended by the Golden Chamber and the famous "Pati dels Tarongers" (orange tree patio), which was to become one of the most representative spaces of this important institution. The patio was later completed with the addition of Saint George's Hall and Saint James' façade by Sant Jaume de Pere Blay (late 16th century), one of the best examples of Catalan Renaissance architecture.

II.6 Barcelona's Rambla

The land to the west of the second town wall was now included in Pere III's enclosure. The linear space left between Jaume I's town wall and the Raval produced the Rambla. Development work was carried out in the 15th century by the Consell and was completed in 1444. It takes its name from the strong runoff that formed in this lower ground during rainy periods as the various torrents running across the Plain sought their outlet in the sea

---

[19] Some years later, Joris Hoefnagle introduced a similar viewpoint in the work Civitates Orbis Terrarum, published by Braun and Hogenberg in Cologne in 1572, that describes Barcelona as one of the world's great cities.

2.a La Rambla.

2.12
Streams and torrents
in the Plain.

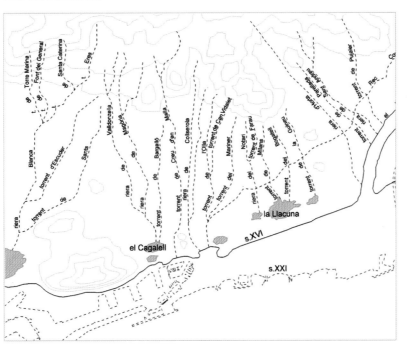

2.13
The Rambla in the second half
of the 17th century; the layout
of the town wall can still be
seen.

2.14
The Rambla, the city's liveliest
public space since e 15th
century.

2.15
Drawing of the remodelling of
the Rambla, turning it from
a space outside the town wall
into a city promenade of the
first order.

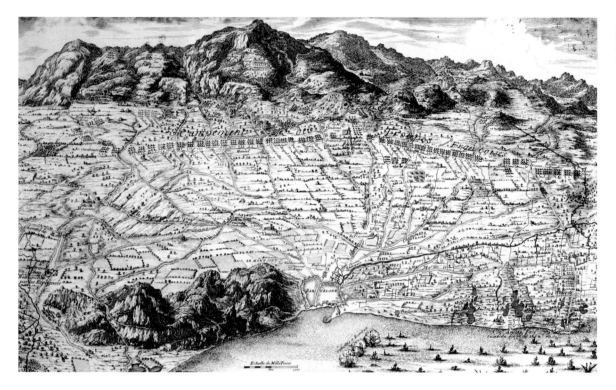

2.16
French map of 1698, showing
the surrounding territory in
detail.

via the Rambla. Its construction signalled the creation of the first large urban space for promenading, recreation and occasional fairs and markets.[20]

It was a space with a singular form due to its relatively irregular ground plan and the buildings of quite different uses, structures, sizes and styles that lined it. The asymmetrical organisation produced by the eastern wall remained for a long time, leaving urban spaces and sites that gradually became built up until the 19th century, another reason for the diversity of its buildings.[21]

The Rambla was initially the site for new monasteries and convents (Discalced Carmelites, Trinitarians, Mercenarians, Augustinians, etc.) on the Raval side.

In the 16th century the University was set up in the building of the Estudi General at the top of the Rambla, in accordance with a privilege granted by Carlos V. The town wall still existed on the east side.

After 1704, the bastion was gradually demolished, making way for new buildings or palaus, or allowing houses built against the old wall to create a façade in the new urban front. It was above all in the 18th and 19th centuries that the most important palaus were built: Palau Moja (1772) opposite the Church of Betlem, Palau March de Reus (1776), built by Joan Soler Fanera in the neo-classic style, and the Palau de la Virreina, constructed for the Viceroy of Peru, the Catalan Manuel Amat, Marquis of Castellbell, during the same period.

---

[20] A. Durán i Sanpere, op.cit.: La Rambla. pp. 486-506. Also Pau Vila: "Orígens i evolució de la Rambla", Miscellània Barcinonensis. Barcelona, 1965. Pere J. Figuerola and Josep M. Martí: La Rambla. Els seus convents. La seva història. Barcelona, 1995.
[21] Various authors: Façana de la Rambla. ETSAB. Barcelona, 1987. Also J. Margarit, Poema per un fris. Barcelona, 1987.

2.17
View of the city from the sea
before the construction of the
military citadel.

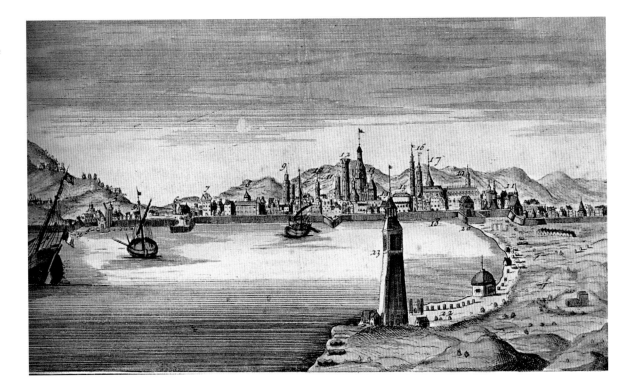

In the late 18th century, between 1772 and 1807, at the time of the Count of Ricla, realignment work was carried out on the Rambla. The engineer Cermeño who later designed Barceloneta was responsible for the technical supervision of realignment work.

This was the basis for further configuration in the 19th century. The widespread confiscation of church property was to add Plaça Reial and Plaça de Sant Josep (today still occupied by the Boqueria market), and the progressive urbanisation of the various subspaces that make up the Rambla continued throughout the century. The Liceu opera house was built on the corner of the Rambla and Carrer Sant Pau, the Canaletes fountain continued as an exclusive point of reference in the city since the origins of the Rambla, distributing water from Collserola; the street furniture was adapted to its context and wrought iron introduced a new touch of splendour.

By means of this slow process, one of the city's loveliest spaces was created, as the result of over five centuries as a central spot where the representation of urban life and commercial and institutional activity have been staged side by side.[22]

---

[22] Among many other references, the great Catalan architect Josep Lluís Sert uses it as an example of "the heart of the city" in his book: Can Our Cities Survive? Cambridge, 1942. He contrasts this type of centre with the functionality of planned modern centres.
For Alexandre Cirici (op.cit., p. 90), "La Rambla de les Flors" is the "quintessence" of Barcelona. "The avenue flanked by great plane trees transplanted from Girona's Devesa Park in 1850, runs between flower stalls which were set up in cast-iron structures in the 19th century. At that time, it was the only place in Barcelona that sold flowers, and each stall had its own circle."

II.7 Barcelona and the Castilian kings

A period of wars against Juan II (1462-1472) gave way to a new phase under the Castilian kings. This situation of change was characterised by the imposition of institutional and religious patterns common to the rest of the kingdom, though the Catalan institutions maintained a degree of autonomy in their own scope.

The establishment of the Spanish Inquisition was a harsh imposition in Catalonia. Despite the opposition of the Consell and the Generalitat, the Kings wanted to ensure Catholic unity at any price. It made a strong impact: its rigid tribunal with a fanatical bent took possession of the Palau Major and caused a mass exodus of conversos, Jewish converts to Catholicism, mostly merchants and dealers, who feared its discriminatory action, with a considerable fall in economic activity as a result.

Fernando II took a more lenient approach to the issue of the remença.[23] In 1486 he established a kind of agrarian reform to pacify the countryside. Peasants were thereby freed from the servitude and obligations imposed by the seigneurs during feudal times and now became usufructuaries of the land that they had worked with their families.

The Consell was remodelled in keeping with new royal tendencies. The system of insaculació was introduced as a more objective electoral procedure, though 1510 saw the introduction to the council of the figure of the military "knight", somewhat devaluing the body's completely civilian makeup.

After the period of regency, the young Flemish King Charles emerged as emperor of a vast empire. Barcelona had a marginal role in this great undertaking as a whole, though maintaining its activities and relations in the nearest reaches of the Mediterranean.

In 1519, the Emperor Charles held the general chapter of the Order of the Golden Fleece in Barcelona. The lavishness of the event left the people quite clear as to the scale on which that great empire moved, and in which the city was basically a mere spectator.

The Catalan institutions still maintained a degree of independence from imperial strategies. The oligarchy represented in the Consell was still able to carry out maritime and trading activity despite the increase in piracy. The houses of the bourgeoisie and the nobles were extended, and work began on new ones in the Rambla and on other sites produced by the demolition of old buildings.

[23] The pagès de remença was a peasant who in this medieval period was enfeoffed to a seigneury that he could only leave by paying a redemption or remença.

II.8 Columbus reaches Barcelona. Catalonia and the Americas

In 1493, the royal family put up in Barcelona after the long conquest of Granada. During their stay in Carrer Ample, King Fernando was the object of a serious attack that almost obliged him to leave the city.[24]

While the monarch was convalescing, Christopher Columbus returned from his first voyage of discovery to the lands known as the "Indies".[25] The circumstances of the king perhaps meant that Columbus' presence in the city with men and women from other cultures, as well as unknown exotic objects and animals, went almost unnoticed. The official chroniclers paid no particular attention to the event, not understanding that a great continent had been discovered, or perhaps with the premonition that Barcelona would have little to do with this new enterprise.

In any case, Barcelona's maritime traders were eager and needed to embark on business relations with the Indies. Catalan exports would have to overcome the difficulties imposed by the Castilians and the Genovese if they were to gain a foothold in this venture. In 1550, the Emperor granted permission to trade directly with the new continent; however, the port of departure had to be Seville, which had obtained the monopoly in 1503. And so the first Catalan manufactured products made their way onto the American market. Full free trade with the Americas did not occur until 1778 with the proclamation of the Law on Free Trade by Carlos III, though, as we will go on to see, trade was already booming.

Nonetheless, the existence of relations between Catalonia and the Americas is still surprising. The Indies depended on the Crown of Castile, which explains why most of the conquistadores were Castilian, though individual Catalans did take part from the very first. This is the case of the adventurer Joan Orpí in the conquest of Nueva Cataluña in Venezuela and it is probably to him that we owe the existence of a new Barcelona in that region. Catalans also took part in the slave trade, operating mainly from the West Indies. Indeed, the hermit monk of Montserrat, Bernat Boil, was the first to celebrate mass on American soil on Columbus' second voyage in 1493 thanks to his position as First Vicar of the Indies.

[24] Agustí Durán i Sanpere: "Cristofor Colom a Barcelona", Barcelona i la seva història. Curial. Barcelona, 1973, pp. 623-625. This documents Columbus' visit in a reference to his logbook: "he was resolved to go to Barcelona, by sea, in which city he had heard that their Majesties were staying, in order to relate to them his voyage..." Later, he mentions the testimony of Pietro Martir d'Anghiera, who writes in his Opus epistolarum: "in Barcelona, the King and the Queen made Columbus, who had returned from such an honourable enterprise, Admiral of the Seas, and they made him to sit before them, which is, in our royalty, a supreme sign of benevolence and honour that is granted for great exploits."

[25] Antonio Rumeu de Armas: Colón en Barcelona. Seville, 1944.

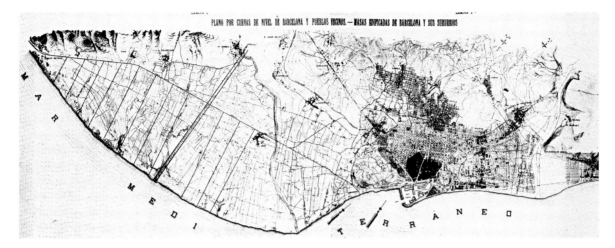

2.18
The city and the Llobregat delta according to a drawing by García Faria in the late 19th century. It proves the importance of the delta as a reserve of farmland and breathing space for Barcelona.

In the 18th century Gaspar de Portolà and a series of Catalan volunteers conquered California and laid the Spanish foundations on the west coast of North America that went on to produce settlements of great interest.[26] The Catalans began to make their presence felt by means of its traders.

The Catalan exodus to the Americas intensified in the 19th century when thousands of young men left their homes in Barcelona and other towns along the Catalan coast to start a new life there, setting up factories and becoming involved in large undertakings. A new term was even coined: indianos[27] were those men who returned from America having made their fortunes; they needed to show off their wealth, which they did by constructing important buildings and contributing to charitable works in the cities to which they returned.

The return of the indianos and their willingness to accept risk and sponsor innovation ushered in the modernisation of the country in the 19th century. For instance, Miquel Biada, a ship-owner from Mataró, was the early champion of the first Spanish railway line (Barcelona to Mataró, 1845) on his return from Cuba. In 1835, Josep Xifré constructed the famous porxos (porches) opposite the Exchange. The cases indianes that they built still afford Romantic villa landscapes in many towns in Maresme, where they were built on prominent geographical spots.

II.9 The Barcelona Plain and its surrounding farmland

At this point in our historical account, the relations between Barcelona and its closest agricultural hinterland require further attention. Fernand Braudel[28] posits that the major land improvement schemes were the work of fast expanding cities concerned with ensuring food supply. He points out the investment of the city's money to boost the countryside, and goes on: "surely this is one of the aspects in Barcelona's economic drama: why did Barcelona's bourgeoisie invest its money in land rather than venturing it in maritime enterprise?"

---

[26] Reyner Banham: Los Angeles. Penguin. London, 1971. Also Jaume Sobrequés: Els catalans en els orígens històrics de Califòrnia. Barcelona, 1992.

[27] Rosa Gil: "Els indians", Revista Girona. Girona, 1991.

[28] F. Braudel: op.cit., pp. 53-78.

2.19
Illustration of the central area
of the Llobregat delta.

2.20
View of the delta in the first
half of the 20th century, when
it was first used for an airport.

The citizens' investment in the countryside was manifested principally: 1) in the purchase of land by a bourgeois class that was successful in commercial activity and wished to own land in order to be like the nobility, which in turn regarded this course of action as controversial, and 2) by means of credit, or the transfer of purchasing power, in the form of money or a deposit with the payment of interest and the return of capital over periods of two to five years. To some extent, the countryside fed the city with products and labour, and the city financed the countryside in a process that sometimes actually hampered farming production.

Investments were centred in Maresme and on land around the Llobregat delta. An excellent study into the territory immediately surrounding Barcelona[29] shows exactly how closely the city and its farmland were interlinked. However, Jaume Codina's work points out that this process took place in the second half of the 16th century, and was very specific: at the end of the 16th century only a third of the owners of farmland were from the delta; the rest were from the capital, more specifically members of the bourgeoisie and some aristocrats.[30] At this moment, "the peasant farmers in the delta began to lose possession of the land, precisely when those in the rest of Catalonia were acquiring it, in a Catalonia that was beginning to emerge from feudal and social struggles (...) Why did the decline of Barcelona have to entail the ruin of the Delta?".[31]

According to this study, rather than representing the rationalisation of the agricultural production process that was now necessary to keep the capital supplied, urban investment in the countryside was merely a mechanism for investment in fixed capital, and agriculture continued to use the old farming methods.[32] It is important to remember that farmland was not habitually inherited. This is partly because church and municipal land could not be sold or transferred until the confiscation of church property in the 19th century when land

[29] Jaume Codina: El Delta del Llobregat i Barcelona. Gèneres i formes de vida dels segles XVI al XX. Ariel. Esplugues, 1971. A detailed investigation of both the evolution in forms of farming and the lifestyles they involved.
[30] The average size of a property was five mujadas, a farming measure equivalent to the stretch of land that a pair of oxen could plough in a day (equivalent to 4,896.5 square metres).
[31] Codina: op.cit., p. 111.
[32] The regime of "sharecropping" (temporary use in exchange for a percentage of the harvest) was dominant in the Delta until the 19th century when irrigation and intensive farming began, and a rent of monies once again governed temporary forms of letting.

2.21
Illustration from the port, 18th century. Engraving by Charpentier.

began to form part of the market system, and partly because the land in private hands was inherited rather than bought and sold. The aim of the Catalan inheritance system was to maintain family heritage with a view to handing down family heritage intact; the figures of the hereu and the pubilla (heir/heiress) were created to correspond to the eldest son or daughter, who inherited the whole property, thereby preventing the progressive fragmentation of the land and ensuring the continuance of reasonably sized production units. This explains the relative unimportance in Catalonia of the smallholding, so characteristic of other areas of Spain such as the Atlantic coast.

It was only in the late 19th century that large tracts of land still afflicted by malaria were drained and, more importantly, irrigation systems were introduced as a result of an increase in local ownership and a new wave of capital from urban sources, this time interested in the implementation of new farming methods.[33] This heralded the golden age of farming in Barcelona's hinterland as a source of food supply for the capital, a model that was also found in other European cities.

Even today, despite the explosion of urban growth and the major interventions to which it has been subjected in recent decades, the Llobregat delta can be seen as a "green lung" for the Barcelona area.[34]

---

[33] To continue this interrelation, García Faria's 1890 design linked Barcelona's sanitation project with that of the Delta.
[34] For greater detail, see the monographic publication by various authors: Proyecto para el Delta del Llobregat. Jano 80. Barcelona, 1976.

2.22
Barcelona besieged by the
troops of Juan of Austria
during the War of the Reapers.
The engraving reproduces an
image of the city seen from
Collserola with its monasteries
situated outside the walled
town. Anonymous, 1640-1652.

II.10 A "difficult century", but one in which the port acquires its definitive form

In this situation of stagnation or low-level dynamism compared to Barcelona's true capacity, the period between 1580 and 1680 is generally considered as "the lost century" due to the city's lack of opportunities in the institutional context. In fact Barcelona had lost its role of political and military power in the Mediterranean and had little involvement in the more international decision-making circuits. However, the city maintained its economic dynamic thanks to the active, broad based network of the guilds. The fall in population was to some extent offset by the influx of French immigrants, who came to represent one in eight of the city's residents. There were, then, different dynamics existing at the same time.[35]

The construction of the port at last began to materialise. At the turn of the century, the port had a perpendicular wharf, 180 metres long and twelve wide. Later, in 1632, it became obvious that a protective dock

---

[35] A. García Espuche: Un siglo decisivo. Barcelona y Cataluña 1550-1640. Madrid, 1998. A detailed study that challenges commonly held views that the city was dormant throughout these decades. It highlights the economic reconstruction behind the sequence of such decisive political events. The description of the city by famous travellers shows just how much interest it excited. Hence Cervantes' praise for Barcelona in one of his Novelas Ejemplares dated 1613, in which he writes: "They admired the lovely site of the city, and esteemed it as one of the most beautiful cities in the world, honour of Spain, (...), an example of the loyalty and satisfaction of one who may ask of a great, famous, rich and well founded city a discreet yet curious wish." See the research into Cervantes' stay in Barcelona that explains how no other city had merited such an appreciation from this illustrious author, precisely the city in which Quijote fights one of his last battles and is defeated. Martín de Riquer, Para leer a Cervantes, Barcelona, 2003.

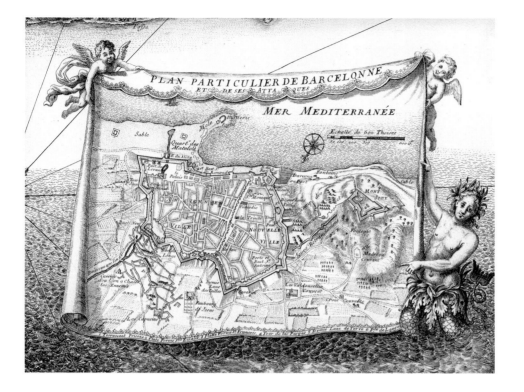

2.23
French relief of the city, 1698.
View from the city towards
the sea.

was needed to provide greater stability for ships moored in the harbour. In order to defray the expense of the work, the Consolat del Mar had levied a tax on goods unloaded in the port. It was not until 1743-1762 however that the port had an efficient working structure of docks.[36]

The city's population rose to 40,000 inhabitants and the Consell set up its first municipally-backed bank that was run in conjunction with the Taula de Canvi.

Relations with the capital of the kingdom became strained when the Madrid-based bureaucracy began to form an unfavourable view of the principality's criteria of independence that allowed it such significant liberties as minting its own coins.

In 1626, Felipe IV travelled to Barcelona and vowed to respect the rights and privileges of Catalonia in the Royal Palace. The city and its houses made a good impression on the courtiers and men of government who proposed higher taxation for "the rich city of Barcelona", with no thought for the centuries of effort it had taken to raise the city.

This signalled the start of an ongoing conflict that came to a head with the attempt to collect a fifth of the levies of the Consell and the Generalitat. The process became very involved, leading to continual confrontations between Catalonia's institutions and the Viceroy. At the same time, the war with France found Spanish troops stationed in Catalonia committing excesses with local properties and even with the civilian population. General malaise increased, and on the day of Habeas Corpus, 7 June 1640, the irate reapers stormed Barcelona and set

[36] According to the project, approved in 1731, by J. P. Verboom, who had already designed the Citadel, as described by Joan Alemany, op.cit. p. 105. The general evolution of the port can be seen in P. Alegre. Atlas del Port de Barcelona. Barcelona, 1998.

2.24
Dutch engraving, 1706,
showing the structure
of the Plain and the outskirts
of the walled town.

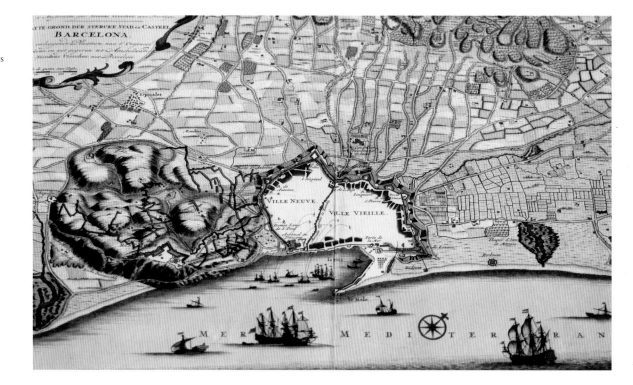

fire to the houses of nobles close to Madrid's royal family; the Viceroy died at El Morrot as he tried to flee the city.

This was the Corpus de Sang (Bloody Corpus). It was marked by its opposition to the central government, but also by social unrest caused by the degradation of agricultural life; there is historical proof of the participation in the events of peasant farmers from the delta and other poor farming areas.

However, while the social revolt began in defence of the social relations guaranteed by Catalan constitutions, it became a revolutionary movement against the entire seigneurial system.[37]

The additional circumstance of a debilitated Spanish monarchy led to a process of rapprochement with the French crown that was to lead to the "War of Separation". Catalonia recognised Louis XIII as Count of Barcelona, and a battle between France and Castile took place in the environs of Barcelona.

In 1651, Felipe IV's troops, in alliance with Juan of Austria, recovered Barcelona. The Spanish king occupied Montjuïc and the shipyard and reserved to himself the port jurisdiction, though construction work fell to the Consell.

The latter half of the century was marked by wars and epidemics. It was only in the last few decades that the economy and manufacturing timidly began to recover when books and tobacco emerged as new sectors in a burst of dynamism that only lasted until the recurrence of struggles for succession at the end of the century.

---

[37] Eva Serra: "Resistència de Catalunya i decadència castellana: la guerra de Separació", Història de Catalunya. Barcelona, 1978.

II.11 Urbanisation of the city

The Consell's task of urban improvements and supplying the city with food was becoming increasingly complex.

Urban planning work included the Passeig de Mar, between Pla de Palau and the Rambla. This intervention took the form of banking up earth around the port's wharves to create this urban front, which then became a popular place with residents and visitors alike.

Drinking water supplies and improvements to the sewerage system became crucial as the population grew. The organisation of water had been guided by a fragmentary system according to the availability of the moment. To maintain this service, the Consell had appointed a mestre de les fonts (master of the fountains), who, in the first half of the 17th century, was the plumber Francesc Socias, who wrote a spectacular description of the city's springs, fountains and conduits.[38]

New palaces were constructed to house the upcoming urban oligarchy, such as Casa Ardiaca, Casa Gralla and Palau Centelles, among others. Nonetheless, they were isolated buildings that replaced the existing fabric rather than presenting an overall development project such as Carrer Montcada, or the aristocratic extensions of many European cities. At the same time, the expansion of the monasteries inside the walled city continued to occupy spaces in the city's suburb and along the Rambla.

II.12 Decreto de Nueva Planta

The adverse outcome for Catalonia of the War of Succession to the Spanish Crown, in which Barcelona had taken the side of the Habsburgs, saw the advent of the military absolutism of Felipe V and a sudden change from traditional political and administrative practices. This conflicting situation was countered by more general changes in the social and economic dynamics.

In fact, according to Pierre Vilar, the 18th century should be defined as 1714 to 1808, marked by a "creative power [...] that ensured the definitive triumph of capitalist over feudal society, not only manifested in the England of the industrial revolution or the France of the political revolution, but in Europe as a whole and in its American annexes".[39]

---

[38] Francesc Socias: Llibre de les fonts de la present ciutat de Barcelona. Written in 1650 and kept in the archives of the Institut Municipal d'Història de la Ciutat.

[39] P. Vilar: op.cit., vol. III, p. 21 and p. 9.

2.25
Final attack on Barcelona
by the troops of Felipe V
in 1714, by the painter Rigaud.

In 1714 the city of Barcelona surrendered to the armies of Felipe V after thirteen months of siege, an event that saw the whole of Catalonia embarked on a change of dynamic. In 1716 the Decreto de Nueva Planta was enacted, abolishing the Generalitat and the Consell de Cent that had hitherto governed the city. The principality was then subject to a military government that acted like a viceroy. The municipal boundary was cut back and other municipalities in the Barcelona Plain were promoted. As explained earlier, the Consell de Cent had governed from Castelldefels to Montgat with regard to infrastructure and supply; its abolition dramatically cut short an indigenous process of great interest, and the city, too, suffered the consequences.[40]

Barcelona then underwent the rapid demographic growth that came to characterise contemporary society: the number of inhabitants rose from 35-40,000 in the 1716-1720 period to 100-112,000 in 1786-1790, representing a spectacular rate of growth. It was accompanied by an economic boom based on manufacturing which was sufficient to lead into the industrial revolution.

The city was the focus for most of the capitalist activities arising from colonial trade and cotton production that formed the basis of proto-industrialisation. Despite its vicissitudes, agriculture too was to some extent a source of capitalist accretion and, most importantly, formed a relatively equal social basis in the country and in the small towns that represented an excellent potential domestic market.

Nonetheless, the brutal introduction of absolutism under Felipe V cut short civic institutions' capacity for action and reduced Catalan autonomy of government. This change was offset by the end of a sterile corporatism that had already been the object of criticism and represented major social change, paving the way for broad based economic restructuring. The imposition of absolutist power actually facilitated the development of institutions that helped to modernise Catalan society.[41] For example, the transfer of the University of Barcelona to Cervera, by order of Felipe V, was an impediment to the city's cultural development but it facilitated the creation of the Royal Academy of San Fernando in 1752, the Barcelona Academy of Science and Arts, the College of Surgeons in 1762 with its headquarters in a building by Ventura Rodríguez,

[40] P. Vila and Ll. Casassas: op.cit., pp. 202-203.
[41] Roger Alier: "Pensament, art i cultura a la Barcelona del segle XVIII", Història de Barcelona, num. 5. Barcelona, 1993.

etc. The founding of these institutions led to a rationalisation of the artistic and academic situation along the same lines as the French Enlightenment. Nonetheless, centralising forces led to the suppression of teaching in Catalan in 1760.

The new dynamic created in Barcelona by the Bourbons, along with the accompanying demand created by major construction work, Italian military campaigns based in Barcelona and an actual increase in colonial trade had the effect of reactivating the urban economy and enabling the modernisation of production structures.

In fact in the 18th century the Catalan economy underwent a major process of specialisation in the production of consumer goods such as cloth, paper and eau-de-vie that were sold to the rest of Spain and overseas.

Textile production had always formed the spearhead of Catalan manufactured goods; now it was the printed cotton cloth known as indiana, which was exported to the Spanish Indies. Wine was another sector that took off in coastal areas; its production involved the use of great stills in which it was distilled. Paper emerged as an expanding industry due to growing demand. It was partly a by-product of the textile industry located near rivers in order to harness hydraulic energy.

The reorganisation of overseas trade at this time led to the creation in 1756 of the "Real Compañía de Barcelona para el Comercio de las Indias" as a way of rationalising the export process.

II.13 The emergence of new ideas and the dawn of the modern city

It seems to be an accepted fact that the 18th century was a favourable time for the most innovative ideas for modern city configuration. In many cases they were concepts rather than actual developments, but the foundations were being laid for the propagation in various ways of the big European cities that came into being in the next century. This was a way of rethinking the rational city in order to leave behind its medieval counterpart, whose urban and organisational structure had ceased to be sufficient.

The French Enlightenment provided the source of some of these new urban planning ideas:

1. M. A. Laugier proclaimed the creation of a new urban order to put an end to the chaotic image of the medieval city: order was to be combined with variety and regularity. J. F. Blondel, in his influential Cours d'architecture, highlighted the same subject.

2. The carrying out of urban reform due to sanitary issues. Pierre Patte promoted urban reform for questions of health, social order and safety. He introduced the idea of the medical metaphor and compared urban design operations to those conducted by surgeons, calling for a scientific basis for this new practice.

2.26
Barcelona during the siege of 1705. Engraving by P. Defehrt clearly showing the town walls of Jaume I and Pere III, the shipyard and the defensive bastions.

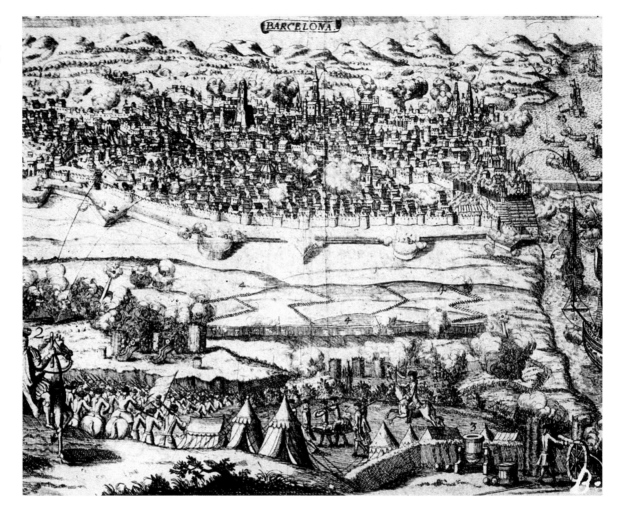

Patte compared the city to the human body, requiring circulation and continual change, and needing ventilation and drinking water without which the urban planning situation became pathological.[42]

3. The urban relocation of monuments. The urban planning doctrine of the Enlightenment in the second half of the 18th century consisted in the extrication (dégagement) of monumental buildings from the rest of the urban fabric.[43]

[42] See P. Patte, Monuments érigés en France à la Gloire de Louis XV. Paris, 1765. This work insists on the need to rationalise the city: it proposes that the cemeteries be moved outside the town walls, which produced new squares near churches. It also suggests the creation of new squares for improved ventilation and sunlighting. It calls for the reorganisation of markets, the installation of drinking fountains, etc. It also includes a sketch of an ideal street in 1769 in which the pedestrians are separated from the carriages. It presents a view of the city as a machine to promote its citizens' health. The authors' works were very influential and in 1769 the city of Paris created the post of city architect, to which P. Moreau-Desproux was appointed.

[43] Barry Bergdoll: L'Urbanisme Parisien au siècle des lumières. Paris, 1997. In Paris it was La Font de Saint-Yenne who advocated Voltaire's influence. And it was Soufflot who applied it by proposing the Louvre's new colonnade separate from adjacent buildings, and finally demolished it so that the monument was freestanding. He later constructed the semicircular square in front of the church of Ste. Geneviève.

These new ideas were actually compared and contrasted for the first time in the reconstruction of the Baixa of Lisbon after the earthquake of 1755, which was a paradigm model for a new form of European city design.[44]

Europe also became the platform for debate between nationalism and the identification of architectural styles. The period between the Enlightenment and the French Revolution displayed a liking for the local, for national culture and folklore, and proposals for patriotic commemoration were made.

According to Bergdoll, the conviction that architecture symbolises the national character is a modern concept that developed after the French Revolution.[45] Its moment came at a time when the map of Europe was constantly being redrawn. Architecture was required to express this identity by highlighting the glories and heroic feats of the past. Hence the apparent contradiction between the 18th century search for architectural "characters" as a universal vocabulary very clearly and firmly established by the Enlightenment and the 19th century formulation of specific styles in keeping with national circumstances. In Catalonia, it reached a peak of splendour in the 19th century with the phenomenon of the Renaixença and in the period of the 1888 World Fair, after the previous century during Catalan had been effectively negated by Bourbon power. Nonetheless, the identification of Barcelona as the symbol of the country remained quite evident.[46]

In this context of innovative ideas, city evolution was dynamic and controversial; the population and economy were booming, despite having to cope with the institutional and political change that the defeat of 1714 meant for Catalan reality.

---

[44] See José-Augusto França, Une ville des Lumières, la Lisbonne de Pombal. Paris 1965. The plan of Eugénio dos Santos, under the guidance of the Marquis of Pombal, implemented in 1758, represented the highpoint of intellectual attention under the Enlightenment. This comprehensive project gave indications for street layout, building heights and forms of construction to stand up to earthquakes, paving, sewerage systems, etc. Dos Santos was also responsible for the impressive Praça do Comercio, beside the river Tajo and on the site of the old palace, representing a great urban forum in the capital of a great maritime empire. It can be seen as an example of the new enlightened government's capacity to design new urban spaces and give form to civic life Lisbon became a symbol of the triumph of reason over the untamed forces of nature This model of new urban planning, already equipped with new urban actors and new technologies, was taken as a reference point for other cities for embellishment, as in the Saint Petersburg of Catherine the Great, or extension, as in the Turin of the Dukes of Savoy.

[45] See Barry Bergdoll, European Architecture.1750-1890. Oxford, 2000. There had already been some episodes of "national orders", such as Sebastien Leclerc's "French order" in 1714, and James Adam's "British order" in 1764. The revision of classical orders in an attempt to find personal nuances led to great pluralism and a stylistic revival. The German Gothic of Cologne cathedral is one example. In London, Wilkins had recourse to the same style, and the Gothic also re-emerged in France, etc. In short, the Gothic made a reappearance as a basis for Central European nationalism.

[46] See Jaume Sobrequés, Història de Barcelona. Introduction. Vol. 5. Barcelona, 1993, when he refers to the declarations of the Baron of Maldà identifying Barcelona as his "fatherland", highlighting the city's capacity to make citizens feel pride in their country and the Catalan nation. The Baron's diary offers a faithful view of the evolution of Barcelona society in the second half of the 18th century, explaining the replacement of the aristocracy by the nascent industrial middle classes, in a desire to leave behind the "old" regime.

According to Joan Nadal and Joan Reglà, the principality's economic revival continued until 1680. The new climate of work and trade made itself felt very strongly and the enlightened travellers of the 18th century recorded the situation: from Townsend to Ponz, via Laborde, they all describe the city's dynamic of activity and endeavour.[47]

It is important to stress to what extent the impetus of the Enlightenment pervaded Barcelona's various scientific, professional and artistic circuits. The sciences, from the experimental to the empirical, at an advanced stage of development in France, were also well received in Catalonia.[48]

II.14 Eighteenth-century Barcelona

A judicious description of early 18th-century Barcelona is provided by the cadastre of 1717, carried out at the changeover to the new administrative structure imposed by the Decreto de Nueva Planta. The census was ordered by the Marquis of Campoflorido and was intended as a fiscal document.

The cadastre[49] describes a city of 57,709 inhabitants occupying something over five thousand houses, in turn distributed throughout 10 neighbourhoods and reflecting the differential occupation of the walled city. The part of the city consolidated before the final wall (what Nadal and Giralt refer to as feudal Barcelona) was very built up (between 30 and 50 houses per hectare). Altogether there were 660 boticas, a term that included both stores and all manner of workshops.

Population studies of a total of 14,474 families show in average terms that the family unit was large, including additional members to the basic nucleus, and reveal the presence of 2,660 servants and 137 clerks. The spatial distribution by neighbourhood explains the social stratification of this almost medieval city.

The 1717 cadastre serves to confirm the inequality of urban occupation of the two sides of the Rambla: on one side, the compact medieval city and, on the other, the Raval, still very sparsely inhabited, occupied by vegetable

[47] J. Sobrequés, op cit., cites Antonio Ponz: "Barcelona, the city in Spain which best gives the lie to the imputations of some foreign writers who are set on broadcasting our slovenliness, abandonment, laziness…" See, among others: Ramón Boixareu: Diario de los viajes hechos en Cataluña. Barcelona, 1978; Alexandre Laborde: Voyage pittoresque de l'Espagne (1794-97). Paris, 1806-20; Arthur Young: Viatge a Catalunya. Ariel, Eslugues, 1970; Antonio Ponz: Viaje de España. Madrid, 1972.

[48] See Jaume Agustí: Ciència i tècnica a Catalunya en el segle XVIII: la introducció de la màquina de vapor. IEC. Barcelona, 1983. Also Horacio Capel et al., De Palas a Minerva. La formación científica y la estructura institucional de los ingenieros en el siglo XVIII. Barcelona, 1988.

[49] Jordi Nadal and Eugeni Giralt: Barcelona en 1717-1718. Un modelo de sociedad preindustrial. Madrid, 1963; Salvador Tarragó: "Barcelona según el catastro de 1717-1719", Cuadernos nº 80. Barcelona, 1971; Biblioteca Nacional, Vezindario general de España. Madrid, 1717.

2.b The Citadel and the neighborhood of the Ribera.

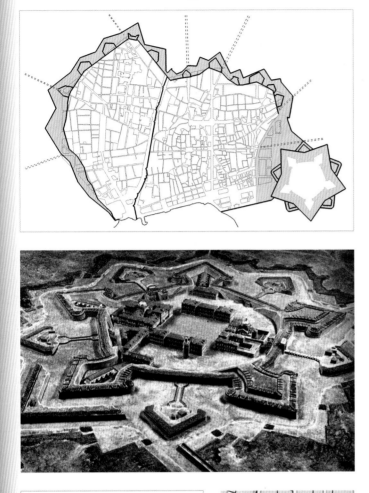

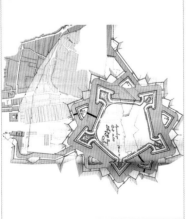

2.27
Layout of the old town with the construction of the Citadel and the neighbourhood of the Ribera.

2.28
Model of the Citadel.

2.29
Verboom's Project, 1715.

2.30
Interpretation of successive urban morphologies in the neighbourhood of the Ribera, summed up in the Born.

2.31
The Citadel, watercolour by
Francesc Soler i Rovirosa,
1869.

2.32
The General's Garden, 1818.

plots and the many religious institutions that were gradually established there in the 16th and 17th centuries. It was to become more occupied in the course of the century, despite being regarded as city outskirts by most citizens.

II.15 The construction of the Citadel

One of the most brutal urban planning transformations was the destruction of the neighbourhood of Ribera, situated to the east of Santa Maria del Mar, one of the city's liveliest areas due to its excellent position near the port. It gave way to the construction of a great military citadel and its parade ground in the interstitial space outside the city.[50]

The fortress design, drawn up in 1715, was the work of Jorge Próspero Verboom, a Flemish engineer, and followed the patterns of French military engineers of the time, principally Vauban. Other city buildings were also constructed or remodelled, mainly around the gates, as barracks or magazines of the Bourbon army. It is important to stress that the basic function of these defences was both to defend Barcelona and to ensure control of the city in the event of a possible citizen uprising. There were also batteries in Montjuïc castle.

The Citadel formed a pentagon made up of five bastions in the shape of spearheads, named after the Queen, the King, the Prince, Don Felipe and Don Fernando.

[50] See Salvador Sanpere i Miquel: Los terrenos de la Ciudadela. Henrich. Barcelona, 1911. Also Manuel Arranz, Ramon Grau, Marina López, El Parc de la Ciutadella. L'Avenç. Barcelona, 1984; Albert Garcia Espuche: Barcelona a principis del segle XVII. La Ciutadella i els canvis de l'estructura urbana. Tesi Doctoral. Barcelona, 1987; Josep E. Hernández Cros, Xavier Pouplana: "La Ciutadella", Cuadernos nº 86. Barcelona, 1971. The article summarises this incident: "Its construction required the demolition of several thousand houses in the district of Ribera (…). Added to this was the absence of compensation of the house owners and the edict requiring all of Barcelona's artisans to work on its construction, providing their own tools and animals, in exchange for an inadequate day's wage and under pain of death if they should refuse. If these motives were enough to justify the unpopularity surrounding work on the construction of the Citadel, the torture dealt out in its cells to patriots and politicians who opposed the Government completed the repressive image of the fortress, and soon carned it the city's unanimous hatred." A situation worth bearing in mind on the occasion of its demolition in the late 19th century.

The complex was surrounded by a ditch with a protective scarp. In order to be effective, a fortification of this kind required a glacis to limit the attacker's visual field. This defensive complex was complemented by the fort of Don Carlos, like a coastal breakwater, and Pienç fort, to the north.

The inside of the Citadel comprised a series of buildings (chapel, barracks, arsenal, magazine, the governor's palace, hospital, prison, etc.) that were constructed in a slower process than the bastions, lasting from 1715 to 1719.

The Citadel and military engineers' work on it in the academic baroque style represented a renewal of the architectural language of important buildings. The inner constructions, mostly designed by Alexandre de Rez, were early exponents in Barcelona of the French classicism that later, duly stripped of decorative excess, was applied in so many 18th-century buildings.

The end of the century saw the urbanisation of the space between the city (the remains of the district of Ribera) and the Citadel in the form of the Passeig Nou or Passeig de l'Esplanada. This intervention, with its rows of trees and fountains, was complemented in 1818 by the Jardín del General, the first space to be specifically designed as a garden with oriental features and small zoological motifs. Promenading and leisure were new pastimes of the Barcelona people and the Teatre de la Santa Creu (later Teatre Principal) was set up by the Marquis of La Mina, an enlightened despot who was very influential in the second half of the 18th century.

Other major planning interventions were the redevelopment of the Rambla and the construction of Barceloneta, described later on.

As we have already seen, the Rambla became a prominent urban space with the demolition of the inner wall, the realignment of its buildings and the new layout, with a central boulevard following the French model that Madrid had already brought to fruition in El Prado. New palaus were built along its façades, shaping the urban image of this seminal space in the city.

At the same time, the space comprising the Pla de Palau was shaping up as the city's new nerve centre: the palace of the Captaincy General was built beside the Portal de Mar as the seat of political and military power. It was later joined by the Llotja (1772-1802), the work of Joan Soler i Faneca, where economic transactions and some of the new teaching institutions were housed. A customs house was built beside the growing port. The promenade around the outside of the town wall was consolidated and the city opened up to the Barcelona Plain, leading to the appearance of second homes in villages on the higher ground, such as Sarrià, Gràcia, Sant Gervasi and Horta, this last with the construction of the Labyrinth, an elegant exercise in the neoclassic style. Areas such as Sant Martí and Sants with their prats d'indianes also provided the function of drying sheds for the spinning processes that still took place inside the walled city.

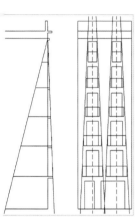

2.33, 2.34
Regulated development.

II.16 Other Baroque transformations in the city. Urban order in the streets and façades

The Decreto de Nueva Planta stipulated that Pere III's 14th-century town walls should be the city limits, making it very difficult to house the growing population in the second half of the 18th century, particularly as the construction of the Citadel had meant the demolition of almost twenty per cent of the city.

Furthermore, there were two different administrative models dealing with the situation, as Bourbon power had transferred to the Captaincy General decision-making capacity for large-scale urban planning.

In this way, then, city development was played out between major urban development projects and a whole string of private initiatives to deal with demographic pressure, especially after 1770. The sheer size of the problem gave rise to constant conflict between military and municipal power.

During the Count of Ricla's mandate as Captain General (1767-1772) an edict was issued prohibiting extension work to houses with a volada, a projection out into the street to increase the limited surface area of some plots. The purpose of this edict was to regularise layout and prevent any further narrowing of streets, partly because there was hardly room for wagons to negotiate them, but also because it enabled the regular forces to control the city. Awareness of this problem had increased since the Esquilache mutiny of 1766 in Madrid. However, the City Council's Works Board opposed the edict and endeavoured to defend the position of property owners as a requirement of local people.[51]

A similar situation arose with the Works Plan,[52] which aimed to establish general rules to control construction within the city. The regular practice took the form of a personal consultation with the corresponding councillor to obtain building permission: this now became unworkable due to the rate of construction required by the city and the need to implement the process officially. The Captain General, conversely, was in favour of liberalising the situation as much as possible and pointed the City Council in the direction of the urban development of the city's vegetable gardens.

[51] Joaquim Sabaté: Op.cit., 1999. In this work he explains in great detail the evolution of building "rules", including "figurative easement" and ordinances.
[52] See Marina López and Ramon Grau: "Barcelona entre el urbanismo barroco y la revolución industrial", Cuadernos nº 80. Barcelona, 1971.

2.35
Map of Barcelona and its surroundings in 1740, clearly showing the medieval urban structure and successive growth.

In 1770 the procurator syndic drew up a series of proposed ordinances for the Captaincy General and the City Council to study and consider. After discussion, the project was disfigured in two main aspects: it neither mentioned the extensions into the street nor did it stipulate building alignment and height. These were serious weaknesses at a time when private initiative was beginning to take energetic action in response to the demands of major growth.

Urban development instruments needed to establish a new urban order. This took the form above all of control of private initiative, establishing rules for the composition of façades and maximum heights, following the French example, and the specific correction of alignments in order to widen streets and improve urban continuity. Though initially difficult to apply, these ordinances represented a turning point for urban form and gradually modified the city's existing typologies. However, these rules concentrated on the relation between the house and the street and did not guarantee the quality of the buildings' interiors.

To a point this represented the start of Municipal Urban Planning in the terms with which we are familiar today.[53]

This period had two singular projects: the first was the realignment of Carrer Argentería, giving rise to new façades along this street between Santa Maria and the gate in the old town wall, and the other was the construction of Carrer Nou de la Rambla (1785-1788), producing the first straight street, lined with regular constructions, following what was to become a widespread pattern in the 19th century.

[53] See Manuel Torres et al.: Inicis de la urbanística municipal. Barcelona, 1985.

Unfortunately, the volume of new construction that took place in Barcelona during the 1772-1791 period was explosive, and neither the City Council nor the military commanders were able to contribute large areas of new land, with the subsequent dramatic congestion of the old town.

According to the Register of Works, of the 4,255 works allowed in the course of these twenty years, only 2% were on clear land; the rest were constructed on previously built parcels, either to improve the house or to enable more intensive use: 33% of applications were for extensions to apartments or further subdivision of built space.

This process of building up the existing city rather than developing new land led to a deterioration of its image and to poorly functioning buildings. The historian Antoni de Capmany, a contemporary of the time, describes it thus: "Noble, polished, magnificent appearance of its buildings and common farmhouses, most of which have disappeared this century, not leaving even the foundations; with the continual rebuilding of houses ruined or battered as a result of the last two sieges and bombings they underwent between 1691 and 1714; with the demolition, thirty years ago now, of many of the old houses that had been left intact, in order to rebuild them and lay siege to a population that is growing day by day, and that is holed up and concentrated in their very rooms, as the military fortifications and their proud walls do not allow the population to expand."[54]

This period saw a major typological change from the artisan's to the plurifamily house with a communal stairway.[55] The artisan's house had been the prototype of the medieval city, combining economic and residential functions with the apprenticeship and propagation of trade; the emergence of the capitalist system removed work from the home, giving rise to a need for other forms of collective housing. This typological revolution in architecture was to evolve throughout the following decades.

II.17 Barceloneta. An innovative project but terribly overcrowded

In 1753, on the initiative of the Captain General, the Marquis of La Mina, Barceloneta was built on military land outside the Portal de Mar to compensate, albeit tardily, for the demolition of the Ribera district. Some temporary buildings had already been constructed in this area for residential and economic uses after the widespread destruction caused by the construction of the Citadel.

---

[54] Antoni de Capmany: Memorias históricas sobre la marina, comercio y artes de la antigua Ciudad de Barcelona. Barcelona, 1779.

[55] Albert Garcia and Manuel Guàrdia: "Estructura Urbana", Història de Barcelona: El desplegament de la ciutat manufacturera, Barcelona, 1993. See also Josep M. Montaner, Escaleras, patios, despensas y alcobas. Un análisis de la evolución de la casa artesana a la casa de vecinos en Barcelona. Arquitecturas Bis. Barcelona, 1985.

A project had previously been designed by J. P. Verboom in the second decade of the 18th century and approved by Felipe V in 1731. According to Manuel de Solà-Morales' article, it was a "model with a square ground plan" constituted by a series of linear blocks and parallel streets; with a central square for the construction of special facilities, including the cavalry barracks.[56]

It seems that construction of this project did begin, though problems in its implementation led the Marquis of La Mina to entrust a new project to the army engineer Juan Martín Cermeño.

This project was organised in the form of a right-angled triangle as a framework for similar street blocks to those foreseen by the original plan, with a base along the port wharf and the hypotenuse in the east to enable easy extension in the late 19th century. This north-south orientation increased sunlighting and protected the streets from the prevailing east wind. Set back from the main façade a square is outlined in which the church of Sant Miquel del Port was built in 1756, thereby defining its subcentre and ratifying the "frontal model" overlooking the port.

This neoclassic design was based on two fundamental ideas: a well-defined housing model and the specific desire to design the city on the basis of layout. This design technique used in the Spanish Enlightenment[57]

2.36
View of the Barceloneta in 1814. Fragment of a painting of the port besieged by the English fleet.

---

[56] Manuel de Solà-Morales, Antoni Font, Mercè Tatjer and Ignacio Paricio: "La Barceloneta", Plans i Projectes. Barcelona, 1983. This is an accurate description of the models of generation and transformation of the district, and a justification of present-day intervention policies to ensure its maintenance and improvement.

[57] Carlos Sambricio, Territorio y ciudad en la España de la Ilustración. MOPT, ITU. Madrid, 1991.

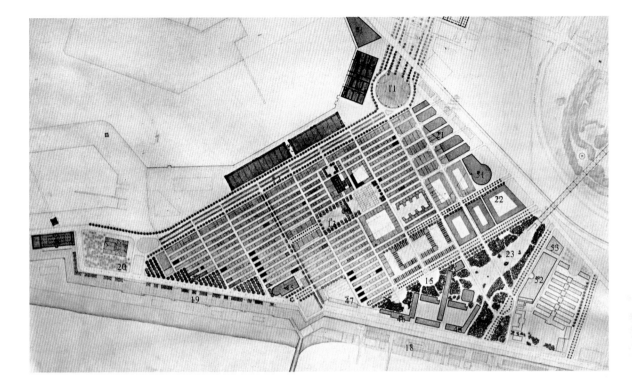

employed very simple instruments and a generic regulation of façades to produce high quality urban results, especially as they were city fragments with a simple brief to be constructed over a long period of time.

The initial house corresponded to a site of nine square vares (8.40 x 8.40 metres) built between two party walls, two façades and one interior wall. The dwelling was distributed over two floors with a central entrance. This unit was organised into a linear block of nine houses along streets measuring eight vares wide crossed by others of ten.

The overall result was a residential district for a population associated with the old town and the port. The port was to play an increasingly important role. The evolution of Barceloneta has been marked by two conflicting factors that have conditioned its fate up until the present day: it is isolated from the central city by the large infrastructures that surround it, and it has become increasingly built up over a period of more than two centuries.

The district came into being outside the city walls as an isolated area, and this was a condition that marked it drastically, first due to the town wall, then the railway line, which prevented any form of connection with the centre. Even its name, "Barceloneta", suggests a little Barcelona by the port, which, curiously, was repeated in other port cities such as Alghero, as well as Tarragona and other cities in the Catalan tradition.

The intensification of the neighbourhood has followed an almost dramatic process, judging by its recent situation. The original house was immediately extended by another floor at the start of the 19th century, with the construction of a second door to enable its use by two family units; this saw the introduction of the casa de mig, or half house. Nonetheless, the double façade and cross ventilation remained and the relation between building height and street width still ensured good sunlighting conditions. However, strong residential pressure in the district and

2.c La Barceloneta

2.38
Barceloneta, aerial view, 1929

2.39
Façades and sections of the proposals contained in the PERI.

2.40
The Barceloneta. Present-day view showing typological diversity.

.41
he Barceloneta and the port,
929.

the permissiveness of urban planning regulations accelerated the fragmentation of the parcel along the interior wall, thereby producing a casa de quart or quarter house, now without cross ventilation. In 1868 the district was comparable to the Eixample in terms of building capacity, and the potential height increased to five floors; in the twenties however the height rose again, and after 1953 as many as seven floors were tolerated, representing a complete break with the district's urban planning structure and letting in brutal property speculation.

At the end of the last century[58] the district was very densely populated, occupying 24 hectares with a population of in the region of 25,000 inhabitants a density of over 1,000 inhabitants per hectare. It comprised some one hundred street blocks occupied by 1,000 houses containing 6,000 dwellings: approximately half were cases de quart with a surface area of 35 m2, clearly very small by today's standards.

In the fifties one of the cross streets (Almirall Cervera) was widened in order to adjust the original layout to the new conditions of use and density, and to provide access to the beaches and the future sea-front promenade. A new built front was created to "bridge" lengthwise streets in their twos, leading to ventilation problems in an already very built-up area.

This diagnosis of the recent situation reveals the importance of the layout and urban planning system in such a singular district in Barcelona for its position and history. Current strategies established by the Special Plan for Barceloneta[59] are committed to a recomposition of its built structure and plot division in an attempt

[58] Mercè Tatjer: La Barceloneta: Del siglo ssXVIII al Plan de la Ribera. Libros de la Frontera. Barcelona, 1973. Idem. Burgueses, Inquilinos y Rentistas. CSIC. Madrid, 1988.
[59] M. de Solà-Morales et al., op.cit., 1983, pp. 42-52.

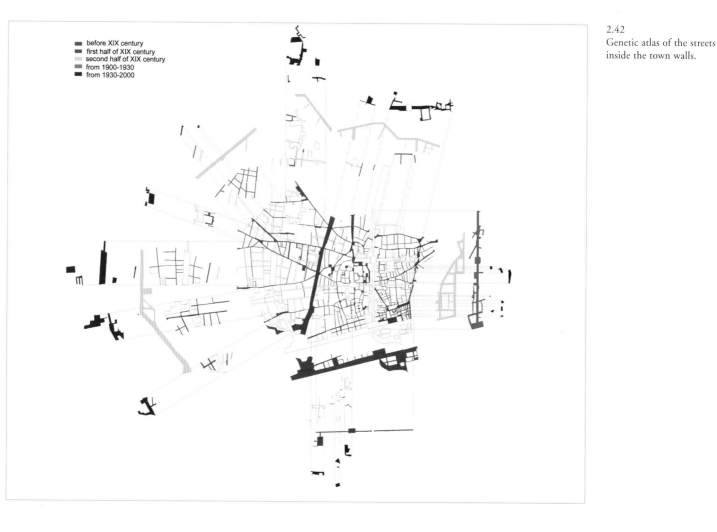

2.42
Genetic atlas of the streets
inside the town walls.

to return to the casa de mig, now as the sum of two cases de quart, thereby opening up the residential fabric. This is accompanied by major interventions around the edges of the district to improve its amenities (with the construction of schools, parks and new housing on the former Maquinista and Catalana industrial sites) and facilitate its connection with the rest of the city (port, Parc de la Ciutadella, Poblenou sector) in an attempt to make the isolation that has marked its urban history a thing of the past.

II.18 The urban forms inside the walled city

As this review of successive historical periods shows, the city is constructed on the basis of dozens of projects, superposed and transforming and complementing each other.

Clearly defined functional requirements (defence, access, supply, hygiene, etc.) have been gradually complemented by the desire to embellish and decorate, which, combined, have produced this highly complex

2.d Identification of the urban forms in Ciutat Vella.

2.43
Enclosures.

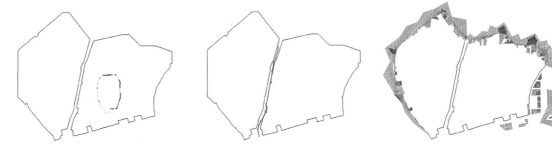

City wall IVth century.

Rambla's city wall

External city wall

2.44
Linear elements.

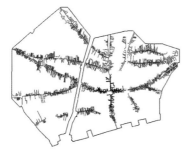

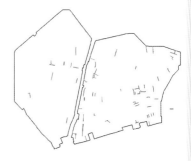

Road streets

Houses streets

Passages, arcs, vaults, and culs de sac

2.45
Functional sectors.

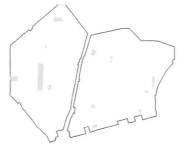
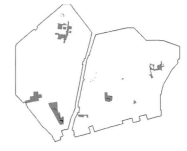

Monumental ensembles

Building voids

Amorphous spaces

2.e The intrinsic values of the walled town.

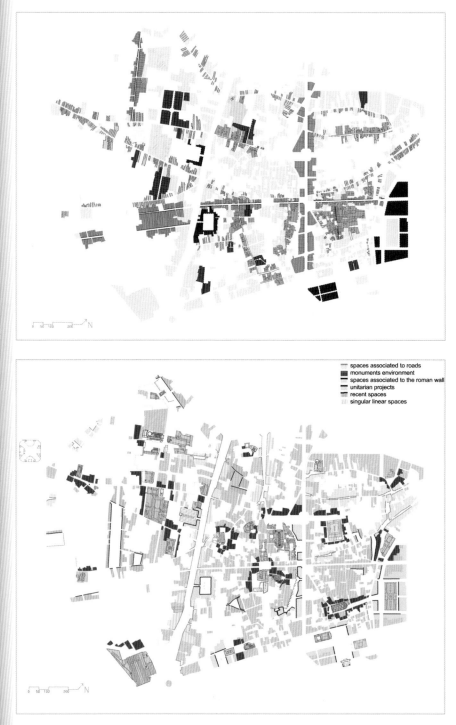

2.46, 2.47
Systems of values in the buildings
and open spaces.

spaces associated to roads
monuments environment
spaces associated to the roman wall
unitarian projects
recent spaces
singular linear spaces

and interesting city that is normally referred to as the historic or medieval city, or old town. These chapters look at overall conceptualisation based on regularity or ideal thought with regard to the city, as in the case of the Renaissance city, but a whole area of work is still needed to clarify the succession of projects and, most importantly, to interpret the instruments used to construct and modify the historic city. Its geometric complexity and spatial richness respond to considered, rational interventions that go beyond the purely organic or local views of the old town as the product of history. The succession of historical facts described here and changes in the city are proof of the relevance of further exploration of these lines of study.

To complement what is intended as a diachronic explanation, below is a summarised interpretation of the structural elements of the urban form that may serve to explain synchronically the parts, footprints and geometries relevant to an understanding of the environmental values of Ciutat Vella.[60]

They form three main blocks: enclosures, linear elements and functional outlines.

The enclosures are basically the enceintes that have left a real or virtual mark on the city's outline: the Roman wall, the wall built along the Rambla during the reign of Jaume I, or the one built under Pere III, today reflected in streets with the name of Ronda surrounding Ciutat Vella.

The linear elements, representing communications and access to buildings, can be divided into three types: historical roads that have become urban streets; streets of housing, designed with geometric regularity to provide access to buildings; and passages, pedestrian routes connecting urban thoroughfares.

A third block includes functional spaces and covers a series of very varied categories: from monumental complexes, usually marking important city events, to the urban spaces produced by the clearing or demolition of buildings to open up the city. Finally, there is also a series of "amorphous" spaces, often produced by conflicts between new ways of organising the old town, but we will return to this subject later.

[60] See Joan Busquets et al., La Ciutat Vella de Barcelona: un passat amb futur". LUB. Barcelona, 2003. It provides a summary of the research work carried out in 2000-2001, and describes the urban transformation of the walled city after the mid-19th century.

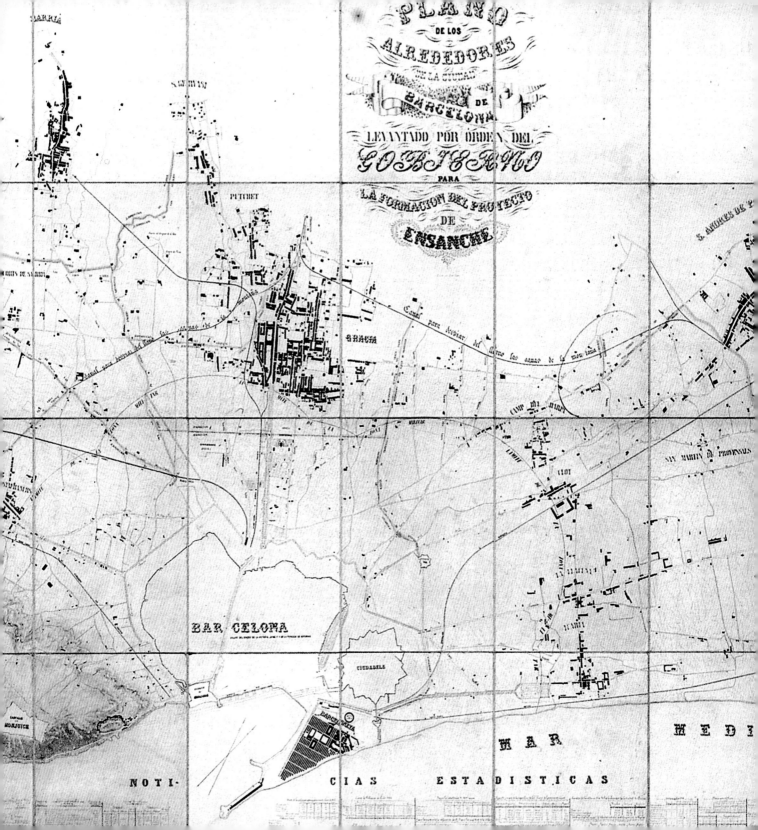

PLANO
DE LOS
ALREDEDORES
DE LA CIUDAD
DE
BARCELONA
LEVANTADO POR ORDEN DEL
GOBIERNO
PARA
LA FORMACION DEL PROYECTO
DE
ENSANCHE

SARRIA

S. GERVASIO

PUTCHET

S. ANDRES DE P.

OLIVES DE SARRIA

GRACIA

Canal para conducir las aguas de la montaña

CAMP DEL HARP

SAN MARTIN DE PROVENSALS

CLOT

BAR CELONA

CIUDADELA

CASTILLO DE MORJUICH

BARCELONETA

MAR

MEDI

NOTI-   CIAS   ESTADISTICAS

II Projects for the modern city and the demolition of the town walls

III.1 The beginnings of modern urbanisation

Industrialisation was set to bring about major transformations in the big city and, above all, give rise to an urban development process of unprecedented characteristics.

Structural changes took place that led unequivocally to the modern city. The concentration there of the production means required by the industrial system entailed the corresponding concentration of labour and the necessary services, thereby producing an essential overlap of industrialisation and urbanisation.

Barcelona represented the main market and, once again, its central position in the country's geography, its port and its services, firmly established it as the emblematic capital. The city experienced major growth and urban transformations that were to shape the present-day urban planning structure.[1]

There is no key date marking the start of Barcelona's formation as a modern city; it began with the accumulation of a series of variables that unambiguously explain the phenomenon of modern urbanisation, like a point of no return.

Urban historians tend to highlight the following variables:

a) the increase in the urban as opposed to the rural population, which, in the case of Barcelona, involved the large-scale movement of persons from the country to the city. This movement was very strong, and the spectacular nature of this absolute growth contrasts, particularly in the 19th century, with the very high mortality rate of the urban population due to the poor hygienic conditions in which the city's working classes lived: it therefore implied a large influx of rural population.

b) the consolidation of the industrial sector which was subsequently linked to urbanisation. The commercial sector too evolved as a result of industrial advances and the potential market generated by urban growth. It is important to remember that in Barcelona and Catalonia this process was a truly singular one since, as we will go on to see, they had no raw materials and found it difficult to maintain a stable open market: America as a market was subject to other influences and the domestic market had a limited capacity due to the backward rural situation of the rest of Spain.

c) this new situation led to an increase in territorial connections, with a strong, stable system of communications in the form of roads and railway that formed the basis for a thorough colonisation of the territory from the central "metropolis", Barcelona.

The expanding city was, in turn, to develop a new concept of urban services, linked first to the industrial sector (stations, warehouses, etc.) and later to a large urban population that became a major consumer of services (transport, gas, the sewerage network, etc.).

3.01
Plan of the surroundings of the city of Barcelona drawn by Ildefons Cerdà, 1854.

[1] Ramon Grau, Marina López: *Revolució industrial i urbanització*. Avenç, Barcelona, 1985.

3.02
Drawing by A. Guesdon of the
city in the mid-19th century,
showing industrialisation inside
the town walls and the first
industries outside the enceinte

In connection with these variables, the specific explanation for Barcelona's growth centres on the significance of urban growth as a form of city production. In this context, the relative importance of factors that produce the city (basically land, work and capital) helps to explain the different use made of it by capitalistic development.

Therefore, without interrupting the sequence of events, there is a latent argument that highlights the dominant or motivating factors represented by the different urban development projects or schemes.

The evolution of infrastructure was particularly outstanding with regard to capital investment in the city, particularly in the case of fixed, usually public capital, intended to last a long period of time: not for nothing did it borrow the attribute of urban "fixed capital" from the production system. Other fundamental investment factors took the form of land and construction, whether of services, housing or industry, and so forth, in a way that explains the relation between industrialisation and urbanisation.

Due to its particular importance, infrastructure is divided by periods into four groups, following the definition established by the work of Manuel de Solà-Morales and José Luis Gómez Ordóñez:[2] "colonial" at the start of the 19th century, urban "promotion" at the turn of the century; "subsistence" after the Spanish Civil War and "exploitation" in the period of development policy in the 1960s.

---

[2] These arguments are based on research carried out by the Laboratorio de Urbanismo directed by M. Solà-Morales and J. L. Gómez Ordóñez: *Crecimiento urbano como inversión en capital fijo: el caso de Barcelona (1840-1975). Ciudad y territorio.* Madrid, 1977. The first version of the work was presented by the author at the Città seminar in Venice (June 1974); a summary of it can be found in *Città-Classe*, Venice, 1975.

.03
Woman weaving, an oil
painting by Joan Planella,
1882, illustrates the great
importance of women's work in
Catalan industrialisation.

III.2 Early industrialisation

The industrialisation process that came to the fore in Barcelona in the first three decades of the 19th century was to turn the city into the centre of an industrial system on a par with that of the major European powers that had experienced this process a few decades previously. The pioneering countries in this innovative experience, known as the "first-comers", must include Catalonia, once again represented by the protagonism of its capital. Not for nothing did it earn the title of the "Catalan Manchester" with which illustrious travellers christened it.[3]

Despite the great difficulties intrinsic in the industrialisation process, according to Jordi Nadal and Jordi Maluquer, "Catalonia is the factory of Spain",[4] as the title of their investigation into the 1833-1936 period reads. This work clearly manifests the seminal role of Catalan industrialisation in the development of other sectors of the Spanish economy. It also explains the important role played by initiative and hard work, the foremost assets of Catalan industrialisation, in the face of an absence of natural resources. Behind the takeoff of industry, the factors listed by Nadal and Maluquer are: 1) the capital produced partly in the American colonies and trade, but mostly from the small

[3] See Richard Ford: *A Hand-book for Travellers in Spain*. London, 1845. He presented Barcelona as "the Manchester of Catalonia", which in turn he called "the Lancashire of the Peninsula". In the early days of industrialisation, Francisco Mariano Nifo (*Correo General de España*, Madrid, 1770), described Catalonia as "a little England within Spain. This no one doubts yet everyone refuses to imitate it, which would be a very useful thing for Spain".

[4] J. Nadal and J. Maluquer: *Catalunya. La fàbrica d'Espanya: 1833-1936*. Barcelona, 1985. An excellent work that provides the guidelines for the following pages and which culminated in an exhibition in Barcelona's Born in 1975, which presented this body of historical research from a long-term viewpoint, focusing primarily on the study of the material aspects of Catalan industrialisation.

3.04
View of Espanya Industrial, se
up in 1847 in Sants; it was th
largest textile firm in Spain.

farming and commercial capital of the artisan ranks;[5] 2) the existence of a Catalan domestic market thanks to a well developed farming sector; and 3) the fact that the country was used to work due to a long manufacturing tradition. In any case, this industrial start-up called for tax protection in order to be able to compete with other European products, due to the high cost of raw materials.

The first time steam energy was used in Spain was at the spinning and weaving mill established by José Bonapla ta in 1833 in Carrer Tallers, inside the enceinte of the Raval town wall. Other factories adopted similar locations during the first half of the 19th century, due to a military prohibition on occupying land in the Barcelona Plain.

The Bonaplata mill was the starting point of a complex industrialisation process in the peninsula.[6] Its innovativeness led to great controversy as a result of the social transformation it represented in ways of working that it represented, and it was burnt down in 1835. Despite its short-lived existence, it was the germ of other establishments such as El Ave Fénix, reconstructed in an annexe and redirected towards metallurgy, later to become La Maquinista Terrestre y Marítima.

However, the process of Catalan industrialisation was conditioned by its lack of energy resources and a shortage of raw materials, mainly textiles, which were mostly imported. These factors make it a truly singular case of industrialisation in comparison with the patterns of other European countries.

[5] The tradition of the *hereu* (single heir) observed in the case of farms obliged other sons of the family to set themselves up in business.
[6] See J. Nadal and J. Maluquer: *op. cit.*, page 163: "The singularity of the Bonaplata factory was manifested in the fact that the establishment was subsidised by the Government to the sum of 65,000 *duros* in exchange for offering free access 'to all manufacturers wishing to find out about the workings of the steam engine and its methods, as the idea is and must be to generalise its use throughout the Kingdom'."

.05
Engraving of La Maquinista
Terrestre y Marítima, founded
in 1855 in the Barceloneta.

In order to understand this process we have to take into account how the Catalan system of towns and cities, with their capital at the forefront, was utilised in different ways by the new social and economic forces of the Catalan "bourgeois revolution". At the same time, an initial wave of expansion took place in a series of towns and county centres that we will refer to as "mature towns".

In this way, limited energy sources called for a stronger regional articulation than might have occurred had the industrialisation process been more local. It began with the desperate search for mechanical energy, particularly coal.

The specific characteristic of modern industry was the use of inanimate energies; until then, man or animals had produced the movement. These new energies were provided by coal or water. The former was the typical energy source of industrialisation in England and Belgium, where it was widely available. In Catalonia, coalmining between 1840-1860 was a frankly negative venture due to the low calorific level of the coal and the difficulty of mining it: Calaf, Guardiola de Berguedà and Sant Joan de les Abadesses were the main coal-producing centres. The coal used came mainly from Cardiff and Newcastle via the port of Barcelona, which thereby became the port of entry for the basic energy resource and of exit for the exportation of the finished product.

In the mid-19th century, coals were the most abundant goods in the port and their distribution to different production points was greatly facilitated by the railway network. The port became a prime infrastructure for concentration and functional rationalisation.

This also applied to raw materials: textile production called for the importing of the bales of cotton that were produced in plenty in the Americas, as well as in other Mediterranean countries. This was also the case of wool when it became a primary product.

3.06
Factories in the Colonia Güell, Santa Coloma.

3.07
The Viladomiu Vell factory in Gironella, making the most of the space along the river Llobregat.

In any case, Catalan industrialisation was clearly marked by its dependence on energy and raw materials, and this was also its Achilles' heel. For example, the shortage of coal was tremendously debilitating to the steel-producing sector, an excellent complement in other cases, including the textile industry, such as the English.

This condition of continual dependence called for great commercial agility both in the commercialisation of products and in the purchase of raw materials.[7] In other cases, it was the Catalan bourgeoisie that developed

---

[7] See Nadal and Maluquer: *op. cit.*, page 41: "The commercial structures created by the Catalans, whether they were established by adventurers (...) or responded to the activity of agents (...) were very specific in nature, defined by a marked centralisation in Catalonia, the strong internal cohesion of each of the mercantile 'colonies'. This is a clear example of the efficiency of an external specialist group, which due to its condition of foreignness and the community of its language and culture, can make its way into the gaps in an economy and take control of a large proportion of trade, particularly in the case of long-distance traffic. It was not in vain that the Catalans were compared, in Cuba for example, to the Scots and the Jews." By way of example, Sabadell's leading role in textile production, especially wool, led to the founding of the Banco de Sabadell in 1882, and this bank opened a central branch in Buenos Aires to control the raw materials that were to be sent to Barcelona.

.08
Terrassa, city of factories
(mainly vapors) and an
example of the strong
industrial dyanmic of other
Catalan towns and cities.

large industrial complexes outside Catalonia in order to implement activities for which it was difficult to find a site here; one example is Josep Vilallonga, *fargaire* (smith) of Darnius, who founded Altos Hornos y Fábricas de Hierro y Acero in Bilbao in 1882.

Modern Catalan industry was to swing between two models: the *vapor*, powered by coal and steam, and the *colonia*, that harnessed water energy. The "machine" of the factory supplied mechanical energy and transmitted movement. The way in which energy was distributed to the various industrial premises produced two distinct urban development situations that co-existed for a long period of time.

The *vapor* presented a compact urban image in which the owner-worker relation was based fundamentally on work, whereas in the *colonia*, the factory contained a small town (school, church, company store, etc.) and even the dwellings formed part of the firm's fixed capital. To a large extent, the workers subordinated their lives to the pace and demands of the factory. These two urban development models obviously produced very differing labour relations, with different types of social and economic costs.

This industrialisation process gave rise to a series of transformations in the social organisation of work that produced conflicts, mainly in Barcelona, but also in other industrial centres. Technological innovation brought with it greater mechanisation and therefore a reduction in the manpower required. Furthermore, the urban congestion produced by the new industries in the walled centre made the living conditions of the urban working classes truly difficult, as described further on. Starting in 1840, major workers' unions came into existence that organised strikes and protests to achieve higher wages and shorter working days. Some of these episodes were violent, as in the case of July 1854, known as the "conflict of the *selfactinas*", coinciding with the progressive uprising, which consisted in an attack on factories and the destruction of the spinning machines of this name (from the English, "self-acting") that had transformed the manual spinning techniques. The events extended throughout Barcelona (particularly Sant Andreu del Palomar) but also to Bages.

Apart from the textile sector, which emerged as the most dominant, there were other strong industrial sectors.

a) The paper sector, located in Girona, began in 1842 to install systems for the production of continuous paper and enabled large-scale production of paper at low cost. This in turn allowed Barcelona to make major advances in book production.

3.09
Industrialisation in the 19th century. Ricart i Cia. factory producing printed fabric in Sant Martí in the Barcelona Plain in 1852.

b) The flour sector, with the changeover from traditional mills to industrial plants that in addition to milling included the classification and grading of flours. By 1900, Barcelona had become the flour-producing capital of Spain.

c) Metallurgy, a vital sector for balanced industrial development; its major limitations due to the lack of energy sources are explained above. However, mechanical workshops, spinning mills and naval shipyards provided the foundations of the metallurgy sector.

In the metallurgy sector, the Maquinista Terrestre y Marítima stood out for its far-reaching influence on the major constructions of 19th-century Barcelona: for example, the Born and other large municipal markets (Sant Antoni, Boquería, etc.). Another of the sector's firms was Nuevo Vulcano, which started out as the naval shipyard of the Compañía Catalana, in 1836 chartering *El Balear*, the peninsula's first steamship. These two large companies were located on the other side of Barceloneta, for many decades marking the industrial orientation of Barcelona's seaside district.

III.3 Urban reform from within

In the first three decades of the 19th century the old town of Ciutat Vella underwent a series of urban transformations that were indicative of the new economic and social dynamic upon which the city found itself embarked. This was an urban reform from within based on the decision to exploit institutional systems and on the substitution of existing urban fabric; similar attempts had been made in the late 18th century.

The city's emblematic buildings were given a facelift, particularly in the form of work on their façades or urban settings, seeking to represent the new condition to which they were called: Pla de Palau in the Portal de Mar acquired its definitive urban configuration at this time.[8]

[8] See J. E. Hernández, G. Mora, X. Pouplana: *Arquitectura de Barcelona*. COAC, Barcelona, 1972.

3.a Former Batlló factory in Carrer Urgell.

.10
ngraving of the Batlló textile
actory, 1870-1875.

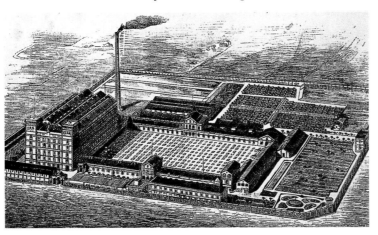

.11
Aerial view of the Batlló
Brothers textile factory in the
920s.

3.12
Industrial macroblock.

Reform of the city fabric was also based on new layouts or rectilinear alignments drawn out to create a street running across the old town (Carrers de Ferran, Jaume I and Princesa), or by turning former convents and monasteries into squares and marketplaces.

Major interventions to colonise the land outside the town walls also took place, such as the construction of Passeig de Gràcia, an exceptional street to begin the urbanisation of the Barcelona Plain.

Pla de Palau acquired its monumental form in 1825 on the basis of a design dated 1818 and was the city's first business centre, with the Royal Palace, the Custom's building (converted in 1902 into the headquarters of the Civilian Government) and the Exchange, as already commented. The square's fourth corner comprises the buildings containing Xifré's porticoes, built between 1836 and 1840, markedly Isabeline in style with a system of arches that shelters the commercial sector on the ground floor, with three floors of dwellings above. This urban space came into being as an intermediate space between the port, the gardens stretching away toward the Citadel and the Portal de Mar. The bastions nearby the Exchange had been demolished in 1834 and the Sea Wall became a promenade raised above the natural level of the port. Beside Pla de Palau, the Estació de França railway station was built in 1848, reinforcing its historical centrality.

The urban planning definition of the present-day Plaça de Sant Jaume also dates from this period. The project was undertaken by the pro-constitution council in the 1820-1823 period, and the small square was extended to form the present-day precinct by means of the demolition of the church of Sant Jaume, a small cemetery and the General Mayor's Office. The new neoclassical façade was the work of the architect Josep Mas i Vila, who immediately afterwards opened up Carrer Ferran with the intention of connecting the new square and the Rambla. The new street consisted of a rigorous ten-metre-wide layout lined by apartment buildings belonging to the nascent industrial bourgeoisie, and the ground floors were occupied by commercial premises. Mas i Vila proposed a series of façades in which the layout of the openings suggested the organisation of the dwellings behind them. A similar model was used for the east-facing openings along Carrer Jaume I (1849-1853) and Carrer Princesa in 1853.

In the mid-19th century, this new street was completed and set to become the important commercial and administrative thoroughfare that it still is today.[9] Demolition and realignment work has to be understood in the

---

[9] Later on, other minor interventions came to reinforce Sant Jaume as an axis, such as Passatge del Crèdit, a wrought-iron arcade that provided a pedestrian link from Carrer Ferràn to Baixada de Sant Miquel, in line with the new European commercial architecture on the limited scale of which Barcelona was capable. Previously, Passatge Bacardí had been built in 1856, joining Plaça Reial and the Rambla. For a contrast in scale of these prototypical buildings in other cities, see Johann F. Geist's excellent work: *Arcades*. MIT, Cambridge, 1985. These two emblematic passageways were joined by another twenty or so in the 19th century with a view to making the existing street system more permeable to pedestrians. At the same time, they allowed the creation of small shopping malls. They were normally vertical in layout, acting as shortcuts between horizontal streets.

3.b Pla de Palau, beside the Portal de Mar.

13
la del Palau, the city's first
usiness centre. Lithograph by
eroy, mid-19th century.

.14, 3.15
iround plan and façade.

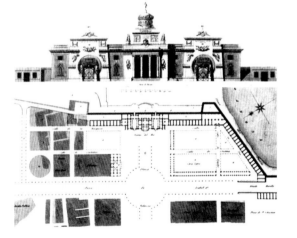

.16
View in 1856.

context of the ongoing reform proposed by Miguel Garriga i Roca, who produced an excellent map of Ciutat Vella in 1858 which is a perfect reflection of the situation of the urban fabric of the time. On the basis of this document, in 1892 Garriga proposed his Plan of Alignments and Improvements, which concentrated on correcting the lack of space in the city's historical layout.[10]

Another development that facilitated urban improvements of the time was the transformation of many convents and monasteries that had become city property as a result of the 1822 Confiscation Act, applied after secularisation in 1835. During the Carlist War news had actually spread among the population that the monastic orders were assisting the Carlists and that in Reus, the monasteries had already been burnt. In 1835, at least six of Barcelona's monasteries were also burned down, and Álvarez Mendizábal's 1837 Act regulated their change of use.

The acquisition of urban space and new facilities on former monastic land was extremely significant: the former Convent of El Carme was to accommodate the university that Felipe V had previously moved to Cervera; the demolition of the Convent of the Trinitarians made way for the extension of Carrer Ferran, connecting it up with Plaça de Sant Jaume; the market of Santa Caterina was built on the former site of the Dominican monastery and the grounds of the Monastery of Sant Josep accommodated the Boqueria market. The former Convent of Sant Francesc provided space for the construction of Plaça de Medinaceli beside the aristocratic Carrer Ample, alongside the port.

Finally, the Capuchin convent at the bottom of the Rambla enabled the construction of one of the city's loveliest squares: Plaça Reial. It was built in 1848 according to a design by Daniel i Molina that established a marked academicist composition, with porticoes on the ground floor and a system of residential distribution that faithfully respected the order of the façades. The square, measuring 84 x 56 metres, is set like an empty die in the confiscated property and is a paradigm example of how to produce a unitary design for a geometrically irregular and difficult space: the differing depths of its buildings engage coherently with the old urban fabric in which it is set.

Also in the Rambla, the Liceu opera house was built on the corner with Carrer Sant Pau, endowing the lower area of Ciutat Vella with a special centrality. The initial project by Miquel Garriga (1844-1848) had to be reconstructed by +J. Oriol Mestres in 1862 after a fire. Though built according to the French canons, it is an

---

[10] Miquel Garriga's map is vital to an understanding of the Ciutat Vella of the mid-19th century. Drawn on a scale of 1:250, it was made up of *cuarterons* (fragments) that were later reworked into a 1:1000 map that was the first precise X-ray of the old town, its spaces and each of its buildings.

3.c Plaça de Sant Jaume.

3.17, 3.18
Map before the remodelling of the cemetery and church of Sant Jaume. Entrance via the Gothic doorway in Carrer Ciutat.

3.19, 3.20
The square today.

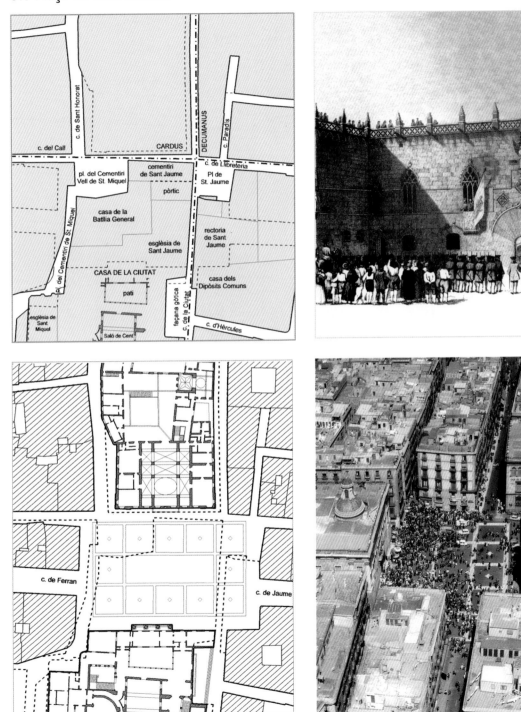

3.d Carrer Ferran.

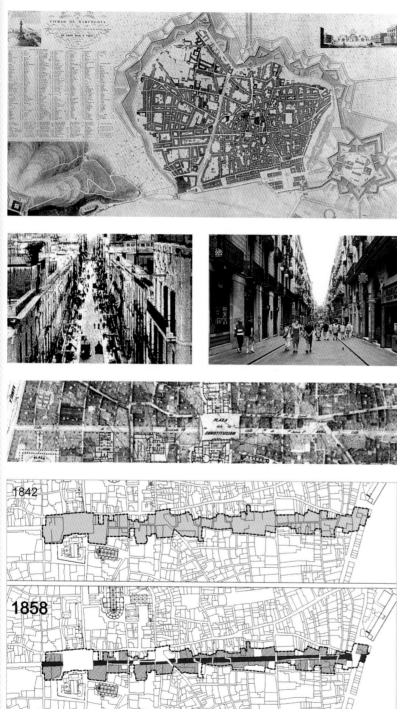

.26
he burning of convents in
835 ultimately freed up a lot
f space in the walled enceinte.

.27
ites confiscated for use by the
ity. They are mostly situated
long the Rambla. The rest
f the perimeters were other
acilities in the mid-19th
entury.

opera house that is set in a fabric of small residential plots, though neither its façade nor its internal distribution are prejudiced by its difficult situation. In January 1994, the same situation occurred: after a fire, the opera house was reconstructed and extended by a team under the direction of Ignasi de Solà-Morales, who died before his time.[11]

Passeig de Gràcia was the most important avenue outside the town walls that linked Portal de l'Àngel and the town of Gràcia, marking out the central axis for the future development of the Eixample, the city extension.

Work began on the avenue in 1824, the year in which the city was also endowed with various parks and gardens.

Its symmetrical profile comprised six rows of trees to define a central space for horse-drawn carriages and two pavements with benches where pedestrians could stop and rest. The avenue's general layout was divided into three subsectors laid out around their corresponding roundabouts on which fountains were built.

Its central position in the Plain and growing relations between Gràcia and the old town meant that this communicating avenue gradually became a place for recreation and meeting. Passeig de Gràcia replaced Passeig de l'Esplanada as the ultimate in public spaces, a place to see and be seen, to look and admire, as the latter became distanced from the new potential axes of Barcelona's expansion.

After 1840 new activities settled along the edges of the avenue and new contents and amenities were added. The municipal plant nursery was set up at the level of the future Gran Via, comprising a series of marquees near the town walls, providing new leisure opportunities for young people. In 1849, the Jardí del Tívoli was opened, offering visitors the chance to stroll among plants and flowers and take refreshment.

The Campos Elíseos were opened in 1853; these large French-style gardens situated between the future Carrers de Aragó and Rosselló introduced the city's first major recreational installations: a boating lake, rollercoaster, café, theatre, gardens, etc. This was a veritable transformation in the system of urban amenities in the up-town area

[11] The renovation of the Liceu was a project of the late 1980s that sought to incorporate a space on one side to extend the stage area and modernise its installations. The difficulty of the administrative procedure and institutional disagreements put paid to the initial project. Unfortunately, it was a fire that forced an agreement, and the opera house was reconstructed immediately. For the story of the project, see Ignasi de Solà-Morales, Lluís Dilme and Xavier Fabré: L'arquitectura del Liceu. UPC, Barcelona 2000.

of the Passeig, built according to a project by Oriol Mestres. On the basis of a similar logic, though on a smaller scale, the Jardín de Euterpe opened in 1857, providing a venue for the choral performances promoted by the musician Clavé.

In 1877, at the bottom near the Ronda de Sant Pere, El Prat Català was the last to open, introducing a new slant on recreation in the form of horseracing.

In any case, the vitality of this civic highway became consolidated in the mid-19th century and has continued until the present day. Despite major transformations to the heart of the Eixample, Passeig de Gràcia is still recognised as one of the city's most representative streets. It has perhaps lost the recreational importance with which it was founded, but it has maintained its civic function as a vital reference in Barcelona's centre.

III.4 Colonial infrastructure. Railways and roads provide urban interconnection

In the modern city that was then taking shape, the railways and roads were the main infrastructures for the conveyance of raw materials and goods, and, later on, also of persons, enabling the interconnection of different centres of production and consumption. This represented a thoroughgoing structuring of the territory that produced an almost definitive organisation of principal and secondary centres, between the industrial coastline and the inland area.

A relatively short period saw the creation of the *vuit barceloní* or Barcelona figure of eight, a railway network centring on Barcelona and two rings that intersected in the capital.

Spain's first railway line was the Barcelona-Mataró route, constructed in 1848, running from the Estació de França train station near Pla de Palau, along the coast to Mataró.[12] This initial layout went on to define the industrial development of the Poblenou area and provide an obstacle to access to the seafront until recent times.

Other sectors of the Catalan network were gradually incorporated: along the coast to Vilanova; in the prelittoral corridor, the Martorell and Granollers lines; and the Maçanet and El Vendrell connections completed the figure-of-eight circuit.

[12] See Santiago Riera: *Quan el vapor movia els trens*. Barcelona, 1998. Also A. Duran i Sanpere: *op. cit.*, and Francisco Wais: *Historia de los ferrocarriles españoles*. Nacional, Madrid, 1974. Also Manuel Maristany: *Un siglo de ferrocarril en Catalunya*. Barcelona, 1992.

3.e La Plaça Reial.

3.28, 3.29
Plaça Reial, designed by D.
Molina in 1848 on the site of
the former Capuchin convent.
Lithograph by I. Deroy, 1865.

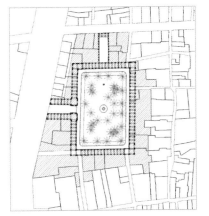

3.30
Aerial view.

3.31
Passatge Bacardí, connecting
the square to the Rambla.

3.32
The square today.

3.f Passeig de Gràcia.

3.33, 3.34
The Campos Elíseos, an example of the recreational areas on Passeig de Gràcia.

3.35, 3.36
The first outdoor space beyond the town walls, in the Plain.

3.37
View in 1923.

3.38
The Passeig today.

By the 1880s, Barcelona had rail connections with France via Figueres, with Aragon and Madrid via Sabadell, Manresa and Lleida, and with Valencia via Tarragona, as well as a new line to Tarragona-Les Borges-Lleida. Finally, the Congost line went to Sant Joan de les Abadesses via Vic and Granollers.

The rail crisis of 1866 made it necessary to concentrate lines in order to ensure coordination and smooth running, leading to the creation of two main groups, MZA (Madrid-Zaragoza-Alicante) and the Ferrocarril del Norte, or Northern Railways. In any case, the transformation of lines represented major investment of foreign capital.

At the same time, the vigour of the Catalan road system is worthy of mention, Spain being historically a country with a scant road network. The Catalan Roads Board was set up in 1848 and existed for twenty years, the only supraprovincial body created with a view to drafting and implementing a Plan.

However, although this was a very necessary action, the work was undertaken on the basis of indirect taxation, leading to a levy on the entire population and establishing a comparative difference with the rest of Spain, where the road network was state financed.

The work begun by the Roads Board was later continued by the provincial councils in an attempt to make the country's inland accessible from the coast where most of the new industry was based.

Spain for its part produced a Roads Plan in 1877, marking the division between networks that still exists today.

III.5 Criticism of the town walls

The density of urban activities inside the town walls and the dreadful living conditions of some highly congested city sectors created strong social pressure calling for the demolition of the walls around the old town.

In 1859, the walled city accommodated over 150,000 inhabitants within a perimeter of something less than had enclosed 64,000 at the start of the 18th century, due to the demolitions in the Ribera: the density of Barcelona in the mid-19th century was 850 inhabitants per hectare, one of the highest in Europe.

Dr. Monlau,[13] a liberal politician and author of the report *Elementos de higiene pública* [Elements of public hygiene] was one of the staunchest champions of demolition: the need to improve hygiene conditions in order

[13] Dr Pere Felip Monlau: *Abajo las murallas!!!. Memoria sobre las ventajas que reportaría Barcelona, y especialmente su industria, de la demolición de las murallas que circundan la ciudad.* Imprenta Constitucional, Barcelona, 1841.

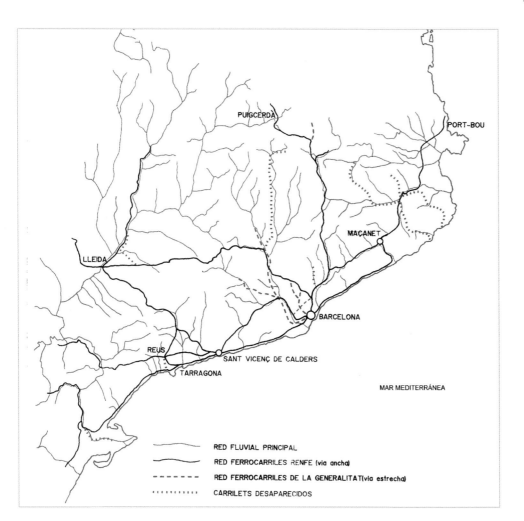

3.39
The railway system in Catalonia, with its centre in Barcelona and the territorial layout forming the Catalan "figure of eight".

to reduce illness was vital. Further, the city's industrial activities required new spaces for production and a more rational organisation of residential forms. This stance in favour of total demolition of the town walls was promoted by a series of articles by the philosopher and priest Jaume Balmes, who used detailed arguments to combat the inadmissibility of Barcelona's continued existence as a fortified town and the insufficiency of partial demolition.[14]

Finally, in August 1854, the Captain General of Barcelona communicated to the City Council its agreement to the latter's repeated request to demolish the town walls, and the city was able to embark on its extension (hereafter Eixample). There had been precedents for partial extensions, as in the case on the site of present-day Plaça de Catalunya, at the request of the City Council in 1844.

---

[14] Jaume Balmes: *Obras Completas*. Barcelona, 1948 (articles originally published in *La Sociedad* magazine).

3.g Spain's first railway line.

.40
The first railway line to run
in Spain was the Barcelona to
Mataró line in 1848.

.41
Fragment of the drawing by
A. Guesdon showing a train
pulling out of the station.

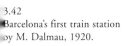

3.42
Barcelona's first train station
by M. Dalmau, 1920.

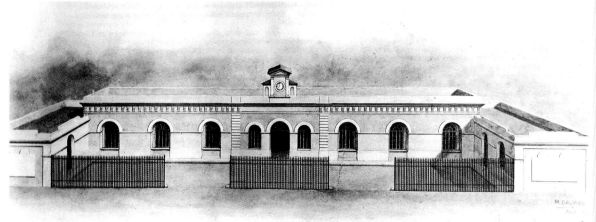

The Eixample project had a difficult and complex gestation, as may be imagined given the situation of the city and the scope of the project. As we will see, it was a fundamental episode in Barcelona's urban development history, and it is difficult to summarise the vicissitudes of a process that began in 1854 and was finally approved on 31 May 1860.[15]

A brief summary of Arturo Soria's study presents a Cerdà preparing for this undertaking as of 1849, when he decided to devote himself fully to the "idea of urbanisation". 1854 marked the beginning of his work on drafting the excellent "Topographic Plan of the environs of Barcelona", commissioned to him by the Civil Governor, and he made the most of the opportunity to submit a Preliminary extension project in November 1855. The political circumstance of the Progressive Biennial (1854-1856) paved the way for the introduction of his ideas both in Barcelona and in Madrid. But the change of political situation sparked off a new trend within Barcelona City Council, which commissioned a second preliminary project to Garriga i Roca, a municipal architect. Cerdà, however, requested authorisation to work on a plan for the Eixample in great detail at his own expense, similar to the case of the railway concessions, enabling him to develop his theory and project. In 1859, the City Council hastily decided to announce am urgent projects competition for the Eixample in order to put a damper on his project. Cerdà, meanwhile, managed to get the Ministry of Public Works and the Economy, by Royal Order of June 1859, to pass his Plan, with slight modifications. The City Council requested that the approval of the project be repealed and the competition, for which 14 projects had been submitted, declared void, in favour of the architect Antonio Rovira y Trias, who drafted a radiocentric design that was perhaps more in keeping with the expectations created by the demolition of the town walls.[16] The battle was on: the competition projects were exhibited in one Council hall, and Cerdà's plan in another adjacent one.[17] The professional confrontation between architects and engineers pervaded the discussion and finally, in 1860, the Ministry of Public Works and

[15] For a detailed version of this process, see the interesting article by Arturo Soria Puig: "El Proyecto y su circunstancia" or, for how Cerdà went about founding a theory and reshaping the city, see Laboratorio de Urbanismo: *Trabajos sobre Cerdà y Barcelona*. Barcelona, 1992. Arturo Soria highlights two phases in Cerdà's life and his relation with the Barcelona project: "one, ascendant and triumphal, that culminated in 1859 with the initial approval of his project, and another of decline, that began right then with a violent and lasting controversy about the project, followed by a gradual loss of support and an increasing financial asphyxia that lasted until his death in 1876." The article also relates in detail the technical and political strategies that Cerdà employed to further his project.

[16] A comparative study of the main projects can be found in Manuel de Solà-Morales: "El proyecto Cerdà frente a sus alternativas", *Los Ensanches I*. Barcelona, 1978.

[17] This confrontation had great political significance for many decades. At that time, the Moderate Party came down in favour of municipal autonomy and against centralist decision-making. The same argument was taken up later by Josep Puig i Cadafalch and the Regionalist League to combat Cerdà in as late as 1927.

43
View of the walled town at the start of the 19th century.

44
View of the city outskirts in 1853. by Enric Ferran Alsina.

the Economy ratified its definitive approval of the Cerdà Project, though seeking a compromise with the City Council that later led to major difficulties in its development: the ordinances and the economic thinking behind Cerdà's proposal were not applied.

Nonetheless, this was a highly singular moment in city development, and the choice of the Cerdà Project undeniably marked the process and the shape of Barcelona. It might be said that the forcefulness of this Plan made it a paradigm model for new towns built in southern Europe.

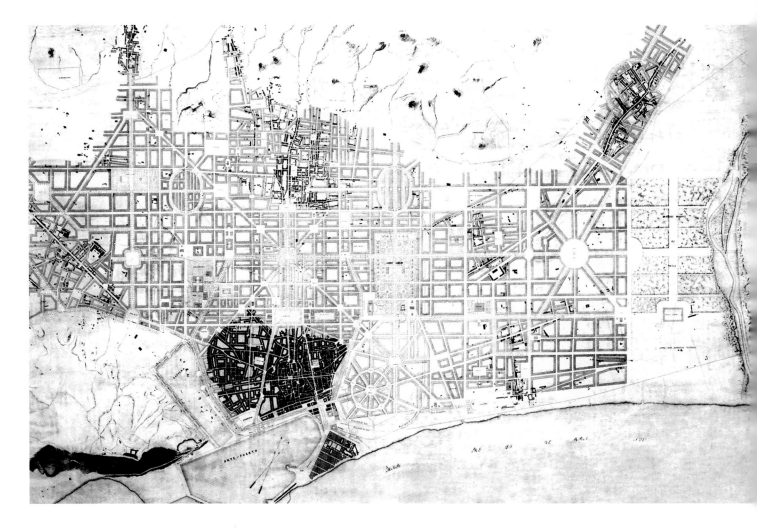

III.6 The Cerdà Plan, a pioneering work in Modern Urban Planning

Ildefonso Cerdà devoted over twenty years to producing the ideas in his project and making its deployment viable. It is undeniably a seminal work for the formalisation of contemporary Barcelona, but it is also a pioneering work in modern urban development theory.

As we will see, Cerdà addresses a thorough reshaping of Barcelona, with the scale and dimension expressed by his forceful city concept. At the same time, he addressed for the first time a modern set of urban planning instruments, which took into account an analytical approach to reality and the city, not in a determinist, unambiguous way, in the design of a new city.

There is no doubt that the dynamic of new ideas informing Barcelona's most innovative cultural trends in the first half of the 19th century involved greater critical commitment on the part of the artist to the changing social context with a view to preparing a better future for the population. The figure of Claude-Henri Saint-Simon, along with his

3.45
Plan for the Eixample, submitted to the municipal competition by Josep Fontseré.

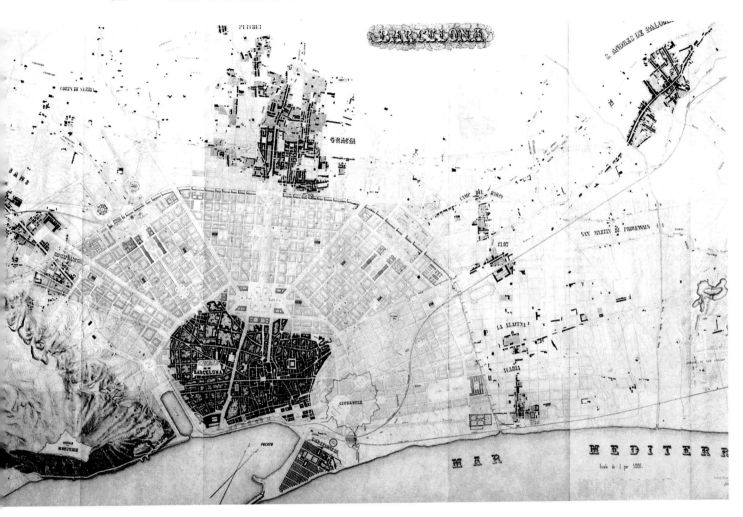

5.46
Plan for the Eixample by
Rovira i Trias, 1859.

followers, was key in this trajectory. His suggestion that artists should attempt to intervene on the side of the new elite of scientists and industrials was to enjoy great influence in the French context. He established a theory of History as a progression of "critical" and "organic" periods that explained social change, as scientists do with the natural environment. This type of discussion opened the eyes of a new generation of engineers and architects, including Cerdà and some of his peers, who began to realise that it was not just a question of repeating the Academy's classical models, but that architecture and the new urban planning science had to include a social component.[18]

Meanwhile, the trend represented by Charles Fourier and Robert Owen, British adherents to utopian socialism, envisaged self-sufficient communities that could be seen as veritable anti-cities, aiming to challenge the class structure and the separation between production means, principally between work and land.

[18] See Chantal Béret *et al.*: "Nouvelles de nulle part", *Utopies Urbaines 1789-2000*. Valence, 2001.

3.47
Cover of Cerdà's Teoría de la
construcción de las ciudades,
1859.

This trend may have inspired a series of proposals deployed at the same time in Barcelona, such as Icària in Poblenou. Utopian thought and action offered an alternative for decades and gave rise to fundamental critical discussion.[19]

The advances introduced by Cerdà are currently being analysed in the light of new documents found in various archives[20] that suggest that he was an outstanding figure in European urban development whose value has been underestimated until recently due perhaps to the difficult gestation of his project. It is important to remember that the "founders" normally named in histories of modern urban planning carried out their work after

---

[19] See, among others, Marius de Geus: *Ecological Utopias.* Utrecht, 1999.
[20] The fairly large bibliography devoted to Cerdà and his work includes: Fabià Estapé: *Teoría General de la Urbanización.* Madrid, 1971; Construcción de la Ciudad (2C): *Cerdà 1876-1976.* 1977; LUB: *Ensanches I y II.* Barcelona, 1978; Ildefonso Cerdà: *Cerdà y Madrid* and *Cerdà y Barcelona* (Facsímil). Madrid, 1992; Laboratorio de Urbanismo: *Trabajos sobre Cerdà y Barcelona.* Barcelona, 1992.

Cerdà (Baumeister, 1874; Stübben, 1890; Unwin, 1909, etc.) and probably did not have access to information about the urban development situation in Barcelona.[21]

Cerdà's Plan studied the following sections: Topographic Plan, General Theory of Urbanisation, the Plan proper, Ordinances and Economic Thought.

a) As already explained, Cerdà drafted his topographical plan of the Barcelona Plain on a scale of 1:1250 and a reduction to 1:5000 with great rigour, thanks to the help of as many as 25 teams of graders which enabled him to produce it in a short period of time. It was drafted with contour lines, presenting an exceptional document for the development of his preliminary project in 1855 and the project itself, presented four years later. In turn, this precise knowledge of the Plain was also of vital importance in making the Plan viable once approved.

b) The Theory of Urbanisation drawn up by Cerdà was a cornerstone of the innovation of his work, including the conceptual formulation that was indispensable to the drafting of city projects. Under this heading we include various Descriptive reports and statistical studies, the Theory of City Construction (1859) and, finally, his General Theory of Urbanisation (1867).

For Cerdà, according to his writings, each work on the "theory of" required its "application to" a specific case and, in turn, theoretical analyses had to be shown to be viable; in his own words, "the best idea is useless unless it is presented alongside the means to deploy it".[22]

With these methodological hypotheses Cerdà developed his theory according to three basic components:

1. hygienism, based on a criticism of the existing urban situation with well founded precedents. Cerdà drew up the *Monografía estadística de la clase obrera* (Statistical report on the working classes) to accompany the preliminary project report, in which he studied in great detail the living conditions in the walled city. To do so, he used the statistical studies of Laureà Figuerola who, in his excellent work on Barcelona[23] presented an extremely

---

[21] City modernisation was referred to as a "science" by Reinhard Baumeister in 1876 and Josef Stübben in 1890, whose 1880 project for Cologne paved the way for the extension of many European cities, such as Naples and Helsinki. These were sound manuals that emphasised the design of the city, new services and technologies and, most of all, strategies for the management of intervention in the existing city: questions of restructuring the plot division, the dimensions of the road network, etc. There was however a good deal of scepticism as to the order and regularity of these proposals, and a critical body emerged mainly in the form of the works of Camilo Sitte of Vienna and Charles Buls, former Mayor of Brussels, in the late 19th century. Sitte attempted to exploit the artistic principles that were to accompany city design. He also highlighted the influence and psychology effects of urban spaces on the users of cities.

[22] In *Despojos* (Facsímil), Madrid, 1991, Cerdà relates the end of his life: "I chose not to content myself with a casuistic answer to questions, as most people do, being the easiest way; rather, when I found I needed a theory to apply to the issue in hand, I invented one, which in most cases, not to say always, involved the most tremendous amount of work."

[23] Laureà Figuerola: *Estadística de Barcelona*. Madrid, 1849.

3.h Research and studies carried out by Cerdà.

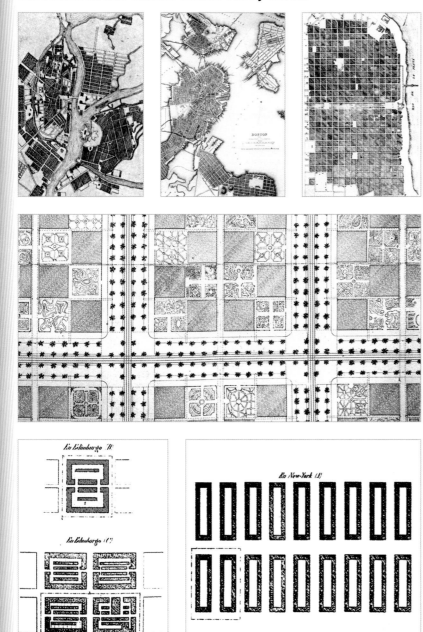

3.48
Saint Petersburg.

3.49
Boston.

3.50
Buenos Aires.

3.51
Model of street block
arrangement.

3.52, 3.53
Images from the preliminary
research and studies
conducted by Cerdà
taken from the Atlas de
Anteproyecto del Eixample
de Barcelona, 1855.

3.i The Plan by Ildefons Cerdà for Barcelona's Eixample.

.54
Map of the Eixample Project
for Barcelona by Ildefons
Cerdà, passed in 1859.

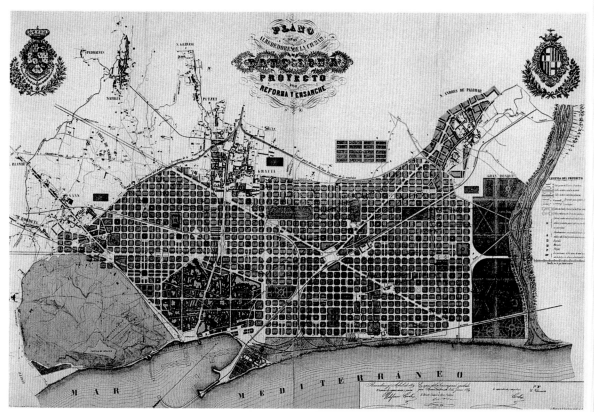

3.55
Fragment of the Eixample
Plan.

3.56
Definitive layout of Cerdà's
project, 1863.

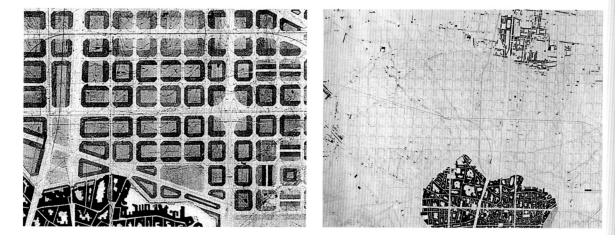

3.57
View of the central sector of the Plan, reworked in 1863 by Cerdà, incorporating the railway layout and adjusting the street blocks and buildings

accurate view of the urban development situation. The same figures were also to be employed by Pascual Madoz in his extraordinary *Diccionario geográfico-histórico-estadístico de España y sus posesiones de ultramar (1845-50)*.

The statistical report highlighted the extremely high mortality rate: average life expectancy between 1837 and 1847 was 38.3 for the wealthy and 19.7 for the working classes. These were, then, truly dramatic conditions that Cerdà analysed house by house and family by family.

Furthermore, the preliminary project report addressed a thorough geographical analysis of the city's position and location, as well as its climatology and sun-lighting conditions. It was, in short, a complete urban analysis that helped him to take planning decisions.

This concern with a disciplined approach to information also led him to study other cities such as Paris, and to personally interpret maps of cities as far flung as Boston, Turin, Stockholm, Buenos Aires and Saint Petersburg, among others.[24]

This almost obsessive preoccupation with an empirical study of real cities also led to an overwhelming accumulation of materials about buildings and construction elements (windows, doors, etc.), not because Cerdà insisted on personal knowledge of everything before undertaking an intervention or a project, but because, in his

[24] The influence of these studies on his proposed Plan has recently been analysed. For example, Javier Frechilla ("Cerdà y el anteproyecto de Ensanche de Madrid", *Trabajos sobre Cerdà y Barcelona*. Barcelona, 1992, *op. cit.*) refers to the influence of the layout of Buenos Aires in defining the size of the street block in Cerdà's project for Barcelona, suggesting the interesting reflection of a colonised city on a metropolis.

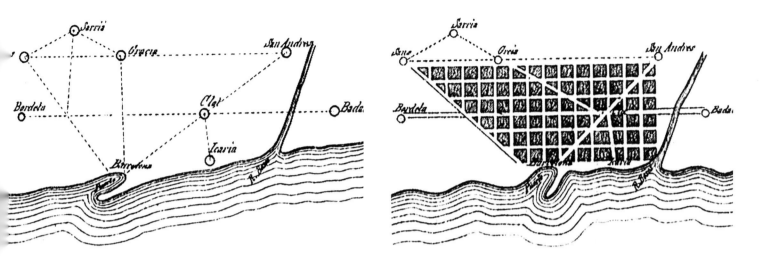

3.58, 3.59
Sketches of the layout of
Cerdà's Eixample.

words, "it is necessary to continually stimulate the rational capacity with empirical data in order to oblige the urbanist to maintain close contact with reality".

2. The second component in Cerdà's theory was circulation. He had become familiar with the steam railway engine upon its implantation in Barcelona and the conditions of which he had to become acquainted in detail when working on the rail layout in Granollers and its subsequent extension to Sant Joan de les Abadesses. The profound impression it made on him caused him to think how the city should prepare itself for this great instrument of mechanical mobility. The leaflet *Necesidades de la circulación y de los vecinos de las calles con respecto a la vía pública urbana, y manera de satisfacerlas* [The requirements of circulation and residents with regard to urban public thoroughfares, and ways of satisfying them], printed in 1863, summarises not only this concern but also the high level of attention that he devoted to the subject.

His proposals for Barcelona were underlain by the force of a well established hierarchy of streets, based on two principles that still apply today: the spaces within a street section devoted to "steam machines", now motorised vehicles, and to pedestrians are equivalent, both in regular 20-metre-wide streets and more narrow ones. The second principle was that all the junctions were built with 20-metre chamfered corners to ease facility of crossing and provide a guideline for building alignment around the edges of the street block.

3. Finally, Cerdà introduced the idea of a city that was to extend right across the Barcelona Plain: the built and the future city, in what was, in a way, a complete reshaping of Barcelona.

This idea of a hygienic, functional city was, according to Cerdà, to produce conditions of equality between all the residents who used it. As a result, the plan was to cover the entire territory, including all forms of settlement in this new homogeneous fabric.

However, his project was also formulated as the "Extension and reformation of Barcelona", since it also embraced the transformation of the existing city with a view to changing the dreadful living conditions of this built-up space. As we will later see, this part of his idea was never approved.

c) The Plan for the Cerdà Project covered the entire Plain without taking into account the jurisdictional limits of the municipality of Barcelona. There was, moreover, a completely empty belt, 1.25 kilometres wide, around the town wall due to military restrictions preventing construction of any kind within firing range of a canon. Beyond this band were the small suburban settlements of administratively independent centres, as we will go on to see.

The existence of this military reserve since the Decreto de Nueva Planta provided Barcelona with all the facilities it needed for expansion. For once, it was able to draw some advantage from the condition of siege that had been imposed on it, forcing it to use up every last space inside the town walls.

Cerdà's proposal for this natural space consisted of organising the city by means of superposed layouts that offered different levels of interpretation:

1. The basic layout consisted of a system of street blocks situated between axes of 113. 3 metres with 20-metre-wide streets. Their guidelines corresponded to the dominant lines of the plain and were oriented at 45° from the north, repeating the Roman layout.

2. The general or regional layout consisted of elements with a larger section of 50 metres that established the main functional relations: Gran Via as a horizontal axis running tangentially above the mountain of Montjuïc and connecting the two river valleys; Diagonal, crossing the city from the Collserola foothills to the sea; and Meridiana and Paral·lel, that met virtually at the port. The two latter layouts correspond, as their names indicate, to their geographical position and explicitly manifested the desire to situate the city in the world by means of an overall conception that integrated different scales of interpretation.

Over these systems the railway layout was superposed with the singularity imposed by its radii of curvature.

In contrast to these systems of "highways", enabling circulation in all directions in isotropic fashion, were spaces with the principal function of offering repose and quietude: the *intervías*, or between-streets areas.[25] These were the sites for both private construction and communal facilities. The latter were implanted in the centre of each residential unit, organising precincts of 5 x 5 street blocks.[26]

d) Construction ordinances. In 1860 Cerdà incorporated for their definitive approval a series of Construction ordinances, as opposed to the Urban police ordinances that had traditionally formed part of a single legal corpus.

This change seemed justified in view of the entity that the construction problem in itself was to acquire from this time on. Cerdà also wanted to guarantee the good hygienic conditions of constructions and proposed that only 50% of the parcel within the street block should be built.

Cerdà was confident that the sheer size of this great Eixample, with the introduction of so much land onto the market, would mean that cheap land would become available for reasonably priced dwellings. He also seriously

[25] In *Teoría General de la Urbanización, op. cit.*, pp. 363-64, Cerdà describes the *intervías* in the production of the complex city as an idea of integrated function that he finds in the *mas*, or traditional Catalan farmhouse.
[26] He writes "in each of the spaces isolated by urban thoroughfares there exists a small world, a small city, or perhaps an elementary city, which, in its whole and its parts, is inhabited by the most admirable analogy and even similarity with the big city".

3.j Some of the instruments proposed by Cerdà.

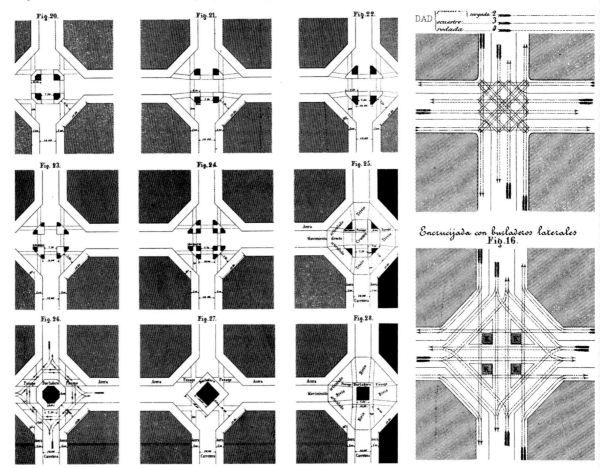

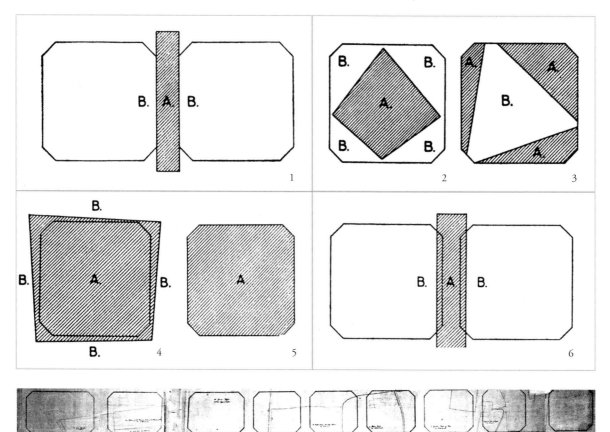

3.63
Different situations of plots in the development of the Eixample, according to Cerdà in Cuatro palabras sobre el Ensanche, 1861.

3.64
Examples of the detail maps or particularios drafted for the Eixample on the Plain.

considered the possibility of producing mass construction elements to bring down costs. His studies of the dwellings in Europe's industrial colonies of Lille and Mulhouse corroborated this intention.

However, Cerdà's ordinances were not approved and those of 1857 prevailed, as a result of which the potential for new building in this fabric was stepped up.

e) Cerdà's economic thought set out to put into practice his constant idea that projects should be viable.

This enlightened engineer's concern with the issue had been revived by his repeated visits to Paris, where he was a guest observer of the fundamental changes being implemented in the French capital by Baron Haussmann.

Cerdà's economic thought was marked by two interesting extremes. One concerned the need for owners to contribute to the task of urban development. According to his text, "the landowner or owners who wish to build a street through their property should meet the costs of construction, with all its attendant sewerage and piping systems of all kinds, paving, etc., and make over the whole to the Municipality, once constructed". It is a description that seems obvious to us today but one that even in the Paris of the time would have been regarded as a bold and extremely socialising proposal.

Another controversial extreme involved his determination to make the rehabilitation of the old town economically viable by interconnecting it with the dynamic and the benefits of extending the city across the Plain. The great ambition of this proposal, that Cerdà[27] wanted to place under private management – like the railways concessions – came up against the strong resistance of the owners in the old town, who finally blocked the situation. Consequently, the "reform" part of Cerdà's Project was never passed. However, Cerdà's interest in Urban Reform continued beyond the passing of the Barcelona Plan and in 1861 he produced a proposal for the centre of Madrid in which he stressed the need to make this kind of scheme viable.[28]

To summarise, this was one of the great urban planning projects of 19th-century Europe which, despite its difficult legal passage, produced an admirable city centre and was capable of inspiring the Act on "Reform, extension and other town improvements", unfortunately not passed,[29] that the minister Posada Herrera presented in the Cortes, and which would have been one of the most innovative urban planning codes of the time. Nonetheless, the New Towns Act was passed in 1864, and the experience of the Eixample was present for all to see.

III.7 Barcelona's Eixample Project in relation to other European cities

In the mid-19th century, Cerdà's Project was set to extend Barcelona beyond its town walls, but other cities were taking different directions towards reform and extension.

Paris adopted the guidelines included in Haussmann and Napoleon III's proposals to restructure the still disorderly centre of the historic city. Taking as its model the Rue de Rivoli (1802) in 1853 it proposed a radial system of broad streets and new buildings with regular façades repeated in a rhythmic pattern. To facilitate their construction, the city established a tax exemption of 20 years for investors in new open spaces. Construction took longer than planned, but in 1867 when the second Great Exhibition was opened, 165 kilometres of new streets,

[27] Ildefonso Cerdà: "Pensamiento Económico", *op. cit.* Facsímil, Madrid, 1992.
[28] See Javier Frechilla, *op. cit.*
[29] Esteve Bassols: "La influencia del Proyecto Cerdà en la Legislación de Ensanche", in Laboratorio de Urbanismo: *Trabajos sobre Cerdà y Barcelona.* Barcelona, 1992, *op. cit.*

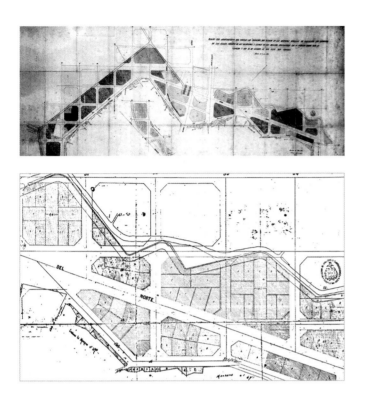

3.65, 3.66
Alignments of the land around
the town walls drafted by
Cerdà in 1865. Detail of plot
division in one sector.

with all the drainage networks, lighting and trees, etc., were completed, marked by junctions with emblematic civil and religious monuments. The increase in investment multiplied six fold and the displaced population was enormous, being estimated at over three hundred thousand people. This major remodelling was proposed in the interests of improved sanitation, circulation and safety in the streets. The ideas proposed in the enlightenment had to wait a century to be carried out.[30]

This urban development scheme was followed at the next Exhibition in 1889 by the creation of a singular landmark, the Eiffel Tower. This great 300-metre-high pinnacle represented a fundamental change in the Paris skyline and, for the crude language it employed, characteristic of the advances of ironworking technology, had many critics - Charles Garnier was one of many - while others saw it as a departure point for the "new" art of modernism, or Art Nouveau.

As of 1900 Paris was to be the model of urbanity for many cities, such as Buenos Aires, Rio, Cairo, Bucharest, etc.[31]

Another model was Vienna which, in the period running up to its Great Exhibition in 1873, had demolished the old fortifications and built a ring system of boulevards, the Ringstrasse, to provide a large site for facilities and

[30] See Jean des Cars *et al.*, *Paris. Haussmann.* Paris, 1991. Also François Loyer: *Paris XIXe Siècle. L'immeuble et la rue.* Hazan, Paris, 1994; David Jordan: *Transforming Paris. The life and works of Baron Haussmann.* Chicago, 1996.
[31] See André Lortie, ed.: *Paris s'exporte. Architecture modèle ou modèles d'architecture.* Picard, Paris, 1995. Also Gianni Fabbri: *Viena città capitale del XIX secolo.* Officina, Rome, 1986. Having recognised the specific nature of Cerdà's proposal, it is now important to see how such an innovative project can be implemented. It will undoubtedly be a path with many ups and downs, but we shall see the city at last with a great New Town, and this project will constitute its fundamental lines.

67
eometric plan of the
risdictional municipality of
arcelona, 1860, showing the
agmentation of farmland on
hich the Eixample was to be
uilt.

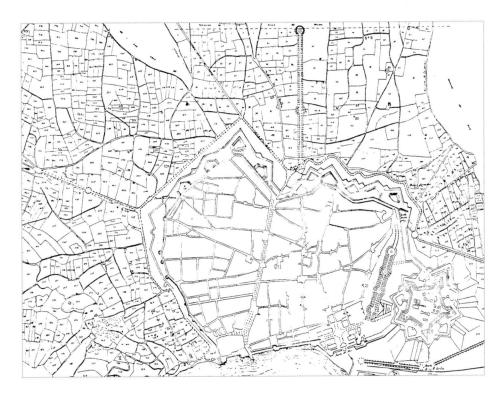

parks that would form a key "urban part" for the city's future development.[32] This Central European model was to be the common referent for other large cities in this context, such as Geneva, Hamburg and Antwerp.

This context highlights the specific nature of Cerdà's project. We will now go on to see how such an innovative project was carried out. It was a path marked by many vicissitudes, but ultimately, as we can see today, the city was to have its great Eixample, and it was this project that provided its basic guidelines.

III.8 The development of Cerdà's Eixample and the Development Societies

The text of the 1860 Act passing the project stipulated that henceforth new constructions in the Eixample would obey Cerdà's plan with regard to alignments and levels, but that prior municipal ordinances would continue to prevail, thereby watering down the technical and innovative forcefulness of the Cerdà Plan.

This heralded a new process which was to put to the test both the capacity of the project itself and Cerdà's personal ability to implement the Plan. Another important issue was the enthusiasm brought to a development of this size by city investors.

Anyone looking at the present-day city will realise that it passed the test, though they will be left wondering about the levels of urban development that might have been achieved had the original project been followed more

[32] See, among others, Renate Banik-Schweitzer *et al.*: *Wiener Atlas*. Vienna, 1980. Also Gianni Fabbri: *Viena città capitale del XIX secolo*. Officina, Rome, 1986.

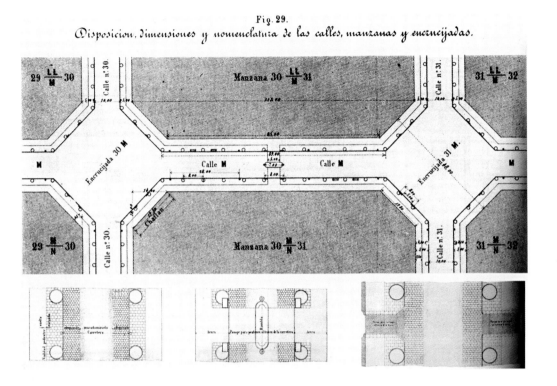

Fig. 29.
Disposicion, dimensiones y nomenclatura de las calles, manzanas y encrucijadas.

3.68
Study of the dimensions of the street blocks, junctions and directory of names proposed by Cerdà in Necesidades de Circulación, 1863.

faithfully. It is, however, important to remember that the city is above all the physical artefact in which social conflicts and economic development take place and is, therefore, the result of that process.

Cerdà continued to work until 1874, as of 1865 as the technical director and representative of the Governor in the municipalities in the Plain. This extraordinary man was very flexible in adapting his "ideas" to the necessary level for their deployment. We will now go on to see how he did this.

a) Designing the plot division. The demolition of the town walls had started in 1854 and farming land in the Plain was subject to very great pressure by the functional needs of a congested city that was gradually casting out activities (*indianes*, industries and small warehouses) and to a large extent by the prospects of the economic value that it was hoped that city extension would bring.

Farmland was made up of small plots as many speculative transactions had taken place, and the agricultural use made of it was frankly backward: two thirds of land was unirrigated. It was a clearly expectant peri-urban situation that only the imposition of military restrictions had kept free of construction.

According to Miquel Corominas's thesis,[33] most plots of land comprised between 3 and 6 *mojadas*, a small area for backward farming, but a large urban site on the scale of development of the Eixample.

Cerdà for his part immediately adjusted the layout plan to continue Passeig de Gràcia (constructed in 1829) and develop new proposals in outlying municipalities to make the development of his project more coherent.

[33] See Miquel Corominas, *La urbanización del Llano de Barcelona*. Doctoral thesis, Barcelona, 1991. "Suelo, técnica e iniciativa en los orígenes del Ensanche de Barcelona". It presents a very precise view of how the land in the Plain was to be broken in order to construct the Eixample. Published by Edicions UPC, Barcelona 2002.

69, 3.70, 3.71
assatge Permanyer in Carrer
au Claris. Layout of a street
lock with houses to the full
ermitted height, built in the
nglish-style, 1864.

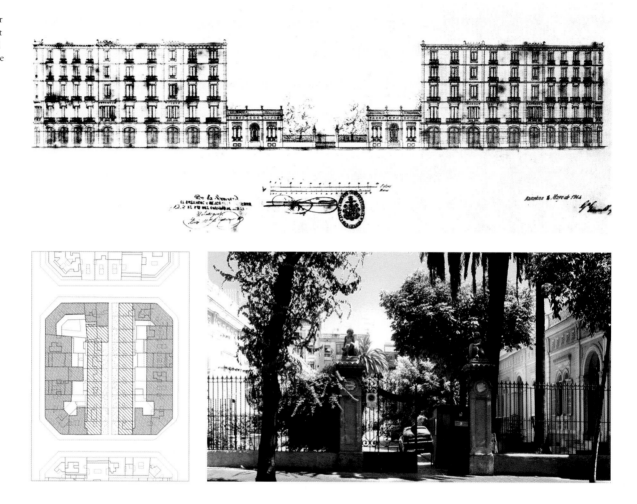

In order to prepare this reorganisation on site, he drafted 28 plans of *cuarterones* or fragments, otherwise known as *planos particularios* on a scale of 1:500 on which he situated with great precision the layout, property borders and topography. This enormous effort was complemented by transversal lines that enabled him to establish the definitive future levels of streets and buildings. The drawings were accompanied by an exact list of the owners of each street block who would receive the necessary information to allow them to act independently.

It was this complex series of technical instruments that enabled the initial construction of the Eixample on the basis of private initiative, but if this was to be possible, first it was necessary to "draft the plan on the land in question".

July 1860 saw the start of redefinition, with the necessary astronomical observations to exactly situate Meridiana. It was later joined by +Avinguda de la Catedral, which was taken as a reference for the implantation of the first junction of streets (Gran Via with Via Laietana, now Pau Claris); in the remaining months of the same year the markers were placed for the main streets. The project was guaranteed, and the effects were not long in appearing: in December, work began on Gibert house by +J. O. Mestres.

b) Forms of construction. In the process of constructing the Eixample, the dividing up of land formerly occupied by the town wall and the glacis provided a splendid test ground. Its 60-hectare extension and its proximity to the old town made it easy to develop. Cerdà carefully designed the plot division according to the overall layout, breaking the area down into 325 plots that were quickly developed. In this case, as all the land was owned by the public authorities, it was divided up in rational, planned fashion. In the remainder of the street blocks there was often a contradiction between the perfect form of the octagonal matrix of the street blocks and the erratic or geographical layout of former farmland. Cerdà fought to regularise the form of plots by means of redivision, and in a few cases he managed to do so: the form of buildings and their gable ends still illustrate this contradiction.

The singularity of the triangular layout in many of the street blocks in the former town wall enclosure imposed a closed street block form of construction.

This represented a marked evolution in the project. Cerdà's initial proposals envisaged street blocks with construction on just two sides, representing very low building levels. Gradually, as he studied the arrangement of the street block in greater detail, Cerdà tended to favour building on four sides without completely closing in the block, in order to allow the use of the inner space as a garden.[34]

Ildefonso Cerdà realised that the development of this new idea of city called for technical arrangement and fiscal instruments that Barcelona had never had. He therefore exerted himself to introduce new ordinances that sought to ensure these principles in the use of built space, but also in the order of urban spaces and development. However, as explained above, these regulations were not accepted, and he had to have recourse to the individual application of some personal projects and to such influence as he could bring to bear when supervising the projects for almost 500 construction sites in the first decade of the Eixample alone.

c) New real-estate mechanisms. The deployment of the project was actually possible due to the appearance of the "property corporations" created to develop the new neighbourhood and comprising Barcelona's new merchant class. Cerdà was well acquainted with them; during the discussion phases of the project there had been attempts on the part of individuals to undertake the town extension privately.

These "corporations" were set up with a large capital and the participation of many small-investment shareholders, traders and minor industrialists who shared in the risk but also in the enthusiasm that the Eixample

---

[34] See Joaquím Sabaté: "Las ordenanzas de construcción de Ildefonso Cerdà", Laboratorio de Urbanismo: *Trabajos sobre Cerdà y Barcelona*. Barcelona, 1992. *op. cit.*

72
ne of the "Cerdà houses"
ilt in 1861-62, owned by
sep Cerdà, unrelated to
e illustrious engineer, and
cently restored.

73
rdà's project for two street
ocks for the Sociedad El
mento del Ensanche.

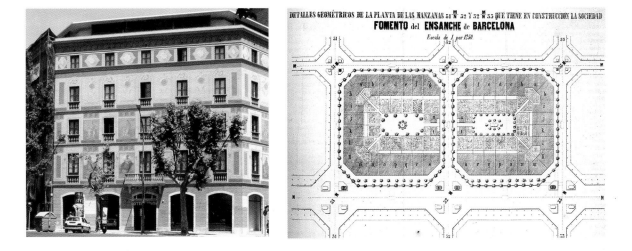

unleashed in the city. Some shareholders were from regions outside the city of Barcelona, but there was as yet no foreign capital.

According to Corominas' study, in this initial period the corporations controlled as many as 57 hectares, mainly between Passeig de Gràcia and Passeig de Sant Joan, around Gran Via, forming the sector that came to be known as the *dreta*, or right-hand side, of the Eixample.

The corporations organised themselves to cover the entire process: from the purchase of farmland and the construction of homes to the corresponding urbanisation, and some of them even incorporated the manufacture of building materials in their brickworks or offered an urban service such as a drinking water network. It was undoubtedly a truly complex undertaking, as the land made available was very extensive and major work was required to develop some areas affected by seasonal watercourses and streams.

In any case, it was during this period that the most interesting examples of developments took place. The participation of Cerdà and other architects employed by the corporations suggested a whole range of very promising foretastes of how the Eixample might have turned out if the scale and the objectives of this launch period had been kept up.

One outstanding example is the street block around Passatge Permanyer, constructed for the Sociedad El Ensanche y Mejora by the architect Jeroni F. Granell, with 16 buildings of five-storeys and 17 single-family dwellings distributed along the passage in English fashion. The result was an excellent example of what was called the *casa de renta* or apartment house, which was very well received by the market.

For the Sociedad Fomento del Ensanche, Cerdà himself undertook the organisation of two street blocks beside Gran Via, each of which was laid out in a U-shape, maintaining the central garden space and employing a shallower depth of construction on the corners to provide better ventilation. He also designed a 211-house project for Josep Serraclarà near the university; the street block was laid out around a passage running the middle. These are paradigm examples to demonstrate Cerdà's capacity for response within the general pattern of the road fabric.

However, the Eixample's splendid beginning was cut short by the general crisis of 1866, signalling bankruptcy for some of the corporations involved, while others were able to retrench and carry on their activity. Tortella Casares suggests as a local explanation of this crisis the continual undercapitalisation of industry due to

3.74
Demolition of the Tallers
bastion.

excessive investment in the railway sector. In the Eixample, the disproportionate purchase of land also weakened corporations' ability to deal with a crisis of this nature.

These corporations rented out the dwellings in the form of deferred purchase, with very low interest rates. The dividends distributed totalled in the region of 6% per annum. The literature published by these corporations explaining their aims and running would still provide a good model today, for their high urban quality and the straightforward explanations with which they presented the many possibilities of access to housing.

Nonetheless, this was the end of a crucial phase for the Eixample, which had proved its viability despite being undertaken by private initiative alone; in a very short period of time, the real-estate corporations had brought some 30 hectares of land onto the market, approximately one seventh of the area of the old town. However, the change in pace that then took place led to a more piecemeal form of management, plot by plot, and a clear separation between firms dealing with land, buildings or urban development. The city was seeing the emergence of the capitalist circuits of the real-estate system, which were to become more generalised later on.[35]

[35] This was the start in Barcelona, as in most big European cities, of a new economic and social phenomenon: real-estate speculation. A discussion took place on this subject in Paris with regard to the development of the land market and incomes from landownership. "If the house were easily transportable, or if they were spread across an unlimited, homogeneous terrain, like ships at sea, there would be nothing to distinguish it from other products", but in addition to the "use" of the plot, which gives it an absolute rent, there is another rent related to its "location", which is produced by the effect of the spatial distribution with regard to other plots, and this is the "differential rent". It is this interplay of values that gives rise to real-estate speculation, which places the owner in a position to "advance and accumulate" a possible future security. Halbwachs would say that the owner acts as though he knew "better than the masses what the masses are going to do". Maurice Halbwachs: *Les expropriations et le prix des terrains à Paris (1860-1900)*. Paris, 1909.

d) **Relations between the real-estate and industrial sectors.** Many differing interpretations have been given of the relations between growing real-estate development as seen in the Eixample and the Catalan industrial sector, due to the lack of specific information about the relative dynamic of these sectors during the 19th century.

One common interpretation is that the development of the Eixample had a belated effect on the industrial sector due to the large amount of capital that the construction sector drew away from industrial production.

In any case, it is evident that in a metropolis growing in both population and industrial development, the interrelation between the different economic sectors was complex. The profits created by industry and trade did of course include the profits produced by the nascent real-estate sector, both by renting buildings and by selling or ceding land.

There has been a tendency to underestimate the major role of land-related profit produced by the huge area of land brought into play by Cerdà's Eixample which, according to M. de Solà-Morales,[36] acted as a great collective loan exchange (in the hands of the commercial and industrial bourgeoisie) that allowed countless exchange transactions.

Xavier Tafunell[37] was the first to introduce a series of cross-related data for the 1854-1896 period, on the basis of which he studied the relations between population movements, number of dwellings built, port traffic, industrial production and estimates of national income and investment.

These variables show that the construction sector behaved in conjunction with other economic sectors and was not an independent sector standing apart, though this does not mean that it did not have a major specific effect on economic accumulation in the broadest sense.

Nonetheless, the figures provided by the study illustrate just how active the real-estate sector was, principally in the Eixample, with a rate of construction of between 750 and 1900 dwellings a year in the second half of the 19th century. It is also interesting to see temporary imbalances in the relative parallelism between the industrial and real-estate dynamic that can be explained either by the existence of a highly competitive sector, as in the case of high-level investment in the railway network in Spain between 1881 and 1883, or by the higher profits offered by "national debt".

As in other advanced countries, Tafunell points out that the high points in construction (1863, 1872, 1876, 1880, 1890, 1893) coincide with the low points of public securities, with the single exception of the 1881-1883 period, known as *febre de l'or* or gold fever, when the country's savings were temporarily held in thrall by grand projects offering spectacular gains.

[36] See Manuel de Solà-Morales: *Los Ensanches* I. *op. cit.*
[37] Xavier Tafunell: "Construcció i Conjuntura econòmica", *La formació de l'Eixample de Barcelona*. Barcelona, 1990.

The other relation to exist between the two sectors was one of complementarity: during periods of relative industrial recession, the real-estate sector expanded, providing a natural outlet for investment.

III.9 Suburban models in the urban development of the Barcelona Plain

The formation of contemporary Barcelona can be explained by means of two major entities or categories that are juxtaposed in the slow-growing, complex old city: the Eixample and the suburban centres (former villages in the Barcelona Plain) that were excluded both in administrative terms (they were not annexed until the late 19th century) and by the fact that they were pursuing different processes of physical construction. Though different, they were strongly interconnected and, in order to understand them, it is important to stress the project variables that characterised each of these. The study of suburban models is divided into two parts; here we deal with the operations represented by the first Barcelona periphery in the 19th century, turning later to those that configured the transformation of the new developments in the 20th century.[38]

The ring of centres in the Plain represented a population of 50,000 inhabitants in 1857 which had multiplied by four by 1900. The functional profile of these centres was very different in the 19th century, marked by their industrial fact: Sant Martí, which in the 1888 census reported more than two hundred factories, mainly in Clot and Poblenou, and whose main sectors were textiles, metallurgy and foodstuffs; Sants, with Espanya Industrial and Fábrica Güell; Les Corts, with Can Batlló in 1867; Barceloneta, with Maquinista Terrestre y Marítima and Nueva Vulcano; and Gràcia, with small workshops and some *vapors*.

Other centres, conversely, remained markedly agricultural, and were affected by residential or summer migration: Sarrià, Horta, Sant Gervasi and Sant Andreu were the most representative.

Despite their functional diversity, these centres were subject to growth and extension dynamics that partook of common "suburban models", very different to those at work in the Eixample, and which produced urban fabrics of a similar size and importance as the latter.

---

[38] The models outlined in this chapter are expanded in a research project carried out in 1981-1982 which produced a summarised map entitled "Lectura de la Barcelona Suburbana", drawn on a scale of 1:10.000. A summary of the work was published by Joan Busquets and Josep Parcerisa: "Instruments de projectació de la Barcelona suburbana", *Annuales ETSAB*, Barcelona, 1983. The work concentrates on a discussion of the elements that make up the first Barcelona periphery, developed in the 19th century, and completed and transformed in the 20th century. An interpretation of these parts of the city sets out to identify the typical "operations" of intervention with a view to appraising the planning instruments employed in its construction.

3.k A general interpretation of suburban Barcelona.

75
general interpretation of
suburban Barcelona that
developed according to
different urban planning
patterns to those of the old
town and the Eixample.

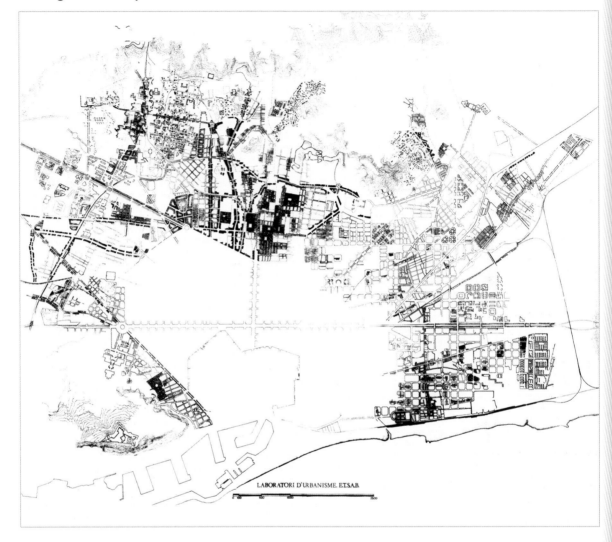

LABORATORI D'URBANISME. E.T.S.A.B.

Cerdà's Eixample occupied a central position in relation to the historic city. There were still however a series of duly rectified guidelines prior to the extension project that do not follow the orthogonal grid: Carretera de Sarrià, Passeig de Gràcia, Pere IV, and so forth. The railways lines also created a series of identifiable guidelines and barriers. However, until 1859 this territory enjoyed the condition of a "non-construction" area, which facilitated the "impression" of the Eixample without having to demolish existing buildings.

There was another entity developed at the same time as the Eixample, though dating from an earlier time, constructed according to a series of much more diverse and discontinuous organisations, but which was very important due to the large surface area it covered. This was the ring that formed the geographical periphery of the Eixample, comprising specific, fragmentary projects and initiatives.

The 19th century saw a series of six model projects that gave rise to the construction of suburban Barcelona. A further four will be presented later on in order to explain its infill and transformation in the course of the following century. Of the first six, three are associated with roads, and the remainder are residential.

Those concerned with roads:

a) urbanisation of roads and rural tracks. The outline has survived of many of the roads and rural tracks that existed before the urban development of the Barcelona Plain, some dating from Roman times.

The roads, with winding, uneven levels and layouts, dictated the original forms of constructions that were built along them.

The roads responded to a more elaborate, unitary and geometrically precise idea of public work. They followed straight lines with gently sloping inclines and transitions, and the buildings constructed along them exploited the advantages of a very solid urban base. They became the "high streets" in villages in the first ring, concentrating activity due to their condition of traffic lanes and through roads (Pere IV, Carretera de Ribes, Carretera de Sants).

b) Streets based on easements. Railway lines, canals, irrigation channels and torrents are elements that impose major urban planning easements on the territory. The fragmentary construction of the first ring had taken place in such a way as to avoid watercourses, which were depressed areas providing a less solid foundation for construction; the railroads and canals were easements but not axes of urbanisation.

The chance to transform these easements arose due to the need to facilitate the interconnection of the city areas they separated and frequently also as a result of pressure to extend and merge urban surfaces, a process which they hindered. This process almost always resulted in a public works project: lowering the existing ground level or canalising the infrastructure underground, in the event that a simple diversion was not chosen.

This type of operation began in the late 19th century, continued throughout the 20th century and tended to create continuity between the Eixample and suburban fabrics: the Riera d'en Malla was covered over to create Rambla de Catalunya, as was the Riera de Vallcarca, now +Carrer del Príncep d'Astúries, etc.

3.1 Origins of the suburban formation of Sant Andreu as an example of suburban development.

...76
...erial view of Sant Andreu.

...77
...rbanisation of rural tracks
...nd streets produced by
...asements.

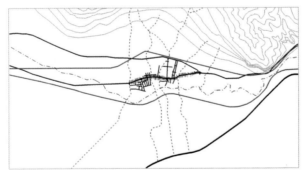

...78
...treets of houses and fabrics of
...reets.

...79
...treets with squares and
...venues.

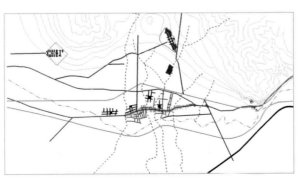

c) Avenues. The deployment in a non-urban territory of a linear layout was a very powerful instrument in the gradual structuring and promotion of urban planning.

It consisted in the expropriation of land, earthworks and construction, and other interventions that formed a new, continuous ground level. A basic constant cross section was decided on, with a precise internal cadence of avenue, pavements, trees and gardens. Their continuity and their breadth made these layouts stand out from the basic networks of streets that organised land for construction. Although interventions of this kind also generated construction on the land running immediately alongside, this was not a basic concern of the project, which was in fact quite independent of the forms of occupation of its edges, which were as a result quite diverse and changing.

Precedents to the 19th-century walled city were Passeig d'Icària, leading to the new cemetery, Passeig de Gràcia, as already explained, and today's Avinguda Mistral, in the direction of Creu Coberta. The three have undergone transformations in section and use, but continue to constitute unvarying bases for the city's general structure.

Similarly, Passeig de Sant Joan Bosco in the south and Passeig de Santa Eulàlia in the north of Sarrià, and Passeig Fabra i Puig leading towards Horta and Passeig de Torras i Bages to the north, in Sant Andreu, were other extended avenues.

The tram system was the first to envisage the importance that these layouts have subsequently acquired as arteries. And, finally, others were proposed as backbones for interstitial occupation: Avinguda del Doctor Andreu and Carrer Mandri are exponents of a form of development in which the shape and position of the avenue are fundamental.

In general terms, at the time of its construction the avenue did not necessarily constitute a strategy for circulation or connection. It was merely the most suitable instrument for drawing together an extensive intervention that would impose structure on a territory that was previously inaccessible, and that would later be occupied by the solid backing of public intervention. It was only later that the "pressure" of growth turned them into central pieces of urban mobility.

The projects of a residential nature include:

d) The street of houses. Any plot of land in a territory with guaranteed access could be used for the construction of a group of similarly typed buildings giving onto a narrow, rather short street, often a cul-de-sac, limited to the dwelling needs of the operation. This was, then, an operation to divide up land for construction on small plots of similar sizes.

This elementary mechanism was much employed due to its low costs and flexible adaptation to the specific requisites of land subdivision and residential construction.

It is found on very varying territories: from the scattered occupation along old roads or forms reminiscent of industrial colonies (El Taulat in Poblenou) to a mechanism to fill in Eixample street blocks in Gràcia and Poblenou, and on the outskirts, the passages of the Eixample in outlying positions.

3.m The different types of project in suburban expansion.

The urbanisation of roads and easements

Avenues

Streets of houses

Fabrics of streets and streets around a square

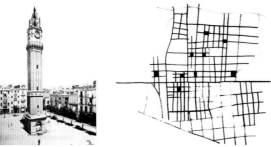

30
rrer Pere IV, the
banisation of the old road to
ance in Poblenou.

31
e Rec Condal irrigation
annel providing the city
ntre with water.

32
sseig de la Bonanova.

33
sseig Maragall in Horta.

34
s Corts, Sarrià, 1929. Streets
houses built along the old
avessera.

35
mp de l'Arpa.

36
aça Rius i Taulet, 1897.

37
e squares of Gràcia.

This process developed construction types that range from the single-family house with or without garden and the house with a ground floor with patio or gallery and one or two floors to the detached house reminiscent of garden city typologies.

e) The fabric of streets. The most immediate instrument for land layout was the intersecting street formation. The idea of forming a relatively small extension comprising a fabric of small streets that left spaces for building was the most elementary way of imposing an urban system. The first Barcelona ring has frequent recourse to this mechanism that historically had been used in the occupation of the neighbourhoods of the Raval inside the walled city.

The streets were narrow, between six and ten metres wide, and varied in length, with multiple T-junctions, producing rectangular or sometimes trapezoid street blocks. The layout of streets and the shallowness of the street blocks indicates that they were accommodated by doubling the depth of the "reasonable" plot depending on the intended typological form. The house façades are in the long street and the gable ends give onto the street orthogonal to complement them. Land occupation was, then, intensive, though the initial construction models were low rise (two or three floors), combining blocks of rented apartments, single-family and artisan houses, warehouses, workshops and detached houses with gardens.

The elementary nature of the system and its intensive occupation signified a lack of public squares and a tendency to grow in any direction by directly prolonging street layouts, in some cases leading to congestion.

This instrument was used to occupy interstitial sites in the first ring, in Poble Sec, for example, and was blatantly generalised in the construction of the entire metropolitan area throughout the 20th century. Nonetheless, a present-day interpretation should stress the precise relation of equilibrium that exists between housing types and the network of streets, due to the judicious use of this suburban form.

f) Geometric plan of streets with a square. The formation of geometric plans emerged in the first half of the 20th century as a way of designing the city by means of categories that had previously proved their viability in the 1700s. A few, very elementary principles were taken into consideration: the network of narrow, orthogonal and basically isotropic streets, forming roughly rectangular street blocks that allowed the organisation of buildings similar in type to the "fabrics of streets" though more homogeneous and without distinction on all sides; and the idea of a central square presided by a public building and including at least a public fountain for reasons of hygiene. These principles were formulated in a fairly unitary project involving the simultaneous construction of streets.

An interpretation of the first Barcelona ring allows easy identification of these "geometric plans" in Les Corts, Poble Sec, Gràcia, Vilapicina, Sant Andreu, La Sagrera and El Clot, places which in this way formed their initial urban nucleus.[39] Despite corresponding to different moments in history, despite the fact that the squares differ in composition and size, the similarity of these occupation projects is irrefutable.

This form of city construction was contemporary to the abuse of the "street fabric", tending to combine discontinuously. Directions that were the mechanical prolongations of layouts frequently marked out borders and

orientations or provided support to the geometric plan, which in turn acted as an incentive to the subsequent extension of some of its main axes in the form of street fabric.[40]

An application of this classification to the old municipalities of the Plain illustrates its efficiency in explaining their formation. The implantation in the territory of Sant Andreu del Palomar, for instance, was guided by the topographic system (hills and watercourses) and the highways, with roads leading from the central city to the prelittoral corridor, starting in the river Besòs gorge, and the irrigation channel that supplied Barcelona with water.

This outline explains the first settlements with their organic, almost geographical layouts; urban development subsequently followed the suburban patterns indicated: highways or easements that became urban to form streets, streets of houses, squares with "geometric plans" and "avenues" that connected traditional nucleuses to new facilities and production sites.

This "suburban" logic shaped the formation of this district until the deployment of the transformation processes outlined below.

[39] See Manuel de Solà-Morales, Eduard Brú and Enric Serra: "Gràcia. Diseño del suelo y forma urbana en los orígenes de la Barcelona moderna". *Arquitecturas bis nº 15*, Barcelona, 1976. The high standard of urban life in these areas is reflected in works of modern literature such as *La Plaça del Diamant* by Mercè Rodoreda. Barcelona, 1962.

[40] This form of city production on the basis of a geometric plan with public squares became more generalised in the second half of the 19th century under the auspices of the New Towns Act and gave rise to interesting extensions to the main Catalan towns and cities such as Mataró, Vilanova, Sabadell and Terrassa, which are later referred to as "mature towns". See Manuel de Solà-Morales and Julio Esteban: *Los Ensanches menores en la región de Barcelona*. Publicacions ETSAB. Barcelona, 1978.

V. Barcelona, city of innovation

IV.1 The demolition of the Citadel

Barcelona, a European City was how Isidre Molas[1] summarised the position achieved by Barcelona in the late 19th century, due to its leading role in industrial development and its reception of the innovative ideas associated with modernity. The Great Exhibition was to be an important catalyst in this process.

"Being the effective capital of Catalonia and the most advanced city in Spain meant fully assuming a governing function and, therefore, achieving external presence and projection in all fields. (…) Barcelona was the door to Europe, modernity, creation and a people's determination to overcome difficulties while still remaining a people, to be universal without ceasing to be Catalan; a situation that to some extent explains the modern life of this stateless nation that was Catalonia in the Spain of the 1900s."[2]

In this process of consolidation of modern Barcelona, Borja de Riquer[3] highlights three periods: the first led up to the 1888 Exhibition, the second was the turn of the century and the third was the Mancomunitat de Catalunya, or commonwealth of municipalities.

The 1880s saw the height of the Restoration, consolidated in 1875 after the "democratic six-year period" (1868-1874). A two-party system held sway, with the alternation of conservatives represented by Cánovas and liberals by Sagasta. In Catalonia these forces were represented by the leading lights of the new bourgeoisie such as the Güells, Girona, Muntades and Ferrer i Vidal on the conservative side, and Bosch, Alsina, Rius i Taulet and Marianao for the liberals.

The years leading up to the Exhibition were marked by a major crisis in the countryside and the desire to continue the protectionist policy that since the Figuerola period had kept up the momentum of "protected" industrial development.

As a result, the Sagasta government's attempts to open up or liberalise the market by seeking an agreement with France or England represented a great danger to the Catalan textile sector: its productivity was lower, since most of the raw materials and energy sources were imported and functioned on a basis of the Catalan and Spanish markets and, to some extent, the Americas.

In 1881 what practically amounted to an urban revolution took place against this "free-trade" policy of the central government, as well as the reform of both industry tax and the Civil Code, that set out to abolish Catalan Law. This led to fully-fledged opposition to Madrid and was even expressed by a resistance to pay taxes.

4.01
View of Barcelona with the project for Ciutadella Park by Antonio Castelucho, 1882.

[1] Isidre Molas: "Barcelona, una ciutat europea", *Homage to Barcelona*. Barcelona, 1987.
[2] *Op. cit.*, page 79.
[3] Borja de Riquer: "La Societat Catalana dels anys Vuitanta", *Arquitectura i Ciutat*. Barcelona, 1988.

In 1885 the *Memorial de Greuges*, or Statement of grievances, with its many demands was presented to Alfonso XII by a group of Catalan representatives, including Valentí Almirall, the founder of *Diari Català* and one of the staunchest opponents of the Great Exhibition.

Another pro-Catalan group, "La Renaixença", which called itself apolitical, represented the pro-Catalan, traditionalist, Catholic project.

The Exhibition served not only to overcome the economic crisis, it was also a qualitative leap forwards. In the cultural world, this leap took the specific form of Modernisme, which extended beyond architectural trends; in urban planning, it saw the affirmation of the Eixample and the establishing of its new urban centre in Plaça de Catalunya and Passeig de Gràcia; and in the realm of national affirmation, it represented a boost to the Catalan language, the use of which once again became widespread in writing. Altogether, they formalised the Catalan *renaixença*, or rebirth, associated with the memory of self-government, as a cultural movement promoted by the well-to-do classes who were in tune with the spontaneous pro-Catalan[4] sentiment of the people.

This produced a situation in which three distinct blocks were formed: the bourgeoisie, a growing proletariat and government, giving rise to a singular situation in the Catalan case: nascent nationalism was to group capital and the workers' sector against the third block for some of this time. There was a degree of dissociation between the representative political structure and the general political sensitisation of civil society, which expressed itself in other forms of associative life, such as cultural associations, choral societies, etc. At this time there were ten daily newspapers, one of them in Catalan, and *Diario de Barcelona* which had been set up in 1792 and was known as "el Brusi", from the name of the founding family.

---

[4] On this theme, there is an interesting description in Richard Ford's *A Hand-book for Travellers in Spain, op. cit.* Describing the situation of Catalonia in relation to Spain in the mid-19th century: "The Catalans are neither French nor Spanish, but a people that differs from both in its language, dress and habits; truth to tell, their abruptness and their activity... suffice to warn the traveller that he is no longer in courteous, indolent Spain... These remains of the Celtiberians sigh for their former independence, and their patriotism is exceedingly 'provincial' and local. Catalonia, with its Cleontes of percale and its Catalinas of cotton, is the strength and the weakness of Spain; and no province in the disunited confusion that forms the conventional monarchy of Spain is less firmly united to the crown than this classical country of rebellion, always prepared to break away."

This development of Catalan awareness took place alongside the structuring of a new capitalist society. These conditions were to mark this process in the booming European capital. But first, the cumbersome Citadel would have to be demolished.

Its demolition had been the constant aspiration of the people of Barcelona due to the inconvenience it represented, but above all for the symbolic value it still embodied. It became possible after the resolution of September 1868, authorising its conversion into a public park for the city as compensation for its former use.

The park was designed by the architect Josep Fontseré, whose project had won the 1872 competition, with the slogan "Gardens are to cities as lungs are to the human body". Construction of the park began a year later, though the demolition of the Citadel only took place gradually.

The aim of Fontseré's project was to define the park as a large open rectangular space closed in by a circular arch to the south. The park was laid out with subspaces according to a central axis comprising the promenade that extended the Saló de Sant Joan. One such was used as a zoological garden in 1898.[5] The rest of the former military land was laid out to dovetail with the most immediate urban fabric. In one of these sectors, Fontseré himself designed a great brick structure as a water tank for the gardens. This construction was designed with a rationality that is still exemplary even today.[6]

Then, in the Ribera sector, covering six hectares, the project envisaged the development of a residential area and the market built in 1874 and known as the Born. Fontseré designed over one hundred sites and established a model façade to allow their construction in stone and a vertical compositional order arising from the axes of the ground floor. The effort being demanded of the city by the Eixample probably prevented the project being carried out completely. However, even today the Born complex is still one of the city's most singular urban spaces.[7]

---

[5] The park suffered from its increased use for the zoo in the 1960s.

[6] The building was restored and enhanced in 1988 by the architects Ignacio Paricio and Lluís Clotet.

[7] The Born ceased to function as a general market in the 1960s and its restoration in the late 1970s once again brought this interesting building by Fontseré to the forefront of attention. However, the reuse of this building with its metal roofing system is not proving easy. The idea being discussed in 2002 was the installation of a light-structured library that would be compatible with the archaeological remains of the old Ribera district in its foundations.

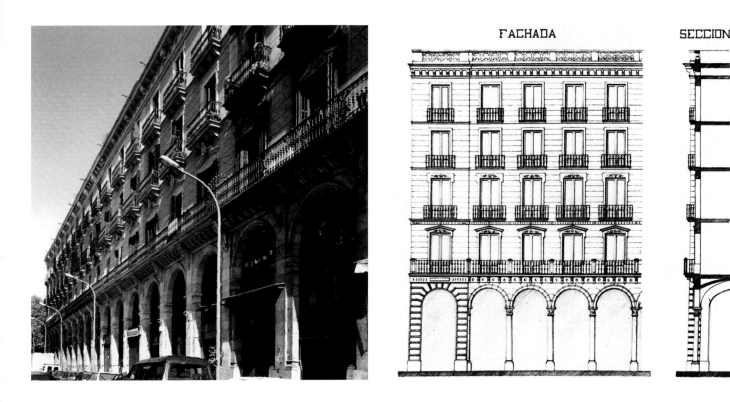

FACHADA   SECCION

4.05, 4.06
Building in Fontseré's
residential complex near the
Born.

IV.2 The 1888 Great Exhibition

The Regent Queen Maria Cristina opened Barcelona's Great Exhibition on 22 May 1888. The spectacular celebration was accompanied by the impressive volley of 432 canon shots from the international fleet anchored in the port.

This signalled the completion of arduous preparatory work on the precinct and the city as a whole, but also the coming of age of Catalan industry and trade, now an established actor on the European stage. Then, as Josep Puig i Cadafalch pointed out, it also marked the start of a architectural and cultural movement that he called the "new Catalan school" and was defined by a special combination of forms and techniques taken from the regional construction tradition and the innovations of modern technology.

Some twenty major exhibitions had been held in Europe and America since the first in London in 1851, at Crystal Palace, when Prince Albert proclaimed that "nations must work together for the benefit of all".[8]

The Paris exhibitions of 1855, 1867 and 1878 also represented great steps forwards and in 1889, a year after the Barcelona event, it was to repeat the occasion on the same site, but with the construction of the Eiffel Tower.[9]

[8] Although there had been important Exhibitions since the late 18th century, particularly in France, it was not until the celebrated London show that the Great Exhibitions opened up to the international scene. The much-famed Crystal Palace stood out for its dynamism and its advanced architecture: the building, measuring 1851 feet in length, one for every year of the event, with its iron and glass architecture, made this great "container" the paradigm of exhibition buildings throughout the 19th century.
[9] The Eiffel Tower became a symbol of "exhibition". In fact Paris presented the tower painted gold for the 1900 exhibition and clad in neon lights in 1937: it was impossible to ignore the urban force of this powerful symbol.

4.a The 1888 Great Exhibition.

07
ew of the port and the city
1888 on the opening day of
e great event.

08
lan of the 1888 Great
xhibition on the site of the
ormer Citadel.

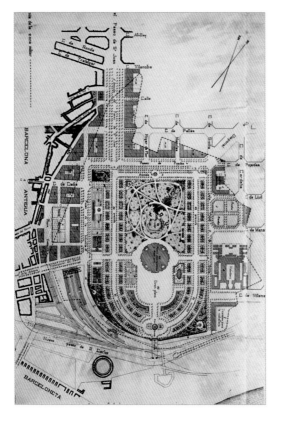

Barcelona in any case moved between the idea of the impact of the big exhibitions and the realism of the "lesser" exhibitions, according to Pere Hereu.[10] A degree of ambiguity marked the dual process through which the 1888 Exhibition was to pass. In the exhibitions in Brussels in 1882, Amsterdam and Nice in 1883, and Antwerp in 1885, second cities like Barcelona had demonstrated to Europe their organisational capacity, but they had also mobilised important sectors of urban development: Amsterdam had opened up to the sea via the river Ij and Antwerp had demolished its Citadel in the south of the city.

The 19th-century exhibitions enabled everyone to visualise, enjoy and partake of the most innovative products and the very latest ideas. They provided requisite points of reference that the advances of the mass media later watered down. Further, the effort they required, from a commercial and architectural viewpoint, allowed cities and companies to set themselves more ambitious aims that those that they undertook in the course of everyday life.

In 1888 Barcelona was materialising its Eixample that extended across the Plain around the old town, with over eight thousand dwellings already constructed. The demolition of the Citadel and its conversion into an urban park represented a good balance between the Eixample and the old town: the construction of the Ronda formed a ring around the city and the urbanisation of Plaça de Catalunya, always an unclear point in Cerdà's designs, completed the

---

[10] See Pere Hereu: *Arquitectura i Ciutat a l'Exposició Universal de Barcelona*. UPC, Barcelona, 1988.

10
View of the cascade in
Ciutadella Park.

intervention. The railway had completed its "figure of eight" circuit centring on Barcelona and the road network had increased considerably. The Eixample was being gradually consolidated, and would finally come together as an excellent extension of the historic city, though Cerdà's idea of overall urban reshaping seemed unlikely to materialise.

The process of developing the Great Exhibition was to be a difficult one, involving two quite distinct phases. The initiative had come out of the private sector and was fairly speculative in orientation.

In 1885 Enrique Serrano de Casanova requested the City Council's collaboration in carrying out an exhibition of this kind. He had the experience of having represented Spain in other European events that had taken place in recent years, getting to know specialists and engineers with the necessary know-how.[11] He thought that if municipal authorisation was given, local capital would throw itself into an initiative of this type.

Initially the City Council viewed the project favourably and provided the land and a modest financial contribution.[12] However, time told the inefficiency of Serrano's group and its project turned out to have many

[11] This was the case of the French architect Alexandre Sallé, who drafted the initial projects; Sallé had been responsible for the Bordeaux exhibition in 1882.
[12] There was of course criticism of this process, as described by Antoni Jutglar in *Els burgesos catalans* (Barcelona, 1966), a text in which he outlines the megalomaniac side of the Exhibition in relation to the problems created by the economic recession of 1886. The build-up to the great event is described in Narcís Oller's *La febre de l'or*. Barcelona, 1890.

technical and economic failings. The buildings designed by the engineering team were in head-on contradiction with Fontseré's park project, by then under construction, to the point that the architect actually resigned from the commission.

This impasse arose a year before the supposed opening of the Exhibition, so there was no going back. Yet the prestige of the city and its trade and industry was threatened by the dreadful management of this private association.

The remarkable mayor, Francisco de Paula Rius i Taulet, applied for help to the Crown and took the reins of the situation when construction work was under way but a long way behind schedule. The poor state of work became evident when a building collapsed after a storm and another had to be destroyed due to an apparent lack of safety.

To face up to this challenge he set up a citizens' "commission" with wide-ranging powers[13] and asked for assistance from the Director of the School of Architecture, the architect Elias Rogent, who had designed the university building in the new Eixample. Rogent formed a team of the School's lecturers and young architects who undertook to supervise the construction process. It was the start of a race against the clock.[14]

[13] Forming part of this commission, of which Rius i Taulet was president, were Manuel Duràn i Bas, lawyer; Manuel Girona, banker; Claudio López Bru, shipowner; Manuel Ferrer Vidal, industrialist, and Elias Rogent, architect.

[14] Rogent immediately changed the face of the intervention; in an initial report, he lamented the state of the buildings and the fact that "the architect is French, the companies are Austrian and the materials are Hungarian...". He also outlined two priority ideas in the operation: firstly, that the "park" should be completed in its entirety, thereby finally ensuring the conversion of the Citadel into a park, and secondly, that the only way for the city to obtain positive results in the medium term was for the buildings to be definitive.

12
Hotel Internacional by
Domènech i Montaner, sadly
no longer in existence.

The change in course of the operation was decisive to its success, though the problems inherited by the new team were such that it was difficult to solve them fast and efficiently. Nonetheless, the exhibition's urban development relation with the city underwent a complete turnaround.

From a closed conception of the park with a single entrance on Paso de la Aduana, the new design introduced an open layout that sought a vertical axis, suggested in the Fontseré project by the Saló de Sant Joan, to join up with the Eixample and a footbridge over the railway track to the sea.[15] In this way, the Exhibition would be laid out in three blocks or sectors: the Saló, the Parc de la Ciutadella and the seafront.

Rogent also set out to turn the opportunity of the Exhibition to good account by promoting the variety of nuances that contemporary architecture was capable of offering.

A series of provisional buildings was built, including the Gran Hotel Internacional, actually built outside the exhibition enclosure, alongside Xifré's porticoes, by the port. This work by Lluís Domènech i Montaner was one of the high points of the event. It was a six-storey building with 800 rooms and a structure that took 53 days to build; its overall construction took four months.[16] The building combined a lightweight iron structure with

[15] P. Hereu, J. Rosell and M. Torroella: "La creació de l'Exposició. Crónica dels esdeveniments", *Arquitectura i Ciutat a l'Exposició Universal de Barcelona 1888*. Barcelona, 1988. Also Jaume Rosell: "La Exposición Universal de 1888", *Rassegna nº 37*. Milan, 1989.

[16] The story of this building's construction illustrates the progress made in the construction techniques applied by Modernisme. The future stylistic trends would camouflage these capacities, and it was only with the arrival of the Modern Movement that these technologies would emerge as the characteristic language of architecture.

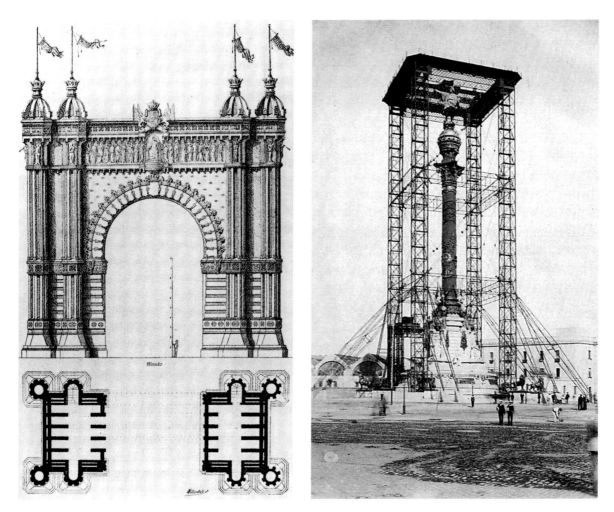

4.13
Triumphal Arch, designed by
José Vilaseca i Casanovas.

4.14
Monument to Columbus
during construction in 1887,
the work of Rafael Atché i
Farré.

hollow brick facings housing a network of chimneys, tubes and down pipes. Many elements were prefabricated and modulation was strict.[17] It is impossible to understand how such an interesting work was demolished after the Exhibition.

One of the most outstanding permanent buildings was certainly Josep Vilaseca's Arc de Triomf, a masterwork in the use of brick, marking the approach from the new city. Josep Fontseré continued to supervise the general construction of the park, a task in which one of his collaborators was the young architect Gaudí.

[17] The construction of this singular building began with the intervention of 200 workers and eventually employed over a thousand people in peak periods. On its completion, six flags were hoisted on the roof of the building, each bearing a figure or letter of the slogan "53 días" (53 days, the time taken to construct it). At the big celebration held, as is customary in the region, to mark the completion of the building's roof, the Mayor, Rius i Taulet, carried away by enthusiasm for this great work, announced that "the Catalans are the Yankees of Europe".

The Palace of Fine Arts was constructed with the idea of providing the city with a permanent museum and the Great Machine Gallery aspired to add the spectacle of the mechanical innovation that had so impressed visitors to Paris.

Another permanent building was the café-restaurant commissioned to Domènech i Montaner, though work was held up by financial difficulties and it was not completed for the Expo.

Finally, the Exhibition did not have its own particular tower, though repeated attempts were made to provide one.[18]

Other last-minute problems arose, including the continuing military use of the centre of the Citadel, even in the church and the Governor's Palace. A final agreement enabled their use for the Exhibition, and explains why these buildings still stand there today.

The situation deteriorated due to worker strikes in December 1887 and the harsh winter. When work resumed it did so at a tremendous pace.

In view of this frenetic activity, the Exhibition had to open without all the buildings being finished; even the monument to Columbus at the bottom of the Rambla, the work of Cayetano Buigas, was presented with the scaffolding still in place.[19]

However, the main objectives had been achieved: four hundred thousand foreign visitors passed through the Exhibition, twenty-five countries had been represented and twelve thousand stands had taken part.

Furthermore, the city had been appreciably enhanced, though perhaps not as much as it might have been. Some institutional buildings had been improved, such as the City Hall, by the hand of Domènech i Montaner. The Rambla de Catalunya came into existence when the Riera d'en Malla watercourse was covered over; Plaça de Catalunya was remodelled after the suppression of the Estació de Martorell station; Passeig de Sant Joan was extended upwards. The port front – Passeig de Colom – was extended to Montjuïc and work started on Paral·lel, after the demolition of the Muralla del Mar in 1881. Improvement work was carried out to city approach roads and the Gran Via was extended westwards.

But above all, the first concerted efforts were made to improve urban furniture. Public space was seen not just as a representative space, but also as a place that should be functional and comfortable. Lampposts, kiosks

[18] The original idea was to build a tower that was 208 metres high, designed by Pere Falqués, the creator of the benches and lampposts in Passeig de Gràcia. It was to be erected at the junction of Passeig de Sant Joan and Gran Via and financed by two Eixample landowners.

[19] According to journalists of the times, what with the confusion at all the unfinished work and the anxiety to be ready at all costs, Barcelona was like a city of "lunatics".

4.15
The university building beside Ciutat Vella, designed by Elia Rogent.

and advertising elements were designed, like in capital cities.[20] The most important streets in the centre, such as Ferran, Jaume I, Passeig de Gràcia and Carme, were paved with a wooden walkway, like floorboards, to facilitate pedestrian access. The gas lighting was improved, and electrical lighting was introduced in the street and in some private establishments. Property owners also received assistance for repair work to façades, for which municipal permission was granted free of charge. The renewal of the sewerage network is absent from this list of operations, and must be considered an outstanding issue.

The city had, however, finally recovered the Citadel and ousted the military use that continued to represent a constraint until just a few months before the Exhibition, an event that provided the city with urban services and development work that would otherwise have taken much longer.

A year previously, no-one could have imagined that a display of this kind was possible.[21] Barcelona had proved to itself and to others that it was the leading European city that the emerging classes so desired. But it had also shown that these concentrated, intense boosts were useful for the development of the city; we will see how it went on to repeat the process.

---

[20] It is interesting here to highlight, for their subsequent importance, some of Gaudí's ideas when he presented his project for the lampposts in the port in 1878, specifying that "the public thoroughfares (...) are places for meetings and transactions, for strolling and for leisure", and must therefore be "perfectly embellished (and) truly monumental". See C. Martinell: *Gaudí*. Barcelona, 1967.

[21] It is unquestionable that the temporary concentration of efforts contributed to the deficit at the close of the operation. The City Council indisputably made a larger contribution to the Exhibition than to three contemporary exhibitions that had enjoyed greater institutional backing.

16
he Jocs Florals literary
mpetition in the Fine Arts
lace, one of the Exhibition's
stive events.

IV.3 The search for a "Catalan national architecture"

The architects who had worked on the Great Exhibition formed part of the trend that favoured a "national architecture" and were very keen to break with the academic eclecticism that had prevailed throughout the 19th century.

Architecture, like the other arts, was fired with general enthusiasm at the changes in Catalan society, in this case expressed by the recovery of images from the past, from the Arabic or oriental world, and Gothic and popular architecture, which, together with the new construction techniques, were to give an image of modernity and cosmopolitan society that the new industrialised Catalonia desired.

This nationalist current was championed in the early 19th century by the writings of Bonaventura ARIBA, particularly in "La Patria". From his position of exile in Madrid, ARIBA clearly subscribed to the Romantic trends that had arrived somewhat tardily in Catalonia. In the 1850s, the *Jocks floral*, a literary competition, provided a thriving means of instating Catalan as the new language of a refined culture. In architecture, this movement burgeoned in the latter part of the century in the form of new commissions for buildings by the nascent industrial bourgeoisie and unique opportunities such as the 1888 Exhibition.

However, in architecture this was a slow process that involved several generations in the definition of a "national architecture", though the cultural and ideological discussion of this "identity" was to gradually turn from Romanticism to Modernisme, Noucentisme, functionalism, and so forth.

Thanks to the open-mindedness of Elias Rogent, the experience of the Exhibition had paved the way for new trends and a whole series of young architects. The frenetic working process produced major achievements despite the pressure of the deadlines affecting all the buildings.

The use of materials and techniques characteristic of the country was manifested empirically: exposed brickwork emerged as a noble material in such noteworthy buildings as Vilaseca's triumphal arch and the Hotel Internacional, regarded as an element retrieved from Catalan tradition with its roots firmly in Arabic and Mudejar architecture.

Elias Rogent was a key figure of the time and can be classified as the foremost Catalan architect to pursue the Romantic style.[22] In 1875 he was named first director of Barcelona's new School of Architecture and was highly influential in changing the classical teaching of the old Llotja art school. One of his finest buildings, the university, in the Gran Via near the old town, is a excellent neo-classical exercise in which he researched the composition and details of Romanesque architecture, so important to the definition of Catalan identity.

Other Romantic architects of the period were Joan Martorell, with his major religious complex dedicated to Saint Francis de Sales, near Passeig de Sant Joan, with its clear neo-Gothic style, and Augusto Font, who designed the main façade of Barcelona's cathedral in the same style.

Particular mention should be made of Domènech Estapà, who opted for greater monumentalism and designed important buildings at this time, such as the Model prison, the law courts and the Hospital Clínic. It is important to stress the novelty of these commissions, as large urban facilities were to be the dominant theme in the capital city's programme of innovation around the turn of the century.

IV.4 Modernisme as an innovative trend

The explosion of Modernisme was a phenomenon with a specific Catalan component that combined this search for "identity" with the urban processes that were emerging so strongly in the city of Barcelona.[23]

In his study of the long gestation period of modern architecture in our city, David Mackay defines the term Modernisme[24] as "the phase, within the overall modern movement, that combined an eclectic relation of historical references with the introduction of modern materials, which brought to decoration and even to construction the undulating lines taken from the original source of nature. It was much more than a local variant of Art Nouveau,

[22] See Pere Hereu: *Vers una arquitectura nacional.* UPC, Barcelona, 1989.

[23] For a general approach to the subject, see: Oriol Bohigas: *Reseña y catálogo de la arquitectura modernista.* Ed. Lumen, Barcelona, 1983; Oriol Bohigas and Leopoldo Pomés: *L'arquitectura modernista.* Ed Lumen, Barcelona, 1968. Also Alexandre Cirici Pellicer: *El arte modernista catalán.* Aymà, Barcelona, 1955.

[24] See David Mackay's summary in his book *L'arquitectura moderna a Barcelona (1854-1939).* Edicions 62, Barcelona, 1989.

17
he so-called street block,
"apple", of discord in
sseig de Gràcia. Different
odernista architects accepted
e general discipline of the
xample, producing strong
listic contrasts.

because it came to be identified as a style with the overall movement of affirmation, as opposed to Spanishness, of the national character of Catalonia and its cultural independence, more in harmony with other European trends".[25]

At the same time, the importance of Modernisme was vital to the modern centre of Barcelona, as it gave a unique shape to whole complexes of buildings within the Eixample network, producing an excellent symbiosis with Cerdà's project. This situation reached a paradigm in the street block formed by Passeig de Gràcia and Aragó, popularly known as the *manzana de la discordia*, in which three buildings were built side by side by the three most emblematic figures of Modernisme: Amatller house, by Puig i Cadafalch, completed in 1900, Lleó Morera house by Domènech i Montaner (1905) and Batlló house by Gaudí (1907), which clearly express different trends both in stylistic terms and with regard to sectors of the bourgeoisie who backed the movement.

Another feature worth highlighting in this Eixample-Modernisme symbiosis is the great proliferation of corner houses in this period. While development led to a continual subdivision of the land in the side façades of the block, the corner tended to provide the showcase for a building that was adorned and magnified by Modernisme, and this was often the house that bore the name of the owner.[26]

At the same time, Modernisme is in fact a label that was applied after the fact, and includes architects and artists of at least three generations who subscribed to sometimes conflicting political schools of thought, despite existing in the same environment.

Ignasi de Solà-Morales[27] distinguished two clearly differentiated trends among the architects of Modernisme. One was a form of architecture in line with the cultural project of the forward-thinking bourgeoisie of late 19th-

[25] In the Europe of the last decades of the 19th century, the battle of styles, "the use and abuse of history", as Nietzsche wrote, led to the burgeoning of a new trend called, alternately, Jugendstil, Modernisme, Art nouveau, Liberty, which accepted the currents of the Arts and Crafts movement championed by William Morris, sought the integration of the various design disciplines and exploration of the capacities of new technologies, etc. It was, in short, an anti-academicist, anti-historicist trend. Fundamental figures in these movements in Europe were Victor Horta and Henri Van de Velde in Brussels, Hector Guimard in Paris, Charles Rennie Mackintosh in Glasgow and Josef M. Olrich in Vienna, alongside whom a large Catalan contingent made its own specific contributions.

[26] In 1990, the exhibition "The Golden Square, the Centre of Modernista Barcelona" (Ed. OCSA. Caixa Catalunya. Barcelona, 1990) highlighted the inroads made by Modernisme in the centre of the Eixample.

[27] See Ignasi de Solà-Morales: "Arquitectura modernista", *Homage to Barcelona*. Barcelona, 1987.

century Catalonia, sharing similar positions to those found in large European cities such as Brussels and Paris. It was an experimental architecture that positively encouraged the intervention in the work of other disciplines and trades influenced by the same dynamic. It represented the search for an "overall design" that highlighted both constructional and decorative values, promoting individuality as a form of creative work.

The key figure in this trend was Lluís Domènech i Montaner, other outstanding figures being Josep Vilaseca, Pere Falquès, Josep Puig i Cadafalch, Salvador Valeri and Jeroni Granell, among others.

This was accompanied by an ideologically different trend: architecture that aligned itself with the ecclesiastic reaction that resisted the innovation being introducing into society, customs and culture by modernity. This current met at the Cercle de Sant Lluc, which catalysed artists with deep-seated Catholic convictions inspired by the figure of the religious writer Torras y Bages. The architecture sought its models in clerical references, and technological innovations, though used, tended to be discreetly masked.

The paradigmatic figure of this current was Antoni Gaudí, who became a referent for the city of Barcelona. Other high-profile figures were followers of his, such as Francesc Berenguer, Josep Maria Jujol, Joan Rubió and Cesar Martinell.

The enormous urban repercussions of this time brought to the fore three emblematic figures whose works were showcased in Passeig de Gràcia, as explained above.

Lluís Domènech i Montaner was one of the leading architects in the 1888 Exhibition thanks to his designs for the Café-Restaurant, still visible on the corner of the Parc de la Ciutadella, and the Hotel Internacional,[28] described above.

He had previously designed the Montaner i Simón publishing house in Carrer Aragó, an interesting industrial building at the very heart of the city that alternated brick walls with openings that combine the Romanesque order with a light metal structure.[29]

In his buildings, Domènech expressed the belief that Modernisme should find its opening in structural, logical clarity, which led him to be considered the most rationalist of his peer group. His firm commitment to Catalan identity led him to write the article "A la recerca d'una arquitectura nacional" [In search of a national architecture], which became a landmark publication in this field. He also wrote a *Historia general del Arte*. His involvement in nationalist politics took him to parliament in Madrid and other posts of responsibility.

---

[28] See Lluís Domènech and Lourdes Figueres: *Lluís Domènech i Montaner i el director d'orquestra*. Fundació La Caixa, Barcelona, 1989.
[29] This interesting building, constructed in 1880, was recently restored by Lluís Domènech and Roser Amadó and converted into the Fundació Tàpies, a vital point of reference in the field of painting in Europe.

4.b The Palau de la Música, designed by Domènech i Muntaner.

8
ew of the concert hall.

19, 4.20
oor plan and view of the
iginal building from the
orner entrance.

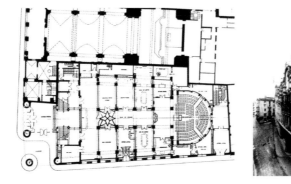

21, 4.22
he extension opens up to Via
aietana.

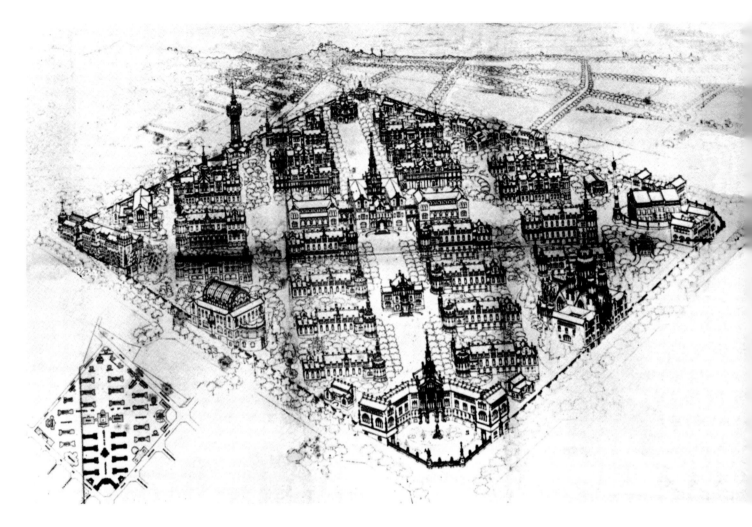

His most spectacular buildings are still the Palau de la Música, completed in 1908, and the Hospital de Sant Pau, begun in 1902 and finished in 1910. The Palau is an emblematic building thanks to its brilliant integration of music and architecture expressed in the continuity between the stage and the hall. The decoration incorporates both Catalan references – the bust of Anselm Clavé, founder of popular choral societies – and European music, with the Valkyries and a bust of Beethoven. It thereby synthesised the contrast that typified Modernisme, combining a taste for the local with a desire to be cosmopolitan and international. Its urban position within the fabric of Ciutat Vella gave the building added significance. How to situate an innovative building in a consolidated fabric? The doorway on the corner can still be seen as a bold and emblematic solution.[30]

The Hospital de Sant Pau, conversely, is a great public building that goes beyond the facile monumentality of the times: on the outer edge of the Eixample, occupying four street blocks, the complex is laid out with an east-

4.23
Hospital de Sant Pau, designe
by Domènech i Montaner.

---

[30] Since 1990, Oscar Tusquets has been in charge of renovating and modernising the existing building and extending it towards Via Laietana.

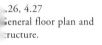

4.24, 4.25
The Güell crypt, designed by Gaudí in Santa Coloma de Cervelló. Exterior reception area and detail of the static study of the temple using the polyfunicular method.

4.26, 4.27
General floor plan and structure.

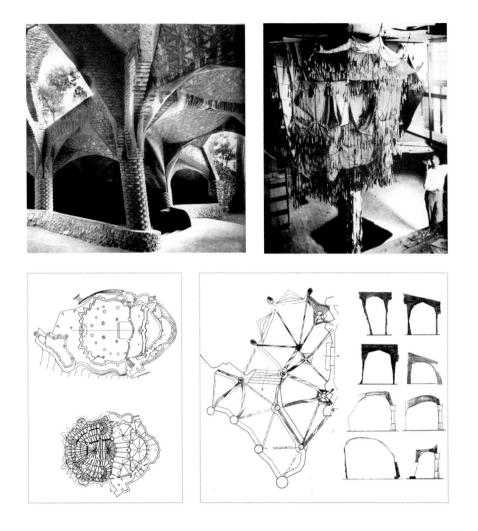

west system of pavilions laid out around a north-south diagonal axis. The individual buildings were complemented by a system of basement connections to ensure efficient organisation. Domènech thereby ensured that the hypotheses of ventilation, hygiene and comfort of pavilion architecture did not compromise its functionality. This intervention, then, formed part of the hospital reform under way in Europe at the turn of the century and which took place here in the form of exquisite building work.

The second figure was Antoni Gaudí i Cornet, who, as the internationally best known Catalan architect, requires little introduction.[31] He represented the most baroque stance of Modernisme and had initially been involved in the Exhibition, designing the park's central fountain.

[31] A very extensive bibliography about Gaudí includes J. E. Ràfols: *Antonio Gaudí*. Editorial Canosa, Barcelona, 1929; George Collins: *Antonio Gaudí*. Editorial Bruguera, Barcelona, 1961; Cesar Martinell: *Gaudí: su vida, su teoría, su obra*. Barcelona, 1967; Ignasi de Solà-Morales: *Gaudí*. Ediciones Polígrafa, Barcelona, 1983.

His body of work is often seen as the fruit of an overflowing imagination and his genius is explained as something out of the ordinary. Gaudí was inevitably a case apart for his individual creative force, but the personality cannot be separated from the Modernist movement – not a style or school – within which he worked, nor should we underestimate the active participation of his followers, Berenguer and Jujol, among others.

Most of Gaudí's work was carried out alongside the works of other Modernist figures according to the ideological guidelines explained above.[32] Only in the latter period of his life, in the 1920s, did he voluntarily take refuge in his final work, the Sagrada Família, giving rise to the mystical image often conjured up by his name. Nonetheless, his architectural activity was truly intense, and his commitment to the use of new Catalan construction materials and techniques exemplary. Gaudí was familiar with the masterfully employed masonry arches and domes of Roman tradition, and he generalised the technique of *trencadís*, using fragments of ceramic tiles, used to produce excellent claddings such as the memorable bench in Park Güell.

The name of Eusebio Güell was very much linked to Gaudí's architectural production, as he was the architect's great sponsor. After Vicens house, completed in 1885, Gaudí designed the stables at Pedralbes and Güell Palace, completed in 1889, two works from the architect's mature period which highlighted his ability to integrate decoration and construction system, and in which he illustrated his aspiration to produce an overall design.

He later designed the School of Saint Teresa and Bellesguard Tower, for which he recomposed the ruins of an old castle. The school was constructed with limited means and can still be seen as an example of the constructional rationality that formed the basic pattern for modern architecture in the following century.

At the turn of the century, he began work on the church of the Güell Colony at Santa Coloma, as part of the Alsina-Güell industrial complex, whose architecture and urban organisation made it the most spectacular of the colonies that decentralised industrial production in search of more accessible energy and cheap labour. Berenguer and Rubió were involved in this project, designing the remainder of the complex. It is probably Gaudí's most spectacular building with its superb spatial integration of functions inside and outside the church. The building was never completed, and the bareness of some of its structural elements give it the intriguing beauty of an unpolished diamond.

To return to his urban buildings, he was responsible for designing two of the best-known buildings in Passeig de Gràcia after 1905: Batlló house and Milà house or La Pedrera, the quarry. Work on Batlló house consisted in the rehabilitation of an existing building that Gaudí transformed completely, giving the façade a new overall

[32] Gaudí's pro-Catalan feeling was undeniable, but in professional terms he was very different to the other great figures of architectural Modernisme who were also actively involved in the world of politics.

4.c Milà House by Antoni Gaudí.

28, 4.29
he main stairway and the
ofs today.

.30, 4.31
levation, section and floor
lan.

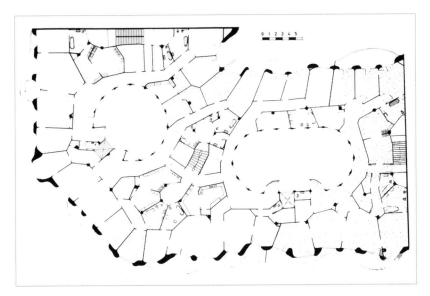

composition and reconfiguring the building's inner patios that change in section and colour as they ascend; the stairs and lifts were elements to unify the building, shunning the idea that an apartment building was the simple addition of superposed floors. The flat façade was completed by the theme of Saint George and the dragon,[33] the quintessential symbol of Catalonia, the final touch to this great work.

Milà house, four street blocks further up, on the other side of the avenue, was the largest residential building to be built by Gaudí. It was designed for the prominent corner site, with an internal metal structure that left the façade free to be addressed by an undulating system of solid surfaces and ironwork balconies. Access to the car park situated in the basement was via a great ramp starting at the main entrance. The building was completed in 1911, not without financial difficulties on the part of the owner, and it was only the unconditional support of Mrs Milà that made this great monument viable.

Milà house, like other of Gaudí's urban buildings, stands out for the way in which the roof is finished, in the case of La Pedrera reaching a paradigmatic situation.[34] The walls of the roof terraces were designed with well positioned openings that point out the buildings' mutual relation and with regard to the Sagrada Família. This visual relation between his buildings is proof both of the importance of this work to Gaudí and the possibility of tabling an intense urban discourse on the basis of just a few pieces of architecture. After the death of his sponsor, Güell, and Berenguer, his close collaborator, Gaudí retired from work on the Sagrada Família, designing the north façade on the same site where he had built the neo-Gothic crypt. In 1926 Gaudí died tragically at the age of 74 when he was run over by a tram. Barely a quarter of the Sagrada Família had been built. If we bear in mind that Gaudí's approach to his work involved personal, on-site control, his individual force could not be passed on in the form of architecture plans alone, because the overall design benefited a great deal from the construction process: work on the Sagrada Família continued at varying paces and the difficulties that this "Gaudí-style" construction caused for the master's original work soon became apparent.

The third character in this history is Josep Puig i Cadafalch,[35] the youngest of the three; his influence was to continue into well into the 20th century. Puig was clearly committed to nationalist political action, leading some historians to place his political career above his architectural work. However, Puig i Cadafalch took his search for the identity of Catalan architecture to its ultimate consequences.

---

[33] According to popular tradition, the dragon is the enemy of gods and men and is fought by Saint George the hero. This was a central motif in Gothic sculpture.

[34] There is a great deal of literature about this exceptional roof; see Manel Armengol *et al.*: *El jardí dels guerrers*. Barcelona, 1987.

[35] Judith Rohner + Ignasi de Solà-Morales: *Josep Puig i Cadafalch: La arquitectura entre la casa i la ciutat*. Barcelona, 1989.

32
ouse of Spires by Puig i
adafalch.

He sought the bases of this identity in Roman and Romanesque architecture.[36] The styles he applied in his buildings were perhaps more literal, hence their frequent medieval flavour. At the same time, his concern with institutionalising modern Catalonia was an underlying concern in both his architecture and in the political arena.

Puig i Cadafalch was a very influential politician in the conservative nationalist party and a councillor on the new City Council of 1901, occupying the portfolio of Public Works. From this post he made important contributions to both the Interconnection Plan Competition and the improvement of city infrastructures. Between 1917 and 1924 he was President of the Mancomunitat de Catalunya, following the death of Prat de la Riba.

This brilliant political profile found its urban planning expression in the development of the 1929 Exhibition, as we will go on to see, and in the drafting of the Jaussely Plan which, in Puig's opinion, was to redress the imbalances created by Cerdà's Plan.[37]

Alongside his political career, Puig i Cadafalch produced a fine body of architectural work which left a strong imprint on the Eixample. The Casa de les Punxes in the Diagonal is still an excellent example, combining the large scale of the intervention with a profusion of refined medieval detail. The constructional rationality applied to Can Casarramona in Montjuïc rivalled that of Domènech himself. Palau Macaya, built at the turn of the century, embodies the sobriety of proportion of the large Renaissance *palaus* and the detail that characterised Modernisme.

---

[36] Josep Puig i Cadafalch: *L'arquitectura romànica a Catalunya 1908-18*, 3 volumes written in collaboration with Josep Goday.
[37] Puig i Cadafalch's persecution of Cerdà's project was well known, partly because it had been approved first in Madrid and then in Barcelona, and also due to the transgressions that the Plan had suffered at the hands of speculators, which were quite beyond Cerdà's control.

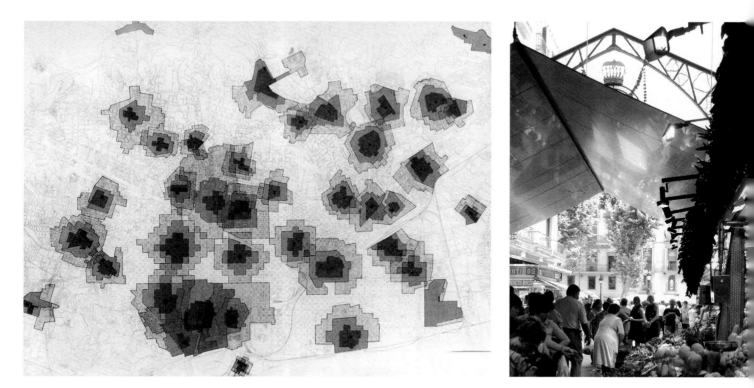

In this torrent of spectacular works produced by the three leading figures, it is important not to overlook the contribution of many other architects who were involved in the movement, which the space available here does not allow us to cover.

Worthy of special mention are the new marketplaces that were built during the last three decades of the 19th century in different sectors of the city in response to a desire to rationalise the distribution of goods and increase hygiene standards[38] combined with the fact that the new buildings represented emblematic constructions of iron architecture with a spatial conception based on modernist principles. These were the markets of Sant Antoni in the Eixample, by Antoni Rovira i Trias; La Llibertat in Gràcia, by Francesc Berenguer, and El Born which, as explained earlier, was Barcelona's central market until the 1960s. This brilliant policy of distribution and the skill of the projects combined with their critical positions in relation to the different urban sectors. The traditional market place stood at the centre of each district, and this is where the buildings had to be sited: as a result, squares were occupied, but used only temporarily, by large-scale avant-garde architectures of wrought iron. Famous markets such as the Boquería in Plaça de Sant Josep, Sant Andreu, La Llibertat and many more occupied squares with mass-use public buildings. However, the stark contrast of their brand-new architecture does not cease to

4.33
Diagram showing the location of the municipal markets.

4.34
La Boquería market in the Rambla.

[38] The rationalisation of the market system and the distribution of foodstuffs had a long tradition going back to the *Consell de Cent* city authority and leading to a present-day situation in which the city has fifty or so markets with a total of over 13,000 stalls. This ensures an evenly distributed and highly competitive supply. The late 18th century saw the introduction of stable markets in the Pla de la Boquería and the Born to eradicate hawking.

amaze us today and calls for conscientious thought about the great capacity for urban innovation that our city has continually exercised in the course of its history.

Modernisme was also followed by many other artists and graphic and furniture designers. It partook of the principles promoted by the English Arts and Crafts movement, mobilising artists and artisans to collaborate in architecture; major developments in wrought iron, stained glass with its leads and tile design, among others, gave richness to building detail, but also to the design of interiors, furniture and household implements. Altogether, it gave way to an overall expression of the Modernista world.

In the field of writing, special mention should be made of Joan Maragall, a staunch champion of the Romantic trend who, in his *Oda Nova a Barcelona*, impresses upon us the Modernista sensibility of end-of-the-century Barcelona.[39]

Another field in which Modernisme manifested itself was painting, one of the most developed branches of the arts. Santiago Rusiñol – painter and man of literature – and Ramón Casas – portraitist of bourgeois society and the foremost social events– were its leading exponents.

As of 1892, Sitges, a coastal town near Barcelona, was the scene of a series of meetings that consolidated Barcelona's Modernista painting movement. After the inaugural "Festa modernista" celebration, it was the headquarters of leading figures from the various schools: Olot, represented by Joaquím Vayreda, the Luministes of Sitges and the painters from the capital. After this meeting, Rusiñol undertook the rehabilitation of an old

---

[39] I strongly recommend a reading of this "Ode" to Barcelona. Joan Maragall, *Poesies*. Barcelona, 1947, pp. 276-80.

house by the port which, with the name of Cau Ferrat, became a symbol of Modernista painting. This major artistic trend underwent an appreciable evolution at the turn of the century, as we will see later.

IV.5 The consolidation of the Eixample

While the development of the Eixample had begun with the Development Societies in which the private sector was the main mover, its consolidation as a specific sector of the city took place with the appearance of the Special New Town Commissions, the result of the New Towns Act of 1892.

This purpose of this act was to reinforce new forms of urban development management not regulated by the earlier acts of 1864 and 1876, and use the bases already established by the Expropriation Act of 1879.

The greatest advance represented by the 1892 act, which remained in force until 1956, was the establishing of joint management in new town developments, involving the municipality and the landowners. This saw the re-emergence of some of the proposals contained in Cerdà's "economic thought" which had never been approved.

The unification of the municipalities in the Plain paved the way for the introduction of increased rationality in the management of the Eixample, and the New Town Commission was its most powerful instrument.[40]

The Commission comprised five city councillors and five landowners in the area, and its main task was to carry out urban development work. For this purpose it had two main sources of income: first, the increase of the Urban Territorial Tax (UTT) for 30 years, and second, a specific tax on the Eixample of 4% of the UTT for 25 years.

This led to the introduction of a specific taxation scheme, but one that required the application of these taxes to the urban development of the Eixample.

The Eixample therefore enjoyed a favourable position in comparison to other areas of the city without a special status and, in turn, the pace of urbanisation was set by that of the construction of houses that basically generated major increases in the UTT.

A powerful management mechanism had been designed, into which specific municipal subsidies could be incorporated, though they did not form part of most of the annual payments.[41]

[40] See the doctoral thesis of Jaume Llobet: *Urbanització i planejament urbanístic a Barcelona 1917-36*. ETSAB, UPC, Barcelona, 1984 (unpublished) and the article by the same author: "Urbanització i finançament públic a l'Eixample (1897-1936)", *La Formació de l'Eixample de Barcelona*. Barcelona, 1990. Also, Ajuntament de Barcelona, *Anuario Estadístico de la Ciudad de Barcelona*. Department of Statistics (to 1916).

[41] Ajuntament de Barcelona: *Memoria de la Comisión Especial de Ensanche 1926*. Barcelona, 1926.

4.d The New Town Commissions and phase-by-phase urban development.

36
onstruction of a street in
e Eixample. The force of
banisation contrasted with
e city's rate of construction.
ne New Town Commission
as responsible for this process.

37
rbanisation work in the area
ound Passeig de Sant Joan.

.38
General plan of plot divisions
y Cerdà. Detail of the area
round Aragó and Pau Claris,
. 1865.

.39
The state of development of
he Eixample in around 1890.

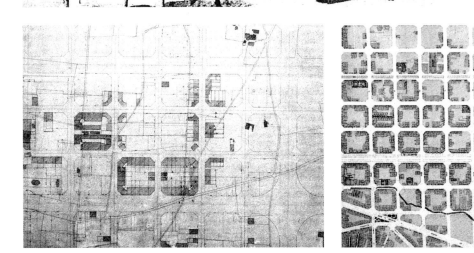

The urbanisation process took the form, first of all, of the construction of streets to provide access to the various plots that were gradually built. Landowners who ceded the land on which the street was built did not have to pay the "specific surcharge", which explains why street construction was not a problematic phase. However, the incorporation of the various services, sewers, mains water and then lighting took place in a step-by-step process.

It was, then, a slow and difficult procedure, that was possible thanks to the existence of unitary infrastructure projects, such as García Faria's, that allowed phase-by-phase development. Thanks also to the superposition of the private provision of services by sectors, such as drinking water, which in some sectors, between Passeig de Gràcia and Passeig de Sant Joan, was provided by a private company, the Sociedad de Aguas, whose water tower still stands in the courtyard of the street block formed by Llúria, Diputació, Bruc and Consell de Cent.

The coincidence with this long urbanisation process of the city's great urban planning event, the 1929 Exhibition, served to accelerate work, promoting the continuity of streets and the completion of some of the most representative axes.[42]

There was, then, a rather slow financing system that could be seen as a consequence of the real-estate economic system underpinned by the *casa de renta* or apartment house, a residential prototype in the Eixample. This required long-term investment to be able to recover the original capital and produce an income from the rents collected. In many cases, the owner and his family occupied the main floor – like the *piano nobile* of the big town houses – with a warehouse and business on the ground floor. The upper floors were occupied by different social classes: office workers, functionaries, employees, etc.; the higher the apartment, the lower the rent.

The capitalisation of that investment came around slowly and as a result there was little reinvestment in the Eixample. Urbanisation took place as the proportional part of the UTT gradually accumulated. Both cycles were slow ones and improvements in the streets and the prime properties came about with the use and running of the house and its apartments. In this situation, the relation between the urban agents was complex and lasting, and the New Town Commission, with its mixed public-private profile and its capacity to maintain a strategy and priorities over a long period of time, contributed to its smooth functioning.

Nonetheless, this process changed radically when the production of houses turned towards sale and the profit returns cycle accelerated as clients sought to capture their capital gains before the product was sold. From this moment

---

[42] See by way of example: *Estudio de orientaciones para el plan de obras que convendría realizar en el ensanche con motivo de la Exposición de Industrias Eléctricas.* Ajuntament de Barcelona, 1914.

4e. The consolidation of the Eixample.

40
e area around the
niversity with Balmes, in the
oreground, and Gran Via.

41
aça de Letamendi under
onstruction, 1880.

42
ot division of the central
ector of the Eixample.

43
otel Ritz in Gran Via.

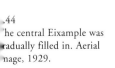

44
he central Eixample was
radually filled in. Aerial
mage, 1929.

on, the various phases of urban construction, land division, urbanisation, the construction and management of houses became quite separate and relations were guided by the well-defined patterns of each submarket.

In any case, the *casa de renta* maintained a degree of protagonism until well into the 20th century, alongside other forms of housing development for sale, first in Barcelona's suburban space, with the division of plots of land in Horta and Sant Andreu for the construction of single-family houses. Later on, "horizontal property" led to the partial sale of houses by apartment and came into full effect in the Eixample when, in 1920, a first rent freeze took place.

The development of the New Town Commission included an interesting discussion in 1917 with the passing of a national decree regulating the imposition of improvement by municipal works, involving a substantial change in the principles of urban planning management: it established that 90% of any municipal investment in urban development work would be paid by the owners of the land or buildings that benefited from its completion. The concept was radically different to what had gone before as it allowed urban development schemes independently of the rate of house construction; it also granted the Council the initiative in projects.

In Barcelona, the Land Registry fought hard against this decree and, after a long dispute, managed to see the new towns removed from this legislation in order to continue with the stipulations of the 1892 Act. As a result, further new towns flourished in 1920, such as Les Corts, Sant Martí, Sant Andreu and Sants. This slowing down of a more modern form of urban planning management represented a major hold-up to the rate of city development envisaged by the Interconnections Plan, a large-scale urban planning project that had been in the pipeline since 1905.

IV.6 Urban utility infrastructures

A new form of investment in infrastructure emerged, centring on urban utilities.

Once the territory was interrelated by the railways and roads, a market for industrial products and raw materials was created, and mobility and competition of production factors, particularly labour and land, were possible, the construction and implementation of urban utilities came into their own.

The moment had come to respond to the latent demand for improved urban quality that hygiene conditions, specifically the drainage network, and transport called for in a growing city.

a) City gas and public street lighting. Gas produced using coal was brought into the city in the form of lighting for the Exchange in 1826. In 1840, Barcelona Council called for the formulation of a street-lighting project for the city. It was awarded to the Sociedad Catalana para el Alumbrado de Gas, headed by Charles Lebon, who for a long time gave gas in Barcelona its everyday name (Lebon gas). In November 1842, the Rambla was lit using gas lamps, which was an irrevocable step towards improving the urban quality of the city streets.

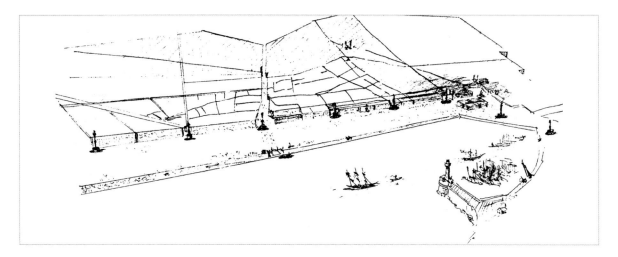

The first gas factory was built in the Barceloneta and was followed by others in Gràcia, Sant Andreu, Bogatell and Sant Martí. At the end of the century, the various factories were grouped at "La Catalana" (Barceloneta and Sant Andreu) and "Eugenio Lebon y Cía" (the remaining three).

Gas factories caught on easily in the most dynamic Catalan towns in industrial terms.

b) Sewers and drainage. The development of the Eixample suffered from a lack of appropriate financial instruments to ensure effective urbanisation, which in turn required technical projects to guarantee their execution. The networks of urban services signified a crucial commitment, especially in view of the hoped-for new city image which was expected to function on modern lines.

The most important of the networks were those for drinking water, drainage and sewerage. The traditional house had its well for drinking water and a cesspool for sewerage; the basic innovation lay in the fact that both services began to function by means of underground networks.

The theme of hygiene in large cities was marked by an underlying social and political dimension in England and France due to the dreadful living conditions of the working class; the statistical reports of Chadwick in 1832 and Villermé in 1840 produced binding legislative proposals that imposed sanitary conditions in new constructions.

The hygienist discussion had played an important role in Barcelona in relation to the demolition of the town walls and the particular attention accorded to this issue by the Cerdà project. For the development of the Eixample, García Faria's Sewerage Network Project was not just an important instrument – it embodied the rationalisation of the logic introduced by Cerdà.[43]

The engineer García Faria had intervened in the "Preliminary report issued by the Western Sub-Commission with a view to proposing a Sewerage Project for Barcelona in accordance with the requirements of Hygiene" and drafted the definitive project in 1891, an overall project proposing a sewerage system that responded to the general needs of the city of Barcelona.

[83] José Luis Gómez Ordóñez: "El Proyecto de los Servicios Urbanos: el de García Faria para Barcelona", Laboratorio de Urbanismo: *Trabajos sobre Cerdà y Barcelona*. Barcelona, 1992, *op. cit.*

The project was drafted on a scale of 1:5000 with great care and precision, employing 29 types of drains ranging from the ovoid, measuring 1.60 x 90 +metres, to the 5 x 3.20 metre model. It was, then, a project that thoroughly addressed the issue of the draining of the Plain. The Plans were accompanied by a Report and the Economic Studies and Building Regulations required for their physical construction. The population studies were based on the 1887 census and the mortality rate by streets for the 1880-1888 period was analysed. This document was also a true representation of the situation of building in the Eixample. The Report comprehensively expounded the situation in over twenty European cities, providing a very necessary point of reference for an operation of this scope.

It was, then, a fundamental project for the city, and despite its fragmentary and drawn-out deployment, it laid the bases for the present-day functioning of the city's sewers. García Faria made a detailed presentation of how the architecture and urban utilities should be approached as a whole, and his section drawings, according equal importance to the drawing of the houses and the services, are still exemplary today.

The most important advance it represented was acceptance of the idea that sewerage should be conducted in underground conduits. This innovation had been introduced in some cities in the mid-19th century and required a plentiful water supply to dilute the sewerage and ensuring that the sewers functioned. Although this called for larger flows of water,[44] it finally assured the integrated functioning of urban utilities. According to Gómez Ordóñez,

---

[44] Regarding this subject, in 1868 the Compañía de Aguas de Barcelona, set up with Belgian capital, was authorised to canalise water from Dos Rius. In 1882, this company became the Sociedad General de Aguas, with the following services: the supply of drinking water; the treatment of wastewater and its use for irrigation, and draining operations. See P. Voltes Bou: *Historia del Abastecimiento de aguas de Barcelona*. Barcelona.

4.f Garcia i Faria's drainage project.

47

García i Faria's project for a sewerage and infrastructure system in Barcelona. It also explains the development of the Eixample in the late 19th century.

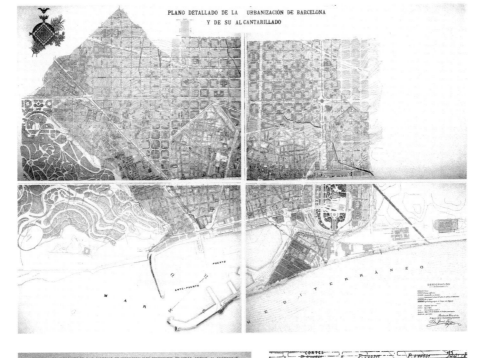

48

Example of new sewerage engineering.

49

Fragment of the project adjacent to Ciutat Vella.

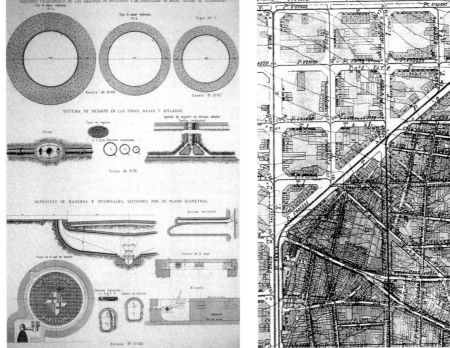

4.50
Integration of urban utilities
the Eixample house.

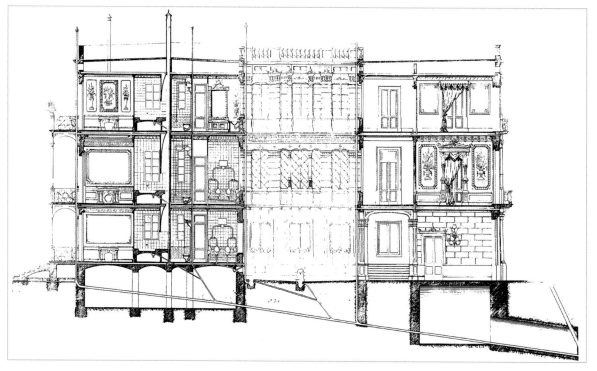

"it is necessary to connect the idea of evacuating waste and rain waters from the city with that of water supply. These are two services which, though differing in form of management, being, respectively, public and private, as in the former the functioning plays no part in its financing, whereas in the latter there is a "metre", a toll, which facilitates its concession, will be internally connected and, almost always, simultaneously managed".

A full understanding of the scope of García Faria's project calls for a comment on his proposals for the Llobregat delta and the drainage of Ciutat Vella.

It proposed that the urban waste from the sewers be recycled to fertilise farmland and laid out a meticulous proposal to provide incentives for the farming of the said delta. Other large European cities also sought to introduce this territorial approach to an integrated idea of recycling that is new to us today: very few managed to implant this system in the 19th century.

Meanwhile, the reform of the old town was still pending. In 1889 the City Council approved the Baixeras Plan, and García Faria incorporated the sewers into the layout proposed by the Reform Plan. In the project report, he wrote: "In Barcelona the question of the sewerage system is intimately related to that of internal reform. The network of existing drains is defective in the extreme, particularly in the oldest districts, with their narrow, winding streets, and it should disappear altogether and be brought into line with the ones that are to be built in accordance with the directions and levels of the streets in the new project. Cleaning is impossible in this narrow, winding streets, since in some there is not even room for the cart that collects the rubbish that is thrown into the public highway, (…) making them a permanent focus of corruption".[45]

[45] Pedro García Faria: *Proyecto de alcantarillado*. Barcelona, 1891. Chap. XVI, page 236.

4.g Urban transport. The tram.

51
he tram in Paral·lel, the focus
night life.

52
oexistence of the new electric
am and its horse-drawn
Ripert" counterpart that
ntinued until the first decade
f the 20th century.

.53
'he tram lines in 1904.

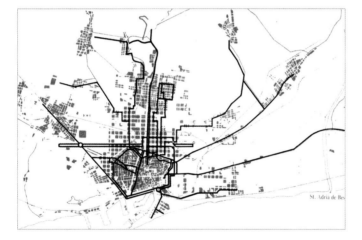

.54, 4.55
volution of means of public
ransport and change in the
ocation of its nerve centre:
rom Plaça de l'Àngel to Plaça
le Catalunya.

This was, then, a project that brought an ambitious response to the needs for extension and reform that Cerdà had tabled. Its practical implementation showed that it was capable of being developed by phases without disrupting the unitary nature of the hydraulic system.

c) Urban transport. Urban transport represented the initial interconnection of the three urban subsystems (Ciutat Vella, Eixample and the suburban annexes) that constituted the growing metropolis of the 19th century.

The implantation of the tram occurred in the final quarter of the century and represented the functional framework for the personal and working relations of the suburban nucleuses in the Plain, firstly with the old town, and then with the Eixample.

The trams, some running on steam and some by animal traction, were introduced between 1872 and 1884, covering with seven areas of operation between the residential annexes situated concentrically beyond the Eixample, in the Plain: two lines to Gràcia-Josepets and Plaça Rovira, another to Sants, one to Les Corts that divided in two to Sant Gervasi and Sarrià, another to Sant Andreu and Horta, one to Poblenou, taking the route to the cemetery and, finally, another to Badalona, testifying to relations with the county towns. Tramlines also ran around the Ronda axes of Ciutat Vella.

These infrastructures were developed by various private companies (Tranvías Barcelona and Compañía General, among other) that ran independent lines that were each concerned with their own profitability.

However, the high cost of tickets meant that for many years the tram in Barcelona was an exclusive means of transport for the upper classes, and only on Sundays and in the summer was it used by the working classes who took refuge in the higher reaches of the city to enjoy the more temperate climate and the leisure activities that were moved out of the centre.[46]

On the basis of this radial structure, the tram encouraged the development of summer residences for the well-to-do classes in the north and north-west sectors of the Plain (Sant Gervasi and Sarrià). Reinforced by the Sarrià train that had come into operation in 1863, these areas gradually became permanently settled.

This process was definitively consolidated by the progressive electrification of the tramlines and the diversification of their routes between 1898 and 1906. This transformation led to a drop in fares and, as a result, a degree of socialisation of the use of the tram. The volume of passengers rose from seven million in 1900 to

---

[46] See Francisco J. Monclús and José Luis Oyón: "Eixample i suburbanització. Trànsit tranviari i divisió social de l'espai urbà a Barcelona, 1883-1914", *La formació de l'Eixample de Barcelona*. Barcelona, 1990. Also: Alberto del Castillo and Manuel Tiu: *Historia del transporte colectivo en Barcelona (1872-1951)*. Seix y Barral, Barcelona, 1959; Joan Alemany and Jesús Mestre, *Els transports a l'Àrea de Barcelona*. Transports de Barcelona, Barcelona, 1986.

56
Example of one of the big
department stores that
benefited from access by
public transport to Plaça de
Catalunya.

thirteen million in 1910, and to seventeen million in 1914. However, it was still far from the mass means of public transport that it was to become in later decades.

In any case, this rationalisation of transport and the increase in the number of lines served to reinforce the Eixample, which became an "intermediate" space crossed by almost all the tram lines, making it the most accessible city sector. This was borne out by the increase in centrality of Plaça de Catalunya as a space of growing urban importance; in 1915, as many as 5,000 trams a day passed through the square,[47] making it the city's new functional centre. This centripetal force of the sector around Plaça de Catalunya was also seen in the location of the innovative department stores that broke with the traditional commercial structure to take up their position in this new centrality.[48]

[47] Fernando Reyes: "Proyecto de ferrocarril eléctrico subterráneo SO-NE y estación central de Barcelona", *Revista Tecnológica Industrial*, 1913.
[48] Sepu, El Aguila, Jorba and El Siglo all confirmed this centrality by setting up in innovative buildings where they offered the most attractive goods. Their shop windows and counters helped to promote not just new products but also new fashions and urban attitudes. A "pedagogical" value was attributed to this type of commercial amenity in the new urban culture of the time. See Mark Girouard: *Cities and People*. Hampshire, 1987.

V.

The turn of the century and Greater Barcelona

V.1 Annexation of the municipalities in the Plain

As well as taking place in the city itself, Barcelona's industrial and demographic growth spread to the various municipalities in the Plain: Sants, Gràcia, Sant Andreu del Palomar and Sant Martí de Provençals. Throughout the 19th century these centres accommodated a large number of industries and workers as housing was easier to find there. These settlements had been built according to the suburban patterns explained above.

The annexation process was a complex and difficult one. Cerdà was already acting as Government representative with a view to establishing dialogue with the municipalities with regard to the development of his project, though a successful outcome to negotiations was always in doubt.

Finally, all the municipalities in the Plain were annexed to Barcelona in 1897 except Horta, in 1904, and Sarrià, even later, in 1921.

In this way, the great extension project finally consolidated its natural space. Barcelona already had 383,908 inhabitants and thereby acquired almost half as many again, exactly 175,681. The surface of the municipality was quintupled, growing from 15.5 to 77.8 km².

V.2 "Gross-Barcelona" and the concept of capital city

The general crisis wrought in big Spanish cities and principally in Madrid by the loss of the colonies did not excite a nostalgic reaction of lamentation or feeling of loss in Barcelona; instead it acted as a salutary lesson that helped the city face up to a change that the Catalan industrial bourgeoisie had been anticipating for some time. It was necessary to modernise the structure of the Spanish State and the Catalan stance on the matter was that decisive action was called for.

Action took the form of radical changes on the Catalan political scene, with the consolidation of the Regionalist League and the republican parties as an alternative to the Catalan bourgeoisie, in the face of the tyrannical structure that had prevailed since the Restoration.

In 1901 the League won the municipal elections, producing, in the words of Vicens Vives, the "generation of 1901", that started at municipal level and went on to wield great influence all over Spain with its presence in Parliament in Madrid. Figures such as Francesc Cambó, Josep Prat de la Riba and the architect Josep Puig i Cadafalch, among others, were in the foreground of the local, provincial and state scene.

But above all, the change of strategy at municipal level was to have evident repercussions for the scale of the city's planning projects. This new "industrial party", as it was later to be called, required an ambitious, connective

5.01, 5.02
Views of central Barcelona,
in the mid-19th century and
today.

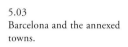

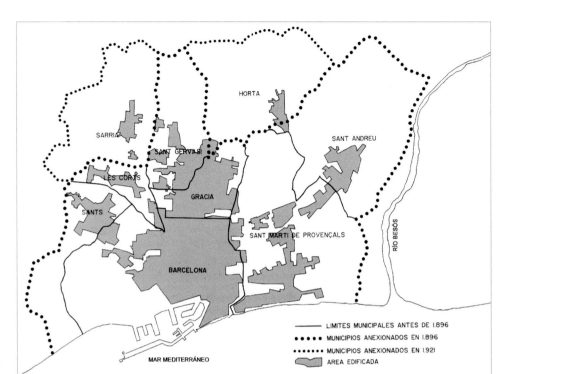

project for Barcelona that was capable of generating an idea of capital city like those achieved in the last three decades of the 19th century by cities such as Paris and New York, and especially Berlin and Vienna. According to Francesc Roca, "Gross-Barcelona", literally applying the Central European city model, had made its appearance in new politics. In his speeches, Prat de la Riba spoke of "Imperial Barcelona"; in the words of Puig i Cadafalch, Barcelona was to become "the new Paris of the South".[1]

The connective project took the concrete form of improving production infrastructures (the free port, railways, etc.) and ensuring basic urban conditions such as transport, facilities and accommodation for the residents and the immigrant population that was beginning to be numerous.

This was the beginning of a period in which the increase in urban population in Barcelona (it doubled in 30 years) was a definitive variable in understanding the present-day city. The arrival of half a million inhabitants in such a short period of time obviously created new urban needs, but it was also a condition of industrial development, which thereby found cheap labour and increased the potential market of consumers.

The city's dominant concern was the development of old projects that had never been implemented, such as opening up areas in the historic city and the introduction of new layouts such as the Plan for Interconnections with the newly annexed towns, but also the definition of ambitious ideas such as the Great Exhibition, which raised Barcelona to the level to which it aspired. It was a complex process, as we will go on to see.

---

[1] See Frances Roca: *Política económica i territori a Catalunya. 1091-1939*. Ketres, Barcelona, 1979. Also Eve Blau *et al.*, *L'idée de la grande ville*. Prestel, Munich, 2000.

In order to achieve these ends it was necessary to extend municipal competences to enable the Council to carry out such a vast programme.[2] It began to consider issues such as schools, parks and culture, which had either been left in the hands of the central government and therefore never reached basic levels of efficiency or remained in the sphere of private initiative. Major advances began to show, though in some fields the proposed aims and the capacity to put them into practice were highly disproportionate.

V.3 The Interconnections Plan

The incorporation of the municipalities in the Plain, whose growth responded to suburban formations and between which there was a great deal of open land, led to the need to study the interconnections between the various sectors in the new municipality.

To this end, in 1903 the new Barcelona Council announced an international competition for preliminary projects to connect Barcelona's Eixample and the annexed towns among themselves and to the rest of the municipal area of Sarrià and Horta (these two municipalities had not yet been annexed). Just five projects were submitted to the competition.

In May 1905 the Council ratified the jury's proposal to award first prize to the Preliminary project by Leon Jaussely, a French urban planner from Toulouse, presented with the heading "Romulus", as a fully-fledged body of urban development theory applied to Barcelona. It included the fundamental criteria of a desire to monumentalise the city and particular insistence on the introduction of green space, until then practically non-existent. Jaussely's Plan was viewed very favourably by a jury including Puig i Cadafalch and Francesc Cambó, which pronounced that the completion of the project would make Barcelona "the loveliest city in the Mediterranean".

The preliminary project presented comprised 29 maps and the proposal had been drafted on a scale of 1:10,000, specifying the zoning of activities (various residential areas, worker housing, industry, facilities, parks, etc.) and basic road layouts. The road system was organised around five radial axes and two ring roads. The project also systematised the rail layout by proposing the connection of the various routes and the undergrounding of inner-city lines.

[2] The experience of the large German municipalities under the influence of the philosophy of *Kathedersocialismus* (socialism from a position of power, also referred to as "municipal capitalism"), according to which the Council can do anything that is not expressly prohibited. With this attitude at the turn of the century, the large municipalities had acquired considerable areas of land in order to apply truly efficient social housing policies. One example was the scheme in Frankfurt under the Adickes Act, named after the Mayor, which in 1902 took the form of a large-scale land expropriation operation to reduce speculation induced by major growth.

Another major area addressed by the preliminary project was that of facilities arranged strategically around a series of focuses defined by the road system. These included the "grand Plaça de les Glories" where the new City Hall was to be situated, the Post Office building and a library. Public or communal buildings were also situated in other subcentres. In order to design a parks system, it compared the distribution of green space in Paris and London with a view to discussing the most appropriate model and standards for Barcelona. All in all, the preliminary project might be regarded as a turn-of-the-century Urban Planning Tract that Jaussely set out to apply to our city.

The preliminary design was redrafted by Jaussely himself with a local team of experts, and the production project was presented in 1907 at a spectacular public exhibition and approved at the end of the same year.[3]

The Jaussely project underwent a whole series of vicissitudes before the Romeu i Porcel Plan was passed in 1917 as a rather watered-down adaptation of its original ideas. A "Parks System" was also proposed, representing a step towards a system of open spaces in the city.

The Jaussely Plan was nonetheless the first to regulate the new administrative area in the first half of the century. Its proposals were adjusted and changed, but the general logic of the idea prevailed.

Jaussely based his proposals on three criteria: the zoning of activities, the systematisation of green spaces, and street and avenue design. These criteria were applied to a territory that had never been designed as a whole and therefore required the addition of further theory to make its urban continuity viable. It also signalled an explicit rejection of Cerdà's Plan and was strongly championed by Puig i Cadafalch himself. The new Plan addressed Cerdà's isotropic grid plan by introducing oblique or diagonal elements.

The same approach can be seen in almost all the cities based on a grid, principally in America: Burnham's ideas for Chicago and San Francisco are paradigm examples, recomposing the old continuous orthogonal layout on a larger scale based on an oblique arrangement, thereby highlighting certain nodes or focuses of generation of these radii.[4]

Jaussely's proposal aimed to combine two principles: to enhance Cerdà's well consolidated layout and table a new dialogue with the belt of suburban towns. To this end, it defined a series of principal and secondary centres from which axes (avenues and main streets) irradiated to connect existing nucleuses with the big new facilities that were so necessary in the modern city. The layout was designed in accordance with the topography reality of the

---

[3] See Manuel Torres et al.: *Inicis de la urbanística municipal de Barcelona*. Barcelona, 1985.
[4] A discussion of these principles in Europe can be found in Eugène Hénard: *La costruzione della Metropoli*. Padua, 1972. Hénard had worked since the late 19th century on the restructuring of the road system in Paris and had drawn up a series of conceptual outlines that were employed by Jaussely. In the American context, the figure of Daniel H. Burnham was key; see Thomas S. Hines: *Burnham of Chicago*. Oxford, 1974.

5.a The Jaussely Plan, connecting the old municipalities in the Plain.

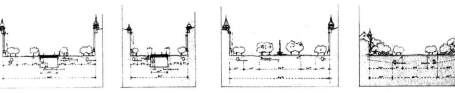

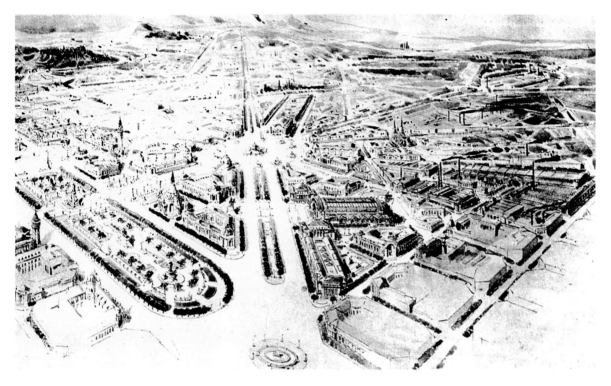

5.07
View of the new city centre
according to Jaussely.

Plain and the Plan was illustrated with a host of drawings and suggestions that, though imbued with the Beaux-Arts spirit of the time, offer the reader a very precise image of how "urban beauty" could be brought about.

Jaussely's project consolidated a new urban reality that differentiated the parts according to their assigned or zoned use or the nearest infrastructures. It also established an excellent system of green spaces that was later nuanced and developed by Forestier and Rubió i Tudurí.

In addition, it also consolidated a splendid catalogue of road and junction sections to ensure the viability of the hierarchical structure of spaces and streets proposed by the Plan (boulevards, landscaped avenues, high streets, and so forth) along with a whole range of squares of different shapes and sizes, representing a far-sighted theoretical and practical approach.

V.4 A focus of cultural innovation

With the new dynamic that emerged at the turn of the century, Barcelona became a major focus of cultural innovation, open to the various European trends.

The field of music, too, received a significant boost in comparison with events in other European cities,[5] with stances ranging from that of Felipe Pedrell, hardly a Modernist himself, and his outstanding students Isaac

---

[5] See Roger Alier: "La vida musical a Barcelona", *Homage... op. cit.* pp. 277-85.

08, 5.09, 5.10
hree paintings by Picasso that
ke Barcelona as a subject:
errats, a faithful exponent of
s blue period; the Barceloneta
each, and Balcón, a cubist
pression of the city and its
ort.

Albéniz and Enric Granados, to that of Enric Morera, a definite sympathiser with Modernist trends, and our most famous violinist, Pau Casals. The Wagnerian Association, founded in 1901, was very influential in promoting the popularity of opera in Barcelona. This productive tradition was continued by Juli Garreta, Frederic Mompou, Eduard Toldrà, Robert Gerhard and many others.

In the world of painting the modernist movement continued to prosper, but a second generation emerged that defined itself by a new attitude and the humbler social backgrounds of its painters. It gave rise to a cultural focus of its own that was greatly influenced by Paris, particularly Montmartre, where the leading Catalan painters worked and visited frequently; Casas and Utrillo were the first, but then Sunyer, Picasso, Miró and Dalí, among others, spent their time living and working in both Barcelona and Paris.[6] Barcelona also became a requisite point on the exhibition circuit for the most innovative European trends, principally with the Sala Dalmau as of 1907 and the Galería Parés after 1877.[7]

Picasso came to the forefront in 1900 with an exhibition of portraits of his friends at the Quatre Gats tavern, which had been started up by the masters of the earlier generation; in fact this exhibition of Picasso's was seen as a challenge to the attitude represented by Ramon Casas. Between 1901-04 Picasso worked on his extraordinary

[6] This was a time of sweeping cultural changes that were expressed by new ways of understanding and experiencing time and space. See in particular the explanation of this transformation in traditional values in the excellent work by Stephen Kern: *The Culture of Time and Space*. Cambridge, 1983.

[7] See the catalogue *Homage to Barcelona*. Barcelona, 1987, *op. cit.*

"blue period" with its main theme of the socially deprived. In 1904 he went to live in Paris but continued to spend time in Barcelona, where he found a great capacity for artistic realisation.[8]

The other great figure behind this change was Isidre Nonell, who concentrated on the study of gypsies, which he turned into a paradigm theme.

There was, then, a new attitude on the part of painters, but the Modernist movement gradually lost momentum before making way for Noucentisme in around 1909.

V.5 Urban reform from the outside

Both Cerdà and Garriga i Roca[9] had used different planning models to address the overall reform of the old town. Garriga applied an intermediate system of renovation to the old town as a whole: substituting buildings and renovating them typologically, building streets, improving the environs of monuments and establishing singular points of connection with the growing Eixample, all project mechanisms that had been tried and tested in the first half of the 19th century, referred to here as "Reform from within". Conversely, Cerdà championed the new urban order of the broad streets of the Eixample as the mechanism to rationalise and restructure Ciutat Vella. The monumental areas were of course recomposed in a finer task of urban "hand stitching", but there was evidently an external planning criterion to be imposed along the lines of Haussmann's proposals in Paris. For Cerdà, however, "extension and reform" formed part of the same project. Sadly, this association was not envisaged when the Plan was passed, and it was applied separately fifty years later and, therefore, out of context and using different instruments to those devised by Cerdà, accommodating far higher densities than those suggested in his original project. The opening up or *sventramento* of the city also took place slowly and with great difficulties, taking half a century to complete.

In 1879, the Baixeras Plan defined a specific strategy for action in Ciutat Vella, with general layouts to restructure most of the existing fabric. The Plan was passed after ten years, thanks to the personal efforts of the developer. However, his death in 1892 meant that it was not until the advent of a new and far more dynamic

---

[8] See Joan Ainaud de Lasarte: *Picasso y Barcelona*. Barcelona, 1981. Also the excellent catalogue (*Avantguardes a Catalunya. 1906-1939*. Barcelona, 1992) of a major exhibition held during the Olympic summer of 1992.

[9] In 1858, Miguel Garriga i Roca, who was involved in the municipal project for the Eixample, drafted a meticulous plan of Ciutat Vella that provided the working basis for his proposals in the *1862 Alignments and Improvements Plan*.

11
eneral view of demolitions in
iutat Vella in the 1920s.

municipal government in the early 20th century that it could be completed as part of the Hygiene and Culture programme.

The situation was a complex one though Ángel Baixeras had been working carefully not just on the road layout and its influence on adjacent plots, but also on the legal and financial problems that an operation of this scope entailed.

The operation was finally undertaken in 1907 thanks to an agreement between the Council and Banco Hispano Colonial. This was Barcelona's first urban renovation operation involving combined public and private initiative, though the railways and utility infrastructures were a precedent.

This agreement enabled the construction of Artery A, also known as Via Laietana, to join the Eixample with the port according to a layout initially proposed by Cerdà.

This street would be fundamental in the urban development of Barcelona,[10] since it connected the city's two focuses of dynamism: the industrial port and an area of new residential growth. Furthermore, the fact that it ran through the middle of the old town increased this area's accessibility. The seminal heart of Barcelona, Plaça de Sant Jaume, continued to play its symbolic and functional role thanks to the innovation represented by Via Laietana: the new street not only provided access, it led to the construction of new buildings, offices and

[10] See the catalogue of the excellent exhibition held at the Museu d'Història de la Ciutat: *La construcció de la gran Barcelona: L'obertura de la Via Laietana. 1908-1998.* Barcelona, 2001. Also Xavier Peiró: *Agents materials, autors dels projectes i referències teòriques de la reforma urbana de Barcelona: 1879-1937. El cas de l'obertura de la Gran Via Layetana.* Doctoral thesis. ETSAB, UPC, Barcelona, 1988.

businesses that gave the old centre a real fillip. The construction of the street also meant that the Metro line could be built beneath it from Carrer Aragó to Carrer Jaume I.

However, the intervention was not all advantages; the construction of this street involved major management problems and represented a great deal of speculation; the association between the Bank and the platform of the industrial party was well known. The layout of the new street involved the demolition of important buildings and some, such as the Church of La Concepció with its cloister, were reconstructed in the Eixample,[11] whereas others were not.

Criticism of the urban planning schemes to arise in the course of the construction of Via Laietana led the Council to commission architects to produce a detailed project for the recovery of some monumental spaces.[12]

In the long term, the operation was justified by the relatively short period of time in which it was completed: in 1930 the layout was practically finished and many new buildings were already occupied. The last building was completed in 1958.

V.6 External transformations to Ciutat Vella

The episode of the construction of Via Laietana goes some way to explaining the different logic of operation applied in the transformation of Ciutat Vella.

The relative success of this operation contrasts with the inefficiency with which other streets through the old town had been opened up. Artery B (also vertical, an extension of Muntaner down towards the port) and Artery C (from the citadel to the foot of Montjuïc) were never actually built and only small remnants of their layouts were actually expropriated. Although these streets were picked up by subsequent plans (the Darder Plan in 1916 and the Vilaseca Plan after the war) they never had the backing of administrative mechanisms or sufficient funds.[13]

In this case, the plans had a plainly perverse effect, since they had been "justified" to rationalise and update the district, whereas their layout was like a planning designation that cast a shadow, never carried out but never

---

[11] The 13th-century Gothic-style church was moved under the direction of master builder Jeroni Granell. See A. Cirici: *op. cit.*, pp. 108-109. Barcelona, 1972.

[12] In an attempt to provide a characteristic urban setting for layout and its edges, in 1914 the architects Domènech i Montaner, Puig i Cadafalch and Romeu produced a series of projects that concentrated on the sectors nearest the Roman remains and endeavoured to tone down this *sventramento* or *rettifilo*.

[13] At the turn of the century, intervention in the form of the construction of new streets through existing fabrics, or *sventramento*, was the course of action chosen for hygienic or speculative purposes in many Spanish cities. Rarely was it carried out in a reasonable period of time, and its impact on the historic city was a negative one. Think of Gran Vía in Saragossa, Calle Molina Larios in Malaga or Gran Vía del Azúcar in Granada and its extension into the district of San Matías, among others.

5.b The construction of Via Laietana.

12
Transformation of the layout and plot division.

13
Aerial view of Via Laietana near the cathedral before the corresponding square was built.

14
Excavation work on the Metro line during the construction of the street.

15
Via Laietana in 1920.

5.16, 5.17
Vistas of the cathedral being opened up.

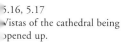

5.c The main plans marking the evolution of Ciutat Vella.

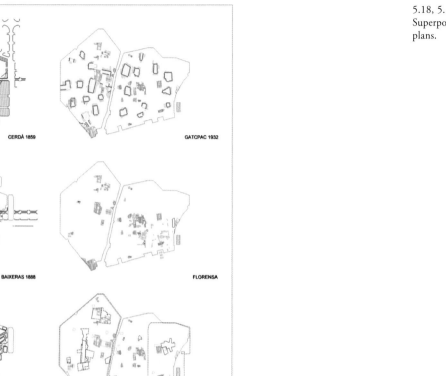

CERDÀ 1859

GATCPAC 1932

BAIXERAS 1888

FLORENSA

DARDER 1918

PLANEJAMENT POSTERIOR AL PGM DE 1976

5.18, 5.19
Superposition of the various plans.

5.d Sequence of transformations to Ciutat Vella between 1858 and the year 2000.

20, 5.21
perposition of the
ansformations.

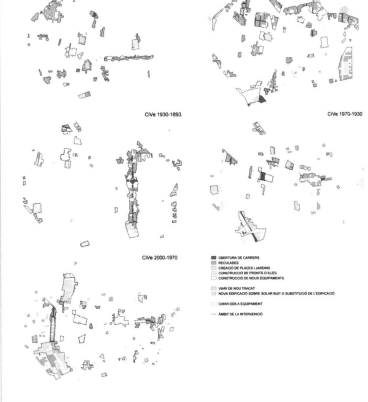

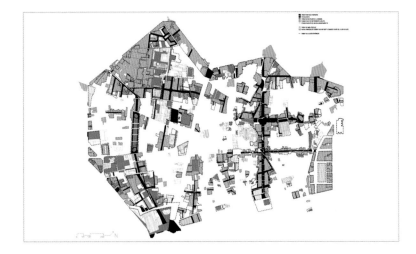

5.22, 5.23
Domènech i Muntaner's proposal for Plaça de Santa Maria del Mar in 1914 and Rubío i Bellver's suggestion for Plaça del Rei, in an attempt to improve existing buildings and reduce the impact of Via Laietana.

entirely erased. This indecisiveness was used by the owners of the buildings in question as an excuse not to repair old structures in poor conditions, which gradually deteriorated into absolute hovels.

This grey area between the planning shadows and actual schemes was one explanation for the existence of run-down areas and amorphous spaces that responded neither to the logic of rehabilitated historical fabrics nor to a new conceptualisation on the basis of innovative ideas.

A recent study carried out[14] on the basis of this hypothesis highlights the relative constancy of transformation projects over the last two centuries of modernisation of the historic town, though accompanied by a succession of notions that supported the different plans for Ciutat Vella as the basis for the various schemes.

Thus in the schemes implemented in the 1840s under the supervision of the architect Mas i Vila, the physical transformations of the fabric of Ciutat Vella corresponded to the following types:

a) streets were opened up, as Mas himself advocated, for reasons of internal logic in the case of Carrer Ferran, or with a view to joining the old and the new cities in the case of Via Laietana.

b) the line of building was drawn back to widen streets and create more practicable road space. This was a slow mechanism, as it was not in keeping with the dynamic of the individual plot.

c) squares or gardens were created by demolishing an urban element or groups of buildings with a view to thinning out the compact fabric.

d) new fronts of houses or street blocks were constructed. Substitution of large unused elements or land awaiting construction, for example beside the town wall in the Raval or in the Rondas.

e) they involved fewer facilities, very often recycling part of existing ones.

These types of projects are constant in the course of the last 160 years analysed, with changes to the location, size and specific morphology of each project.

The study was carried out on the basis of reliable cartographic documentation, establishing five periods: 2000-1970, 1970-1930, 1930-1893 and 1858-1842. Over this long period at least 115 hectares of land in Ciutat Vella were transformed, equivalent to half of its total surface area. The grouping of years reveals a rate of

[14] See J. Busquets *et al.*: LUB. *op. cit*, 2003, chapter 4.

24, 5.25
oject for Plaça de Catalunya
907) and Can Casarramona
021-1923), by Josep Puig i
dafalch.

transformation of between 0.6 and 1.2 hectares a year on average, and the spatial distribution responds to the dominant concerns of each period since, as explained above, interventions were based on plans that were operative during a given period. The transformation of the city in the modern period took the form of different notions of urban reform.[15]

Without purporting to reproduce all the plans under way during this period, we can outline the main ideas contained in them.

In the first half of the 19th century, the work of Garriga i Roca and Cerdà represented two very different options: Garriga advocated specific reform "from within" to introduce clear compositional rigour into city improvement, whereas Cerdà proposed that Ciutat Vella should be part of the new city using shrewd administration mechanisms explained elsewhere. Both aimed to improve hygiene and health by means of different instruments.

Reform ideas in Europe were evolving in keeping with changes in urban development culture. While major reform work in big cities such as Paris and London focused on the historic centre as the space of transformation, in Barcelona the force of the Eixample project made this a harder decision to make.

City reform on the basis of demolition to create streets continued to play a major part in various plans: first Cerdà's plan, then Baixeras' plan to adapt it, as already explained, then Darder's in 1918, among others, sought to reduce the impact of straight lines in the district and construct building alignments that were drawn back from the streets.

The continuing use of road-building instruments as a means of reform was to change in the 1930s with the proposals of the GATCPAC, who advocated rationalisation on the basis of thinning out by constructing urban spaces instead of road axes. After the Civil War, the pattern once again changed with the imposition of road layouts over urban fabric. Heritage was also accorded greater importance in the last century, leading to the meticulous task of grouping buildings and spaces carried out by Florensa and his team. Unfortunately, in the

---

[15] See our article: "Rehabilitación urbana. Evolución de su contenido teórico e influencia en la práctica urbanística reciente", *La reconstrucción de los centros urbanos*. EU especiales de urbanismo no. 2, Las Palmas de Gran Canaria, 2002.

5.26, 5.27
Carrer de Barcelona by
Joaquim Torres-García, 1917
and Carrer de Pedralbes by
Miró, 1917.

major "development" years, there was no great interest in Ciutat Vella and we can detect unconsidered plans such as the 1953 General Plan, for which the old town was no more than an area with rules about construction levels, leading to very heavy-handed and often blatant systems of substitution and intensification.

What remained as an outline was the succession of notions about Ciutat Vella that very often acted as shadows on the urban fabric which were not completed in a reasonable period of time and therefore produced a more negative effect than may have been expected. Because very often these shadows were superposed, creating a great complexity of situations that cancelled out the possibility of improvement that they purported to bring. Further, the study of transformations shows us firstly an insistence on certain key sectors and secondly reveals big differences between what the plans purported to change and what they actually modified.

Finally, it is important to highlight that during this long period, Central European ideas about rehabilitation and reform took a long time to reach Barcelona and be applied. This tardy arrival may have been due to the fact that the city was constantly prioritising other urban sectors. This situation did however change to some extent to judge by the impetus witnessed by Ciutat Vella in later decades, as we will go on to see.

V.7 Noucentisme

The political and social changes to emerge at the turn of the century deflected the importance of Modernisme as a dominant cultural trend, despite the fact that the movement's foremost buildings were constructed in the first decade of the 20th century.

The search for a new cultural framework for Catalan identity was now expressed by Noucentisme. This current with its literary origins was to a large degree represented by the person of the writer Eugeni d'Ors ("Xenius") who, to some extent, replaced the figure of the poet Joan Maragall, who had died in 1911. D'Ors published *La ben plantada*, which became the inspirational work of Noucentisme with its protagonist, Teresa, as the symbol of this pro-Catalan trend.[16]

The Institut d'Estudis Catalans was set up in 1907 and very soon Eugeni d'Ors became its executive secretary, a post from which he played an active role as leader of the new Catalan intelligentsia. To some extent he became the ideologist of the Regionalist League of Prat de la Riba and Puig i Cadafalch.

Noucentisme was anti-Modernist, following the lead of parallel movements in Europe, including the Viennese Sezession headed by the architect Otto Wagner, which gave the development of Vienna a tremendous boost at the turn of the century with impressive schemes of great scope and quality.[17] It also adopted the more theoretical positions defended by Adolf Loos in 1908 in favour of aesthetic clarity and the rejection of Art Nouveau, reaching the extreme of identifying ornament as a social ill to be overcome.[18]

But above all for Puig i Cadafalch and his followers it was necessary to return to a classical, more neutral order than the individuality mooted by Modernisme, making architecture capable of "institutionally strengthening" the country, an end that was pursued programmatically. This determination was expressed in the facilities (schools, parks, etc.) that were constructed during this period.

This neutral or classical order contained the specific characteristics of the Mediterranean condition of which Catalanness formed a part. This heralded the search for the Mediterranean garden to which Forestier and Rubió i Tudurí gave concrete form, and the repertory of stylistic approximations produced by various architects of the Noucentisme movement, combining several classicist styles with a taste for the rural.[19]

[16] See E. D'Ors: *La Ben Plantada*. Ed. 62. Barcelona, 1980. This work caused quite a stir, both for its literary quality and its content. The atmosphere surrounding its female character produces a landscape that brings together different places of Mediterranean geography.

[17] Wagner restructured the city on the basis of elements ranging from infrastructure (Metro, embankment and hydraulic system of the Danube) to important buildings (churches, banks), including the public and the private sector. This sweeping dynamic of Otto Wagner and his team did not differ so much from that of some of our foremost architects of the time. See *Otto Wagner*. Academy Editions, London, 1979.

[18] See Adolf Loos' articles, published – not without great difficulty – in Austria in 1932 with the title *Ins Leere gesprochen*. A series of critical articles about the 1898 Vienna exhibition held to commemorate the fiftieth anniversary of the accession to the throne of Emperor Franz Josef. These articles, which are of great importance as a theoretical basis of modern architecture, are radical and sometimes irreverent in tone to Austrian tradition and formulate the radical statement that "ornament is a crime".

[19] See Esteban Castañer: "Catalogne: À la recherche d'une architecture nationaliste" in François Loyer and Bernard Toulier ed., *Le Regionalisme, Architecture et Identité*. Paris, 2001. Also Jean-Pierre Epron, *Comprendre l'Éclecticisme*. Norma, Paris, 1997.

5.28, 5.29, 5.30, 5.31
Graphic images by Joan
Miró, Rafael Barradas, Salvat
Papasseit and J. V. Foix.

The key figures in this architectural current were Durán i Reynals, Rubió i Tudurí, Florensa, Puig i Cadafalch and Rafael Masó.[20]

An outstanding figure in this new dominant framework of Noucentisme was Josep Maria Jujol, who produced an architecture that stood out from the mainstream, maintaining the expression of modernism – he had worked on many of Gaudí's creations – but establishing a unique expressive constructional process.[21]

In the field of painting, too, Noucentisme influenced the leading artists. In 1917 Picasso spent some time in Barcelona where he painted *Harlequin*, regarded as an authentic neoclassical painting. Joaquim Sunyer, too, alternated between Paris and Barcelona and moved from Modernisme to the classical movement.

When in 1912 Eugeni d'Ors published the *Almanach dels noucentistes*, Picasso, Gargallo and Torres García formed an integral part of the movement. The latter was famed for his paintings of rural Catalonia.

In sculpture Enric Casanovas marked a return to classical references in his female busts, and Josep Clarà and Arístides Maillol also followed this line.

Periodical publications flourished, including the weekly *Papitu*, edited by Feliu Elias, that combined drawings with political satire. The painter Juan Gris contributed to this weekly publication between 1908 and 1911.

But Barcelona was gradually establishing itself as an artistic centre of international repute. In 1912 the Galería Dalmau organised an exhibition of cubist art, including the work of Marcel Duchamp. A few years later during World War I, the city was home to scores of exiled artists such as Francis Picabia and Albert Gleizes, and many others.

This breeding ground spawned a new generation that included Joan Miró and Enric Ricart, who showed at the Dalmau in 1917. Miró stood out from the very first for the two-dimensional nature of his work and his cubist inclinations which later led him to surrealism alongside Salvador Dalí. Later, the avant-garde, cubist-inspired Agrupació Courbet was constituted as an alternative to the Cercle Artístic de Sant Lluc, with the participation of Llorens Artigas (a ceramist and collaborator with Miró), the sculptors Manolo Hugué and Pau Gargallo, and the poet Joan Salvat-Papasseit.

[20] See the monographic issue of *Cuadernos de Arquitectura y Urbanismo*, "Noucentisme". Barcelona, 1970.
[21] See the interesting catalogue by Josep A. Llinàs *et al.*: "Jujol 1879-1949", *Quaderns 179-180*. Barcelona, 1989.

5.e The railway lines with their centre in Barcelona.

32
Much of the railway system was constructed in the 19th century.

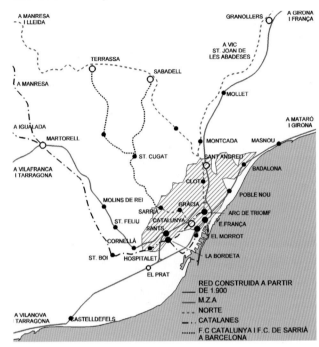

A MANRESA I LLEIDA
GRANOLLERS
A GIRONA I FRANÇA
A VIC ST. JOAN DE LES ABADESES
TERRASSA
SABADELL
A MANRESA
MOLLET
A IGUALADA
A MATARÓ I GIRONA
MARTORELL
MONTCADA
MASNOU
ST. CUGAT
SANT ANDREU
A VILAFRANCA I TARRAGONA
BADALONA
CLOT
MOLINS DE REI
POBLE NOU
GRÀCIA
SARRIÀ
ARC DE TRIOMF
ST. FELIU
CATALUNYA
E.FRANÇA
SANTS
CORNELLÀ
EL MORROT
ST. BOI
HOSPITALET
LA BORDETA
EL PRAT

RED CONSTRUIDA A PARTIR DE 1.900
——— M.Z.A
– – – NORTE
–··– CATALANES
······ F.C CATALUNYA I F.C. DE SARRIÀ A BARCELONA

A VILANOVA TARRAGONA
CASTELLDEFELS

.33
Carrer Balmes with the Sarrià railway line.

5.34 5.35
The railway line along Carrer Aragó was originally uncovered; its undergrounding in 1960 led to use of the street as a major traffic artery.

V.8 The infrastructure of development: electrification and suburbanisation

Major investment in infrastructure continued with improvements to urban services and an increased interest in infrastructure to support urban growth and extension.

By this time, the suburban railway was the protagonist of the incipient structuring of the counties surrounding Barcelona, a process in which the Ferrocarriles de Cataluña, running between Barcelona-Sarrià and Sant Cugat, Sabadell and Terrassa, played a major part. This was a railway built with the international gauge with the aspiration – still today unrealised – of connecting Paris and Barcelona with the European gauge. Another narrow-gauge rail system known as the "Catalans" joined Barcelona with the towns in the Llobregat valley to Martorell.

The importance of these axes was vital to the development of a series of low-density residential urbanisations outside the city.

Then the electrification process was to radically change the distribution and scope of Catalan industrialisation. In the mid-term it also influenced the form of city organisation and particularly mobility between the centre and its outskirts.

The turn of the century was an important moment in Barcelona's electrification process and one that ushered in improvements to urban conditions.[22]

This was also the period of the second energy transition to have an appreciable impact on Catalan territory; although not a new energy source, the possibility of its distribution over long distances was to be decisive.

It was the Catalan rivers (Segre, Noguera Pallaresa, etc.), with the construction of reservoirs and falls in their upper basins, that provided energy for consumption in the cities and the rest of the territory, thereby promoting the development of a fully industrial society.

It allowed the region to overcome much of its dependence on imported energy in the form of coal. In turn, this greater availability of energy led to the development of energy-intensive industrial sectors which had to a large extent been impossible in the 19th century.

Although the textile sector was still important, it had branched into knitwear and was fully immersed in a process of industrial diversification: mechanical constructions and heavy industry were now possible, and the cement industry received a major boost, as did the chemicals sector in response to a widespread need of fertilisers for farming. The foodstuffs and publishing industries responded to the new demands of urban society. Long-lasting consumer goods (automobiles, sewing machines, etc.) entered the Catalan production systems and the

[22] See J. Nadal and J. Maluquer, *op. cit.*, p. 175. "The production of electricity began with a power station to provide public street lighting in Barcelona in 1875 (...) though it was not used intensively until the early years of the 20th century."

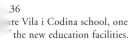

buildings in Barcelona's new Eixample began to devote sophisticated shop windows to the products that defined industrial society in the first decades of the century.

Furthermore the extraordinary flexibility of electrical conduction and its easy transformation allowed domestic consumption, which was to gradually but completely modify housing patterns.

Electricity production was initially fragmentary, until in 1913 the company Energía Eléctrica de Cataluña was created on the initiative of Emilio Riu with the protagonism of the North American, Fred Stark Pearson. The holding company, Barcelona Traction, Light and Power Co., known as La Canadiense, was set up, and work began on major hydraulic works in the Pyrenees. Pearson also made his importance felt in garden-city developments on the slopes of the mountain of Collserola.

Another large firm, Hidroeléctrica de Catalunya, was formed by Catalana de Gas and a group of Catalan industrialists.

The presence of electrification in the city was quite patent in the urban images of the new street lighting and the tram, but it was above all the electrification of the railways that triggered the metropolitan explosion, creating a greater capacity for mass transport and, as a result, increasing the possibilities of further urbanisation of Barcelona's hinterland.

V.9 New urban services and facilities

In the new Council's connective project, urban services and infrastructures were a priority, and councillors and specially created commissions alike devoted their efforts to them. Themes such as transport, culture and teaching were central axes for discussion, though never overriding more ambitious projects such as "the interconnections" or the Great Exhibition, which we will look at further on.

While the Moyano Act of 1857 had recognised the public school system as an obligatory service, the real situation differed a great deal to its stipulations and the school structure was markedly elitist and organised fundamentally by religious orders. However, it was in this period that public schooling was seen as one service more to be offered as part of the new logic of the big industrial city.

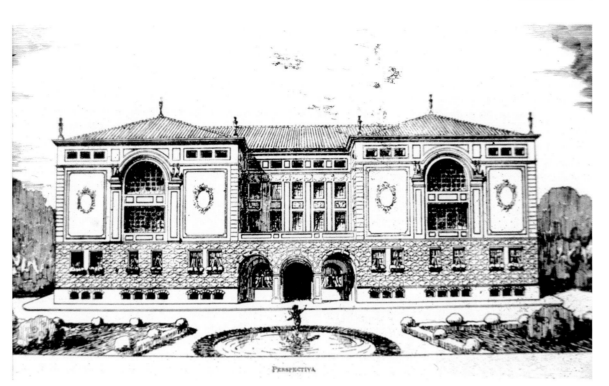

PERSPECTIVA

5.37
Goday's school complex, an example of Noucentisme.

In the urban planning programme of the League, but also of other pro-Catalan sectors, school was regarded as a fundamental culture medium for the development of a national awareness.

The Culture Commission of Barcelona Council, created in 1916, and the Mancomunitat de Catalunya that implemented the schemes; the latter played a particularly salient role in the periods in which the Schools Board was most active, between 1922-23 and later between 1930-36.

This renovation of the school system brought about a substantial change in the buildings and internal organisation as well as in the pedagogical system. Worthy of mention here is the figure of the architect Josep Goday, a follower of Puig i Cadafalch, who in the 1916-20 period designed seven schools in the city of Barcelona, of particular interest both for the architectural language employed and the functional structure adopted. They were absolutely modern buildings in their organisation and constructional rationality and were built in the style of Noucentisme. Some of these schools (Pere Vila and Ramon Llull) are paradigm examples of the movement.

In his 1917 report, Goday himself pointed out that the quality of the school building contributed to the "moral training of the pupils (...), to the spirit of the future inhabitants of Barcelona, in a pleasant and tasteful atmosphere".[23]

There was the excellent example of the Escoles Municipals del Bosc, founded between 1914 and 1916; this impressive institutional effort produced thirty-seven new schools. Particular mention is worthy of the Escola del Mar in the Barceloneta, constructed in 1921 beside the beach in order to promote a form of teaching more

[23] Cèlia Cañellas and Rosa Toran: "Una nueva escuela public para la normalización cultural", *Cuadernos* no. 113. Barcelona, 1976.

in keeping with the natural environment. During the summer it was used for children's holiday camps, thereby making full use of the facilities.

Private initiative also underwent renovation with the setting up of the Modern School at the start of the century, due particularly to the dedication of Ferrer i Guàrdia.

Public transport also increased in response to the growing demand for mobility in an increasingly metropolitan situation. We have already seen how the trams were electrified in this period, but then, most strikingly, the metropolitan railways followed suit, ushering in the definitive suburbanisation of the counties adjacent to Barcelona.

And, finally, the Metro arrived, with the construction of the first two lines: the first, Gran Metropolitano, started in the Rambla and travelled up Passeig de Gràcia to Lesseps at the top of Gràcia, and the second, Línia Transversal, following the horizontal axis marked out by the Gran Via and the axes of the Great Exhibition, was built in 1926 from Plaça d'Espanya to Carrer Marina in the east of the Eixample.[24]

Conversely, social housing operations were practically non-existent and it was only in response to the Exhibition that five complexes of small *casas baratas*, or cheap houses, were built; as we will later see, the living conditions of the urban immigrant population were difficult in the extreme.

V.10 The parks system

The Interconnections Plan had made the definition of Barcelona's open spaces a priority issue for the city. Furthermore, the daily press at the close of the century provided a platform for discussion as to their necessity, and tentative projects had been drafted for Montjuïc and Les Glòries.

The consideration of green areas as a systematic public place for the specific activities of promenading, leisure and representation was an innovation in most European cities in the mid-19th century, with such spectacular cases as Adolphe Alphand's works for Paris with its promenades and gardens.

The impact in Barcelona was less; apart from the Citadel, the only exponents of a system of urban open spaces were Passeig Nou and the Jardí del General in the 18th century, the excellent Passeig de Gràcia in the first half of the 19th century and some avenues in other municipalities in the Plain.

[24] The railway lines to Sarrià, Martorell, Terrassa and Sabadell were electrified during this period, becoming faster and more frequent as a result. The Sarrià line was also undergrounded as far as Sant Gervasi. See Marc Andreu and Josep Maria Huertas *et al.*: *La ciutat transportada*. TMB, Barcelona, 1997.

5.f The Parks System, 1920. Rubió i Tudurí and Forestier.

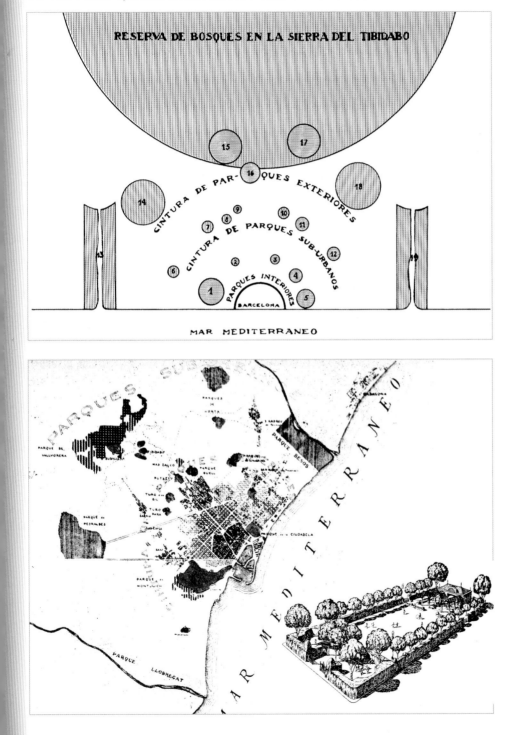

5.38
General layout of parks.

5.39
Location of proposed public parks.

5.40
Example of garden design.

41
eneral plan of the Tibidabo
arden city, Marià Rubió i
ellver, 1907.

42, 5.43
iew of Vallvidrera in 1930
nd Avinguda del Tibidabo
oday.

However, intensive use was made on high days and holidays of certain areas near the city, such as the mountain of Montjuïc, where excursions to natural springs, private picnic areas and so forth offered an outlet, though not publicly organised, for this latent demand for recreation.

However, there was no systematic reflection as to open space in the city until the beginning of the century, when it found its expression in the work of Nicolau Maria Rubió i Tudurí and the French landscaper Jean-Claude-Nicolas Forestier, conservator of the Parks of Paris, who in 1915 undertook the design of park elements for Montjuïc and collaborated most effectively in municipal organisation of the theme.[25]

---

[25] Nicolau Maria Rubió i Tudurí: *Jardines de Barcelona*. Ajuntament de Barcelona, 1929. See also Cèlia Cañellas *et al.*: "Nicolau Mª Rubió i Tudurí, entre la razón y la sensibilidad", *Cuadernos* no. 113. Barcelona, 1976. Also Various authors: *N. M. Rubio i Tudurí (1891-1981)*. Barcelona, 1989; Ajuntament de Barcelona: *El problema de los espacios libres*. Barcelona, 1926.

5.44, 5.45
The "blue" tram and a funicular railway provided a fun approach to Tibidabo.

In 1918 the Council created the Directorate of Public Parks, of which Rubió i Tudurí was appointed director. This department promoted both the conceptualisation of the theme and the construction of new parks.[26]

In this context, mention must be made of Cebrià de Montoliu, who, despite being a minor figure in established power relations,[27] played a very important role with regard to organicist theses and what he defined as "civic science".

Montoliu was very much influenced by the English reform tendencies of Morris and Ruskin; in addition to studying their work he also translated it (1901), and was moved to enthusiastically follow in the footsteps of Ebenezer Howard, the garden city theorist, ideologist and author of the famous *Garden Cities of Tomorrow*, published in England in 1898.[28] He also put the work of pioneers into practice by applying the theories of

---

[26] The discussion of the parks system in big cities came to the fore in the American city after the Civil War, as part of the cultural and ideological "Parks Movement". The leading exponents were the great designers Olmsted, Vaux, Eliot and Burnham, among others, who produced a series of interventions in cities such as Boston, Chicago and New York that still stand out today. There was in fact a deep-seated change in the significance of the park, which ceased to be simply an urban facility for recreation and pleasure and became an essential element of social reform, seeking to ease social problems. Parks were distributed in different areas with functions geared to the various users, according to age and gender. In this way, it became an amenity with a specific functional content, be it sport, children's games, etc. This major movement probably also encouraged European landscapers to undertake more specific, better defined interventions. See Galen Craz: *The Politics of Park Design. A History of Urban Parks in America*. Cambridge, 1982.

[27] See Francesc Roca: "Cebrià de Montoliu i la Ciencia Cívica", *Cuadernos* no. 80. Barcelona, 1971.

[28] The idea of an urban model created by a constellation of medium-sized towns and cities scattered across a territory of farmland was accompanied by the idea of administering urban land so that the increase in its value for urban use would revert to the community. The ideas that Edward Bellamy expressed in 1888 in *Looking Backward* were a definitive influence on Ebenezer Howard's book.

5.46, 5.47
...or plan and view of the Park
...the Labyrinth, Horta.

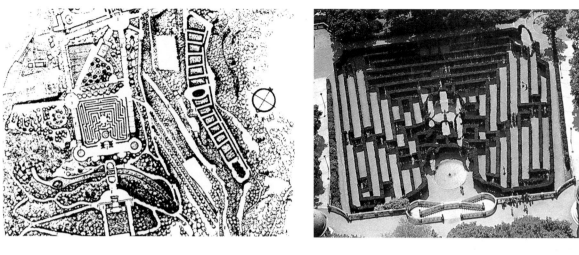

5.48
...iew of a sector of the park.

Howard, Unwin and Parker. An indefatigable worker, Cebrià de Montoliu was constantly in the press and giving lectures; his efforts later found a platform in a journal, *Civitas*, that he himself founded.

When the first garden city estates such as Frare Blanch at the foot of Tibidabo were developed in the uptown part of the city and connected by new means of transport, Montoliu did not tire of publicising their good points and benefits, seeing an affinity with the processes that he had observed in England. However, to judge by the results, in the case of Barcelona this form of urbanisation was too closely associated with the direct interests of large landowners, who were unlikely to share the decentralising, environmental principles advocated by the theory of civic science.

In 1912 he founded the Sociedad Cívica La ciudad jardín (Garden City Civic Corporation) and established contacts with similar bodies in Europe[29] to make headway in this international trend.

[29] Cebrià Montoliu: *La ciudad jardín*. Barcelona, 1912.

A year later he published the book *Las modernas ciudades y sus problemas*, a comprehensive analysis of the situation faced by industrial cities. It also broached a new perspective emerging in some countries where the reformist trend represented criticism of the unregulated industrial city and sought formulas for collaboration and decentralisation to improve living and environmental conditions.

In 1920 Cebrià de Montoliu left Barcelona to settle in the United States where he founded the town of Fairhope, based on the ideas of civic science and a single tax. Three years later, at the age of fifty, he died without having achieved the results that the same innovative ideas had obtained in the European context. Francesc Roca has compared him to Cerdà for his determination and abnegation. It is necessary to recognise the practical difficulties of implanting the garden city in Barcelona in order to understand the vulgarisation of these ideas and the high profile role of land ownership on the urban scenario of this growing metropolis.[30] The Civic Corporation lived on for some years with a new secretary: Nicolau Maria Rubió i Tudurí.

The systematisation of open or green space was, then, seen as being necessary both to alleviate the ills of the industrial city and to further embellish it.

As Rubió i Tudurí pointed out when writing about his work with the Council: "As the big modern city grows, it crushes and destroys the landscape. The formidable forces behind urban progress – industry, overpopulation, traffic – demand all available space for themselves."[31] He goes on to add, more radically: "We in the services of this Directorate of Public Parks of Barcelona stand by the motto that 'land intended for construction is land lost'". "One excess has to be combated by an equal and opposite excess."

In formalising the parks system, Rubió sought first to rationalise existing green areas and then to superpose optimum models of distribution.

As a basis for intervention he established a category of open spaces with facilities, defining two types: urban garden-parks, including squares, district gardens and children's parks, and large spaces, including urban parks, between 8 and 10 hectares, and natural reserves.

He also sought an organisational model of park belts, in which those closest to the existing city were smaller but more continuous, increasing in size and relative distance apart the further they lay from the centre. However, when it came to applying these principles, he came up against a fairly consolidated geographical and urban

---

[30] As opposed to the lack of real interest in garden cities as a form of residential decentralisation, the second half of the 20th century saw the rise of entire estates of second homes, representing a big threat to the landscape as they were very often located in areas of natural interest.

[31] Nicolau Maria Rubió i Tudurí: *El problema de los espacios libres. Divulgación de su teoría y notas para su solución práctica*. Ajuntament de Barcelona, 1926.

structure. Furthermore, the average levels of green areas existing in the city were very low, despite the fact that the Municipal Statute stipulated that ten per cent of urban land should be given over to open space.

Rubió i Tudurí and his team came up with the definition of a clear conceptual scheme of concentric semi-rings that sought to create, in accordance with the opportunities that presented themselves, both municipal and easy-purchase properties.

His proposal envisaged three levels: 1) the inner-city parks, comprising two principal ones, Ciutadella and Montjuïc, and three minor ones (Letamendi, Sagrada Família and Glòries); 2) the belt of suburban parks, including: Hipódromo, Turó Park, Turó Gil, Font del Recó, Vallcarca, Güell Park and Guinardó Park; 3) the outer belt of parks, including: Llobregat, Pedralbes, Vallvidrera, Tibidabo, Sant Medir, Horta and Besòs; plus, finally, the natural reserve of woods on the Tibidabo hill range.

The result was a clear, possibilist scheme that was implemented with great emphasis on the purchase of land and interventions in certain parks.

Whereas in 1910 the city had just 72 hectares of open space, acquisitions up until 1924 multiplied this area by six, which, broken down, produced 103 hectares of land for inner-city parks and 347 for parks in the outer belt.

Thus a powerful scheme of open city space was formalised and a considerable amount of land accumulated for the development of subsequent projects. However, the administrative and intervention mechanisms were still embryonic, as Rubió himself often said.

It might be said that at that time in the inner-city area, apart from Ciutadella Park and some fragments of Montjuïc, there were hardly any other parks than the Desert de Sarrià, Hort Labyrinth and Güell Park. These were in fact small parks that had come into being with the vogue for private open spaces and were later turned over to public use.

One such was Güell Park, designed by Gaudí, who had set out to develop a residential area in the style of the garden city, a pioneering idea when it was conceived in 1900. It covered 20 hectares on one of the higher slopes of the Montanya Pelada, or bald mountain. It was divided up into 60 triangular plots with a series of central services such as its raised terrace and a covered market. The estate was never used for this purpose and it became a park on the death of Eusebio Güell, when it was purchased by the City Council and incorporated into the parks system. The whole is a spectacular combination of trees and landscape forms;[32] the viaduct and the square offer magnificent vistas of the city.

---

[32] Gaudí recovered Mediterranean vegetation and built tracks and paths using stones found on site in a return to the traditions of the Mediterranean countryside. The classical tradition emerges in the structures that support the square with a characteristic interpretation of the classical style and the system of slanting columns. See the complete work of Conrad Kent and Dennis Prindle: *Hacia la arquitectura de un paraíso: Parc Güell.* H. Blume, Barcelona, 1992.

5.g Güell Park: from garden city to public park.

5.49, 5.50, 5.51
Views of the plaza with the bench around it.

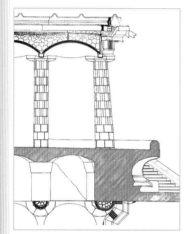
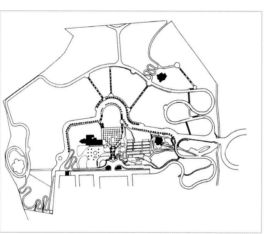

5.52
Section of the hypostyle hall.

5.53
General floor plan.

5.54
Viaduct.

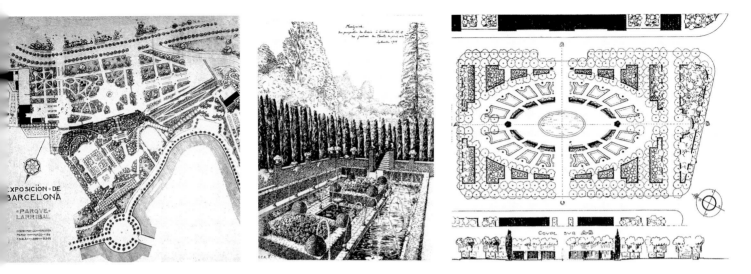

5.55, 5.56
Laribal Park by J. C. N.
Forestier.

5.57
Ciutadella Park.

The Labyrinth in Horta is one the city's most interesting classical gardens which developed in the late 18th century around a medieval fortified house. It was a landscaping work of great complexity, apparently undertaken by its owner, J. A. Desvalls, Marquis of Alfarrás, and completed in a short period of time and with a great deal of effort due to the difficult topography. The composition of the garden is based on three interrelated elements: the labyrinth, the great terrace and the pond, set in a thick wood. Today it is still an outstanding example due to its size and its compositional interest.[33]

The Forestier-Rubió i Tudurí team was decisive when it came to action. In 1915 the French landscaper had agreed to produce a project for the park of Montjuïc as part of his work for the Great Exhibition, and his contribution was a lengthy and productive one. Rubió started out as a student of Forestier, and this close collaboration produced new bases for reflection on the Catalan component within the wider spectrum of the Mediterranean garden. Their work sought to engage the existing vegetation with introduced species with a spectacular adaptation to the topography, seeking to minimise the walls and differences in levels that always seek urban perspectives and relations.[34]

Their work in Montjuïc could be called a project of parks within a park. The mountain's irregular topography, the existence of large quarries and springs and so forth, suggested a division of the overall project into parts with their own cadences and contents. These included Laribal Park, Passeig de Santa Madrona, the Amargós gardens with their Greek theatre and the Miramar garden with its steps down to the port, elements that became attractions in themselves during the 1929 Exhibition.

Forestier's influence also made itself felt in other of the city's gardens, such as the Plaça d'Armes in Ciutadella and Guinardó Parks; Rubió also intervened in both projects before going on to become the principal designer, with a team of assistants, of Pedralbes Park, Turó Park and today's Plaça Francesc Macià.

These events marked the start, albeit a tardy one, of the introduction of urban open space into the city, though the theme would continue to call for concerted effort, as we will see.

[33] Joan Villoro: *Guia dels espais verds de Barcelona*. COAC, Barcelona, 1984. Also Patricia Gabancho and Ferran Freixa: *La conquesta del verd*. Barcelona, 1995.

[34] See Nicolau Maria Rubió i Tudurí: *Del Paraíso al Jardín Latino*. Barcelona, 1981. Jean Claude Nicolas Forestier: *Grandes Villes et Systèmes de Parcs*. Paris, 1997.

5.58
Plan for the 1929 Great
Exhibition, drawing by J. Pu
i Cadafalch, 1915.

V.11 The long march towards the 1929 Electrical Industries Exhibition

The idea of a Great Exhibition was latent in the urban planning programme of the industrial party, and Puig i Cadafalch voiced it in a front page article in *La Veu de Catalunya* newspaper, calling for votes in the 1905 elections: "Come and vote! For the Great Exhibition." In the article he justified the exhibition as a way of implementing the main body of ideas in Jaussely's Interconnections Plan.

The urban development process of the exhibition was long and complex; for an explanation of that process we will follow Ignasi de Solà-Morales' brilliant analysis of the period.[35]

In the event of an undertaking of this magnitude, the city was fortunate to have an exceptional protagonist in the architect and politician Josep Puig i Cadafalch who, directly or indirectly, guided the process for over two decades.

The urban location of the exhibition was a vital issue. The experience of the 1888 exhibition had revealed the attendant difficulties, but also the attraction of the urban improvements that an event of this kind could bring about.

The initial hypothesis centred on the eastern sector of the city with a view to urbanising the Besòs park as suggested by Cerdà's project, then described as the "Great Wood". In 1909 the architect Manuel Vega i March presented a project to develop this sector, including the Plaça de les Glòries Catalanes: the point of convergence

[35] See Ignasi de Solà-Morales: *L'exposició Internacional de Barcelona 1914-1929: Arquitectura i Ciutat.* Fira de Barcelona, Barcelona, 1985. A summary of this work can be found in "L'Esposizione Internazionale del 1929" in the new monograph of *Rassegna* magazine. Milan, 1988 (published in English and Italian).

of the three main axes of Cerdà's layout – Gran Via, Diagonal and Meridiana – which both Cerdà and Jaussely coincided in appointing as the great future centre of the city.[36]

At the same time, Montjuïc was gaining in stature as an alternative with the possibility of condensing the urbanisation of a great park on the mountain – also zoned by Cerdà – and recovering for the city an emblematic but little known feature, a hill that was close by but intriguing, from which the Bourbons had laid siege to Barcelona.

The two options were clear opposites: Besòs or Montjuïc, the east or the west of the existing city. In 1913 a mixed commission was created, comprising Cambó, Pich i Pon and Puig i Cadafalch, that decided on Montjuïc. This decision represented Barcelona's future development towards the west, at the same time creating special conditions for the exhibition project: it would be built on sloping ground, and this would be the first time that an exhibition of this scope took place on a mountain of the characteristics of Montjuïc. However, this singularity was probably the project's greatest attraction.[37]

We do not know exactly how instrumental this factor was in choosing the site, though we do know that the Board of Directors of the Electrical Industries Exhibition was created in 1914 and Puig i Cadafalch presented an initial project in 1915. Puig's intuition was key to the entire process, because although changes were introduced into the buildings, the general layout of the exhibition plan maintained the same principles.

It is interesting to note that some famous exhibitions had purposely chosen conditions of urban limits: one such was the famous 1893 Chicago Exhibition, held to celebrate – a year late – the fourth centenary of the discovery of America on the shore of a lake, with a monumental layout that was the work of Daniel Burnham, with closed salon-type spaces and long vistas of the great buildings constructed there.

Puig i Cadafalch was responsible for several key operations in the overall layout. He designed a main axis, the Gran Avenida, which, starting out from the centre of present-day Plaça d'Espanya, non-existent at the time, drew out a forceful line from the north towards the mountain. He also designed the square with a colonnade and exedra, forming an imposing façade for the exhibition buildings. Starting at the Gran Avenida, the main buildings were laid out in a system of terraces that moulded the mountainside. At the end of the axis stood a suitably monumental building with a great dome to crown the whole. Below the terraces, a perpendicular axis provided a side approach to the upper slopes of the mountain, where a further two Exhibition sectors were located: the first on the centre of the hill and the second on the south-facing slopes, in the Miramar area, at mid-height above the port.

The language of the complex presented other great similarities, as Solà-Morales points out, to the "Art city" project of Otto Wagner, another figure who exerted a great deal of influence in the tastes of Catalan Noucentisme.

[36] This is still a city sector with a great deal of potential today, which is currently being developed.
[37] Estanislau Roca: *Montjuic, la muntanya de la ciutat*. Barcelona, 1994.

5.h The 1929 Electrical Industries Exhibition.

5.59
Aerial view of the complex.

5.60
View of the main avenue.

5.61
The lighting of the 1929
Exhibition.

But above all, the forceful formalisation of Plaça d'Espanya ensured a suitable context for the Exhibition complex and its future utility. In fact the square was not yet urbanised and was a difficult meeting point for three other axes: Creu Coberta, the core of the suburban growth of Hostafrancs along a medieval road from the old town; Gran Via, Cerdà great horizontal axis, and Paral·lel, which, together with Carrer Conde del Asalto, had since the end of the century been a very busy thoroughfare with its theatres and popular attractions.

In order to complete the project, three groups of architects were invited to take part to develop the three above-mentioned parts: Puig i Cadafalch and Guillem Busquets designed the bottom part around Plaça d'Espanya where the General Spanish Exhibition was to be held; Manuel Vega and Lluís Domènech i Montaner undertook the central part for the Electrical Industries Exhibition; and, finally, Agusto Font and Enric Sagnier were responsible for the Miramar sector.

However, the coordination of the three projects was minimal, and the monitoring of the developments was uneven. In 1917, construction work began with the idea of completing it in 1919 under the direction of the engineer Marià Rubio i Bellver. However, the pace of work was impermissibly slow and the date was set back to 1923, though political events were also to change the course of the exhibition.

Spain was not involved in the World War, a fact that redounded to the benefit of its industry, producing an artificial wealth that created a strong dynamic in Barcelona; however, there were serious social conflicts. After the Morocco Disaster of 1921, the democratic process was interrupted and the Dictatorship of Primo de Rivera was imposed with the approval of the King and the most conservative sectors of the country, including Catalonia.

The Dictatorship of Primo de Rivera introduced far-reaching changes into municipal and Catalan administration. The Mancomunitat de Catalunya was dissolved and construction work was blocked until 1925,

5.i The Barcelona Pavilion by Mies van der Rohe.

5.63
Opening in 1929.

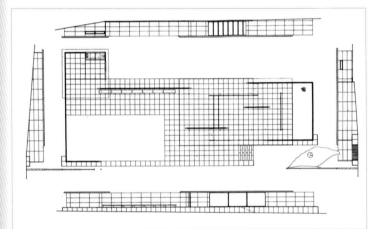

5.64
Floor plan, façade and sections.

5.65, 5.66
Views of the Pavilion, in 1929 and today.

when the Catalan bourgeoisie was able to make a pact with the dictator and resume work on the exhibition, which was rescheduled for 1929.

By 1923, the urbanisation of the Gran Avenida and the streets had been carried out, the earthworks were completed and some buildings were fairly advanced. These included the two pavilions designed by Puig i Cadafalch, dedicated to Alfonso XIII and Victoria Eugenia, situated one to either side halfway along the visual axis that defines the National Palace.

These pavilions and the interstitial development, including the four allegorical columns with winged victories in reference to the four stripes of the Catalan flag[38] were completed and their first exhibition use was for the Salon of Agriculture and the International Furniture Salon. This marked the beginning of the trade-fair activity that later became the central use of the exhibition enclosure.[39]

These first buildings were located in excellent positions, as a plinth to contain or retain the mountain and the central pavilion, and were built in the academic style with a fine use of stucco and Catalan construction techniques. Inside, they employed modern structural concepts that engaged in an attractive interplay of light and volumes.

The exhibition project continued in 1925, with the appointment of the Marquis of Foronda as the royal curator, at the same time as its counterpart in Seville, which was working on its own exhibition, also for 1929.

The resumption of work on the palaces involved public competitions and commissions once the basic urbanisation work had been completed. The competition for the National Palace project was won by Pedro Cendoya, who designed a monumentalist building that followed the lines of Puig's early concepts.

---

[38] In fact these columns were not present at the 1929 exhibition, having been demolished "for fear of angering the dictator". See Ignasi de Solà-Morales: *op. cit.*, 1985. p. 74.

[39] The Fira de Barcelona is the trade fair institution with the longest tradition in Spain. Since its beginnings in the 1920s it has organised its exhibitions in the precinct built in 1929, adapting or constructing new buildings. The precinct currently has 20 pavilions with a total built surface area of 120,000 m². Every year it holds an average of forty shows, a very intensive use compared to the European average.

In the eighties, comprehensive improvement work was done to the buildings, though the need for more exhibition space led the institution to consider extending to the other side of Montjuïc with more modern pavilions and approaches.

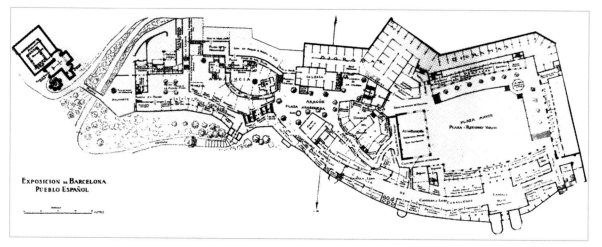

A total of fourteen palaces or groups of buildings were constructed, a task that involved both functionary architects and professors at the School of Architecture. The palaces varied a great deal in size – from 5,000 to 30,000 m² – as did their styles and construction methods. However, this was not what the exhibition had to offer; these buildings were mere containers for many small stands.

With regard to the general evolution of the exhibition phenomenon, this was still a time in which these events were organised in a large constructed space that was occupied, decorated and beautified by the various commercial or institutional users. The exhibition was an urban planning and architectural feat, as opposed to later times when the exhibition would become an urbanised space in which objects or small pavilions were arranged.[40]

In fact pavilions or small buildings with a monographic content were present at the 1929 exhibition, though their role was to complement or enhance the main buildings or palaces that still stand in this urban space today.

The purpose of these small pavilions was to represent institutions, nations or commercial brands. They sought to transmit a direct, effective advertising message and their architectural content was in many cases ephemeral or of scant interest.

However, in this city of advertisements, one pavilion stood out: the German Pavilion, designed by Mies van der Röhe and known as the Barcelona pavilion, which has been recently reconstructed. It is in fact a masterwork of modern architecture, a small building that combines the various ideals that inspired the movement: the purity of the planes used to define a space characteristic of neo-plasticism, and the fluidity or continuity of the space, all with a sophisticated use of materials.[41]

The building stood on a small podium, near the walls of one of Puig's pavilions, in accordance with the location chosen by Mies himself, with a minimum of expository content – the building and its construction provided the theme. Its innovative value evidently made it a controversial building during the exhibition. As in

[40] See Laurence Zimmermen's summary ("The seven eras of World's Fairs: 1851-1976", *P. A.*, vol. 8, no. 74, 1980) in which he enumerates as many as seven generations of exhibitions, marking this change in urban and functional direction.
[41] It was reconstructed in 1985-87 on the same site, using the original foundations. Cristian Cirici, Fernando Ramos and Ignasi Solà-Morales were the architects responsible for applying Mies van der Röhe's plans under the supervision of the MOMA.

the case of the Hotel Internacional built for the 1888 Exhibition, today it is impossible to understand how a building of such noteworthy intrinsic qualities could have been demolished.

Around this pavilion and among the great palaces, dozens of small buildings jostled for attention: firms such as Nestlé, Hispano Suiza, Aromas de Montserrat and Codorníu presented a direct image of their products, converted into macro-architecture.

A full account of the 1929 exhibition has to include three singular facts that underpinned its spectacular nature: the "Pueblo español" or Spanish village, the sporting and recreational activities and the lighting.

The Spanish Village was one of the main attractions; although it had a precedent in the 1900 Paris Exhibition, in Barcelona it became a fine art. An area of 20,000 m^2 was built under the direction of the architect Francesc Folguera, with the collaboration of Ramon Raventós and the draughtsmen Miguel Utrillo and Xavier Nogués.[42] It was a collection of Spanish urban architecture and spaces brought together in a unique project. With the assistance of the Mas Archive and trips to the original sites, the team was able to produce an extremely interesting synthesis of such characteristic spaces as the town square, the monastery, the streets of artisans, the town walls, the church square, etc., and to insert the most miscellaneous buildings into this structure by adjusting and distorting their scale for inclusion in a new project. Interesting reproductions of famous stairways, colonnades and pavements produced a false object, but it was a singular product within the overall exhibition, because unlike so many hypotheses of architectural collage used as a stage set, the Spanish Village was designed as a small functional complex.[43]

Another interesting fact about the 1929 Exhibition was the inclusion of sporting and recreational activities, as a spectacle in the case of some lesser known sports such as "tennis", or as a mass activity in others, such as swimming. The emblematic building was the stadium designed by Pere Domènech i Roura, with capacity for 62,000 spectators and Gargallo's sculptures, an equestrian group, to enhance the marathon gateway. The more cultural recreational activities were represented in the Teatre Grec amphitheatre and the Projection Hall.

[42] See Josep Maria Rovira: *Arquitectura catalana de la modernidad*. UPC, Barcelona, 1987.
[43] The Village still exists and since its recent rehabilitation has become a tourist attraction of the first order.

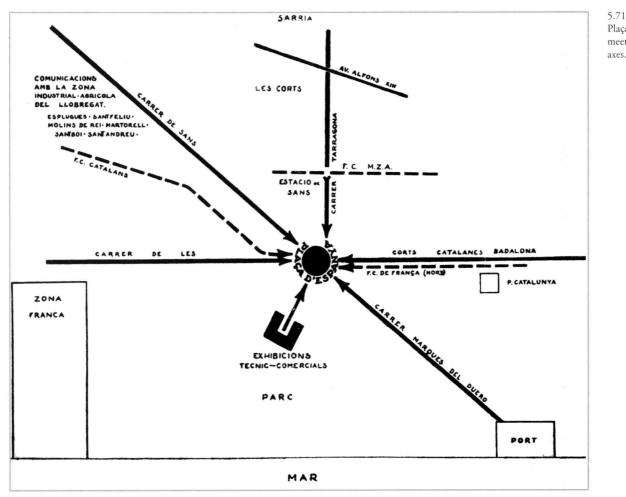

5.71
Plaça d'Espanya, the difficult meeting point of three urban axes.

But the star product of the image of '29 was the spectacular lighting of the buildings and fountains, which led to it being called the "magical exhibition". The same technique was used as had been employed in Paris in 1925 to outline the Eiffel Tower in neon. This time, the project carried out by the engineer Carles Buïgas and the Westinghouse technicians was to delight visitors and the people of Barcelona alike.[44] From behind the National Palace emerged great beams of light that inverted the shape and shadows of the building, making it seem to float in the air. The central or magic fountain was made up of hundreds of nozzles to spray water, giving the light a whole new form of expression: its movements were controlled, and light and image followed the rhythm of the music. Finally, at Forestier's suggestion the Gran Avenida was lined by lights popularly known as "asparagus shoots", which were reflected in the pools of water that gradually climb the slope of this central axis.

---

[44] See the leaflet *Fuentes luminosas.* Ajuntament de Barcelona, 1972.

V.12 From Plaça d'Espanya to the river Llobregat

For Barcelona, 1929 was the year of the Electrical Industries Exhibition, but it was also a time of major changes in the international arena and for the new political dynamic of the 1930s.

As regards the city's urban development, the exhibition had made an impression that was to last a long time. The city's finances were in a serious state and received harsh criticism, but Barcelona had been given a new lease of life, and the mountain of Montjuïc began to be used by the general public and become irreplaceable as an urban park: the mountain's oppressive image had been erased, though the castle was not to give in to the city until the 1960s.

Furthermore, the dynamic of the exhibition had spread to a good many urban agents, mainly public corporations and institutions that were firmly set on bringing about urban improvement.

Thus many of the city's representative buildings were remodelled or rehabilitated: the Council itself rebuilt some sites and Josep Maria Sert painted the Hall of Chronicles, telling in epic tones of sepia and gilt the

5.75
Project for the layout
of Avenida 14 de Abril
(Diagonal).

5.76
Construction westward of the
Diagonal.

expeditions of the Almogavars. Elements of the Generalitat Palace (the Diputación or Provincial Council at the time) were reconstructed and the controversial, eye-catching bridge was built over Carrer del Bisbe to the Canons' House. The Captaincy General in the port was remodelled by Florensa and the Post Office building by Goday. The Estació de França station changed its configuration completely to acquire the structure of an important terminus in keeping with the scale of city it served. Pedro Muguruza and Duran Reynals were the men behind this new building overlooking the avenue, with its great four-domed foyer.[45]

While urbanisation work on the city was stepped up, the Parks Service had undertaken some of the internal elements it had programmed, such as three squares: Letamendi, Urquinaona and Tetuán. The urbanisation of some principal elements such as the Pont de Marina bridge, the Passeig Torras i Bages in Sant Andreu and the Saló de Sant Joan in the Eixample went ahead thanks to the dynamic established by the New Town Commission. Plaça de Catalunya acquired its definitive form with a project by Francesc de Paula Nebot, completed in 1925, after years of debate about the project begun by Puig i Cadafalch in 1918. This nodal point in the city, a meeting point between the old city and the Eixample, is the symbol of a disproportionate contrast between its functional and symbolic value as the communications centre of Barcelona and Catalonia, and the indecisiveness of the urban projects drafted for it, and is perhaps still an ongoing theme for debate.

The Exhibition certainly meant good prospects for two large sectors in the west of the city, Diagonal and Plaça d'Espanya, which went on to be protagonists in contemporary Barcelona. In the post-war years, Diagonal was to extend westwards to join up with Esplugues and create a great hundred-metre broad boulevard that enhanced the properties of the big landowning families, such as the Güells and the Gironas. In fact it was the Güells who offered the estate of today's Royal Palace, which, duly remodelled by Eusebi Bona and landscaped by Rubió i Tudurí, acted as the residence of the King and Queen during the Exhibition.

The initial colonisation of this territorial axis marked out the arrangement of future residential developments in the sector, as we will later see.

Plaça d'Espanya, on the other hand, materialised with the development of the exhibition. It took the form of a ring comprising Puig i Cadafalch's colonnade on the Montjuïc side and a series of brick-built constructions designed by Rubió i Tudurí as exhibition hotels.

[45] The building of the train terminal underwent further rehabilitation to bring it up to date in the Olympic year of 1992.

77
[Ru]bió i Tudurí's futuristic city:
[gr]eat buildings along the river
[Ll]obregat.

Entrance to the Gran Avenida was marked by two brick propylaea in the style of the campaniles of Saint Mark's in Venice. This axis was completed by the central fountain designed by Jujol, a powerful organisational element. The configuration of the square took into account the only pre-existing building, Las Arenas bullring, which had to change its entrance due to the new gradient created by the final urbanisation of the square. Despite the presence of the two coexisting orders in the layout, it is one of the city's few squares to have a well-defined image.

The consolidation of Plaça d'Espanya as a new centre signposted expansion towards the Llobregat delta and the lower part of Hospitalet. A considerable number of projects addressed this city sector: the competition for the free port in 1930, involving the extension of the port and an industrial area of almost one thousand hectares; Puig Gairalt's plan for Hospitalet using a mixed system of residential types, the subject of debate for both the GATCPAC and Le Corbusier's minimum dwelling project. In any case, *de facto* suburban growth followed the guidelines already marked out but with scant attention to any of these projects. However, the desire for a new tertiary centre was so explicit that Rubió i Tudurí designed a project in conjunction with Durán Reynalds to restructure the exhibition spaces as a strategic centre for the city.

The leaflet *La Plaça d'Espanya, centre actiu de Barcelona* [Plaça d'Espanya, the active centre of Barcelona][46] presented a proposal for skyscrapers of offices and dwellings on 8.5 hectares of the lower space of the exhibition plot beside the square.[47]

Rubió's conviction with regard to this axis led him to design futurist perspectives of great buildings beside the river Llobregat, drawn with heavy river traffic in the image of Hood's great American downtowns. This seems to be an accurate premonition to judge by the results of the Baix Llobregat urbanisation process, though it is unfortunately proving more controversial than any of the ideas put forward in the 1930s.

[46] Nicolau Maria Rubió i Tudurí: *La Plaça d'Espanya, centre actiu de Barcelona*. Barcelona, 1990.
[47] In 1935, this sector was the object of a series of proposals made by Folguera and Sert with the GATCPAC and Rubió himself. See Manuel Torras Capell *et al.: op. cit.*, 1988, p. 266.

I.

The Barcelona of a million inhabitants

VI.1 Metropolitan problems and the new social dynamic

The 1930s witnessed major transformations and new approaches in the territorial and urban realm. First of all, the city reached the figure of one million inhabitants in 1930, thereby psychologically joining the ranks of the big cities. But this also meant the attendant problems that big European cities suffer from: lack of residential space and facilities, a growing demand for transport, etc.

At the same time, the international panorama was marked by the economic crisis of the Great Depression, which was compromising expectations of industrial development and trade.

This period saw a major increase in the participation of the masses in Catalan political life, particularly in the city of Barcelona. Large sectors of the working and artisan classes became involved in political and social life. The elections at the turn of the century had reported an electoral roll of just 20% of the population; in 1933, the census represented 60% of the entire population and effective participation was verging on two-thirds, which was a very significant percentage.

Barcelona had closed the 1929 exhibition; despite the many difficulties it had entailed, it served to promote westward urban development. However, the economic exertion represented by the initiative had taken its toll on municipal finances. The Council budget for 1930 included an outstanding debt of 44% of the overall budget.[1]

Added to this situation, the urban model supported by the industrial bourgeoisie during earlier decades had not resolved the major needs for infrastructure and facilities required by the growth of migration. The housing problem, as we will go on to see, was joined by those of schools, hospitals, etc. Although these issues had been the subject of intense cultural and social concern – with some initially satisfactory results – they fell a long way short of the massive scope required by the metropolitan scale.

Now, in the thirties, political changes came energetically to the fore and created a platform for discussion of new models of city and territorial organisation. With the proclamation of the Second Republic in 1931, after the triumph of the left in the municipal elections and the restoration to government of the Generalitat de Catalunya, emerging metropolitan problems were to received renewed attention.

Previously, the social and political model had been dictated by farming and industrial forces;[2] now, in 1930, new prospects began to emerge, at least in the early years, and most particularly within the Catalan

[1] Francesc Roca: "Primer, importem; després, exportem. La política urbana, 1917-1939", *Homage to Barcelona*. Barcelona, 1987.
[2] Francesc Roca: *Planificación territorial en Catalunya (1901-1939)*. Ciudad y territorio, Madrid, 1975. It includes Joaquim Maurín's opinion of 1932: "from 1874 to 1917, for almost half a century, Spain has been trampled by the heavy boots of the Andalusian boyars and the Castilian hidalgos." Roca continues: "After 1917, 'boyars' and 'hidalgos' were joined by 'industrialists'. While the territorial policy of the agrarians consisted in defending – and sometimes revaluating – land ownership (agrarian and urban), the industrialists had a very different overall proposal: they sought to transform general production conditions in order to favour the process of accumulation." p. 63.

6.02
Our skyscrapers by Gabriel Casas, 1930.

6.03
Photomontage of the Gothic Quarter by the Sociedad de Atracción de Forasteros, 1935

borders. In this period, discussion of the territorial structure and the deployment of the work of the GATCPAC[3] were illustrative of a dynamic that, with avant-garde artistic components, verged on urban utopia, particularly due to the renovation represented by the alternative models that this group of artists and technicians promoted.

This innovative cultural trend had come to the fore in the final years of the previous decade: during the 1929 exhibition the Galerías Dalmau had shown a compendium of works of modern architecture and a version of Barcelona that was clearly an alternative to the official one presented in the City of Barcelona pavilion. This was the work of young architects who then joined together to form the GATCPAC. Then the decidedly futurist Yellow Manifesto, written by Dalí, Montanyà and Gasch, represented a challenge to the decadent official culture. It practically amounted to a Dadaist manifesto calling for a new attitude in the era of modern production means and criticising institutionalised, traditionalist Catalan culture. In 1929, *Un chien andalou* was premiered in Paris to great acclaim; this film with its extremely innovative content was directed by Buñuel with the assistance of Dalí and filmed in Cadaqués. These were some of the signs of the changes that were to occur in the course of the thirties.

The ADLAN (Amics de l'Art Nou – Friends of the New Art) was created in 1932; this artistic association represented the formation in Barcelona of a surrealist group, backed by Joan Miró and with a degree of

[3] GATCPAC (Group of Catalan Artists and Technicians for the Programme of Contemporary Architecture), a Catalan group under the umbrella of the Spanish group GATEPAC. For their work, see *AC/GATEPAC 1931-37*. Facsimile re-issue. Gustavo Gili, Barcelona, 1975.

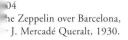

independence from the Paris movement.[4] The association grouped together avant-garde artists and intellectuals such as Salvador Dalí, Josep Lluís Sert, Joan Prats, Joan Miró and Joaquim Gomis, among others, and even Federico García Lorca on his visits to Barcelona.

VI.2 Regional planning in Catalonia

The strong dynamic of urban and industrial growth implicitly involved reflection on a larger scale than that of the city. The phenomenon of suburbanisation went beyond the limits of Barcelona and reached the perimeter of what in the 1950s was to be known as the *comarca*, or county, of Barcelona. Industrial development had specific needs that called for a strategy to transform the territory, creating a distribution that would make it more rational from a production point of view; this involved the electrification of the railways, river valleys used as sites for industrial colonies, and so forth.

Ideas for the structural organisation of the Catalan territory became an everyday thing in the 1930s, though evidently based on existing hypotheses mainly formulated during the period of the Mancomunitat.

[4] See the monographic issue of *Cuadernos*, "ADLAN. Testimonio de una época". Barcelona, 1970. Published on the occasion of the exhibition at the COAC organised by J. Corredor Matheos, S. Gasch, J. Molas and C. Rodríguez-Aguilera, on the theme of the mutual influence of the ADLAN and the GATCPAC. Also the excellent catalogue of the exhibition *Avantguardes a Catalunya. 1906-1939*. Barcelona, 1992.

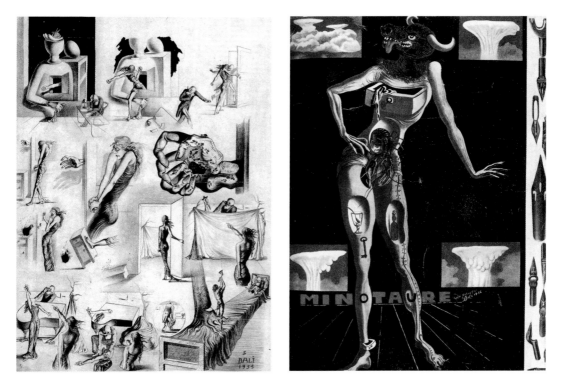

6.05, 6.06
Treatment for a screenplay,
1935. and cover of the
Minotaur by Salvador Dalí,
1926-1927.

There were two basic documents informing this situation: the *Regional Planning* document of 1932 and the *Territorial Division of Catalonia* of 1936.

Regional Planning[5] was drafted by the Rubió i Tudurí brothers in 1931-1932 as a general attempt to zone the Catalan territory. It sought firstly to protect the most attractive landscapes and natural areas and, secondly, to assign specific functional contents to certain territorial sectors with a view to reducing imbalances.

This idea of zoning or planning the territory had been advocated by Cebrià de Montoliu, whom Nicolau Maria Rubió i Tudurí succeeded as president of the Societat Cívica Ciutat Jardí. The idea of redressing the territorial balance by means of planned interventions also had an obvious precedent in the work of the Mancomunitat de Catalunya. In its Six-year Plan, dated 1920, the Commonwealth had launched a series of special programmes with a view to reducing existing imbalances.

In 1920, Nicolau Maria Rubió himself had appealed to the Mancomunitat for the need for a Catalan regional plan to organise Catalan territory in the same way that a city was planned.[6] The Mancomunitat was by no means unaware of these arguments, as its tremendous concern with the transformation of the territory showed.

[5] Nicolau Maria and Santiago Rubió i Tudurí: *Regional Planning. El Pla de distribució de zones del territori català*. Generalitat de Catalunya, Barcelona, 1932. (Re-issued by Novatecnia, Barcelona, 1976).
[6] Rubió i Tudurí: *Regional Planning, op. cit.*, p. 81. "It is a question of considering that the region or nation is like a city, that the constructions built there, be they factories, houses, mines, etc., should last a long time, and that they should therefore be subject to planning regulations."

Zoning as a planning tool had been employed in the capital in the form of the 1927 ordinances that instituted a thorough classification of urban development (industrial, residential, mixed zones, etc.) along the lines of German patterns from the beginning of the century that had been implemented by famous urban planners such as Josep Stübben, who had visited Barcelona Council.

The Rubió i Tudurí brothers' *Regional Planning* was a preliminary plan for the distribution of zones and comprised a series of works and hypotheses that they had produced during their years of professional and theoretical experience.

The precedents they cited were American, particularly the Philadelphia Tri-State; Patrick Geddes' strong influence as a practical promoter of the garden city movement, and a champion of proposals for new towns in England; and Patrick Abercrombie, the first professor of urban planning at Liverpool University and founder of *The Town Planning Review*, who was to make his mark on this process. Another reference was the experience of Doctor Luther, of Essen, and his Ruhr Regional Plan, passed in 1920 by a special act.

The document was divided into 10 sections comprising 58 plans. The sections presented a judicious analysis of the country and included basic geographical maps, covering agriculture and stock-keeping; mining; natural resources; industries; commercial and sea ports; major regional traffic; monuments and archaeological reserves; natural beauty and tourism, and health and culture.

After these analytical summaries, the Rubió i Tudurís addressed structural ideas to enable the Regional Plan to overcome the detached superposition of partial statistical studies. Of note among these ideas was the combination of industrialisation and farming, shunning the "furious industrialisation" that threatened to put paid to much of the country's natural beauty; and the decentralisation of Barcelona in order to construct what they referred to as "Catalonia-City" in which "Barcelona is no more than a great district".

6.a The 1932 Regional Plan.

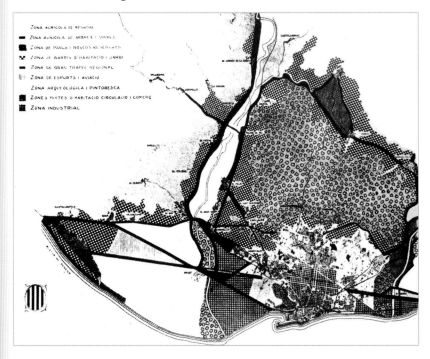

6.09
Zoning of the Barcelona area.

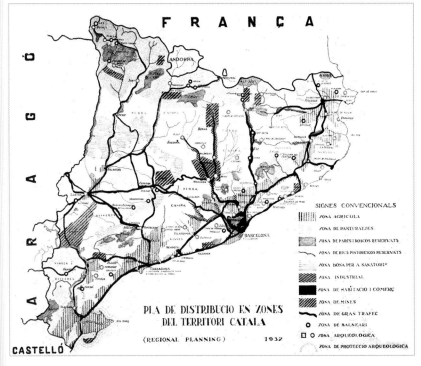

6.10
Plan for the distribution into zones of Catalan territory.

37 Territorial Division Plan.

Regional Planning concludes with an example, "the Barcelona region", by means of which the authors endeavoured to apply the ideas expounded. At the end, the document called itself a non-definitive project that required the addition of a decision-making and administrative process as an open, living plan; to this end, they proposed the creation of a Regional Plan Service to facilitate the development of such a process.

The Territorial Division of Catalonia[7] is another fundamental work to the structuring of Catalan territory; it stemmed from a commission by the Generalitat de Catalunya in 1930 to a team led by the distinguished Catalan geographer Pau Vila i Dinarès[8] to draw up a territorial division of Catalonia on the basis of scientific and political criteria.

The purpose of the spatial organisation was to ensure the efficient functioning of public services, particularly administration, and the Commission was requested that the "parts" of the division not be too numerous, with similar surface areas and populations. According to this document, at that time Catalonia had a population of 2,920,748 inhabitants and a surface area of 32,049 kilometres, representing an average density of 91 inhabitants per square kilometre, and included 1,070 municipalities within its borders.

[7] Conselleria d'Economia: *La divisió territorial de Catalunya.* Generalitat de Catalunya, Barcelona, 1937.
[8] Among his various works, see Pau Vila: *La fesonomia geogràfica de Catalunya.* Comissariat de Propaganda, Generalitat de Catalunya, Barcelona, 1937, and *La divisió territorial de Catalunya.* Curial, Barcelona, 1977. See also the prologue by Lluís Casassas that so judiciously sets the figure of Pau Vila in the Catalan geographical movement.

The division was drawn up on the basis of a survey of the municipalities, a comprehensive study of Catalonia's economic and social reality, and an excellent appraisal of the history of the political and administrative distribution of Catalonia.

The Territorial Division proposed 9 regions and 38 *comarques*, or counties, of roughly equal surface area. Each municipality was assigned to a *comarca* and, from then on, was dependent for administrative matters on the new county town.

The purpose of the *comarca* was to clarify and, henceforth, it became associated with Catalan identity. The definition of the *comarques* was based on a synthesis of a geographical approach, closely linked to the territory, and the urban polarities implanted in it; and based on market relations and the existing communications network.

But above all, the document offered an interesting synthesis of the "old territorial divisions", on which it most specifically insisted. These included the medieval division into *vegueries* established in the late 13th century and introduced under Jaume I, and continued until the imposition of the *corregimientos* in the time of Felipe V and the Decreto de Nueva Planta.

For Pau Vila and Ignasi Iglesias' group, the concept of *comarca* never had the legal and administrative force of the *vegueria*, yet, within the possibilities of the territory and influenced by traditional links, the term *comarca* had been created according to an extension of territory that was rather imprecise but that adapted better to the needs and conveniences of everyday life: the *comarques*.[9]

This new distribution was seen as an alternative to the uniform division into provinces established by Napoleonic influence in the 1821 Cortes, when Catalonia was divided into four provinces, and Spain as a whole into fifty-one.

The Territorial Division was completed in 1933 and was implemented as an administrative structure after the events of 19 July 1936, when the Catalan Ministry of the Economy for the coordination of new economic decisions and territorial decentralisation adopted the division.[10]

---

[9] According to Pau Vila, in 1708 in "Descripción y planta del Principado de Cataluña", Josep Aparici wrote that "the best known division is that of the *comarca*, and he notes thirty".

[10] Josep M. Bricall: *Política econòmica de la Generalitat*. Edicions 62, Barcelona, 1970. Also, Francesc Artal, Emili Gasch, Carmen Massana and Francesc Roca: *El pensament econòmic català durant la república i la guerra (1931-39)*. Edicions 62, Barcelona, 1976.

12
"heap housing" quarter in
e neighbourhood of Baró de
ver, 1924.

VI.3 Accommodation as a problem in the modern city

High levels of migration in the first three decades of the century to industrial regions and particularly to Barcelona city were set to create a high housing demand that was not satisfied, and therefore spawned suburban forms and substandard housing.[11]

This heralded a new issue for the modern city: the suburb, which made its appearance in rapidly growing cities with few resources, to the point that these abnormal forms of urban fabric came to constitute a quantitatively dominant sector.

Production had received a boost as a result of World War I. The fragility of the Spanish industrial structure, masked by the country's wartime neutrality, became evident in the crisis of 1921.[12] However, expansion continued thanks to the support of effective protectionism and a thriving policy of public works.

In this period, Jutglar[13] highlights the evolution of annual average immigration in areas associated with Barcelona, from 3,400 inhabitants in the first decade of the 20th century to 20,000 inhabitants in the 1910-1920

[11] Reworked chapter from J. Busquets: *Urbanización marginal en Barcelona*. LUB, Barcelona, 1975. The analysis covers the first three decades of this century.

[12] On this subject there is a plentiful historical bibliography; see J. Vicens Vives: *Coyuntura económica y reformismo burgués*. Ariel, Barcelona, 1968.

[13] A. Jutglar: "Perspectiva històrica de la fenomenologia immigratòria a Catalunya", *La immigració a Catalunya*. Ed. de Materials, Barcelona, 1968.

6.13
Shanties provided a temporary
solution to an insufficient
housing supply.

period. This increase continued in the 1921-1929 period of public works (the Metro and the Great Exhibition in Barcelona) with an annual average of between 25 and 30,000 immigrants.

The majority of this migratory wave gravitated to Barcelona capital, due to its greater job opportunities and the difficulties in other places of fast transport. Towns close to the capital suffered the induced dynamic of the city's growth and because optimum locations for industrial decentralisation involving companies that were less competitive with regard to the workforce, which was protected and provided with accommodation.[14] The consequences of this type of growth affected mainly the old town.

It is difficult to imagine how Barcelona capital absorbed this notable increase in residential space arising from a very specific demand: immigration. We will go on to outline how this demand was "satisfied", but first let us look at the measures taken by the public or corporate sector and the availability of housing for immigrant labour.

From the Decree of 31 July 1813, backed by the liberal spirit of the Cortes of Cadiz, until the 1920 Bugallal Decree, complete freedom reigned with regard to the contracting of rents in urban property (a position established in 1843). In this situation of an apparently well-balanced market, the country reached the early decades of the 20th century with a highly precarious accommodation situation for the working classes. "There is no doubt about it, the corridor houses of Madrid, Barcelona's shanties and Seville's shacks offered their tenants comparable conditions to those of the European proletariat at the most relentless moments of the 'Industrial Revolution'."[15]

[14] Some workers' colonies in the *comarca* of Barcelona were formed in this way.

[15] For an analysis of the situation in this period, in the publication of his doctoral thesis, see A. Cotorruelo: *La política económica de la vivienda en España*. CSIC, Madrid, 1966.

14
shanty district on Eixample
nd.

This ongoing situation called for the attention of the authorities, which can be divided into two types: 1) **advisory**; for example in 1853 the Ministry of Government urged the Councils of Madrid and Barcelona to construct low-rent houses for the poor in outlying districts; and 2) **incentive-based**: in the form of the 1888 and 1892 Acts, and such diverse legislation as the Low-cost Housing Act of 12 July 1911. Although this legislation lacked in efficiency, it represented the start of direct state intervention in the problems of worker accommodation.

Its insufficiency was corrected by the Low-cost Housing Act of 1921 and then, during the Dictatorship, with an increase in incentives in the form of Decree-Law of 1924 and 1925.[16]

Although the housing problem was considered to be very serious,[17] the policy of low-price housing produced scant results up until the time of the Dictatorship since its developments covered, almost exclusively, the needs of a few chosen sectors and not exactly the most needy ones – for example, the houses in La Salud and Horta for journalists. It did increase under the Dictatorship, though the housing demand was also higher. The Generalitat de Catalunya later constituted the Housing Commission, whose policies did not have sufficient time to prove their validity. The period described here did, then, represent incipient attention on the part of the state to the housing problem, despite its scant effects. Another complementary measure was the Bugallal Decree (1920), which initiated the rent freeze.[18]

---

[16] F. López Valencia: *El problema de la vivienda en España*. Ministerio de Trabajo y Previsión, Madrid, 1929.
[17] As C. Massana notes (1971) in an analysis of "Los Anuarios Estadísticos de la Ciudad de Barcelona (1902-1923) y el socialismo municipal". *Cuadernos*, no. 80. Barcelona.
[18] See Miquel Domingo and Ferran Sagarra's compendium: *Barcelona. Les cases barates*. Barcelona, 1999.

Forms of substandard housing

What, then, was the answer to the demand for accommodation generated by the high levels of migration in this period? It took an anomalous form with regard to the usual types of residential growth in the city. On the one hand, the typical apartment house of the liberal period of the second half of the 19th century was feeling the effects of the rent freeze, and at the same time rents were excessively high and inaccessible in relation to the wages of the economically weaker classes; a similar evaluation could be made of the garden city proposals made at the time and the suburban dwellings subject to ground rent; and low-price housing was not yet mass produced. Given this situation, the most common forms of "accommodation" were:

a) **"dosshouses"**. This was generally the solution for workers without families who were offered a bed in common dormitories at a very low cost. This was the most flexible form of "accommodation" for the immigrant without regular work, but the hygienic conditions of these "pensions" left much to be desired.[19] Furthermore, at times of peak immigration or job shortages, a considerable number of immigrants were obliged to sleep in the open. Under this "accommodation" heading, the municipal dormitories were a more rationalised version of the dosshouses.

b) the **densification** of certain sectors of Barcelona's **old town** and the annexed centres (Sants, Sant Andreu, Poblenou, etc.), and the building of complementary constructions with a view to letting them to immigrant families or, principally, sharing houses. According to E. Lluch,[20] the capital's **subtenants** in 1927 numbered 100,000 people. The studies carried out by the GATCPAC and reproduced in *A.C.* review in relation to district V bore witness to the dreadful conditions of these dwellings.[21]

c) the **barraca, or shanty**, in Barcelona (a type of accommodation known as *chabola* in the rest of Spain). These were very precarious constructions built using waste materials (reeds, pieces of wood and tin, etc.) with a very small surface area and minimum stability. They usually had a single interior space, mostly with no divisions, where all the functions of the family or resident group were carried out. Short-lived constructions did exist in isolation, but the most usual version was the formation of districts comprising a hundred or so shanties, on average. Some such examples were Somorrostro and Pekín by the sea in the Poblenou area, inhabited at the start

[19] A description of the city in a magazine of the period (*Barcelona-Atracción*) notes: "This city has a series of 'private houses' where, for a small sum, they provide (...) beds, houses which, we might add as an aside, ought for the most part to disappear due to lack of hygiene and morality..."

[20] E. Lluch: "La vivienda", *Promos* no. 43. Barcelona, 1966.

[21] There is a summary in *A.C.* nos. 6 and 25. Barcelona, 1937.

15
Plan showing "Satalia",
Montjuïc.

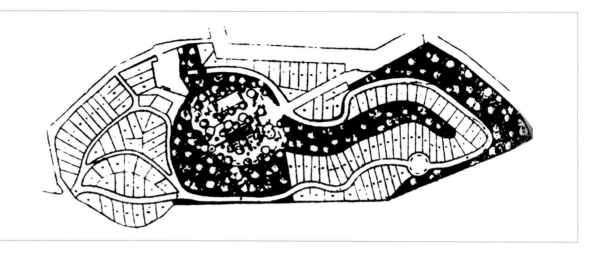

.16
Marginal, self-constructed
lot divisions began in the
periphery.

of the century by people who worked in professions related to the sea. The founding of the Pekín district dates from the late 19th century; its name was taken from the first people to settle there, who were Chinese. The change in residents and functional role of these districts has been very variable.

High immigration was accompanied by an appreciable growth in shantytowns. The press of the time described and commented on districts that appeared in La Llacuna, Floridablanca, Poble Sec, Can Tunis and Hostafrancs, among others. According to Rubió,[22] there were as many as 6,500 shanties in Barcelona in 1927, though other less formal sources give higher figures. The conditions of overcrowding, lack of services, poverty, and the terrible location of some districts on land prone to flooding, etc., were amply reflected in the material published at the time.

[22] Rubió i Tudurí: *La caseta i l'hortet i dos altres treballs*. Barcelona, 1933.

There were two main types of shanty district at this time: 1) those built on public land, where shanty-dwellers had a firm control of their dwellings and very high possibilities of individual transactions. In these cases, the Council merely collected a small sum by way of rates or taxes, and on repeated occasions attempted to eliminate them. They were grouped to form narrow alleyways with a very compact organisation. Accommodation in "caves" dug into sloping land could be converted into shanties. Their layout was very closely linked to the morphology of the terrain on which they were sited; 2) those built on private property, where users' control of the shanty was generally more limited. They paid a daily rent which was collected regularly by force, and anyone failing to pay was physically expelled from the shanty the following morning. They were laid out around the patio,[23] where the few poorly equipped communal places were situated.

This situation was accompanied by endless articles, lectures and discussions on the subject, either reporting the tasks of charitable social boards, calling for improvements (installation of drainage, drinking fountains, etc.) or condemning the profit being made at the cost of the shanty-dwellers.

The Council, too, issued orders and prohibitions[24] but with minimal effectiveness; the shantytown was a consolidated phenomenon that accompanied the economic development of the time. The most radical condemnation that appeared in the press generally took the form of impassioned reports based on a concept of ideal city where there was no room for shanties, which were a problem to be wiped out, dissociated from the social relations of which they formed part and the alternatives on offer. In this context, the shanty districts grew and were constantly renewed, disappearing only as a result of Council action in relation to conflicts with major public operations, such as the destruction of the shanties in Carrer Floridablanca for the 1929 exhibition and around the Jaume I barracks, or in order to improve hygiene and prevent the propagation of infections, etc.

d) The first **self-built** plots or illegal urbanisations appeared in around 1910 in the areas of La Trinitat, El Carmel and some sectors of the Muntanya Pelada, among others. This involved the sale of plots of unurbanised land for very low sums, with no provision of utilities, where the buyers gradually built themselves very modest and quite illegal dwellings. This typology subsisted in some areas with larger buildings that were used as weekend residences.

[23] For example in the shantytown between the streets of Floridablanca, Viladomat and Entença, there were at least five "patios" (del Alcalde, del Carboner, del Calderer, de la Gallega, dels Gitanos).

[24] One such dated 1904 gave shanty owners three days to "destroy those foul dwellings, constructed without permission", giving them notice that otherwise the Council would undertake to do it and the shanty dwellers would have to meet the cost. On another occasion, a different mayor absolutely prohibited the use of shanties as dwellings, ordering owners to shut them up and the municipal police force to prevent anyone entering them.

7
e Barcelona urban system,
30s.

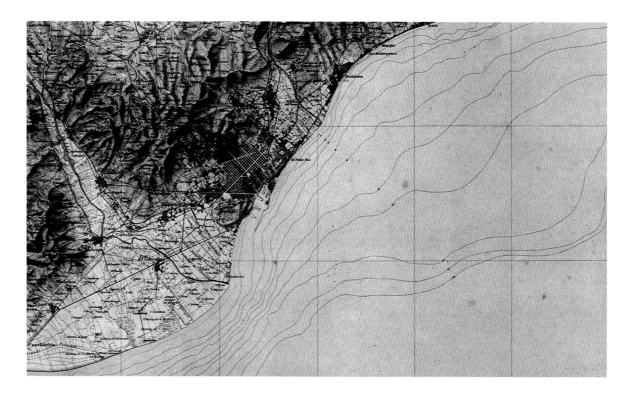

This represented the occupation and construction of very isolated fragments of land with poor building conditions. In some areas, development masqueraded as the sale of plots for weekend vegetable gardens and, as we will go on to see, the first tool shed turned out to be the "home" of the family who had bought the plot.

The public repercussions of this phenomenon in the period described were much lower than in the case of the shanties. In general, it was limited to newspaper reports denouncing the state of abandonment of these areas. One example, a broad-based report, is the series of articles with graphic documentation, by +F. Dalmases Gil in May 1913; under the title of "Peor que en el Rif" [Worse than in the Rif], it described the situation of the slum of El Carmel.[25] It tells in great detail of the dangers of walking through the district's "streets" due to their terrible condition and goes on to state the situation of illegality with regard to planning permission and the lack of urban infrastructure.[26] It traced the problem back to the lack of services provided in the area on the part of the Barcelona authorities and called for intervention with a view to remedying this lack.

The importance accorded to the appearance of these districts was, then, limited on the one hand to calls for urbanisation and, on the other, to recognition of them as dwellings that were developed and administered by the users themselves. At this point, there was no critical appraisal of the city that was being created in this way.

[25] Published in *Las Noticias.*
[26] With regard to these last two themes it describes, firstly, the case of one local resident who: "Wishing to build on a plot that belonged to him, went to the Council offices to apply for permission and be informed of the lines of gradient and façade. The municipal employees, after consulting a good many maps, declared that the street in question did not exist, nor had a plan of the district been accepted by the municipal corporation." With regard to the state of the district, it read: "There is no lighting, no sewerage network, nor any trace of urbanisation. It is evident that there is no health or social service, no clinic and no policing."

VI.4 The GATCPAC and the functional city

A group of Catalan architects comprising Josep Lluís Sert, Josep Torres Clavé, Ricard Churruca, Germà Rodriguez Arias, Pere Armengou and Sixt Illescas, among others, set up the GATCPAC,[27] which, together with other regional groups, principally in Madrid and San Sebastian, constituted the GATEPAC (Group of Spanish Artists and Technicians for the Promotion of Contemporary Architecture) in Saragossa in October 1930. One of the larger group's most important agreements was the decision to publish a quarterly review, *A.C.* (Actividad Contemporánea – Contemporary Activity), of which 25 issues were published between 1931 and 1937. The Catalan group was responsible for both organising and producing the review. Once again, Catalan identity seemed to act as a differential fact that encouraged a feeling of solidarity in this group of young architects committed to a common cause.

This, then, was the first and very forceful instance of an avant-garde artistic group being created to debate architecture and the contemporary city. There had been brilliant precedents in the worlds of painting and literature in the first two decades of the century (after 1912, Barcelona had hosted exhibitions by Gris and Léger), but curiously the major architectural advances in Europe scarcely altered or influenced the eclectic trends prevailing in our city.[28]

Now, not only was the transformation set to be a big one, it would also influence the international debate: Le Corbusier became a more frequent visitor, both to Barcelona after 1928[29] and to Spain, thanks mainly to Sert[30], and in 1932 Barcelona hosted the preparatory meeting of the 4th CIRPAC Congress,[31] which was supposed to be held in Moscow but ultimately took place on board the packet boat "Patris II", which set sail from Marseilles in late July 1933 headed for Athens, returning to the same French city on 15 August.

This Congress, patently directed by Le Corbusier and with the active contributions of Sert, Torres and Bonet, primarily addressed the "Functional city". Thirty or so of the world's cities came under study, with observation of their historical formation processes and the new problems created by mechanisation and traffic circulation. The city's principal "functions" were outlined, namely: 1) habitation, 2) leisure activity, 3) work, and 4) circulation.

[27] Oriol Bohigas: "Homenaje al GATEPAC", *Cuadernos de Arquitectura* no. 40. Barcelona, 1960 and *Arquitectura española de la Segunda República*. Tusquets ed., Barcelona, 1970. Also Various authors: "GATCPAC 1" and "GATCPAC 2", new monographic publications of *Cuadernos de Arquitectura y Urbanismo* nos. 90 and 94. Barcelona, 1972 and 1973. They include a series unpublished works about the GATCPAC archives that have been available for consultation at the History Archive of the COAC since 1971.

[28] Ignasi de Solà-Morales: "GATEPAC: Vanguardia arquitectónica y cambio político". Prologue to the re-issue of *AC/GATEPAC 1931-37*. Gustavo Gili, Barcelona, 1975.

[29] Various authors: *Le Corbusier y Barcelona*. Fundació Caixa Catalunya, Barcelona, 1989.

[30] The international profile of the GATCPAC is important for its coverage in innovative journals of the time, such as *De 8 en opbow*, Amsterdam.

6.b The Macià Plan, the GATCPAC's "New Barcelona", 1934.

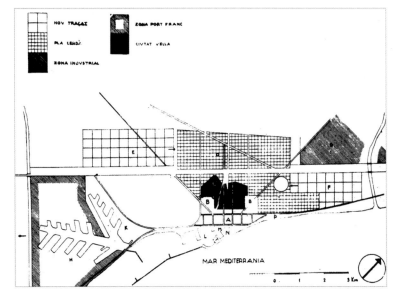

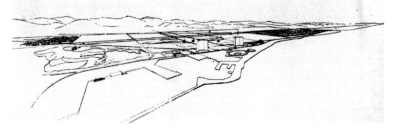

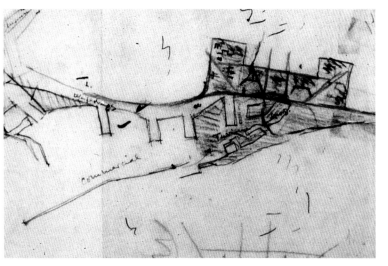

Each of these functions was analysed in great detail at the Congress, highlighting the most salient defects in each of the cities. The CIRPAC defined a series of principles to correct these dysfunctions. These principles compiled the famous Charter of Athens, which became practically the Bible of functionalist architects.

These discussions were reflected in issue 12 of *A.C.*, explaining both the general requirements of the city and each of the elements – the functions – that made up the "Functional city". These criteria were later applied to Barcelona in the form of the Macià Plan.

A.C. was a faithful reflection of the ideas and activity of the avant-garde movements of that decade and exceptionally published a series of almost monographic issues to present "contemporary urban planning". The public school, the history of the bathroom, the minimum hygienic dwelling and open spaces were some of the themes set forward with a critical viewpoint but also with convincing arguments in favour of the new models. The GATCPAC was basically convinced that "art is capable of changing urban lifestyles" and a great deal of ingenuity and enthusiasm was invested in this end. The fundamental leitmotif of *A.C.* was innovation in design and in the resulting form of modern architecture, giving rise to demands for different administrative mechanisms that did not yet exist in the early 1930s.

The new guiding principles for architecture and the city project were simplicity and economy: urban problems had reached such dimensions that their solution called for the marked priority of serialised production, improved hygiene and the judicious use of natural spaces. Hence the rejection of specious aesthetic speculation, which was seen as superfluous and contradictory.

Both in stance and format, *A.C.* followed the guidelines of *Das Neue Frankfurt*, a magazine that had promoted residential renewal in post-war Germany in the previous decade.[32]

In addition, the analysis of the problems facing the city of Barcelona and the projects that sought to resolve them began to appear regularly in *Arquitectura Contemporánea*. Some of them, such as the "Notas previas a un estudio urbanístico de Barcelona" [Preliminary notes for an urban planning study of Barcelona] gave widespread coverage of the principal contents that were presented systematically and comprehensively in the Macià Plan.

---

[31] CIRPAC: Comité international pour la réalisation des problèmes d'architecture contemporaine.

[32] Between 1926 and 1930, the architects Ernest May and Fritz Wichert published *Das Neue Frankfurt* magazine that published new concerns and social housing projects being carried out in the city. This was one of the most innovative urban development processes in Europe, producing such important residential complexes as Römerstadt (completed in 1928) and influencing both new residential typologies and new ways of designing dwellings. See for example its studies of the rationalisation of the kitchen. Berlin, at the hands of Martin Wagner, was another proposed paradigm for the modern city.

32 Macià Plan.
w 400 x 400 module.

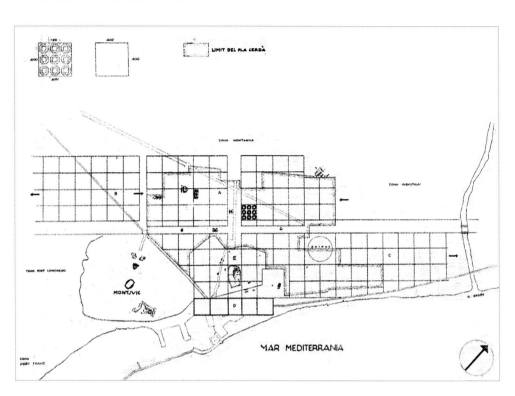

VI.5 The Macià Plan and Le Corbusier

The Macià Plan, or the plan for the "New Barcelona" was the GATCPAC's most ambitious project for our city. It laid down an alternative or critical urban planning strategy with regard to the models that had guided Barcelona's spurt of growth at the start of the century.[33]

In this respect, the GATCPAC was absolutely opposed to the urban model represented in the City Pavilion at the 1929 exhibition, where "Urban development in the Barcelona Plain", according to an outline prepared by Rubió i Tudurí, was directed towards the interior hinterland, by means of the suburban mechanisms of "caseta i l'hortet" – a little house and garden, the Catalan version of the English garden city – and the reform of Ciutat Vella was envisaged on the basis of new axes in the Baixeras Plan (according to which Arteries C and A, Avinguda de la Catedral and Avinguda Drassanes had yet to be constructed). The GATCPAC sought to avoid the patterns that had been at work in the city for several decades and set out to establish a policy of integrated action for Ciutat Vella, involving the effective airing of its residential fabric in order to create lower density. This was a constant theme in *A.C.*

The Macià Plan, meanwhile, found its analytical basis in more precise, advanced information sources:[34] these included the new "Martorell Plan" maps drawn up in 1923. They featured new aerial views of the city, both

[33] Francesc Roca: *El Pla Macià: de la Gross-Barcelona al Pla Comarcal.* Edicions La Magrana, Barcelona, 1977.
[34] Salvador Tarragó: "El Pla Macià" and "La Nova Barcelona 1931-38". *Cuadernos de Arquitectura y Urbanismo* no. 90. Barcelona, 1972. Also the monographic issues of *Cuadernos de Arquitectura y Urbanismo* nos. 141 and 142, entitled *Homenatge a J. Torres Clavé.* Barcelona, 1980.

6.22
The Eixample, reinterpreted
according to the macroblock
the Sant Martí area.

photomaps and oblique flight views, which were used as working documents. It made confident reference to the demographic analyses of Josep Vandellós and municipal statistics from the Year book that had been published annually since 1902. Interpretations of the historical formation of the city had also been written by Durán i Sanpere, and by Sanpere i Miquel and Carreras Candi.

Furthermore, the monographic projects under way in the city were the object of careful study: the canalisation of the river Llobregat, the consolidation of the airport in the delta and the free port, according to the winning project by Blas Sorribas in the 1928 projects competition then being developed by the Free Zone Consortium. Altogether, they formed a veritable arsenal of systematised information to underpin planning hypotheses.

The intervention of Le Corbusier was key to the Macià Plan. This master of architecture had offered his collaboration back in 1928 on his first visit to Barcelona at the invitation of a group of young Catalan architects, including Josep Lluís Sert, who was later to work in his studio in Paris on the project for the Society of Nations.

Work on the Plan lasted from 1930 to 1934 and represented a process in which the Plan practically drafted itself. In theory, the municipal authorities had other ideas and constituted the Urban Planning Council, which commissioned Rubió i Tudurí, Adolfo Florensa and Vicens Martorell to come up with a comprehensive body of reflection about Barcelona and its future.[35]

The project for the "New Barcelona" gradually unfolded in the form of various themes and sectors that were published over time in A.C.: a historical interpretation of the city in 1931, the Recreation and Holiday Resort in 1932, etc.

The first interview between Le Corbusier and the President of the Generalitat, Macià, took place in 1932 thanks to the offices of Josep Lluís Sert. In 1933, Le Corbusier worked on much of the Plan in Paris while the GATCPAC concentrated on the rest in Barcelona. Finally, in July 1934, the Macià Plan was publicly exhibited in the gallery beneath Plaça de Catalunya.

---

[35] For the Macià Plan in the context of the CIAMs (Congrés Internationaux d'Architecture Moderne), see Eric Mumford: *The CIAM Discourse on Urbanism, 1928-1960.* Cambridge, 2000. See particularly pp. 66-73 where he describes in detail the project for Barcelona and the personal enthusiasm of Le Corbusier for the new Catalan situation.

3, 6.24, 6.25
e GATCPAC project
ablished the rationalisation
Ciutat Vella as a basic
ority.

The Plan's basic contents were contained in a series of interpretative plates about the city's historical development and the schematic scale proposal of the *comarca*, or county, of Barcelona.

The "Functional city" proposal classified the city according to the following areas:

a) an area of habitation, with dwellings and hotels;

b) a production area, with the port, industrial areas and the city;

c) a civic centre;

d) a recreational sector, with green and beach areas, and

e) traffic and circulation areas to interconnect the above.

The functional distribution of the areas was organised in accordance with the horizontal axis of Gran Via as a connective element in the Plain from the river Llobregat to the river Besòs. This axis was extended by the elimination of a street block in the Eixample to increase its capacity for restructuring. Particular emphasis was laid on two avenues of the existing road structure, Paral·lel and Meridiana, which crossed at the port to constitute the "City", the new strategic centre of Barcelona. A Y-shaped series of skyscrapers was posted in the lower area of

Ciutat Vella, presenting a new seafront image. During this period, Le Corbusier presented this paradigm solution for other port cities such as Algeria in 1931 and Buenos Aires in 1940; it was a generic solution for the new "City" – located at the gateway to the city, which was still the port – but with a specific formalisation in each city.

The Macià Plan, conversely, promoted the industrial area to the west behind Montjuïc, including a new free port to extend the city's production space. The coastal front was seen as a great resource that was exploited in the form of the project for Gavà and Castelldefels beaches.

Meanwhile, a distinction was made in the existing city between Ciutat Vella and Cerdà's Eixample. The first was addressed by major efforts in the field of sewerage systems and hygienic renovation. It was proposed that the more insalubrious areas of the old town be renovated to create green spaces and facilities such as public libraries, schools, clinics, etc.[36] This was certainly a justified obsession among the GATCPAC which had meticulously analysed the poor living conditions of most of the area's inhabitants, principally in the Barrio Chino, or the Raval. It was even said that President Companys, on the occasion of the exhibition of the Macià Plan, commented to Sert: "Take my word for it; if I could, I would knock it all down with canon fire."[37]

With regard to Cerdà's Eixample, the GATCPAC at all times respected the quality of the original project while repeatedly condemning the way in which the landowners had built up and blatantly misused such an interesting project.

In this case, the Macià Plan reinterpreted the Cerdà layout, seeking a superior hierarchy in the street system – the supergrid of three streets by three streets – in order to allow a more hygienic, less built-up form of construction.

In this way, in the parts of the Cerdà project that were not yet filled in, such as Poblenou and Sant Martí, a new, larger grid was proposed to restructure a layout that would include open construction according to the principles of the Ville Radieuse that Le Corbusier had just endorsed. The modern city required more space for traffic and the form of residence called for annexed spaces that would give it greater urban quality. The radical nature of these proposals must be seen to lie more in the comparison and contrast of models than in the hypothesis that a single pattern should be applied to resolve this area of the city.

Furthermore, a residential proposal of great interest came to the fore in the western sector, between Gran Via and the bottom sector of Hospitalet, above the free port.

---

[36] The GATCPAC itself, with a project by Sert, Torres and Subirana, constructed the Tuberculosis Clinic (1934-38) in the upper reaches of the old town as a critical contribution to improving the centre. This was one of its most innovative projects which, with the contrasts in its language of modern architecture highlighted the need for this rationalisation process.

[37] Quoted from Salvador Tarragó, *op. cit.*, 1972, p. 29, referring to the more insalubrious parts of the old town, particularly the Raval.

6.c Le Corbusier's low-cost residential expansion project: "for every house, a tree".

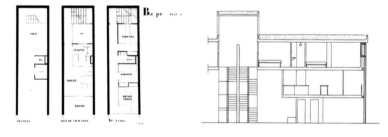

This was a project for low-rise, high-density minimum dwellings that Le Corbusier entitled "for every house, a tree", set in a supergrid generated on a scale with Cerdà's Plan. It seemed that discussions between the master and his young students produced an exceptional synthesis. Some members of the GATCPAC may have doubted the universal viability of the Ville Radieuse pattern for a population with limited resources, recently arrived from the countryside, and Le Corbusier reacted by producing a more piecemeal version of the city that would make for less traumatic urban insertion.[38]

Though unfortunately still not enacted, this project represented a real alternative to the residential peripheries that sprang up around Barcelona and so many other cities in the 1950s and '60s and is worthy of consideration in greater detail. A comprehensive interpretation of this project is still pending: the low-cost dwelling with communal services calls for relatively high density and is still needed in our context. It is not in vain that Le Corbusier seized this opportunity to propose its application: Barcelona was and still is a city that shares the conditions of all big cities and at the same time in its hinterland has had to deal with similar problems to cities with fast, congested development. The traditional models of modern dwellings – high-rise blocks or single-family homes – are antagonistic proposals that need to be reconciled: Le Corbusier's project offered a point of reflection that is still relevant today.

The suggested model of dwelling adopted the 400 x 400 metre module, corresponding to three by three complete street blocks in Cerdà's layout. On the basis of this unit, the district produces six groups of row houses with narrow facades, comprising a ground floor and two storeys. This scheme produced a density of over 60 dwellings per hectare, making it possible to calculate the optimum repercussion of the cost of urban services per house, with regard to both construction and maintenance.

This great macro-block was divided up into smaller units based on a very diffuse system of plot division: each house would have a façade of three and a half metres and a depth of four times this measurement. The function of the ground floor was open and undefined for the user to establish; the kitchen and sitting room were on the first floor, and the bedrooms and a bathroom on the second. The stairway at the rear of the plot facilitated cross ventilation and coolness in summer. The cost of the prototype was very reasonable, as the facings were structural elements of maximum simplicity.

The dwelling was the sum of three floors, of equal surface areas, making it highly adaptable to any changes the user wished to make. The complete integration of each house into the whole with regard to services and structure

---

[38] See Joan Busquets: "Cada casa un arbre, un model actual d'habitatge en el Pla Macià", *Le Corbusier y Barcelona*. Fundació Caixa Catalunya, Barcelona, 1989.

6.e Bloc House in Sant Andreu.

30
rspective of the GATCPAC's
oc House, 1932-1936.

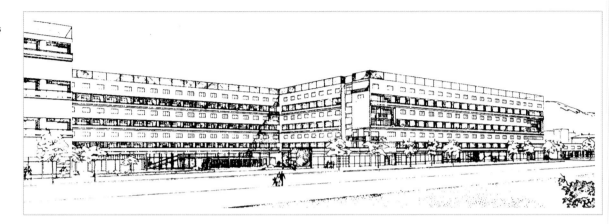

.31
xonometric of a housing
odule.

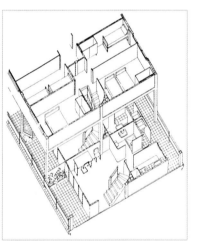

.32
resent-day photo of the
ehabilitated dwellings.

contrasts, then, with the great privacy enjoyed by each. The dwellings would share communal services distributed within the macro-block, and the urbanisation of the public spaces was complemented by the planting of a tree in front of each house to mark the plot division and provide a common element that changed in the course of the year to generate differing outward expressions.

The ambitious nature of this project, always associated with the idea of a provisional settlement, seems to substantiate the hypothesis of evolutive housing – that is, a process of construction over time – as a way of constructing cities that is absolutely necessary in countries with a rapid increase in urban population.

Le Corbusier, who had always championed high-rise construction with open spaces between blocks, found in Barcelona the need for a different arrangement.[39] He had always had recourse to the concrete structure, whereas here he accepted mixed construction systems; he had always designed model dwellings with definite spaces, and now he was presenting highly adaptable spaces. Barcelona was the context that suggested to him a new way of organising low-cost housing.

The very expression of the Barcelona housing model presents all the force of Le Corbusier's method. He taught us to use the aerial view – in this case axonometric – to interpret and design cities as of 1930. He said: "When the eye sees clearly, the spirit decides clearly." His admiration for technical inventions and particularly for the aeroplane allowed him to incorporate the general outline of the city in his working instruments.

VI.6 Bloc House and the Recreation and Holiday Resort

The series of proposals set forward by the Macià Plan has left us with a reflection of the "Functional city" in Barcelona and a series of planning experiences that signified the coming of age of modern architecture in our city.

Some of these episodes stand out for their lively proposals and the interest of their execution process. Bloc House, built in Sant Andreu opposite Avinguda Torras i Bages and commissioned by the Institute against Compulsory Unemployment is an interesting example of a high-density urban worker's dwelling (equivalent to 1,140 dwellings per hectare).

The site is elongated with its frontage on the avenue and is laid out in the form of a linear, shallow toothed construction to ensure good sunlighting and cross ventilation.

---

[39] Le Corbusier's interest in Barcelona is undeniable if we look at the study of his *Cahiers* by Jordi Oliveras: *Le Corbusier y Barcelona, op. cit.* In turn, his commitment to the dramatic political evolution of Barcelona led him to paint his interesting work *La chute de Barcelone*, a forceful expression of his feelings. See Daniel Giralt-Miracle: *Le Corbusier y Barcelona. op. cit.*

6.f The Recreation and Holiday Resort in Castelldefels.

33, 6.34
e Recreation and Holiday
sort as an innovative way of
aling with mass leisure.

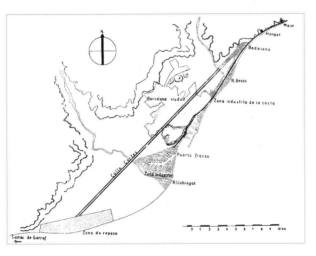

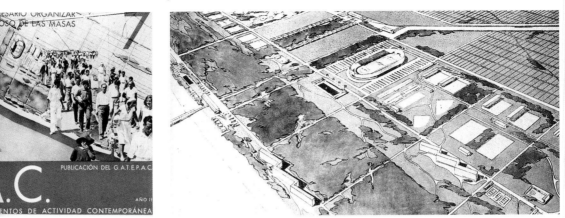

35
ap showing its location on
e axis of Barcelona's Gran
ia, 1932.

.36, 6.37
artial perspective of
he proposal and model
ismountable beach house,
933.

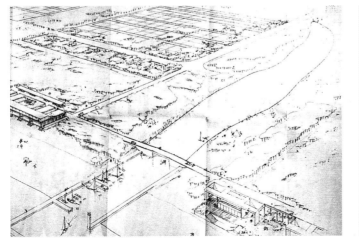

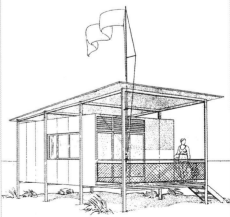

The dwellings are organised in duplex form, with corridors every two floors, producing a total of 207 dwellings. The ground floor is left free and is used for communal services: company store, library, crèche, swimming pool, etc.

The metal structure is designed to be separate from the facings, seeking the corresponding functional independence of the construction systems.

The project was presented at the CIRPAC congresses and responds to broader-based reflection on worker housing in Barcelona, an ongoing concern of the GATCPAC. On this point, the *Ensayo de distribución de la zona edificable en una manzana del ensanche de Barcelona* [Essay on the distribution of the building area in Barcelona's Eixample][40] is interesting reading, making urban form compatible with the orthogonal geometry of the Eixample.

The project for the Recreation and Holiday Resort was a response to the organisation of leisure time and recreation of the urban masses. This was a new need in big metropolitan conurbations, where the individual represented an increase in movements towards the countryside or the coast.

The GATCPAC took this initiative in 1931 in the Llobregat delta, where the engineer García Faria had wanted to recycle the land in the late 19th century and which by the start of the 20th century had been repopulated by the State. The fact that the land had recently been formed made it public property, and this eight kilometre long, 800 metre wide strip could be converted into a site with a great future as a public facility.[41]

The project envisaged five main areas organised along the prolongation of Gran Via over the delta and the existing railway track communicating inland towns: 1) the bathing area to accommodate the agglomerations of people on public holidays; 2) the week-end area, with a further two kilometres of beach for people wishing to spend a couple of days there; camping sites and demountable houses encouraged this use; 3) a residential area for hotels and children's holiday camps; 4) an area for rest cures, with sanatoriums and spas, and 5) an area of farmland for cultivation, in a strip below the other areas, for those wishing to spend their free time growing vegetables, a regular practice in the environs of Barcelona (in Montjuïc, Gràcia and Sant Gervasi) where there were rented allotments for cultivation at weekends or in the holidays.

The project was laid out with buildings that differed in size according to their use, arranged in a great seafront park with priority of access to the on-site facilities. The complex had an anticipated capacity for in the region of 300,000 people and it was planned to reinforce the public transport system accordingly.

[40] Both projects can be consulted in issue 11 of *A.C.*, 1933, re-issued in *GATEPAC*, Barcelona, 1975.
[41] Emili Donato: *Cronología y bibliografía del proyecto de Ciutat de repòs i de vacances para Barcelon*a". Ciudad y Territorio, Madrid, 1971.

38, 6.39, 6.40, 6.41
vilion of the Spanish
public. 1937 Great
chibition, Paris. Ground and
st levels, images of Guernica.

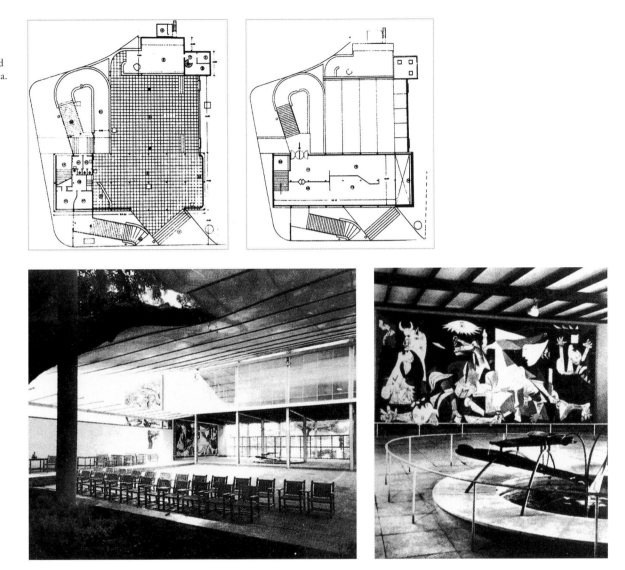

The project was exhibited publicly in the spring of 1933 in the gallery beneath Plaça de Catalunya and caused a great impact on the city's people. At the end of the year, the Recreation and Holiday Resort Cooperative was formed, bringing together 600 Catalan associations with a total of 800,000 affiliates.

Despite this immediate implementation, political and administrative difficulties with regard to drainage and the expropriation of some of the land prevented this important project from flourishing. It did however mark out the guidelines for a type of development that the private sector implemented, in quite a different fashion, in the 1950s.

6.42
Ode to Barcelona, illustration
by Joan Junyer of Pere Quart
work, 1937.

6.43
The fall of Barcelona by Le
Corbusier, 1939. Constructiv
forms are used to express the
city's agony.

6.44
Poster by Miró.

VI.7 Dissolution of the GATCPAC and the Civil War

Though the exhibition of the Macià Plan in July represented a major breakthrough for the implantation of GATCPAC ideas, in October 1934 a substantial political change took place and the right wing came to power until 1936. The Statute of Catalonia was then suspended.

The so-called black biennial did not help the progress of the Catalan group's urban planning projects. However, the constitution of the Popular Front and the establishment of a left-wing government created potential for these innovative ideas. However, the uprising of military groups based in Morocco and headed by General Franco plunged the country into a Civil War with tragic consequences.

During the initial period, the Generalitat Government was able to deploy markedly progressive collectivist policies, including the municipalisation of urban property and the construction industry.[42]

The new organisation of this industry saw the incorporation of the GATCPAC into the SAC (Societat d'Arquitectes de Catalunya – Architects' Society of Catalonia) as a new professional organisation. But most importantly, its avant-garde stance changed,[43] and the priorities established by its existing projects were transformed in the light of the new social order. The war also changed the focus of interests of the group members. The one who was most committed to recent events was Josep Torres Clavé, who died at the front in 1939. Other architects were forced to go into exile: Josep Lluís Sert[44] was a foremost example, taking his theoretical and professional activity to the United States, where he became Director of Harvard Design School.

Previously, in 1937, Sert had designed the Pavilion of the Spanish Republic in Paris in collaboration with Luis Lacasa.[45] This was a building with a simple structure that combined the principles of modern architecture with

[42] Joan Grijalbo and Francesc Fàbregas: *Municipalització de la propietat urbana*. Edición UGT, Barcelona, 1937.
[43] Ignasi de Solà-Morales: *GATCPAC*. 1975, *op. cit.*, pp. 26 and 27.
[44] Shortly after going into exile he produced an excellent summary of this important body of reflection begun in Barcelona. See: Josep Lluís Sert: "Can Our Cities Survive?", *ABC of Urban Problems, their Analysis, their Solutions. op. cit.*
A general compendium of his work can be seen in Josep M. Rovira: *José Luis Sert: 1901-1983*. Electa. Milan, 2000.
[45] This pavilion was reconstructed in 1991 in the Vall d'Hebrón, in one of the Olympic areas.

5

nsolidation of the old
nicipalities in the Plain.

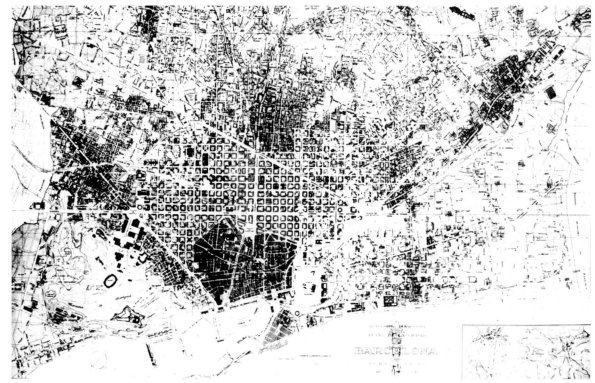

the lightness of great awnings to filter Mediterranean light. This pavilion housed Picasso's famous *Guernica*, that expresses with great dramatic quality the brutality of fascist actions.[46] Miró, too, with his work *Still life with old shoe* expressed his indignation at the dissolution of the democratic political process of the 1930s.

This was the end of a highly dynamic situation – markedly revolutionary, according to many – that had extended a flourishing critical attitude to the field of the arts. At this point, there were many European artists who, moved by this dynamic, joined the progressive movement in favour of the Spanish Republic.[47]

The outcome of the Civil War meant the end of democracy for a long period in Spain and also the interruption of a process of innovation in architecture, urban planning and modern art, which lacked sufficient time to mature and develop to their full potential.

[46] Fortunately this painting is once again on show, now in Madrid, symbolising democratic normality in Spain and bearing witness to difficult times past.
[47] Spanish and European artists acted in favour of the Spanish and Catalan progressive bloc. Other moved to Barcelona to live or even to fight for the cause as a sign of their solidarity. One of many contributions was *Homage to Catalonia* (Penguin, London, 1949), the work of George Orwell who as of 1936 fought on the Republic front, where he was wounded. Lor alit inciliquis nis aliquatet iurem at.

The grey post-war years and the formation of the metropolis

VII.1 Autocracy, reconstruction and shantytowns[1]

The end of the Civil War gave way to a lack of economic resources and political repression. "The implantation of a new economic order that broke first with market economy mechanisms and then with political and economic relations with the rest of the countries in the world"[2] was more important in explaining the penury that prevailed in the post-war period than the physical destruction of production means.

This led to an autocratic state policy with regard to the industrial sector, encouraging self-sufficiency, and entailing protection of industries to ensure they had no domestic competition and that all consumer goods were produced nationally. At the same time, the countryside found itself plunged into crisis due to a lack of means and adverse climate conditions.

This framework promoted a continuing trend of migration from the countryside to the city; due not exclusively to the lack of industrial labour, but to greater possibilities of subsistence in the city, despite the drawbacks it involved. Problems caused by lack of residential space were becoming increasingly serious.[3]

In these conditions, official action on the part of the Reconstruction Board tended fundamentally to promote the representative values of the dominant ideology.[4]

As part of the General Plan for national reconstruction, the construction of dwellings with state assistance was envisaged in the Protected Dwellings Act of April 1939. This act set up the National Housing Institute and was passed for contractors involved in solving the problem.[5] The benefits involved were basically grants and loans for financing, tax exemptions and the priority provision of materials. The effects of this measure had little effect in relation to the initial problem. Only five years after the passing of the act, a new legal code appeared to address another kind of demand: the Discount Housing Act of 1944 (which can be seen as a continuation of the 1935 Salmón Act), aimed basically at the middle classes, also affected by the shortage of housing.

[1] Reworked by J. Busquets. Barcelona, 1975, *op. cit.*, pp. 68-75.
[2] See particularly the work of Clavera, Esbeban, Montserrat and Ros Hombravella: "Capitalismo Español: De la Autarquía a la Estabilización", *Cuadernos para el Diálogo*. Madrid, 1972.
[3] Jutglar (1968), *op. cit.*, page 14, numbers at 45,000 the annual average of immigrants to arrive in the province of Barcelona.
[4] The 1941 Madrid Plan is an obvious example. See V. Simancas and J. Elizalde: *El mito del Gran Madrid*. Guadiana de Ediciones. Madrid, 1969.
[5] A summary of the contents of these acts can be seen in J. del Barrio: "Legislación especial de viviendas de protección estatal". *Vivienda* no. 4. Barcelona, 1962.

7.01
An outlying neighbourhood in the post-war years.

7.02
Image of Verdum in the nort[h]
of Barcelona, representing m[a]
residential growth of various
types without urbanisation o[r]
facilities.

The existence of these acts channelled and ensured the provision of materials for the few housing developments at the start of this period[6] but it was not until 1945 that a slight increase in the number of dwellings being built made itself felt. The housing issue was so crucial that a catch phrase appeared among people who obtained an apartment: "M'han donat un pis" (They've given me a flat), though it was, evidently, rented or bought.

In this situation, the homeless floating population was accommodated in pensions or "dosshouses"; subletting became very common in urban centres; warehouses were fitted out as "dwellings", and shantytowns and caves became vitally important, with the number of shanties in the municipal area of Barcelona being quoted as 20,000.[7] Self-built districts also multiplied and existing cases were consolidated, though an initial shortage of materials curbed this dynamic. In this way, districts such as Roquetas and Can Caralleu in Barcelona's municipal area underwent considerable expansion.

In this context, reconstruction schemes and tolerance of shantytowns were set against a backdrop of recognition of migration as something natural and inevitable. Demonstrations were organised, such as the Spanish Social Week in Burgos in 1945, and the prevailing mood was one of general acceptance of the phenomenon, but without any real action to rectify its deficiencies. It was still many years before an official stance on worker housing was

---

[6] There is no breakdown of figures by province, but according to A. Cotorruelo (1966), *op. cit.*, the national average was 20,090 for the 1941-45 period and 31,940 a year over the next five years. Remember that the operators were relatively small in this period. At the same time, a work by the Study Service of the Banco de Urquijo (1952), *La economía española y la reconstrucción 1947-1951*, places the national shortage at one million five hundred thousand dwellings.
[7] "Evolución y datos fundamentales del barraquismo en la ciudad de Barcelona", *Vivienda*. 1969.

to produce results. However, without contradicting this general stance of recognition with no effective action, there were two schemes that provided guidelines for a new way of dealing with the phenomenon:[8] 1) the Council edict of 1949, which once again entrusted to municipal forces the responsibility for "demolishing any work or construction presumed to be intended as a shanty", and 2) the authorities showed themselves to be aware of the worsening problem of continuing immigration and introduced measures to directly curb immigration: people were forced to return to their towns and villages under threat of arrest and imprisonment in the event of recidivism.[9]

VII.2 City and *Comarca*

The end of the international embargo signalled a degree of opening up to the outside world, and its most direct repercussion was industrial growth due to the entry of foreign capital. The result was an intensification of mass migration, not just of labourers but also of small landowners from rural areas, to the cities where industrial growth was polarised.

Immigration then began to be tolerated as a potential labour supply that fed this industrial development. This period also saw the transfer of much of Barcelona's industry to a new physical area: its *Comarca* – which was legally recognised by the 1953 Barcelona County Plan – and nearby towns and cities in Vallès, such as Sabadell and Terrassa, with existing industrial settlements.

The process triggered off by the dynamic in the national context led to the formulation in 1954 of the First National Housing Plan and the passing of the Low-Cost Housing Act and, later, the Subsidised Housing Act, in 1957. The process began of "channelling private initiative into the task of building homes by increasing – with a considerable profit margin – the funds that the private sector invested in low-cost dwellings".[10]

Barcelona was witness to a singular housing scheme before the implementation of the above-mentioned legislation: the Eucharistic Congress Housing (2,719 dwellings) built over the 1953-1962 period, with the intervention of state subsidies and the cooperation of other bodies and institutions, such as banks and savings banks. This scheme and others carried out at the same time served more as prototypes than any kind of real

---

[8]   Reproduced in *Barcelona informa*. Supplement of the Municipal Gazette (October 1972). Barcelona.
[9]   In the Housing Report of Barcelona's Eucharistic Congress (1954), the delegate of the Civil Governor stated: "6,248 persons were evacuated from their home towns, but 5 per cent of them did not request it voluntarily (...) If they returned, they would be punished by ninety days of prison (...) It may be considered [a measure] that was much needed, since it prevents greater ills..."
[10]   J. del Barrio (1962), *op. cit.*

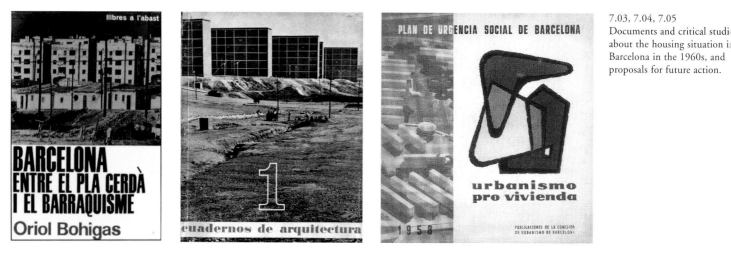

7.03, 7.04, 7.05
Documents and critical studi[es]
about the housing situation i[n]
Barcelona in the 1960s, and
proposals for future action.

solution to the problems of the low-cost housing sector; most of these dwellings were adjudicated to middle-class families or employees of the sponsors.

Throughout this period the shantytowns continued and increased in importance, as did other "abnormal" forms of housing, which had a greater effect on the municipalities in the *Comarca*. Self-built districts were consolidated and new plots appeared in poorer outlying areas.

Alongside the real forms of "accommodation" various "formulations" were suggested to solve the problems arising from migration. When discussing Barcelona's disproportionate growth, for instance, the architect Manuel Baldrich[11] proposed the *Comarca*-city model with a view to solving those problems, raising the following issues: how to check immigration to the cities? How to fix the rural population? How to avoid migratory movements and their serious consequences and introduce a new, more balanced kind of settlement? The idea of Barcelona as a *Comarca*-city was never more than a hypothetical formulation because the territorial scope of the *Comarca de Barcelona* was to be addressed on the basis of very different criteria by the 1953 County Plan.

The County Plan represented the establishment of an urban system that was in actual fact being constructed and directed according to the criteria of functional zoning. The Plan was based on a series of sociological and economic studies. Each city, town or village was configured by a system of blots allowing each municipality access to practically all areas. The result was a "multinuclear" system that was to be promoted by the prospects of the land market, given the practical non-existence of urban planning. The Plan was drafted on very mixed scales with an imprecise topographical basis, and its implementation in a totalitarian political framework inevitably led to adjustments and changes to zones that were clearly reprehensible.

The 1953 Plan did serve in part to establish the concept of *Comarca* that was later institutionalised in 1974, but its capacity to regulate urban planning was slight, as we will go on to see.[12]

[11] M. Baldrich: *Ante el crecimiento desmesurado de los aglomerados urbanos: la ciudad-comarca.* Barcelona, 1952. An architect and urban planner who made a great professional contribution to the planning of this period and particularly to the Barcelona Provincial Plan.
[12] See Manuel de Solà-Morales: "De la ordenación a la coordinación", *CAU* no. 10. Barcelona, 1971.

VII.3 The dawn of the development policy

The 1959 Stabilisation Plan promoted a series of internal changes that strengthened the industrial and finance sectors to the detriment of farming, and heralded an increase in tourism. This period also saw the external emigration, to European countries, of the cities' qualified labour force, which was replaced by a huge mass of labourers who had recently arrived from the countryside. This was a peak time for migration in Catalonia: immigrants arriving in the 1961-1965 period numbered 800,000, of which 50% settled in Barcelona province. Compare this to the figure given for the 1950-1960 period: in the region of 440,000 immigrants to Catalonia as a whole.

The destination of this body of immigrants divided up as follows: 32 per cent in Barcelona city; 40 per cent in its *Comarca* and 28 per cent to the rest of the province. This illustrates perfectly the role of the *Comarca* as an industrial and working-class residential periphery, taking over from the city of Barcelona itself.

Also in this period, in 1954 and 1957, the Central Government took measures to stimulate housing. The Social Emergency Plan of 1958 delimited areas for expropriation to obtain cheap land and implement major housing programmes.

In this way important social housing schemes went ahead, known as *polígonos* or housing estates, with the subsequent change in scale of the contractors and construction techniques.

The administration and financing of housing construction now became independent, being taken over by property developers. In this way, development moved from the hands of small or family agents to larger contractors, encouraged by the housing acts[13] and increasingly began to be linked to or dependent on the finance sector.[14]

Initially, the estates tended to be located within the municipality. Between 1955 and 1965, 25,911 dwellings were built on estates in Barcelona, as opposed to just 18,205 in its *Comarca*. Conversely, from 1965 to 1972, this situation was reversed, with the construction of a mere 9,767 dwellings in the municipality of Barcelona as opposed to 91,351 in its *Comarca*.[15] To these figures for mass housing schemes we have to add the existence of smaller developments, but in this period, in the *Comarca* it can be attributed a similar quantitative importance: suburban developments of three- or four-storey blocks using traditional construction systems and with a sales price that competed with mass housing developments.

[13] One of the benefits of subsidised housing was a direct grant of 30,000 pesetas per dwelling, which could represent as much as 15 per cent of its cost at that time.
[14] One example is the district of Sant Ildefons, which housed as many as 45,000 people. For a description see C. Masana: "La formació de Sant Ildefons". *Serra d'Or* no. 163. Barcelona, 1973.
[15] See A. Ferrer: *Los polígonos de la comarca de Barcelona*. Monografías ETSAB. Barcelona, 1974.

7.06
The Barcelona coastline in the
1960s between the Barceloneta
and Poblenou. Industrial
installations and the shanties of
Somorrostro. The present-day
site of the Olympic Village.

There was, then, an appreciable increase in housing construction, which actually multiplied by five in just seven years,[16] but the shortage of low-cost homes continued. The "abnormal" forms of accommodation, such as shantytowns and subletting continued. Self-built and poorer outlying districts came to the fore during this period for two reasons: 1) the construction of existing districts continued and actually intensified in the *Comarca*,[17] the supply of materials returned to normal and in general the municipal authorities continued their tolerant stance; 2) the first measures were taken to legalise and transform them, generally by the drafting of a Partial Plan, in the oldest districts and in the municipality of Barcelona.[18]

The outset of this period of development policy, during which mass housing construction and self-built districts took great steps forwards, was marked by the appearance of a series of critical works and studies that begin to prefigure future action.[19]

Particular mention is worthy of the critical view taken of Barcelona's evolution by Oriol Bohigas in 1963[20] when, in the appendix entitled "Praise of the shanty", he highlighted the dire living conditions of immigrants

[16] See *Vivienda* P.M.V. Barcelona, nos. 29 and 30, 1969. The total number of dwellings constructed in 1959 in the province of Barcelona was 10,933, whereas in 1966 it was 52,627 dwellings.
[17] For example, the districts of Vistalegre and Costeras.
[18] For example, the districts of Roquetes and Sant Genís dels Agudells.
[19] For a summary of these works see CEDEC (Centro de Estudios para el Desarrollo de la Comunidad). "Las Roquetas", *Promos*, Barcelona, 1964; "El barrio de Vallbona". *Promos* no. 28. Barcelona, 1964, among others.
[20] O. Bohigas: *Entre el Pla Cerdà i el barraquisme*. Edicions 62, Barcelona, 1963.

forced into the shanties and +*coreas* that constituted the suburb of complete abandonment, but most of all he criticised the type of solutions introduced to deal with them, and the fact that they now formed part of the "paternalist" suburb – that is, shantytowns with the signature of an architect, "new suburbs that emerge from macroshanties without services and remote from the city, while that city's land continues to await an increase in value".

Another interesting viewpoint is that represented by the Francesc Candel's well-known work[21] *Els altres catalans*. It relates with realism and colour the "accommodation" conditions of immigrants, their lifestyles and difficulties in integration. It describes the life of shanty-dwellers in Barcelona, the poor conditions of low-cost housing or apartments administered by cooperatives, highlights the problems of sublets in suburban centres and of people who lived in pensions or as lodgers.

Between these two approaches are a whole series of interesting initiatives, such as the two monographic issues of *Cuadernos de Arquitectura* in 1965[22] which were of great significance at the time of their publication. Specialist

[21] F. Candel: *Els altres catalans*. Edicions 62, Barcelona, 1964. On page 254 he describes: "Beside Sant Vicenç dels Horts (...) there is a working-class district called San José, popularly known as 'Mau-Mau'. The residents of 'Mau-Mau' are people from Extremadura, Murcians from Collblanc and La Torrassa and also Andalusians. This is a district situated on a hillside, an almost vertical slope, with hanging houses like a miniature Cuenca. The poor, arid, rough and mountainous plots are cheap. They say that it was the Council of Sant Vicenç or the councillors themselves who sold them, overlooking the obligation to urbanise. This is true. This areas will never be urbanised, not with the best will in the world, because it is impossible. The streets – if these spaces between rows of houses can be called such – are torrents."
[22] Various authors: "Los Suburbios". *Cuadernos* nos. 60-61. COAC, Barcelona, 1967.

publications[23] and daily press[24] were also a platform for ongoing criticism, paving the way for broad-based citizen awareness that later came together in the form of urban social movements.

VII.4 Top-heavy Barcelona and the system of Catalan cities

This interpretation of the **metropolitan formation of Barcelona** is based on a discourse that serves structurally to explain the great wave of development affecting this singular urban agglomerate.

When we speak of Barcelona's top-heaviness in relation to Catalonia as a whole, we refer to the fact that it represented 65% of the population, 60% of net production and 50% of the active population according to figures from 1980. This polarisation is identified as a clear expression of present-day territorial imbalances, of which this top-heaviness is the most representative effect of the interplay of dominant forces within the economic system which seemed to find in it the most appropriate territorial model for its reproduction.

A discussion of these categorisations reveals that: 1) the production of this urban phenomenon took place at a high social cost; 2) it represented spatially very concentrated investment that excluded the possibility of an alternative location in other points of the territory; and 3) as a result resources tended to be drained towards this growing centre from areas that become progressively more hierarchised in relation to it.

Our thesis here suggests that if a description of the more recent growth of Catalonia can be summarised by continuing concentration in Barcelona, this concentration is identified with the development of the county

---

[23] Various authors: *La inmigració a Catalunya*. Edició de Materials S.A. Barcelona. It contains a series of topics including the significance of this process in Catalonia, "land of the marriage of cultures", throughout its history. In 1972 a monographic issue of *CAU* was published on emigration, also as a collective work. Worthy of particular mention is *Promos* magazine which in issue 43 on housing (1966) published two interesting articles by the economists Enric Lluch and Jacint Ros Hombravella. The first was an interesting summary of the historical evolution of housing deficits. The second outlines the problem of the suburb on the basis of a consideration of the cost of settlement in the city of each immigrant. He estimates that each inhabitant required over 35,000 pesetas (1954) of investment to be able to provide the facilities and infrastructure for his home and movement around the city; a further 70,000 pesetas (1954) had to be taken into account for housing per inhabitant. Bearing in mind that the average family had two working members, this means 210,000 pesetas (1954) per person of investment were required in "housing, urban life and movement". The author considers this figure to equal the investment required to create a job in the city, 200,000 pesetas (1954), (the job that attracted the immigrant to Barcelona). He thereby draws our attention to another aspect for consideration when addressing the incoming labour that served to balance out the market, because it was ultimately immigrants who were affected by this imbalance.

[24] Series of nine articles by J. M. Huertas Clavería published in *Tele/eXpres* in relation to the nine districts affected by the Partial Plan for Torre Baró-Trinidad-Vallbona, in which he critically describes the characteristics of each district. Other relevant articles to appear in the daily press of the time were "Vallbona desde la Universidad".

suburb as an expressive, valorative phenomenon of it; and, in addition, that this process has not, to date, cancelled out the capacity of other Catalan towns and cities to undertake a more rational form of growth.

It is a question, then, of expressing the "logic" of the economic and territorial "model" of configuration of top-heavy Barcelona in terms of factors of city growth – such as population and urban land growth – and the construction of infrastructures, significant factors in a discussion of the possibility of a less unbalanced urban territorial structure.[25]

It is important to bear in mind that the concentration of population in Barcelona was consubstantial to the Catalan urban model, apparently the only way of explaining how it undertook industrialisation without resources or aspired to be a capital without strong political support.

Barcelona's importance in terms of population in comparison to Catalonia as a whole became consolidated in the second half of the 19th century in keeping with the guidelines of urban concentration promoted by industrialisation. In mid-century, smaller municipalities of under 2,000 inhabitants dropped from almost half of the population to one third. Conversely, towns of more than 10,000 inhabitants and Barcelona – including the municipalities in the Plain – underwent major growth. Barcelona grew from 12 per cent in 1857 to 27 per cent of the total Catalan population, while the Catalan industrial towns and cities rose from 28 to 41 per cent; it was principally the industrial towns and cities well communicated with Barcelona by railway (Mataró, Terrassa, Sabadell, Badalona, Manresa, etc.) that constituted the "mature" cities described below.

This meant that urban population then stood at 78 per cent, and of the population growth in Catalonia in the second half of the 19th century, 90 per cent settled in the Barcelona area (286,000 persons of a total increase of 314,000).[26]

The city entity was, then, an object of the territorial phenomenon and the construction of infrastructure was largely attributed to the urbanising dynamic.

After a summary analysis of the county suburb as a suitable representation of top-heaviness, the work categorises a series of types of cities and towns within Catalonia, considering that the growth dynamic goes further to explain the problems arising than the mere question of size. It identifies four types of cities, according to their growth dynamics: A, mature cities; B, recent cities; C, stagnant cities and D, empty cities.

[25] This is a summary of the article "La Macrocefalia barcelonesa" presented by the author at the Congress of Catalan Culture in 1975 and published in *Ciudad y Territorio* no. 2. Madrid, 1977 and in *Cuadernos* no. 2, COAC. Barcelona, 1980. The work was updated according to the 1981 census and presented at the International Conference on the North-western Mediterranean in Barcelona in 1983, and it is these most recent results that are presented here. The latter work contains specific hypotheses with regard to the Catalan urban system that contemplate both the problems facing the conglomerate of towns and cities around Barcelona and in the rest of Catalonia, principally up to 1980.

[26] Figures summarised by Borja de Riquer in his "Societat catalana dels anys vuitanta". Barcelona, 1988, *op. cit.*, page 18.

7.a Barcelona and Catalan towns and cities.

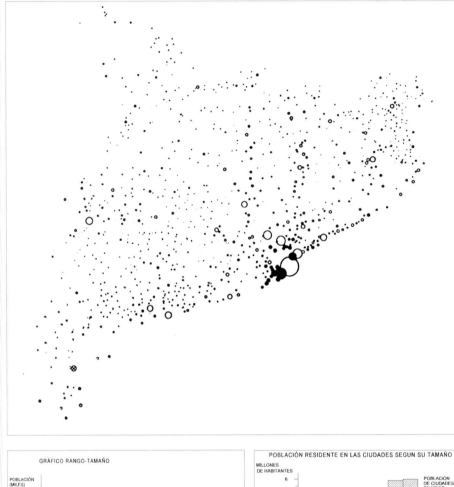

7.08
Barcelona and the rest of
Catalonia's towns and cities,
represented by population size
and rate of growth.

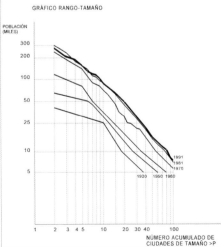

GRÁFICO RANGO-TAMAÑO

POBLACIÓN
(MILES)

300
200

100

50

25

10

5

1991
1981
1970
1920 1950 1960

1   2   3 4 5   10   20 30 40   100

NÚMERO ACUMULADO DE
CIUDADES DE TAMAÑO >P

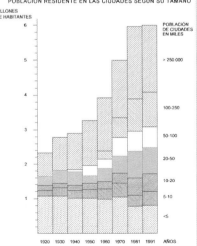

POBLACIÓN RESIDENTE EN LAS CIUDADES SEGÚN SU TAMAÑO

MILLONES
DE HABITANTES

6

5

4

3

2

1

POBLACIÓN
DE CIUDADES
EN MILES

> 250 000

100-250

50-100

20-50

10-20

5-10

<5

1920 1930 1940 1950 1960 1970 1981 1991   AÑOS

7.09, 7.10
Graphs showing relations
between towns and cities. The
position-size graph shows the
relative order of towns and
cities smaller than Barcelona.
The other graph represents
how the population gradually
concentrated in other large
towns and cities. The last
decade has been marked by a
stabilisation of the population
and an increase in "second"
cities.

1
ᵗᵉs of town and city
ᵒrding to the rate of
ᵖulation growth, a variable
ᵗ summarises some specific
ᵃan development projects
type.

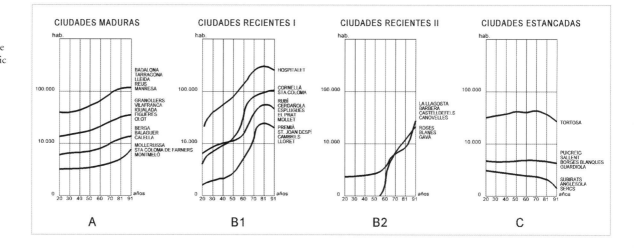

1. The materialisation of Barcelona's top-heaviness, mainly in the latter decades, involved the progressive differentiation of two plainly opposing sides of the problem.

a) The land in its centre, the municipality of Barcelona, was filled in by intense densification, seeking to extend and shape the strategic centre of Catalonia, with the construction of luxury residential areas and remodelling attempts (by means of intervention in infrastructures, in most cases supposedly required by the collectivity). The infrastructural works underpinning these transformations were those of internal restructuring (extension of the Metro network, the First Beltway, more or less isolated responses to traffic conflicts), with an overall view to achieving a level of efficiency that would allow more intense use and increased capital gains; although apparently intended to promote territorial structuring (new railway stations, new city approach roads, motorways and so forth), in fact they merely accentuated further the hierarchy of this centre.

These supposedly decentralising development schemes, concentrating mainly on the road structure, in fact led to the densification above all of the facilities in the centre, which acted almost like a monopoly, dominating the entire country's consumption.

b) The consolidation of the county suburb that protagonised growth in terms of population (in the 1960s representing 70% of the total increase) and of land (65% of total urbanised land) as the generic place for new industrial investments and relocation from the centre.

It is important to remember that the urban continuum in Baix Llobregat and Barcelonès extended almost without intermediate spaces over a strip of between 4 and 15 kilometres from the centre of Barcelona; it represented the requisite location of the residences of a low-paid workforce, this being one of the fundamental factors informing the "development" of this top-heavy concentration. This form of growth led to the destruction of the urban fabrics of the old rural centres (here we refer to type B cities) which were overlain and acted as the only form of scant support for the various residential parcels that now form this "residential" suburb around Barcelona. The "ministerial" operators of local government and private developers were the contractors involved in this peripheral, deurbanised, chaotic building process, dominated by speculative mechanisms of real-estate management and promotion, of which block upon block of dwellings without services (estates) and marginal urbanisation (districts practically built by the residents themselves) were the most common expression.

7.12
Vilanova i la Geltrú, a
prototype of the mature tow

The consumption of land represented by this suburb was highly intensive, a process in which land appraisal mechanisms played a very significant role. Conversely, there is a general lack of public and communal spaces and access to services and facilities was very poor, not to say non-existent.

By way of contrast with these two facets of the problem we have sectors such as Vallès, with marked differences: recent (B) and mature (A) towns and cities coexist and are interconnected in hierarchical form and with a functional and technical division between nucleuses, with a major dependency of the strategic centre and presenting, particularly in B cities, appreciable phenomena of suburbanisation. The urbanistic degradation of the aggregate growths of the towns and cities in Vallès, however, took place, despite the compensatory action that the general elements of recently constructed infrastructure purported to provide. We have to take into account the impact on the rural land of these motorways and connections; they were more effective in generating expectant land value than connecting the region as they were intended to. This situation can only be explained by the predominance of land and speculation in this general process.

A more complete assessment may be provided by the consideration, in these terms, of the transformation process also undergone by the towns and cities in Maresme and along the other axes affected by Barcelona's top-heaviness.

Before addressing this problem more specifically from the viewpoint of the cities, we might provisionally assume that the spatial concentration of population, the investment in infrastructures and urban growth in Barcelona represented first and foremost the consolidation of the county suburb and that the above-mentioned actions to decongest it led to a high level of land consumption – even more than its high occupation – when they were supposed to decentralise industry and residence, with few guarantees of urbanisation, thereby inducing rather irrational trends and types of growth.

13
iew of the urban space
etween Cornellà and
Hospitalet, two cities
ith important population
ynamics.

2. The second part of the argument centres on Catalan towns and cities not directly involved in the top-heavy centre. The exclusive mapping of towns and cities by sizes suggests that the incontestable importance of the Barcelona agglomeration has to be nuanced to take into account the resources and the potential that the urban network has had historically and still possesses, despite this polarised distribution. The top-heaviness of Catalonia cannot, without mystification, be regarded directly in the same light as the Latin-American models, to cite the most appropriate and frequent framework of application and discussion, with their broken, dislocated urban networks and an even more accentuated hierarchy between their urban nucleuses.

However, if we consider the time scale of the dynamics of each town or city and of the changes in numbers of towns and cities with regard to size, we see how at each level (of size) there are towns and cities marked by a strong dynamic in the last twenty years and also how levels include a growing number of towns and cities in the last fifty years. That is, there is an increasing number of towns and cities of all sizes over 2,000 inhabitants; "urban" concentration therefore takes place at all levels.

With a view to assessing the role of this system of Catalan towns and cities in a broader-based territorial structuring, we will now go on to essay an interpretation of their historical formation, with particular reference to the infrastructure schemes that underpin and inform it.

We will centre our discussion on cities A and B (recent and mature), on the understanding that types C (stagnant cities) and B (empty cities) call for specific assessment that goes beyond the scope of this work.

Type B or "recent" cities characteristically presented a very high rate of population growth between 1960 and 1970 (150-200% approximately), with high rates, too, for the period between 1950 and 1960 (around 80%). Growth over the latter twenty year period took place around small urban centres with precarious infrastructure levels. We might say that these towns or cities came into being in 1950. Some of them, which had already achieved a degree of entity and size by the 1930s, had reached that situation at a similar rate of growth in the twenties and thirties. The dynamic of the eighties presented two subtypes (B-1 and B-2) according to a fall in or maintenance of population.

This group included the towns and cities in the Barcelona continuum and some others which, in a similar relationship of dependence with regard to nearby secondary agglomerations, had previously served to characterise the county suburb. These were towns and cities that had grown with no infrastructure except that which was produced by the juxtaposition of vital individual services; given the proximity though without contiguity to Barcelona of these cities, strong general infrastructures such as the suburban railways in the 1920s generated processes of degraded growth.

Mature towns and cities, or type A, are characterised by a growth curve with appreciable dynamics in the 1920-1930 and 1950-1970 periods (around 20%); their growth in these periods centred around urban centres – that is, around a stock of urbanisation work – of considerable size and entity with regard to new growth. They were urban structures that were gradually generated in a historical process that has left the imprint of the transformations in social and productive organisation on these cities, particularly in the types of construction, of streets and squares, and in services present and past. They are cities of very differing sizes – between 5 and 50 thousand inhabitants – which have had a particular significance in the history of Catalonia, denoting the general meaning of successive works of urbanisation. Between the 1850s and 1884, then, the construction of the railways saw decisive investment in the construction of a network and an urban hierarchy in the system of towns, interconnecting them and linking them with Barcelona in a radial scheme that was the spatial transposition of general economic integration. The construction of the railways gave way to a hierarchical system of towns and cities. While there is no denying the importance of the relationships supposed by this infrastructure, it is vital to understand that the railway was also an urban element that structured the interiors of towns and cities. The station, originally built at some distance from the centre, became accessible, monumental even, thanks to the construction of an avenue linking it to the centre of that mercantile town; it also highlighted the axes of expansion of the town which, from this moment on, aspired to be and in fact became industrial. After the railway, constructed in some cases in the early decades of the 20th century in its narrow-gauge form, it was the new town plans that characterised the physical shape of these mature towns and, most of all, provided the means to regulate transformation and deal with the growth dynamic. Further infrastructures were then built: networks for sewerage, electricity, water and gas; it was on the basis of this built fabric of services to the residence and industry (that is, to the factors of land, work and capital) that cities can be understood as generators of agglomerative economies in their homogeneity and scale economies in their hierarchy.

3. A study of the distribution of population by groups of towns and cities reveal two specific situations: one constituted by Barcelona and the towns and cities in its environs; the other created by a group of thirty or so towns of between 10 and 100 thousand inhabitants situated outside Barcelona's urban continuum.

These "thirty towns" had an overall population of more than a million and offered the potential capacity to constitute a basic complement to the central nucleus, or even provide an alternative location for many activities that are not compatible with urban congestion. It can be seen as a scattered, dispersed, discontinuous "city" but one that overcame the internal imbalances affecting the capital and the disadvantages it imposed on the rest of the territory. This was viable due to the large potential for growth that urbanisation accumulated over time, like fixed capital, was offering in those towns, where new extensions were produced with low cost margins and new urban land could expand in relatively controlled fashion.

At the same time, however, the central urban system was the space where most conflicts and accumulated deficits converged: firstly due to the difficulties involved in constructing the suburb or the county periphery, and secondly because the actual scale of the infrastructures introduced in the sixties and seventies called for a new form of urban interconnection.

It was, then, a metropolitan whole that might be seen once again as a system of towns and cities with high levels of interconnection that continued to call for attention as the central theme of Catalonia.

VII.5 The evolution of large infrastructures

In the phenomenon of top-heaviness, an understanding of the imbalances in population is closely linked to the concentration of investment in infrastructure within the Barcelona area which, due to its "exploiting", low-level urban nature, generated serious problems of balance in the central city.

If, however, we look at the mature cities, we see that they have fundamentally been the object of infrastructural investment plans that were never carried out: the "arterial networks" envisaged for towns of over 20,000 inhabitants, and the drainage and water supply projects for towns of over 10,000 inhabitants did not, in most cases, proceed beyond the planning stage. It is important to remember that the idea, never implemented, was to fund infrastructures of the same type and nature as those planned for the city centre, and responding to the same type of aims; the impracticability and inapplicability of these standard proposals, then, comes as no surprise.

Likewise, it is hardly surprising that all that was in some cases ultimately constructed of those arterial networks was the typical relief road or occasional motorway approach roads, in cases near cities, constructed and designed with independent finances that have frequently disrupted the order of the existing road network.

Nonetheless, it is also important to point out that while infrastructural investment was limited to the top-heavy area it was above all the model nature chosen for the infrastructures that led them to be located, for reasons for internal profitability, in the congested traditional centre of Catalonia. While it is not necessary here to go into a detailed discussion of the financial and speculative mechanisms that have often accompanied the development and construction of large infrastructures in this country, it is basic to highlight the absurdly autonomous functioning with which such operations are approached: in this way, the consumption generated by the selfsame infrastructure and the profit produced by its actual construction are the sole stimuli to explain implantation.

To follow through with this logic (motorways, large hypermarkets, etc.), the ultimate "beneficiary" always turns out to be the Barcelona area. And if they are outside this area, they represent such a strong concentration (nuclear power stations, recreation areas, and so forth) that they constitute forms of colonising one piece more of the territory for the capital.

To return to the above-mentioned article about the valuation of infrastructures as fixed capital,[27] in the 1940-1975 period there were two distinct phases in the implantation of infrastructures: one of subsistence in the years immediately after the war, and one of exploitation beginning in the sixties and associated with pro-development expansion.

In fact the subsistence phase produced scant investment in infrastructure, while the city underwent major population growth: half a million inhabitants between 1940 and 1960 did not receive the corresponding necessary public investment in urban development and services. The minimum infrastructure to be constructed took the form of the extension of certain streets which was vital to support further growth and the minimal increase in transport demanded by the growing population. Furthermore the construction industry had scant capacity, leading to serious residential problems for the labour force immigrating from the countryside, and particularly from the south of Spain; the precarious solutions adopted by public and private agents are explained elsewhere.

This was, then, a period marked by serious urban undercapitalisation, in that existing infrastructure was the only fixed capital at hand to face up to the new urban development situation.

[27] Manuel de Solà-Morales and José Luis Gómez Ordóñez, *op. cit.*, pp. 56-61.

7.b Large infrastructure: the motorways as the radii of metropolitan expansion.

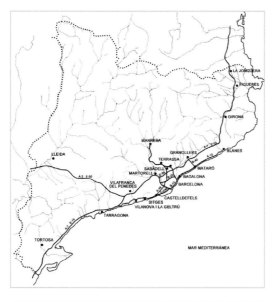

6
...agram showing the Catalan
...torways in the 1990s.
...th Barcelona as the centre
...gravity, they repeat the
...ial lines marked out by the
...ways.

7
...jor infrastructures emerge
...he residential fabrics in
...periphery. An element in
...rcelona's Arterial Network.

8
...e rigidity of various projects
...to their rejection by the
...people that brought them
...a standstill. The example
...he second beltway in Nou
...ris.

7.19, 7.20
The major deployment of infrastructures was geared towards the car, whereas public transport was inefficient. In 1971, the trams were replaced by buses.

A far-reaching change emerged in the 1960s with exploitation infrastructure, which corresponded to the new political and economic situation of Stabilisation and Development Plans. Exploitation referred to the use of the system of infrastructure, focusing more on financial gain than on the functionality of urban growth. The autonomy of "toll-style" operating accounts took precedence over the global urban development results achieved by these infrastructures.

Meanwhile, Barcelona's county area underwent a growth explosion: almost one million inhabitants between 1960 and 1970.

One particularly outstanding investment at this time was the 1962 Barcelona arterial network as a communications plan drawn up by the Central Government, enabling the construction of the radial motorways that extend out from Barcelona to the Metropolitan Area: the Vallès, Llobregat and Maresme axes were given their first stretches of motorway – approximately 15 kilometres – that were later extended to form the present-day system.

It is not a question here of speaking for or against the motorways, but of taking into account the fact that their urban and regional impact would have been very different if their layout and construction had responded to a more integrated, complex decision-making process. We have already seen how it was the toll concession that governed the layout, and it is important not to confuse the profitability of an investment with its short-term internal accounts.

This arterial network of motorways actually linked up directly to Barcelona's system of main streets – Meridiana, Diagonal, Gran Via – with no mediation or interrelation between this powerful new system of mobility and traditional urban axes, and, as a result, these axes have for decades now been city through roads. It is quite fair to say that this aggression substantially modified the system of uses and relations between central and suburban Barcelona. It might even be said that the absence of mediation of this kind imposed the construction of the city ring roads (the Ronda Litoral and the Second Beltway) as the only possible way of redistributing the traffic on today's radial motorways.

However, this initial model was joined in the seventies by the Third Beltway, the remainder of the motorways and Vallvidrera tunnel; work on the latter was paralysed for twenty years due to its financial "unviability". The Council, for its part, built the First Beltway, which came to a standstill in Guinardó due to problems of expropriation necessitated by its passage.

Once again, then, the various motorways were elements that, in seeking their own internal logic, overlooked the colonising effect they promoted on the surrounding and the not so immediate land. This, then, heralded the exploitation of expanses of land in the form of numerous housing developments comprising second homes in Barcelona's large Metropolitan Area, with the added value being appropriated by the landowners, and frequently without the most basic investment in local services.[28]

Attempts were made in the 1960s to rationalise this situation in the context of a possible Metropolitan Area, as we will explain later. Also during this period and with a major impact on industrial land, the port was extended westwards and the land on which the free port stood was restructured in the form of the industrial estate known as Zona Franca, or free zone, which became the country's largest production area.

In the city, the continuing expansion of the Metro and the Railway Interconnections Plan were beginning to introduce incipient strategies of restructuring, though as yet with limited effects.

VII.6 The residential periphery

In the contemporary city, the term urban periphery refers to residential forms that are incomplete, lacking services, centrality and/or symbolism and image. Major growth in cities in the last century was based on a single main protagonist: housing. Its problems and difficulties were generally far removed from the overcrowding and insalubrity so common in the 20th century city; however, they offered a whole spectrum of issues that required detailed analysis

---

[28] See the monographic issue of *Cuadernos* no. 98. Barcelona, 1973, particularly the article "Querida familia" by Ll. Cantallops. Also the work by C. Martí and J. Sanmartí in *Cuadernos* no. 102. Barcelona, 1974 and the article by M. Herce: "El consumo de espacio en las urbanizaciones de segunda residencia en Catalunya". *Ciudad y Territorio*. Madrid, 1977.

7.c Urban forms of residential suburb: suburban growth, marginal urbanisation and housing estates.

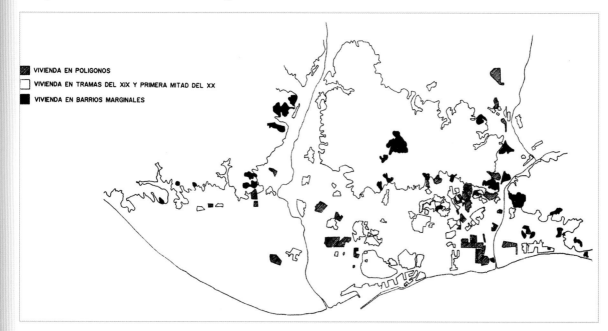

VIVIENDA EN POLIGONOS

VIVIENDA EN TRAMAS DEL XIX Y PRIMERA MITAD DEL XX

VIVIENDA EN BARRIOS MARGINALES

7.21
Identification of the residential types in the Barcelona suburb: estates, suburban fabrics and self-construction areas.

7.22, 7.23
Street in a suburban neighbourhood and view of Cornellà.

7.24, 7.25
Views of the neighbourhood of Roquetes.

7.26
Residential estate in La Verneda, 1955.

if the existing city was to be reclassified. A separate section should be devoted to the forms of provisional housing more associated with precarious urbanisation, such as the shanties and other temporary forms.

In this respect, southern European cities present a singularity that has to be taken into account: their urban structure is closely interrelated with the traditional centre and highly specific patterns are applied to residential development, enabling a fairly straightforward interpretation.

In Barcelona, various forms of periphery coexisted throughout the 20th century, varying in importance depending on the urban planning situation and the development of the real-estate sector. There are at least three radically different types:[29]

a) Districts of suburban expansion, the result of a form of plot division that followed a rectilinear layout of narrow streets and small squares allowing the construction of between 2 and 6 dwellings on narrow plots using a simple construction system. This was very common as a form of proletariat residence at the end of the last century and one that continued until the seventies. Originally the house was shared by a resident owner who rented out the rest of the dwellings, in a process of mass generalisation of the suburban extension of the 19th century. This was a very economic system of urban development produced on the basis of small production units, that advanced by means of "self-promotion" and practically family-run construction companies.

b) Districts of marginal urbanisation or self-construction in which dwellings were constructed on pieces of land that were parcelled up irrespective of urban development regulations and with no planned utilities. The dwellings were mainly self-built and were constructed by phases as the family's spending power increased.[30] The same process existed in many rapidly growing countries[31] with the common denominator of, on the one hand, the difficulties created for families who were obliged to follow this residential pattern, and, on the other, the fact that they ultimately became established districts within the city. Both conditions require serious analysis, avoiding facile interpretations that suggest it was a passing phenomenon or else praise the flexibility of this type of dwelling without attending to the overexploitation to which their users were submitted.

---

[29] This work is based on the hypotheses contained in the book *Evaluación de las necesidades de rehabilitación*" (MOPU, Madrid, 1984), and arose from research that began in early 1980 in the framework of the Laboratorio de Urbanismo, directed by the author, based on the Barcelona area. An initial version was published by the ITEC as a presentation at the 1st Rehabilitation Conference held in Barcelona in 1983. The text was taken from a reworking of the article "La periferia. Che cosa è, che cosa fare", published in two volumes: *La riqualificazione della città in Europa*. Rome, 1990.

[30] J. Busquets: *La urbanización marginal*. Laboratori d'Urbanisme, UPC, Barcelona, 1999.

[31] This process is given different names in the various countries in the Mediterranean area but the same characteristics are common in all cases: *abusivi* in Italy; *clandestinos* in Portugal; *grecekondu* in Greece, etc. A summary of the process can be found in LUB: "Teoría y experiencia de la urbanización marginal" in D. Lewis: *El crecimiento de las ciudades*. Barcelona, 1972.

7.27
Photomap of Nou Barris in t
1960s, showing low levels of
urbanisation in the residenti:
periphery.

c) Mass housing estates: groups of dwellings built in a unitary style and arranged in linear and/or high-rise blocks responding to a repetitive, very homogeneous building type. These estates were constructed by private or public developers, usually formed part of subsidised social housing programmes and configure a stereotype image of the modern periphery of our cities.

An analysis of the implantation of the three principal forms of periphery in the Barcelona area could be summarised as follows.

Suburban districts

Here there are two quite distinct groups differentiated by their density and level of infilling:

a) **built-up suburban fabrics**. These mainly correspond to processes of suburban growth in the mid-19th or early 20th centuries.

Today's high indexes of residential surface area in these fabrics are the result of intense building processes arising from the development of the real-estate sector that followed on from Catalonia's industrial transformation. Today, they represent densities of up to 150 dwellings per hectare.

They mostly correspond to nucleuses that originally formed according to a typological structure based on the model of the "artisan's house" (small buildings on narrow plots with a workshop or business premises on the ground floor and living quarters on the first floor) that gradually underwent major transformation processes. These dwellings were mostly rented and tended to grow over time.

One of the most marked elements of the homogeneity of these fabrics was the structure of their layouts, in which the form and measurements of the public space invariably adapted to the use and the image of the 19th-century suburban city. The districts of Gràcia and Poble Sec are two obvious examples.

There are specifically two types of urban spaces: streets with a small section of between 6 and 12 metres, and small squares marked out by the fabric's road network. The percentage of public space, for the most part streets, is very high, the ratio of public land to land divided into plots being one to three.

As a result of the high densities and the urban position of these fabrics, the use of public space was a variable differential that came to characterise them, and in which major traffic conflicts and parking problems were clearly seen. A second important shortcoming was the general lack of open spaces, as the squares, due to their limited size and capacity for use, did not satisfactorily meet the needs of the resident population. In general, it might be said that the environmental and urban planning value of public space was acceptable and appealing, though the problems varied substantially according to the levels of density.

b) unbuilt-up suburban fabrics. This group was characterised by lower indexes of density and residential surface area, generally less than 80 dwellings/hectare. They came into being at the same time as the fabrics in the first group, and their original morphological characteristics are very similar.

In general they correspond to outlying urban sectors that did not come under such strong pressure from the expansion of the property market in the late 19th and early 20th centuries. Consequently their present-day structures still preserve much of the original fabric of the small single-family house between party walls. It was in the 1960s that transformation processes as a result of intensive property speculation made themselves felt, taking the form of a vigorous dynamic that replaced certain of the fabric's important sectors or roads.

Unlike the dense fabrics, in which the impact of modern replacements tended to merge in with large old buildings, of just a ground floor and two storeys, the contrast of the new high-rise constructions was extremely controversial, with the subsequent break-away from basic morphological relations.

With a predominance of single- or two-family buildings, the typological repertory was less varied than in the built-up fabrics. It is widespread in certain areas of Sant Andreu or Camp de l'Arpa, for instance.

The form of tenure of the old dwelling was more evenly divided between ownership and rental than in the built-up fabrics, with a greater incidence of ownership in the case of the smaller types of houses. This is one of the reasons why major property development in the sixties and seventies came up against less resistance to the replacement of old buildings by large blocks of apartments for sale.

The form and characteristics of public space were comparable to those of the built-up fabric, as they originally obeyed planning processes that employed similar criteria and instruments.

Levels of urban development were also relatively satisfactory. Differences to the built-up fabric lay primarily in the reduced importance of public space due to a lower density of population. Traffic and parking problems were also less significant, enabling a more evenly distributed application of superficial solutions over the existing road system.

Districts of borderline urbanisation

The situation of urban planning illegality, the precarious nature of urbanisation and poor conditions of habitability were the main problems facing any policy for intervention and improvements in these districts.

In order to identify the typical situations, two main families of districts can be established:

a) those that had kept up a process of **consolidation** and had a strong enough dynamic and local initiative to address improvements.

7.d Neighbourhoods of marginal urbanisation in the comarca of Barcelona.

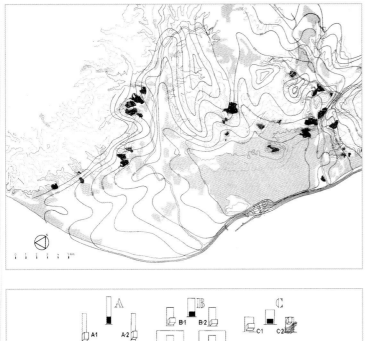

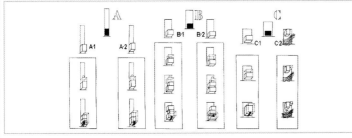

7.28
Neighbourhoods of marginal urbanisation and levels of accessibility.

7.29
Different housing typologie

7.30, 7.31
The neighbourhoods of Vallbona and Singuerlin, wi their difficult topographica situation.

2, 7.33
e self-construction
ghbourhood of Sant Josep
Sant Vicenç dels Horts on
other side of the railway
e, on the mountainside. A
all housing estate was later
lt there.

b) those that had undergone periods of **stagnation**, and were now run down with high levels of abandonment.

The construction dynamic of the first group of districts produced more continuous building with compact areas, unlike the second, which was, in general, more scattered in its organisation, with the corresponding difficulties of establishing criteria to plan and improve the urban space.

The two districts did however share the common characteristic of a high percentage of roads, poor levels of urban development and disorderly processes of land occupation that led to serious difficulties in creating new green spaces and facilities that were not residual plots.

The dwellings varied a great deal in typology, obeying evolutive models in keeping with the plot characteristics (gradual occupation of the land and upward growth of construction). The services and finishes were often extremely deficient and the possibilities of rehabilitation were more favourable in consolidated districts, as in the case of Sant Josep, where practically 90 per cent of dwellings were eligible for improvement work; in districts that had stagnated for many years, however, such as Torre Baró, the percentage of dwellings that could be rehabilitated was fewer than 70 per cent.

The form of tenure did not present major administrative problems, as most of them, despite their illegal status, were "owned" (almost 70%), though there were cases of unclear or controversial ownership that hampered the regularisation of some plots.

Mass housing estates

There are as many as five clearly differentiated groups of mass housing estate corresponding to consecutive periods of history:[32]

---

[32] For a broader-based view of this form of peripheral growth see Amador Ferrer: *Los polígonos de vivienda en la comarca de Barcelona, I y II, op. cit.*

7.34, 7.35
Eucharistic Congress housing
built between 1953 and 195?

a) **Post-war housing developments**. These include estates built between 1945 and 1954, and the *casas baratas* or cheap houses of the twenties, which were the first example of public housing in Spain. They were public developments undertaken by councils or the state body, Union Housing Association, which was specially constituted for this purpose.

They were constructed in very remote, marginal locations which have however since been integrated into the city as a result of subsequent growth. These are small estates: the surface area is in almost all cases less than 10 hectares, with no more than a thousand dwellings per development.

As they were the first public housing operations, they were clearly experimental in nature. The absence of established regulations and precedent led to the search for a variety of possibilities. This explains their typological variety: from single-family dwellings, via the traditional house between party walls, to the first multi-family apartment blocks, using a wide variety of systems to join the dwellings. The dwellings themselves were relatively small (less than 40 m²) and had all the problems arising from the low quality construction characteristic of the time.

b) **Residential extension estates**. This group includes those built in Barcelona in the second half of the fifties, in developments coordinated by the schemes of the 1957 Social Emergency Plan. The foremost developer of the period was the Urban Development Commission of Barcelona and Other Municipalities, set up in 1953 to manage the County Plan.

A high urban content was brought to these operations, which were located in positions to continue and extend Barcelona's residential fabric; they represented the urbanisation and rise in value of large urban sectors that had, until then, been unoccupied. As a result, these estates now form a fully integrated part of the city. They are medium-sized (10-30 hectares), containing a large number of dwellings, normally over 1,000.

The buildings are laid out along roads. The construction types show strong signs of the influence of the traditional house between party walls found in Cerdà's Eixample. Other resources were the toothed and high-rise blocks in the Congress Housing development, the blocks of duplex housing on Montbau estate, or the combination of row houses and linear blocks used on the Besòs estate.

Higher quality in construction was accompanied by an increase in the size of the dwellings, between 60 and 75 m², which from this moment on became the typical size of apartments in blocks.

36
lineueta estate. 15-floor
ock on Passeig de la Vall
Hebron surrounded by
developed land.

37
esòs estate on the eastern edge
Barcelona. This view from
e 1970s shows the lack of
frastructure.

c) **The first metropolitan estates** were developed by Union Housing Association and constructed in Barcelona in the 1960s, along with other privately-funded estates that obeyed the same intervention guidelines.

These interventions were characterised by their location in relation to the historical urban nucleuses of Barcelona's wider county context, in what might be termed a dual position: the Sant Ildefons estate in relation to Cornellà, the Can Serra estate in relation to L'Hospitalet, the Neighbourhood Absorption Unit of San Cosme in relation to El Prat de Llobregat, etc. In this way, the developer could supplement the estate's facilities and services with those of the nearby town. This deficit was particularly prevalent during the early years of these estates, subsequently undergoing a gradual decrease.

These were large estates (20-25 hectares), with a large number of dwellings – over 2,000. Most of the problems that these estates faced were related to the low technical quality of the projects and the inconsistency of their arrangement. The very high percentage of empty land of indeterminate use, inappropriate proportions and scant urban context created major problems for maintenance and interventions to improve urban development.

The main construction types were the free-standing linear block of 4-5 or 7- 8 storeys, and the tower block of 11 or more floors, with a relatively high index of dwellings per block, contrasting with the low overall density. The overall quality of construction was low.

The dwelling, with a prototypical surface of 60 m², consolidated certain distributive and functional characteristics (the kitchen-living room and bedroom-bathroom relationship, etc.) with three bedrooms.

d) **Speculative estates**. This group mainly includes the projects of private developers and semi-public bodies such as savings banks, cooperatives and others. These initiatives represent the vigour of the construction sector in the latter half of the sixties and the creation of property developers with the capacity to undertake the construction of large housing developments.

The estates occupied small areas of land (less than 15 hectares) on which they concentrated a large number of dwellings (between 1,000 and 3,000), taking the overall densities to more than 150 dwellings per hectare, and as many as 320 in some cases.

They occupied isolated, fringe positions in the territory and were directly dependent on main highways. These locations, which are unusual in small, high-density housing estates, can often be explained by an incorrect interpretation of the densities and building levels stipulated by planning regulations.

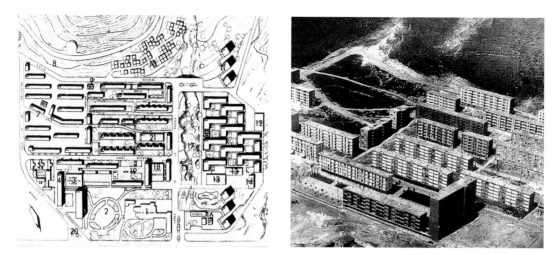

7.38, 7.39
Montbau estate, marked out
by the Social Emergency Plan
(1960). The orthogonal layout
was superposed onto the slope.

The predominant construction type is the high-rise block (normally between 12 and 20 floors), with a large number of dwellings per block. The characteristic layouts are four dwellings per stairwell in the linear block, with a single façade per dwelling, and six or eight dwellings per stairwell in tower blocks. These constructions did, nonetheless, represent a slight improvement in the quality of construction in comparison with many of the buildings on the estates in the previous group. The surface area and the functional characteristics of the dwelling followed the same model.

e) The metropolitan estates of the seventies. These are the major public housing developments undertaken in the early seventies by various state or local bodies, such as the National Housing Institute, the National Urban Development Institute or the Barcelona Municipal Housing Board.

The large surface of land occupied by this type of interventions (20 to 60 hectares) was a determinant factor in the choice of their location, outside the city.

The number of dwellings was also large – always above 2,500 dwellings per development – with on average very uniform gross densities of between 120 and 150 dwellings per hectare.

As a result of their sheer size, the projects anticipated large reserves for communal facilities, most of which were a long time coming. This led to major functional deficits, with important repercussions for the adjacent urban areas.

The construction type employed was a direct derivative of the previous groups. The linear block and the high-rise block were refined by planning regulations and emerged from the process with undeniably improved intrinsic conditions (a single bay, large patios for ventilation, better installations, etc.); nonetheless, this accentuated the importance granted to the building as part of the whole, making it increasingly autonomous.

The number of dwellings per block was over 30. The dwelling was identical in size, layout and facilities to those on the estates of the sixties.

Different forms of city periphery

The role of each of these processes in the various areas of the city and in relation to the centre is, in itself, a major field of discussion.

The peripheral fabrics of the Metropolitan Area of Barcelona added up to a surface area of in the region of 2,500 hectares – that is, more than twice the surface of the city's Eixample. A breakdown by types give us: 1,000

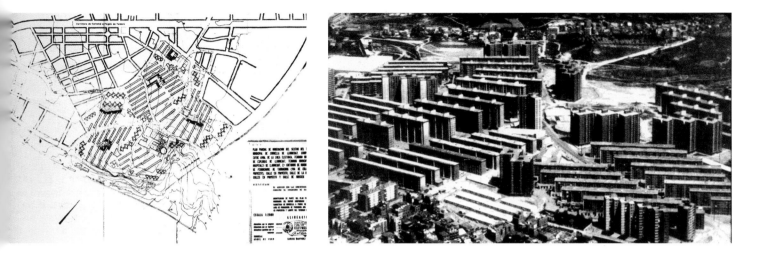

7.40, 7.41
The Sant Ildefons housing
estate in Cornellà de Llobregat,
1960.

hectares of suburban expansion districts; 650 hectares of marginal areas, including housing and precarious urban developments, and 900 hectares of generally high density mass housing estates.

If we consider these three categories in their "normal" terms – that is, separating out the singular data that can make an area very different to its counterparts, we see the "profile of urban reclassification needs" by types of periphery.

Different profiles serve to explain the most urgent problems or priority issues for the rehabilitation of the periphery.

a) The dwelling in suburban expansion districts has a rehabilitation profile that features modernisation of the dwelling itself – general antiquated – and the difficulties created by the form of tenure, generally an old fixed rent, due to which the owner is not interested in investing in improvement or rehabilitation. Conversely, the urban space is usually very good.

b) the dwelling in marginal districts has a profile that features the need for both primary urbanisation and the legalisation of the district. Studies of these areas show that only a fairly low percentage of the buildings had insalubrious conditions (approximately 10 per cent) whereas the rest only requires a relatively simple process of improvement and extension.

Rights with regard to the dwelling can in general be ascribed to the owners, except situations of condominiums or special contracts which require careful study in each case.[33]

c) The mass housing estate has a relatively different profile of rehabilitation needs. The major issues are the dwelling and urban space. The former may present serious repair problems due to poor construction during some periods, as described above. Furthermore, the urbanisation deficits are, in general, serious.[34]

[33] See the example of application to the district of Sant Josep, published in issue 82 of *CAU*. Barcelona, 1982. Also see the summary "La Urbanizzazione marginale a Barcellona" published in the reader edited by A. Clementi and L. Ramírez, published in 1985 by F. Angeli: *Abitazioni e periferie urbane nei in via di sviluppo*.

[34] Both themes gave rise to major problems in the 1970s and 1980s in the field of mass housing rehabilitation, for example on Barcelona's Besòs estate or the UVA of Sant Cosme in El Prat. The problem of "aluminosis" of concrete was also concentrated intensively in some high-density estates of low quality construction.

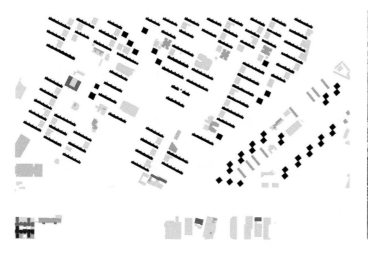

Conversely, although the form of tenure – normally deferred access to ownership – does not present problems in the short term, it has yet to be seen how this situation affects the transformation processes which in some cases will have to be dealt with in the longer term.

The general layout of the estate and the size of the district may definitively condition the process of urban enhancement. This was the periphery in its planned form, and the reality and its possible modifications have to be assessed on the basis of the hypotheses contained in the project.

7.42, 7.43
Bellvitge, one of the large estates to be built using a French prefabricated system, repeats the model dwelling as basic module.

VII.7 Speculation with land and suburbs

The role of land and the capital gains on its income go a long way to explaining the existence of different residential fabrics and the urban planning processes of transformation and/or replacement taking place in them.

The relation between the evolution of the real-estate sector, as regards the land, and the development of the property sector, as regards the construction of dwellings, is undeniably a structural whole that varies from region to region, and one that must be understood in order to interpret the periphery and proceed to a positive intervention in it.

The differing ways in which land and housing construction operated in each form of the periphery does in fact call for a more detailed explanation. Attention should in any case be paid to the interplay established at a given moment between the subsectors of the land and the housing markets since, although it is obvious that they act in integrated fashion, they combine well-defined subsectors that acquire great protagonism. Think of the so-called "informal" sector in housing, which scholars have on occasion chosen to see as being autonomous,[35] when in fact it is a well defined subsector within the broader construction field.

[35] This is an attitude normally represented by the work of the English architect John Turner: see for example *Freedom to build* (The Macmillan, New York, 1972); and M. Boyars: *Housing by people* (London, 1976). While they address the subject of substandard housing in fast growing countries with few resources, they tend to suggest an alternative or autonomous condition that does not correspond with the real role of the unregulated sector in those countries.

In this way, for example, the phenomenon of marginal urban development, so widespread in some Mediterranean regions,[36] reveals the strategy of producing income from increased land value in relation to the legal status of more general urban land.

In the case of the Metropolitan Area of Barcelona, in the sixties marginal urban development districts were the perfect excuse for landowners to sell "marginal", non-urban land at a good price. But then, in the mid-term, the very existence of this marginal district enabled the creation of an Urban Plan to "acknowledge reality" and always incorporated new, unoccupied land, thereby attributing further capital gains to expectant land adjacent to the district, often belonging to the same property that spawned the marginal process.[37]

These days, a full discussion of the issues merely outlined here would highlight our cities' vacant, interstitial or peripheral land[38] which hosts processes that start out as provisional and end up becoming consolidated as a well-defined system of occupation.

The peripheral dwelling and housing policies

A study of the periphery also requires further thought about the housing policies that led to or intervened in their construction.[39]

It is true that a policy will often conceal a fairly precise project image, particularly if we look at policies in the 1960s, inspired by the ideas and slogans of the Modern Movement. Much has been said of the force behind this movement, which saw its principles become laws and its residential models adopted by mass housing policies, though this may also have been its weakness.

Analyses of the minimum housing conditions and typological models introduced by modern architecture were incontestable, and their direct translation into a housing programme and acts was, at the very least, little meditated, and still serves as an alibi for inflexible housing programmes in many countries. The difficulties of

---

[36] The work "La Metrópoli 'spontanea': il caso di Roma", dealing with Rome, for example, highlights both how widespread the phenomenon was and the variety of forms of the periphery. This situation suggests the need to introduce more specific meanings to separate the essential *abusivismo* of housing from merely speculative *abusivismo*, or from the *abusivismo* that refers solely to the procedure of legalisation, without overstepping legal stipulations.

[37] On this subject, see the work of M. Solà-Morales: "La urbanización marginal y la formación de plusvalía del suelo", *Papers-Revista de Sociología.* Barral, Barcelona, 1974.

[38] An issue that was developed in the English-speaking world in the late 1970s with the term "derelict land", paving the way for larger scale infill projects.

[39] See the author's article: "Políticas de vivienda vs. urbanización marginal", *Ciudad y Territorio.* Madrid, 1975. Also in "La urbanización marginal", *op cit.*, 1999.

7.44
Location of marginal neighbourhoods (represented by an asterisk) in the 1970s and prospects for land consumption generated by them.

7.45, 7.46
Vistalegre in Castelldefels. The appearance of this neighbourhood changed the growth dynamic, introducing partial plan for the interstitial area.

such centralised policies should be set in the context of the optimism of an epoch and the determination of a real-estate sector that addressed a major process of expansion in this way. This however is the key to many of the problems being faced by the periphery today in sectors which served as a matrix for mass housing operations, but also, indirectly, for the development of other peripheral sectors that emerged simultaneously in the absence of any kind of response from central planning policies.

Regarding this subject it is important to remember certain innate difficulties in central policies, for which a parallel can also be seen in rehabilitation policies in the seventies and eighties that have run up against the administrative and juridical embargo of the urban complexity which is so difficult to assess at central level. Recent experiences, such as the Spanish case, that implement grants for rehabilitation are even leading to the development of specific companies and agents to administer these resources. In any case, these are situations that required detailed assessment to see to what point these matters call for analysis and evaluation at central level, but also a more open form of development that may be local.[40] There is room here too for a discussion of generic policies and specific programmes.

There is another comment to be made on the theme of non-spatial policies with a major impact on the dynamic of the periphery. It is a reflection that goes beyond the scope of this text, but it is evident that

[40] It would be interesting to undertake a rigorous evaluation of the French programmes such as the Banlieu 87 for its contributions to the reclassification of the "Grandes Ensembles", as well as more complex programmes such as the ANAH development with the coparticipation of central and local sectors.

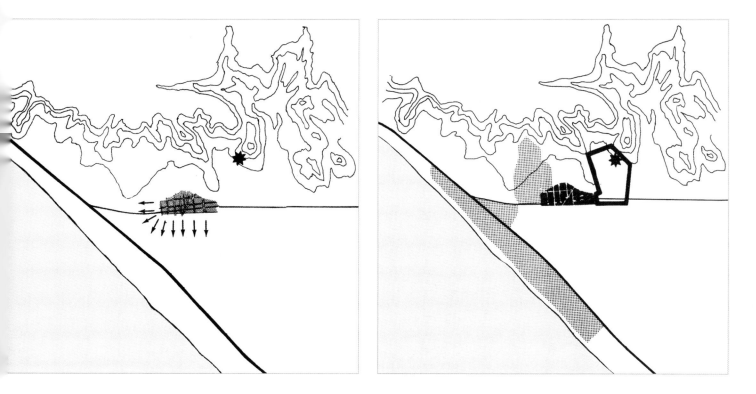

in some countries, such as ours, land and housing are a structural refuge for many savings and financial transactions that are not entirely transparent. In this way, schemes apparently unconnected with urban planning – related to taxation, for instance – can substantially alter these markets and establish specific demands of a very different nature and speed that affect the behaviour of land and real-estate agents, and must be taken into account.

VII.8 The transformation of the Eixample and the suburban plain

There were initially a series of important modifications to Cerdà's project for Barcelona's Eixample: the reader will remember that its proposed building regulations (ordinances) and economic reclassification were explicitly left out when the project was approved. It had to trust to the strength of the layout and the personal efforts of Cerdà in the first decade of its implantation.

In this process, the street blocks, initially with an open layout, became closed blocks and the inner courtyard was built up rather than remaining a garden, which was Cerdà's idea. Building grew in height and depth with changing ordinances. Some of the land set aside in the project for facilities and parks was also gradually transformed.[41]

[41] Various authors: *Cerdà. Urbs i territori*. Electra, Madrid, 1994. Catalogue of the exhibition of the same name.

7.e Rehabilitation of the residential periphery.

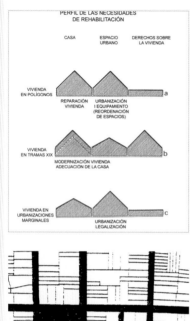

7.47
Different rehabilitation processes according to specif "needs".

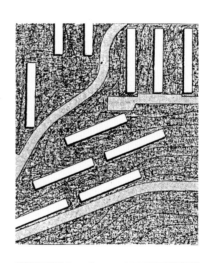

7.48, 7.49, 7.50
The different fabrics in the urban residential periphery.

7.51
Rehabilitated suburban house.

7.52
The redevelopment of Sant Josep.

7.53
Arrangement of open spaces. Valldaura estate in Nou Barris

.54
The Eixample has become a
fully-fledged CBD (Central
Business District), maintaining
correct level of residence.

.55
The permissiveness of higher
building levels destroyed the
existing suburban fabric.

Nonetheless, today's Eixample is still an emblematic part of our city. The rigour of its geometric order has enabled the production of an urban element in which a wide variety of urban uses have been installed with admirable architectural flexibility: the Eixample is an ongoing laboratory of architectures that has room for the most diverse styles and trends, all within the general coordinates of alignment and ground levels established almost at the very start. Further, the morphological adaptability of the square grid with chamfered corners has proved itself to be a powerful one, judging by the many different solutions applied to plot division and the use of the passages running through the middle of the street blocks, etc.

In terms of its extension, today's central Eixample is only half of what Cerdà actually designed; nonetheless, the amount of building and activity are perhaps greater. We might even controversially posit the idea that there are two entities in central Barcelona: Cerdà's project with its innovative criteria and the Eixample, a reality produced by the social and economic contradictions of its development. This approach enables a better understanding of the strength and the interest of the two entities. Below is an outline of what the Eixample is today.

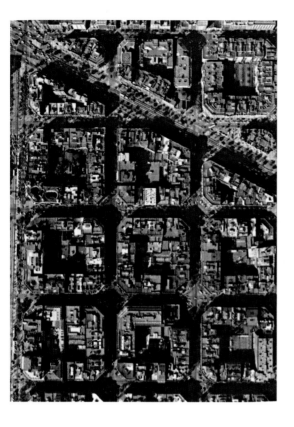

7.56
Image of the central Eixample
from the poster for the 1993
exhibition to launch its
recovery.

It covers 880 hectares – approximately 550 street blocks, and in the order of 125 kilometres of street; roughly speaking, it has a resident population of 350,000 inhabitants and 300,000 jobs. Another indicator of use and activity, as well as structure, is traffic: approximately 600,000 cars per day circulate around the area. This highlights the powerful dimensions of the centre and the strong simultaneous presence of residence and work.[42]

These magnitudes have different dynamics; whereas the population is falling slightly and ageing, non-residential activities are flourishing, as traffic has also done to a larger extent. The amount of building housing these activities has also grown, though at a slower rate than residential building. And, very importantly, over the last twenty years, the number of public parking places in the Eixample has grown from 20,000 to 50.000.

Furthermore, the Eixample is a very busy commercial area. The analysis of the census of settlement produces an average of 300 m² per establishment, taking into account the usual downscaling involved in tax information. This average conceals a very wide range: for example, over 10% of the activities are carried out in premises of over 1,000 m². On the basis of a sample of 20 street blocks, the average number of commercial premises is 40 establishments per block, varying between 20 and 100. If we compare these two figures, we deduce that in the Eixample there is, on average, 11,500 m² of business activity per block – that is, almost one and a half floors if we were to locate these businesses around the perimeter of the ground floor, with 75 per cent occupation, leaving

[42] Figures taken from the comprehensive study of the evolution and current state of the Eixample, carried out by a team headed by J. Busquets and J. L. Gómez Ordóñez: *Estudi de l'Eixample*, 2 vols. Ajuntament de Barcelona, 1983. There is a publication that summarises the work "Estudi del Eixample", Barcelona, 1983, translated into Spanish (MOPU, Madrid, 1984), and a catalogue of an exhibition that travelled to Genoa, Venice, Rome, Lisbon, Oporto, London, Bordeaux and Hamburg (with translations from the same time, 1985-86).

7.f Infilling and densification of the Eixample.

57
volution of Eixample building
dinances. Speculative
nsification increased building
els and promoted excessive
ansformation.

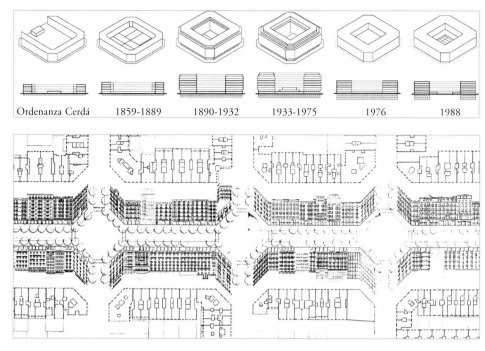

Ordenanza Cerdá   1859-1889   1890-1932   1933-1975   1976   1988

58
eometric composition of the
çades.

59
volution of Eixample housing.

60
Drawing of the types of
reet block and their plot
morphology.

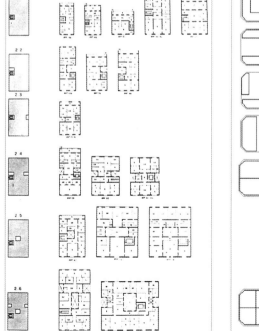
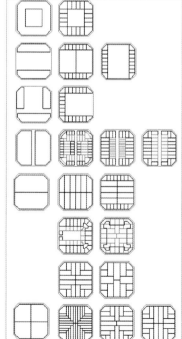

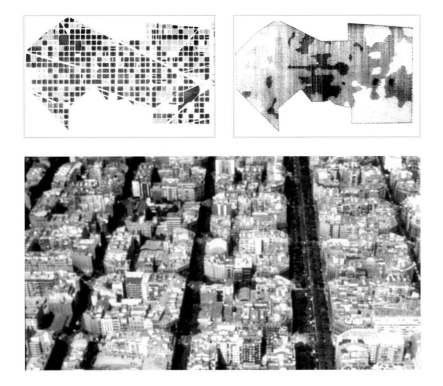

7.61, 7.62
Interpretative images of the
situation in the Eixample
in 1983. For example,
prospects of densification and
summarised diagram of the
ageing of the population.

7.63
The aerial view reflects
functional and morphological
complexity.

the inner courtyard free.

In addition to these densities, the strong residential component and the large surface area it represents in relation to the metropolis make this area a special centre, more complex and perhaps less specialised than other urban centres that become spaces of almost exclusive central activity.[43]

In any case, the enormous capacity for transformation that can be attributed to it is even greater than the exaggerated transformations that it has undergone since its implantation, 140 years ago. Nonetheless, the centre of Barcelona has a more favourable structure than that of other European and North American metropolitan centres. This does not however mean that the Eixample is not a dense urban piece; any treatment is difficult and must be strictly controlled and nuanced, because it is both a metropolitan centre and the heart of various residential districts.

The main transformations in the Eixample have taken place with the intensification of private construction on the block in accordance with changes in construction ordinances. There are four main periods, coinciding with different legislation:

a) Plot ordinances (1860-1890) allowed the construction of 50 per cent of each plot to a height of 20 metres – the same as the usual street width in the Eixample.

[43] This is the typical downtown, a modern city centre that is very active during office hours and absolutely deserted during the rest of the day and at weekends in a disproportion that often produces serious social problems, but above all which does not represent a good use of the centre as accumulated historical heritage.

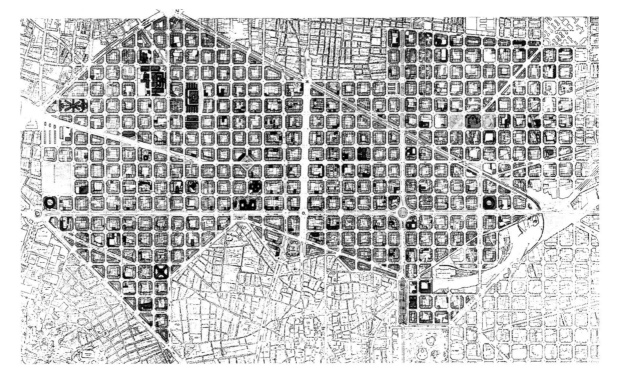

b) Block ordinances (1891-1941) allowed occupation of the block to a level of 73.6 per cent, taking building depth to 28 metres. The courtyard was then occupied to a height of 4.4 m.

c) Congestion ordinances (1942-1976) saw the height rise to 24.4 metres (with ground floor and seven storeys plus penthouse and top-floor apartment). The courtyard came to be occupied to a height of 5.5 metres, with the possibility of a ziggurat-style construction above this limit. This ordinance broke with the skyline of the Eixample and promoted the disastrous upward extensions of previously existing buildings to reach the new height limit which has done so much to fragment the urban image of the whole. Evidently, the resulting densities increased dramatically.

The history of the Eixample is full of additions and reinterpretations of the existing buildings, but the experience of these operations brought with it a coherence and an overall interpretation. This period also saw interesting examples with the new heights but this architectural production tended to depart from an overall approach of the building as part of a whole and introduced a new skyline dotted with penthouses and other added volumes that created complete formal disorder.

d) The ordinances of the General Metropolitan Plan (1976) reduced occupation slightly and the regulatory heights were brought back down to 20.75 metres for the overall construction and 4.5 metres in the courtyard.

Unfortunately, the period of infilling in the Eixample coincided with the days of development policy and ordinances allowing greater congestion, as explained above.

Despite the difficulties arising from these inappropriate transformations, the results of the above-mentioned study show that the Eixample retained important attributes. In addition to the elements of transformation listed as being produced by changes of ordinance, a present-day diagnosis includes the following factors, necessary in directing rehabilitation and improvements:

1. The overall form has strong urban consistency. In urban planning terms, it is important to understand the Eixample area as a unitary entity in order to strengthen its structure and image: the successive rhythm of streets and corners, and the visual continuity of built land are elements that configure its general form and must be taken as dominant in any treatment of it.

2. The street layout is the most fixed part of the project. There are two clearly perceptible orders: one of 105.20 metre wide streets with internal passages that establish the basic order of the layout and larger streets responsible for interdistrict connections.

3. The surface use of streets; intensity of use is a cause for concern. The Eixample is crossed by one in five of the total number of trips conducted in the Metropolitan Area with a population equivalent to one eighth and almost 1,000,000 journeys of a total of 5,000,000). Over half of these journeys in the Barcelona area are on foot.

On a daily basis, residents in the central sector make 300,000 journeys on public transport (100,000 within the Eixample) and 100,000 journeys by car (25,000 within the Eixample).

Other economic activities also attract journeys in this central area. The result is that every day 500,000 people go to the Eixample for reasons of work and a further 150,000 specifically to shop. Of course, over half of these journeys begin within the Eixample. There are a great many – approximately 20 per cent of journeys – that actually have nothing to do with the city of Barcelona, but simply cross through it via the Eixample.

The use of the road network by cars is uneven depending on the areas or streets of the Eixample and the direction they follow. Horizontal relations (for car journeys) are in the order of 300,000 cars a day, whereas vertically the sum of traffic on all streets is almost double this figure, or 540,000 vehicles. In this central area there are of course twice as many vertical as horizontal streets of an average length of approximately half.

4. Car parking is intense, as corresponds to an important central area. Almost half – 40 per cent – of the street blocks include public car parking.

Underground car parks beneath public thoroughfares, first built in the late 1960s, represent overall more than 2 kilometres of street and a surface area equivalent to the land occupied by ten Eixample street blocks, or the built surface area of two.

5. Public transport creates greater accessibility. Both under ground and on the surface, the Eixample is the area of the city best communicated by public transport. Over ground there are fifty bus routes that practically coincide with the most important axes of private traffic. The routes are closely associated with the continuities established between the streets in the Eixample and those in the surrounding districts.

7.g Central use of the Eixample street system.

7.65
Distribution of car parking in the Eixample.

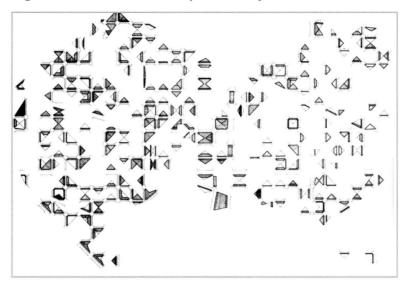

7.66
The Eixample as a turning place for different central flows.

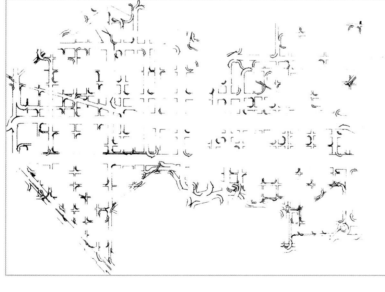

7.67, 7.68
Verification of the orthogonal streets and main axes in today's Eixample.

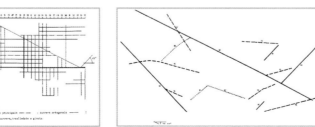

7.69
Illustration of the use of
underground spaces in a central
fragment of the Eixample.

7.70
Underground layouts in the
streets and avenues.

The subsoil is occupied by the railways, both through lines stopping at Sants and Passeig de Gràcia stations, and the Sarrià and Sabadell lines and the metropolitan network. In the Eixample and its outskirts there are 10 kilometres of railway tracks and approximately 15 kilometres of metropolitan trains.

The network of lines produces a point of interconnection and concentration in Plaça de Catalunya; the city's dual rail passage via Carrer Aragó and the Ronda beltways, the first built in the twenties and the second in the seventies, turned what was the Plaça de Catalunya terminal for trains from Sabadell in the twenties into a new junction of difficult functioning. The Metropolitan railway also comprises two longitudinal Barcelona crossings, with their extremes in Sagrera and Sants.

A stocktaking of the occupation of the subsoil of the streets and avenues of the Eixample highlights the need for an overall distribution of the various urban services, and outlines the possibilities of rationalisation of the Eixample in the future. Today it is possible to see the relative independence of each urban utility (water, gas, etc.) with regard to the others, representing major functional imbalances.

6. The activities of the Eixample. An overall interpretation of the present-day content of the Eixample street

7.h Plaça de Catalunya, a central place.

1, 7.72
ial views, in the 1930s and
ay.

73
 underground infrastructures
e it great centrality.

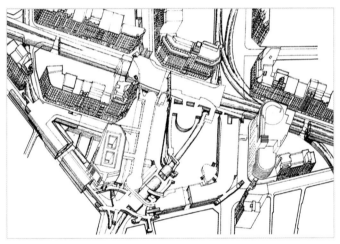

74
ontinuity between the
ambla and Rambla de
atalunya.

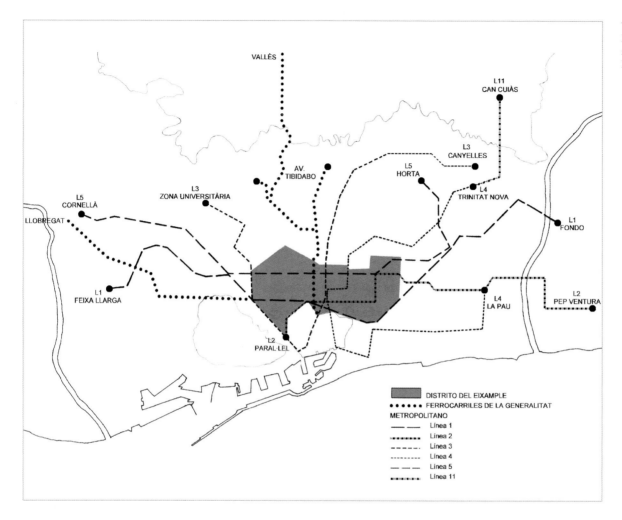

7.75
In the 1980s, the Metro line mostly passed through the Eixample.

blocks presents new images of the continuous, best distributed aspects of the centre of Barcelona, highlighting the huge variety of activities based there. It also reveals an even balance between residence and tertiary in absolute terms.

7. The distribution of facilities and open spaces. The Eixample is a very built up central city complex with few unoccupied spaces for services and facilities, though its use is evidently very intense.

As we know, Cerdà's proposal was laid out on the basis of street blocks devoted to facilities that were laid out in isotropic fashion. Although this model is not applicable in itself today, the positioning of new facilities has to provide the opportunity to introduce a model of complementary structure. Likewise, the idea of subcentres based around facilities emerges quite clearly in the Eixample and its districts even identify with them, principally the markets. The result is a structure of axes or clusters centring around these facilities.

8. The reserve of courtyards inside the street blocks. The Metropolitan Plan had set aside courtyards or fragments of street blocks for communal use. It is also possible, by studying the present-day plot division systems in the Eixample, to extract the most appropriate pattern and form for the recovery of the courtyards inside the street block. Modification of the ordinances would ensure their conversion into green spaces or local gardens, as we will go on to see.

9. The specificity of the centre of Barcelona. Specific recognition of the Eixample is called for. Its large size and formation process, the richness of its invariants, its complex but strong nature, and its capacity for residential use are characteristics that make it singular, among modern centres, and fundamental in the Barcelona area.

The densification of the suburban fabrics

The developments in Barcelona's suburban plain described above followed patterns of densification not unlike those of the central Eixample. However, their urban structure – the form of their streets and squares – made explosive intensification more difficult.

Nonetheless, a series of instruments or specific schemes can be detected on the basis of which transformation took place, unfortunately almost always in congestive or inappropriate terms.[44]

a) *Sventramento,* **or opening up** is a traditional planning instrument used in city reform and one that has been used with quite distinct effects due to different attitudes to the design of the intervention, ranging from Carrer Princesa-Ferran and Via Laietana, a case commented on above, to the First Beltway in the district of Putxet.

A central theme here is what happens to the adjacent strip of land. Too broad a definition would lead to suspicion of a strategy of extensive land remodelling which is always debatable and remote from the justification of the thoroughfare (such as García Morato's project for the Raval). Yet a mechanical, minimal definition that only addresses the road surface affected would produce an undetermined meeting of the street edges and the fabric to either side, with regard to ground level, form of the street and conflicting ownership interests, basically aggravating the intervention's impact on the fabrics through which it passes.

b) Drawing back the façade. This operation consists in establishing a new alignment on one or both sides of a street.

The purpose is in almost all cases to increase a street's capacity. This kind of designation of public property is therefore mooted for an entire street, not just for certain street blocks.

This measurement is not effective until it is complete. The real difficulty lies in the need to substitute each and every one of the buildings lining it. This process is not carried out imperatively, rather it is the result of the individual decisions of each site in question. To offer an incentive for replacement building, new regulations allow higher building levels (by means of the simple mechanism of the height corresponding to the width of the street).

[44] This is a reworking of the second part of J. Busquets + J. Parcerisa: *op. cit.,* pp. 63-80, 1983.

7.i Types of project in suburban densification.

Sventramento.

7.76, 7.77
The first Ronda beltway
running through El Putxet i
Gràcia.

Drawing back façades.

7.78, 7.79
Carrer Gran de Sant Andreu
replacement and withdrawing
of buildings.

High-density extensions.

7.80, 7.81
The area around Turo Park is
one example.

Enclosures.

7.82, 7.83
Comparison of Pedralbes
and Les Corts in the form of
a collage of enclosures with
different functions.

Even so, experience shows this mechanism to be ineffective in achieving its aims in a reasonable time period (for example, Travessera de Gràcia). Temporary situations become never-ending, the street becomes a sequence of party walls and the original problem remains unresolved.

This is one of the most common instruments to be applied in Barcelona to deal with the modern increase in the need for traffic space in very extensive areas of the first periphery. However, it has never incorporated a planning management mechanism to ensure the transformation of plots that present greatest inertia; it then becomes a speculative process, since the increased building intensity does not bring the expected general result.

c) High-density extensions. The modern phenomenon of the systematic intensification of Barcelona's first periphery incorporated a new, specific planning instrument. This was the mainly residential extension to occupy new interstitial areas that had hitherto simply been wasteland. When this initiative began, built-up residential typologies were already widespread in the city, calling for a corresponding change in scale of plots, street block, streets and junctions. Transformations of residential typologies were empirically endorsed by the fabric of the Eixample, which then became the point of reference for high-density extensions.

This new instrument was characterised by the transposition of these elements, as they were in the Eixample, taking them out of context in a partial development plan that guaranteed the public-private definition and the recomposition of land rights for building according to traditional criteria.

It crystallised in a system dotted with multiple tiny operations, as at the junction of Diagonal and Les Corts with the Turó Park development, a former sports complex, perhaps the only complete formalisation that aspired to be a representative residential area. Common to all of them is the absolute geometrical irregularity of the street block, added to the dubious solution of the inner courtyards.

d) Enclosures. Fragmentary city construction facilitated the ascendancy of the characteristic forms of each element. There is a prevalence, then, of large pieces, plainly situated here and there, enclosing areas of land in an autonomous arrangement, that do not respond to general guidelines. This process of land occupation was very convenient for the individual pieces, but in many cases conditioned the capacity to create a more connected and rational territory. They tend to respond to a monographic, almost exclusive use – a sports complex, a hospital or even specialised housing.

The hermetic nature of these enclosures took the form of one or various entrances in the perimeter, which was often fenced. This also led to the effect of barriers and "rears" onto all the adjacent areas.

More complex was the transformation of pieces of this scope when the use that gave rise to them changed without the immediate response of a clear alternative arrangement: the former football ground in Les Corts is an obvious example.

Some common points of suburban transformation

7.j Suburban transformation in Sant Andreu by way of example.

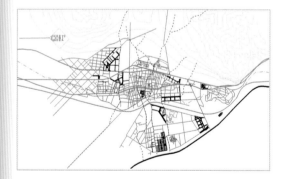

The suburban densificatio of Sant Andreu.

7.84
Plan by Vicenç Martorell, 1929.

7.85
Extension and urban transformation of Sant Andre

7.86
Transformation of old industrial elements at the end of the 20th century.

7.87
Photomap of the sector.

This is obviously a way of constructing the city in fragmentary but not spontaneous fashion. Land occupation obeys projects or plans, albeit on a lower scale of initiative and scope. Similar behaviours can be identified in different places and at different moments in time. These were, then, generally applicable planning operations and, above all, they had the potential to be updated.

In the absence of a unitary project or intention, city forms have gradually changed and even today the superposition of partial models is frequently seen. Altogether they manifest themselves as a continuous substratum, though this is not the result of a prior planning process.

The progressive interrelation of these peripheral operations has generated conflicts between the operations themselves and with the central city. It is important to remember that rather than being dual, these processes differ in their planning instruments. At the same time, the level of overlapping and copying leaves no doubt that they were both produced within the same economic apparatus: the passages in the Eixample and the chamfered corners on the periphery are examples of this mutual influence.

Disregard for these forms of more partial intervention has in fact been one of the most serious deficiencies of recent urban transformation; the construction of a series of new streets would have been the basic minimum project by means of which to extend our cities, for example. Conversely, the meaningless, stereotypical transposition of these sectoral instruments, such as drawing back façades to widen streets in general plans, has sentenced much of the development of the original residential fabrics.

VIII.

Patterns of pro-development expansion and political change. Urban development and the Plans

VIII.1 From County Plan to Partial Plans

The 1953 County Plan set out to respond to the new supramunicipal reality that metropolitan Barcelona called for. The drafting of the Plan followed the guidelines of the Barcelona Provincial Commission, constituted in 1945, which empowered Barcelona City Council to carry out the Plan. The architect, José Soteras, assisted by Pedro Bidagor, drew up this Plan.[1]

The ideas of a strict zoning of functions and the formation of district nucleuses provided the basis for the drafting of the County Plan, passed by a Special Act on 3 December 1953, and the Barcelona Urban Planning Commission was created to deploy the Plan, with the engineer Vicente Martorell as first in command.

The County Plan established a model of functional distribution to provide each municipality with the principal functions as though they were independent units.

The deployment of this Plan seemed to force out the initial organicist tendencies that had invaded the urban development of the immediate post-war years, associating the shape of cities with various beings, as though a problem of this complexity could be reduced to such a banal concept: Barcelona was shaped like an archangel, Valencia like a fish and San Sebastian like a bird.[2]

Another important innovation in that period was the promulgation of the first Land and Urban Planning Act on 12 May 1956, which, despite its difficult application, gave city development a framework of rationality. However, the protagonism of land ownership in this country and in those political circumstances could only hinder the deployment of rational planning.[3] The very title of the "Land" Act indicates just how fundamental this variable is in urban development in Spain.[4]

In this context, there was no firm central management of the County Plan, which was implemented fairly autonomously by municipalities according to the partial plans. The partial plans were dependent on the specifications of the County Plan but in many cases they altered it, yielding to the pressure of landowners. In its

[1]   Fernando de Terán: *Planeamiento urbano en la España contemporánea: historia de un proceso imposible.* Barcelona, 1978. The book illustrates Bidagor's clear role in post-war urban planning, first in the Ministry of the Interior and then the Ministry of Housing. Also by the same author: *Historia del urbanismo en España. Siglos XIX y XX.* Ed. Cátedra, Madrid.
[2]   *Op. cit.*, pp. 269-280.
[3]   Manuel Ribas i Piera: "La planificación urbanística en España", *Zodiac* no. 15. Cremona, 1965. On page 163 he describes the situation as follows: "The private sector at this time saw Urban Development as an instrument of legalised self-enrichment, rather like speculation within the law."
[4]   Compare this to other countries that tend to pass "planning acts". The power of land is so important that for example in Catalonia, urban land is usually measured by square spans instead of square metres, 1 m² being equivalent to 26.5 square spans, if this offers an indication of the "appreciation" of land...

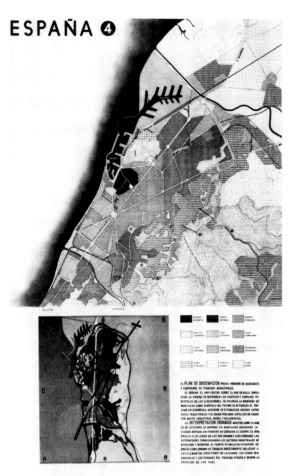

ESPAÑA ❹

BARCELONA 1550000 HABITANTES. CAPITAL DE REGION, CIUDAD ADMINIS-
TRATIVA Y COMERCIAL. CENTRO PREDOMINANTEMENTE INDUSTRIAL

8.02
Proposal for Barcelona and its "organic interpretation". International Housing and Urban Development Congress, Lisbon, 1952.

classification of the territory, the Plan evidently assigned different values to the land in keeping with the zoning of activities; a change in classification from a green area or facilities to residential or industrial use could represent a major increase in value for the agents or intermediaries in question.

In other cases the change was made *de facto* in collusion with the powers that be, who tolerated forms of land occupation that went against the Plan's stipulations, consequently leading to the appropriation of large speculative profits.

A study carried out in 1971 into changes in zoning with the application of the County Plan pointed out that "in most cases the changes take the form of a leap from a classification included in the '53 Plan to another that allowed higher building levels and, therefore, increased densities, representing, to date, an increase of 1.8 in the overall density of population foreseen by the County Plan".[5]

[5] See Carlos Teixidor, Marçal Tarragó and Lluís Brau: "Barcelona 1953-1971. Introducción a una visión del desarrollo urbanístico", *Cuadernos* no. 87. Barcelona, 1972. Also Amador Ferrer: *Los Planes Parciales*. COAC, Barcelona, 1972.

8.a The 1953 County Plan.

3
e Development Plan for
rcelona and its area of
fluence (1953).

04
entral fragment of the
ounty Plan. The urban
efinition is very piecemeal
nd therefore leaves a great
al of freedom for subsequent
artial Plans.

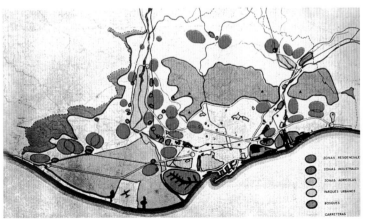

.05
roposed functional scheme.
esidential centres and
reas of production in each
unicipality.

8.06
Sector of Sant Martí.

8.07
Example of one of the
developments proposed by the
County Plan. Eastern sector
Gran Via.

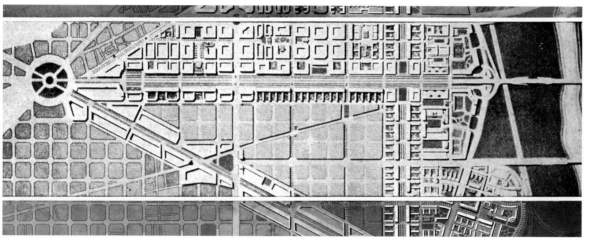

8.08
Partial Plan of the Eastern
Area.

The situation was serious, since the increase in density was not accompanied by a corresponding increase in services to make the new, more intensive use compatible. Further, the lack of effective public control meant that the partial plans concentrated construction in spaces where building was permitted – that is, private space, and that in most cases facilities and green areas remained mere reserves of land. Alongside the 1953 Plan, another two in-depth studies were carried out about the two ends of the Diagonal, indicating the unequal protagonism of the two sectors.[6]

Urban development in Barcelona in the fifties threw in its lot with the Diagonal. It saw the first planning attempts since the Civil War that aimed to improve the city's connectivity. World Urbanism Day in 1950, celebrated with a major exhibition in the city's Great Hall, was a possible sign of this change.[7]

[6] J. Busquets: "Diagonal 1953", *Semanario de La Vanguardia*. Barcelona, 1983.
[7] In fact the small gardens and some emblematic schemes in the Gothic quarter under the direction of the architect A. Florensa moved on to a fully-fledged discussion of models and patterns of growth. The slim volume by Francisco Folguera: *Urbanismo para todos*. COAC, Barcelona, 1959, reflects the urban planning theory that inspired the plans of the 1950s.

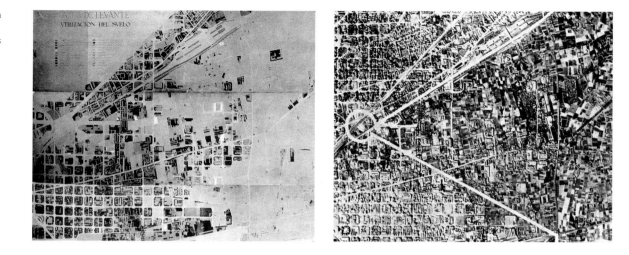

However, there was still a contrast between the documentation about the city that went on show and the reality: Barcelona and its area of influence were, above all, the first port of call for an immigrant workforce with very few resources and living in dreadful conditions. The real-estate sector was incipient and the protagonism of land owners overweening; the districts on the present-day periphery were becoming consolidated. How were these problems to be dealt with? How could residential conditions be improved? Disorder and irrationality in the city were evident, but instead of seeking the causes, it was decided that the generic need was to strike a balance between "artificial and natural".

With regard to specific solutions, the major development options centred on either end of the Diagonal: the uptown or western sector – in a reworking of the 1946 Plan – and in the eastern sector around Plaça de les Glòries, creating an industrial and worker housing sector. Both areas were presented with spectacular models and integrated planning: these were the goals of the Barcelona of the fifties.

Fifty years later, the projects are apparently well resolved in themselves but fail to respond to the city's problems; despite the passage of so many years, those models were never realised. As the city developed, it disfigured the model that was publicly exhibited, some priority sectors are still wasteland, and what were reserves of land have to a large extent been built on. There was no intervention of public management to supervise the planning quality of these projects.

In hindsight, viewing the urban planning process of the Diagonal's uptown or western sectors from a distance, we see that attempts to develop this sector as a luxury residential area in the forties received an impetus from the location there of the new University Campus[8] in the early 1950s, along with a series of sports installations (the

---

[8]   The Ciutat Universitària, or university campus, now covers 60 hectares of land and has followed a process of gradual construction since the acquisition of land in 1951-52 (part of the land of the former Güell estate from which Pedralbes Palace had already separated). Development began with the construction of the Pharmacy section and the hall of residence. The latter was the theme of a projects competition (1954), won by a monumentalist project of little interest, when the previous competition had been declared void despite including the submissions of young architects such as Bohigas, Giráldez, Martorell, and Corrales and Molezún, who had put forward frankly innovative designs. It was not until the construction of the Law Faculty (1958), designed by the architects Subías, Giráldez and L. Iñigo, that more ambitious architectural proposals were accepted. Most of the existing buildings were constructed in the 1960s.

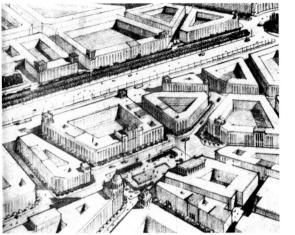

8.11, 8.12
Proposed westward extension
of the Diagonal in 1954.

Polo Club, Turó Tennis Club and even Barcelona Football Club's Nou Camp), which provided a good setting for this residential area.

Added to the implantation of these installations was the development work which, on the occasion of the 1952 Eucharistic Congress, centred on the Diagonal (Plaça Pío XII), thereby completing work begun in 1924. The 35th Eucharistic Congress was also a great event for the city insofar as it reopened the doors of a society that had been completely closed and controlled.

The uptown stretch of the Diagonal had been constructed in 1924 as the extension of the avenue then called Alfonso XIII, later changed to Avenida del 14 de Abril by General Franco and now Avinguda Diagonal, the popular name that coincides with its geographical position in the city.

This axis connects the former Camp d'en Galvany, now Plaça Francesc Macià, with Pedralbes Palace; it has an average width of 84 metres with an asymmetrical layout: the sunny, 27-metre boulevard to its north makes it Barcelona's most pleasant avenue. The complete project had been completed in the 1920s, though the plot organisation produced by the street has changed a great deal in the decades that have passed since the avenue was an esplanade (1921-24).

The opportunity of the urban development of this sector was not put to good use. It is impossible to overlook the imbalance between the satisfactory result of the urban intervention and the formal disorder of the buildings lining Diagonal. There were various proposals, including one made by the GATCPAC, that suggested an overall organisation of building in keeping with the principles of Modern Urban Planning.[9] Despite the substantial innovation introduced by this new type of construction, the GATCPAC project sought to dovetail it with the traditional city in the form of the district of Les Corts, specifically in the Travessera, continuing it as far as Plaça Francesc Macià and Gràcia, an option which unfortunately is now impossible.

The prototypical value of this project is still open to many different readings, many of them nostalgic to judge by existing results. In 1946, the Council formulated a Sectoral Plan that introduced the closed street block as the

[9] Compared to the very high quality types of single-family dwellings envisaged in the initial outlines in the twenties, its proposal, presented at the 1932 Moscow Congress on the functional city, addressed an open model of construction with a linear structure parallel to Diagonal, avoiding the difficulties of building in a closed street block. The model ran westwards from Urgell in an attempt to overcome the specific determination of each plot, as far as the environs of Pedralbes Palace, to make the most of the views of the city from this splendid enclave.

3, 8.14
.TCPAC plan for the
.gonal in the 1930s,
.trasting with the
.npositional principles of the
.t-war period.

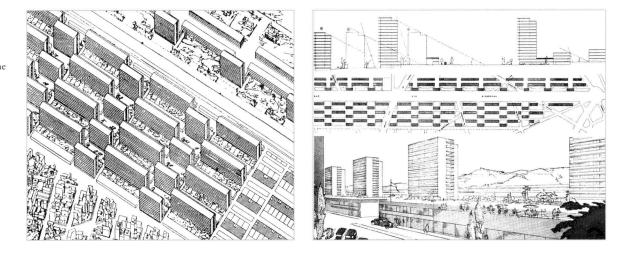

dominant form of construction. A Decree of 1949 introduced a special discount for real-estate developments in the sector.

In 1954 the Plan was revised with a view to incorporating new institutional uses and once again proposed an open form of construction. However, subsequent development shows the fragmented history of this part of the city, today full of morphological discontinuities.

VIII.2 A fresh impetus in architecture and urban development

Post-war architecture once again found itself plunged into academic monumentalism, as though returning to the situation of the late 1920s with the architecture of the Great Exhibition's pavilions. There was an explicit rejection of the innovative lines that had been expressed in the thirties.[10] This was apparent in the architecture that was built but also in the teachings of the School of Architecture, with figures such as Nebot, Florensa, Bona and even Jujol representing this situation.

Architecture centred on representative buildings, such as banks – mainly in Plaça de Catalunya and Passeig de Gràcia – and luxury residential constructions.

It was not until the 1950s that modern styles and conception of architecture and the city were recovered. Grupo R, founded in 1951, was the platform for renovation throughout that decade.[11]

[10] See the exhibition catalogue *Arquitectura para después de una Guerra 1939-1949*. Barcelona, 1973, particularly the article by Roser Amadó and Lluís Domènech, produced by the organisers of the exhibition "Barcelona, los años 40: arquitectura para después de una guerra". The article points to the ambiguity with which architecture and ideology are sometimes identified, to the point of confusing modern architecture with republican architecture, certainly an exaggeration. The theme of city reconstruction can be seen in Carlos Sambricio's article with the expressive title "¡Qué coman república! Introducción a un estudio sobre la Reconstrucción en la España de la Postguerra" [Let them eat Republic! Introduction to a study of reconstruction in post-war Spain] in the same catalogue.

[11] Its statutes define as the group's field "the study of the problems of contemporary art and particularly architecture". Foremost members were Josep Partmarsó, Oriol Bohigas, Josep Maria Sostres, Josep A. Coderch, Antoni de Moragas and Manuel Ribas Piera, among others. See Oriol Bohigas: *Polèmica d'arquitectura catalana*. Barcelona, 1969. Also Carme Rodríguez: *Grup R*. Barcelona, 1994.

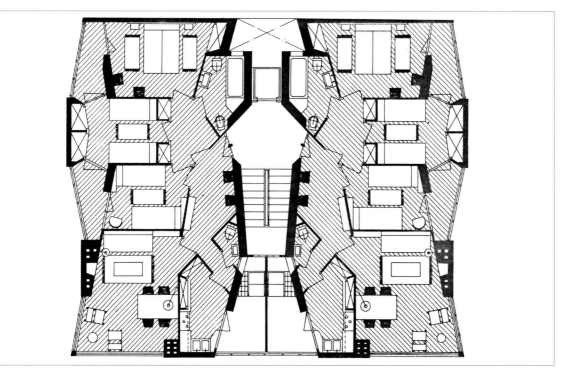

From that moment on, the group constituted the central nucleus of architectural renovation. It concentrated on the promotion of exhibitions of work by young architects, and the organisation of competitions for architecture students, giving rise to discussion between future professionals.

Against this backdrop, the new post-war generation of architects featured three master figures: Josep Maria Sostres, with his great capacity for theory and criticism who, despite producing few works of architecture, gave the group its theoretical consistence and went on to introduce a spirit of renewal into the School of Architecture.

Antoni de Moragas was a very active architect, both professionally and in disseminating the field. His most innovative early works were the Fémina cinema with its marked Nordic lines and Park Hotel, near the Estació de França railway station, in which he applied the particularities of organic architecture. His work was later to lean more towards a development of local technology which he applied in masterful fashion in numerous projects for dwellings in the Eixample. His work in the field of industrial design was invaluable, both with regard to the works themselves and to his promotion of ADI-FAD.[12]

A presentation of Josep Antoni Coderch, the third master, has to be based on the consistence of his architectural work, always in association with Manuel Valls. Except in the later years, his work concentrated on the scale of small buildings, which he controlled and resolved with simplicity down to the last detail. Particularly outstanding are a series of buildings in Sitges and, above all, the Fishermen's building in the Barceloneta (1959), still a paradigm example of a residential solution of great functional and compositional interest. The planes of the façade are perforated to increase the force of the building's corner position. Coderch's ethical stance was

[12] Association for the improvement of industrial design and the promotion of the decorative arts.

8.b The architecture of Grupo R.

8.20
Dwellings in Carrer de J. S. Bach by R. Bofill.

8.21
Atalaya tower block by Corre and Milà.

8.22
Building by Moragas.

fundamental to his architecture: his article "It is not genius that we need"[13] was a strong advocate of a form of architecture that was committed to action. Coderch was the best-known architect on the international scene at that time; he was a foremost member of Team X, an essentially European group that followed the principles of modern architecture showcased in recent CIAMs with a view to heralding in a spirit of renewal.

Apart from these personal links, Barcelona and its most qualified professionals became more isolated from the innovative trends taking place in Europe and which at other times they had formed an active part of. Nonetheless, the city of Barcelona was taken as one of the referents in the planning exercises carried out by Constant in the sixties and exhibited in The Hague in 1970.[14] They were however to have little influence on the local panorama.

In the 1960s, this local panorama changed, and while the spirit of Grupo R lived on, its practical actions were individual or represented by various practices made up of groups of two or three architects. As of 1959, they organised "small congresses" in the form of informal meetings to present and discuss different works. Then 1958 saw the start of the FAD prizes to recognise the constructed work of greatest interest.

In 1962 Oriol Bohigas published an article in *Serra d'Or* entitled "Towards a realist architecture" which constituted a kind of manifesto in favour of architecture that was committed to the country and economic context in which it was set. This approach was also in line with the innovative trends taking shape in Italy which were faithfully reflected by the new phase of *Casabella*, directed by Ernesto Rogers.

This proclamation also meant the revision of some of the important forerunners of Catalan architecture in the last 100 years, particularly from the Modernisme period, representing its commitment to the materials, techniques and language of the time, and from the period of the Modern Movement under the Republic.[15]

[13] See the Italian magazine *Domus*. Milan, 1962
[14] Exercise of superposition carried out with a dozen European cities as part of the New Babylon project that defined the "Situationism International" trend that was so influential in radical thought on the European city and which came to the fore once again at the start of the new century in an academic context. See, among others, Mark Wigley: *Constant's New Babylon. The Hyper-Architecture of Desire*, Rotterdam, 1998; Simon Saddler, *The Siuationist City*, Cambridge, 1998.
[15] This concern is expressed in Oriol Bohigas' work in relation to Modernisme. See *Arquitectura modernista*. Barcelona. For the GATCPAC period, see: *La arquitectura de la Segunda República*. Barcelona.

23
rcelona was one of the cities
mulated in the outlines for
:w Babylon.

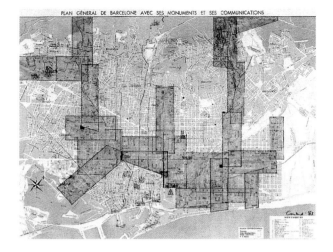

PLAN GÉNÉRAL DE BARCELONE AVEC SES MONUMENTS ET SES COMMUNICATIONS

However, this "realist" practice also took the form of some emblematic interventions by the Martorell-Bohigas practice, later joined by David Mackay, such as the house in Carrer Pallars (1959) and the Metalúrgica de Seguros building in the Diagonal. The team constantly responded to the theme of the low-cost dwelling between party walls, with great architectural expressivity, using common materials and layouts; the house in Avinguda Meridiana or the one in Ronda del Guinardó are excellent examples. In 1965 a special issue of *Zodiac* magazine devoted to Spain came out, with a large feature on the Barcelona group.[16] Ricardo Bofill contributed an interesting article about the situation of architecture in Spain, providing an insightful analysis of the Spanish and in particular the Catalan scenes.

This issue featured Bofill's early works which are of great interest in his search for a physical expressionism in architecture, at the same time demonstrating his concern with the internal functional transformation of the dwelling that produced ambitious district-scale projects in the early seventies.

In addition to Coderch and Valls who have already been presented, it featured other interesting teams such as Federico Correa and Alfonso Milà, who made a great impact in the interior design world of the time; Josep Maria Fargas and Enric Tous, who achieved great quality in the rationalisation of architecture; the Subías-Giráldez-López Iñigo team with large-scale buildings; and Emili Donato, Francesc Mitjans and Antoni Bonet, among others.

In the late sixties the Barcelona School came to the fore as a trend that aspired to bring together a series of working lines that partook of the same political and economic conditions, seeking architectural innovation in the expressiveness of materials and detail.[17]

From exile in America, Josep Lluís Sert also contributed to this renewal of the architecture scene with the Fundació Miró located on Montjuïc (1968-1975).

[16] See *Zodiac* no. 15. Cremona, 1965. With a prologue by Vittorio Gregotti, and articles by, among others, Carlos Flores in Madrid, and O. Bohigas, F. Correa, M. Ribas i Piera and J. A. Solans in Barcelona.
[17] Ignasi de Solà-Morales: "La segunda modernización de la arquitectura catalana" (1939-1970), *Ecleticismo y vanguardia*. Barcelona, 1980. Also Helio Piñon, *Arquitecturas catalanas*. Barcelona, 1977. Out of the Barcelona School a new generation burst forth in architecture, with groups of architects such as the PER team, with Tusquets + Clotet and Bonet + Cirici; Bach + Mora; Garcés + Soria; E. Torres + J. A. Martínez-Lapeña; Piñon + Viaplana; Sabater + Doménech + Puig + Sanmartí; E. Borrell and F. Rius, among others.

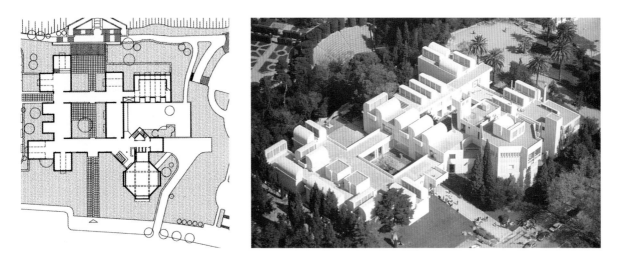

8.24, 8.25
The Miró Foundation on
Montjuïc by J. L. Sert.

In this way, despite adverse political conditions, a highly interesting cultural breeding ground was forming, since the Barcelona School also extended to other fields such as literature, film, painting, etc.

This stance of professional concern and social commitment gradually produced changes in the university world, with the admission of innovative lecturers to the School of Architecture, and with regard to criticism in seminars and journals, as the bibliography for the sixties and seventies proves, and also in the field of action. One instance was attempted renovation in the planning field, as explained in the next section.

VIII.3 The major plans of the sixties: the Metropolitan Area

Catalan urban development received a new lease of life in the sixties in the form of the Barcelona Metropolitan Area planning process in the 1964-1970 period.[18]

This process initially took the form of a revision of the 1953 County Plan and it was the planning team itself that introduced the concept of Metropolitan Area,[19] thereby recognising a planning reality that went beyond traditional municipal and county level to be found in urban agglomerations of a certain size with an appreciable dynamic. The Metropolitan Area as a field of study corresponds to 3,000 square kilometres along a 100 kilometre coastal strip of Barcelona province. The history of this discussion in Barcelona can be seen as "the progressive struggle between the experts who created it [the Metropolitan Area], a reality that developed independently of planning work and a Government that was reluctant to accept it".[20]

[18] To explain this interesting period, we refer to the series of articles by the LUB in issue 87 of *Cuadernos de Arquitectura y Urbanismo.* Barcelona, 1972.
[19] A much-used concept in North America since the definition of the Metropolitan Area Standard in 1950, and also in Europe. Kingsley Davis: *The World's Metropolitan Areas.* Berkeley, 1959, and A. Acquarone: *Grande città e aree metropolitane in Italia.* Milan, 1962. For its application in Barcelona, see Antoni Font: "Delimitación de las Areas Metropolitanas: el caso de Barcelona", *Cuadernos* 87. Barcelona, 1972.
[20] "Breve historia del Área Metropolitana de Barcelona", *Cuadernos* 87, *op. cit.*, pp. 7-8. In this first phase, the coordination of work fell to J. Soteras, M. Baldrich and J. Ros Vila, and the technical presentation was made by E. Lluch, M. Ribas, M. de Solà-Morales and A. Serratosa, among others.

The initial phase (1964-1966) produced the Master Plan for the Metropolitan Area of Barcelona, which was then hushed up for more than two years: work was marked by the implicit recognition of the state of urbanisation of the region and of a new administrative reality that clashed with the existing power structure. The proposal of a specific management body was even removed from the text of the report that suggested the idea.

Finally, in 1968, the Ministry of Housing approved the work as a Preliminary Master Plan and a second phase was brought under way dividing the work into two fronts: the County Plan itself, within the scope of the 1953 plan, and the Metropolitan Area Plan, which in turn divided into the General Infrastructures Plan and the Immediate Action Plan. The latter was to be applied to the various *comarques* or counties in the metropolitan area.

At the same time, Barcelona City Council had commissioned a revision of the General Municipal Plan (PGM) to an internal team. The difficulties of coordinating so many levels of technical and institutional development made collaboration between already very distant parties even more laborious. In turn, the problems arising from political mistrust at the end of the first phase continually cast doubt on the work being carried out.

Furthermore, decision-making was moving in another direction: in 1970, the Madrid-based Ministry delimited the special Riera de Caldes area between Mollet and Santa Perpetua as a large-scale urbanisation scheme, outside the urban continuum of Barcelona, in the image of the new towns being created in Europe in the post-war years.[21]

This scheme was a prelude to the Decree of June 1970 on "Urgent Urban Development Schemes" (ACTUR), which represented a step on the part of the Ministry of Housing towards joint public and private schemes on the large scale.[22] A similar ACTUR scheme was drawn up for Sabadell-Terrassa in the space between the two municipalities. This highlighted a major incoherence in ministerial action with regard to the Third Development Plan, which aimed to organise strategies for urban redistribution on the basis of "metropolitan areas" and "balancing metropolises".

These decisions, so contradictory to efforts to enhance the urban fabrics of Barcelona's peripheries, triggered off a generalised process of resignations among the technicians involved in drafting the Metropolitan Area Plan, which definitively aborted any possibility of the plan being carried out. It was followed by other partial studies in the

---

[21] This phase of work was coordinated by J. Soteras, A. Serratosa and M. Ribas and the three blocks directed by M. de Solà-Morales and J. A. Solans (County Plan); Ll. Cantallops and E. Lluch (Immediate Action Plan), and García-Rosales and A. Font (Infrastructures Plan).

[22] The new town as an *ex-novo* foundation of a large urban precinct has a long tradition in urban planning practice, but it burgeoned after the war as an easy response to mass housing construction and the decentralisation of activities. See E. Galantay: *New Towns: Antiquity to the present*. New York, 1975. Also C. Stein: *Toward New Towns for America*. Cambridge, 1973. For the ACTURS see E. Leira, A. Rodríguez-Bachiller, I. Solana: *El Decreto de Actuaciones Urgentes*, and Julio Esteban: "La nueva ciudad de Riera de Calders", *Cuadernos* 87, *op. cit.*, pp. 50-52. Criticism of this type of scheme should not be considered merely as a negative valuation in itself, but also for its incoherence with the guidelines of urban recovery that the Master Plan attempted to introduce.

8.c The Master Plan for the Metropolitan Area.

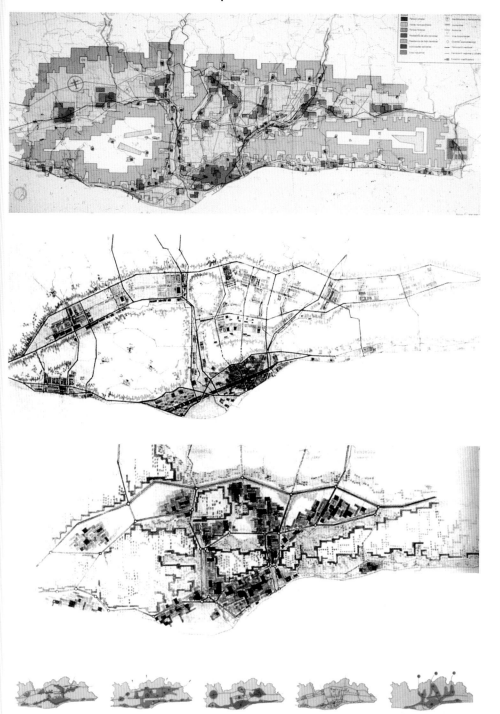

8.26
1968 Master Plan.

8.27
Example of one of the scenarios in the Planning Map for the Barcelona Metropolitan Area.

8.28
Another, more concentrated scenario.

8.29
Various schematic models for the Metropolitan Area.

early 1970s, but this represented the end of an era that, albeit utopian or impossible, did a great deal to introduce renovation and aimed, on the basis of far-reaching, complex technical reflection, to introduce some rationality into urban development decision-making in a rather ragged metropolitan reality. However, the urban planning history of Barcelona contains a series of works of the first order that still represent an invaluable contribution.

For example, with regard to the Master Plan, there are several dozen volumes explaining the monographic analyses that signify an updating of an urban planning reality that lacked basic data. Monographs on "population typology" or the "tertiary sector" also represented appreciable progress.[23]

The work team, with an intentionally multidisciplinary basis – as was typical in those years–, ultimately organised its work in groups according to discipline, and, as Manuel de Solà-Morales so expressively writes,[24] the architects – professionals of the pencil – concentrated on the physical study of the urban form and structure, concerned with the "location" of activities; the engineers directed their prediction techniques towards the "reserves of land" and the economists and sociologists joined together in the common technology of "statistics".

The Plan's propositive phases also offer incisive discussions with regard to the urban planning organisation models possible at the time. The ideas of "territory-city" and "region-city" were tabled alongside closed planning systems of the old type.[25] Two basic ideas are present in these works: **a)** the decongestion of Barcelona: as opposed to the commonplaces of spontaneous growth and traffic congestion, the idea was posited of industrial decentralisation, in the belief that residence would follow the movement of production activity; and **b)** the location of the tertiary sector, as a way of balancing the territory. These were important principles whose articulation called for studies to check their effective capacity. The Plan proper also contained certain ambiguities: the idea of the parallel city (like the Sant Cugat-Cerdanyola strategic centre), the rosary of new and old cities and towns, and the support of existing subcentres, giving them new contents or differential accents, might be contradictory. But this was a "Master Scheme", requiring subsequent working processes that could not be carried out. Nonetheless, the core idea of the "territory-city" and the Metropolitan Area were there, and in their present-day form stem back to this initial hard work.

On another front, the Barcelona municipal authorities were carrying out initiatives of a very different order: the leaflet *Barcelona Año 2000*[26] summarises the Municipal Plan and the ideas that drove the city. Sweeping urban

---

[23] The precise study of the metropolitan reality uncovered situations like those of 600 residential estates outside Barcelona, of which just 25 per cent were legal.

[24] Manuel de Solà-Morales: "La metodología del Plan Director", *Cuadernos. op. cit.*, pp. 19-26.

[25] The almost contemporary experiences of the PIM 63 (Piano Intercomunale de Milano) and the Schéma Directeur de Paris (1964) were a major influence on this discussion which was approached in very innovative fashion.

[26] See the leaflet published by Barcelona City Council, 1971. The work was supervised by Xavier Subías.

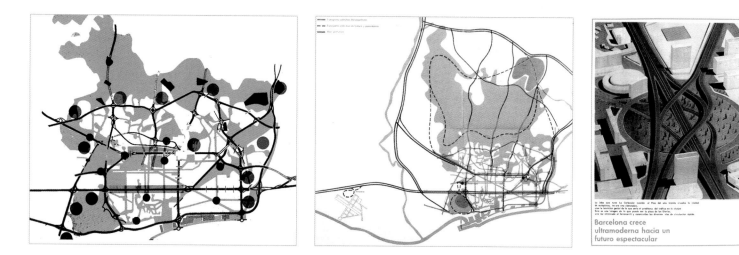

development transformation was taking place, with the presentation of major projects that were difficult to carry out. The document, with a prologue by the Mayor, José María de Porcioles, constituted a summarised proposal of a city embarked on large-scale pro-development transformation. The Plan's overall aim was to "adapt the City to its new function, in a metropolitan context of over 6.5 million inhabitants".

In 1970 the Cabinet had carried a motion to apply for a Great Exhibition in 1982. The project never came to fruition, but it did spark off important plans for urban transformation and the design of major road axes.

The 2000 Outline Plan presented a city crossed by segregated roadways, like motorways, that divided it into parts. Gran Via de las Exposiciones was designed as a vertical axis connecting Plaça d'Espanya with Vallès via the Vallvidrera tunnel; Travessera de Gràcia joined Avinguda Tarradelles, becoming appreciably broader as it passed through the old suburban centres to Santa Coloma, forming "Gran Via North"; it was proposed that the original Gran Via be widened by demolishing a built street block along its entire length. It was the road system, then, that served as a vehicle for urban transformation.[27]

VIII.4 Speculative transformation and urban social movements

The contrast between these planning trends also reflected the difficulties involved in the urban planning situation that underwent a brutal speculative transformation in the 1960s as the result of an unprecedented real-estate dynamic in the city, in the period referred to as "the Barcelona of Porcioles".[28]

This major period of development took place under the mandate of the mayor of this name, from 1957 to 1973. This phase saw the introduction of new legal and administrative conditions such as the 1960 Municipal Charter, which finally granted the city a special economic statute that it had been requesting since the time of

8.30
2000 Barcelona Municipal Outline Plan.

8.31
Proposal for a Great Exhibition in 1982, setting forward the ideas of the "Barcelona 2000" project, highlighting the construction of three tunnels in Collserola and a project with two Expo focuses, one in Vallè and one on Montjuïc.

8.32
Outline plan of Les Glòries from the same project, drafted in 1971. The predominance of private mobility.

[27] The maximalism of the transformation proposals is such that the prologue, by Porcioles, calls it the "first version", and points out that "the technical services are even preparing other variants to be able to offer alternative solutions".
[28] Here we use the title of the monographic issue 21 of *CAU* produced by J. M. Alibès, M. J. Campo, E. Giralt, J. M. Huertas Claveria, R. Pradas and S. Tarragó, and published in 1973, which takes a critical look at this period, organised in the form of a vocabulary.

33, 8.34
overs of CAU magazine.

Cambó. The Council's financial precariousness meant that in 1959 the budget was smaller than in 1930, with no allowances for the extremely high rates of immigration.

The Charter granted the city a larger budget, but most importantly greater financial and administrative agility: the Council could intervene actively in many urban development schemes which it had previously been unable to, due to the lack of both resources and competences. This positive characteristic had a marked effect on the urban developments of this period: the Council promoted schemes that involved the active intervention of Catalan and national capital with final results that were often highly speculative.[29]

We can understand the positive aspects for the dynamisation of the city during this period of development policy, yet there was no apparent concern with controlling either the belated impact of many projects which implicitly involved the designation of public property or the expulsion of many low-income residents, or with finding out who benefited from the capital gains generated by each transformation.

Thus a whole series of major works was carried out to improve or enhance the city: the covering over of Carrer Aragó, which had until then run along an open channel; the extension of Gran Via towards the Maresme, improvements to Montjuïc on its sea-facing façade; the division of the Barceloneta seafront façade despite the construction of Carrer Almirall Cervera, breaking up the original district; the promotion of the Zona Franca[30] as an industrial estate, etc.

Other reform operations specifically concerned the road network, such as the First Beltway, constructed as a segregated roadway, that created a huge potential for construction on the empty sites it served; no one at the Council supervised the huge capital gains generated. Likewise, the purpose of the three Tibidabo tunnels was to pave the city's way into Vallès, with the slogan "Faith moves mountains", but there was no one to supervise either the future use of the land or how financing was organised. During the construction of the Rovira and Vallvidrera tunnels, the company folded and the operation was frozen until the 1980s.

[29] See issue 10 of *CAU*, collected by Jordi Borja: "La Gran Barcelona". Barcelona, 1971. See also Salvador Tarragó: *En defensa de Barcelona*. Barcelona, 1978.
[30] This area has the forerunner of the Free Port in the twenties. Its new use for industry received a boost from the installation there of SEAT in 1950 and the Consortium of the Zona Franca was reactivated in 1965, extending its activities to the creation of industrial land.

But in some cases transformation also involved an increase in building levels with no corresponding public services: an ordinance governing outstanding buildings allowed higher building levels if construction took the form of a tower block than if it followed the regular pattern of the fabric.[31]

Remodelling usually took the form of "Plans" for large sectors of the city. These were the elements that were most directly rejected by the city people, as they were the operations with the most transparent procedures: the Land Act stipulated a mandatory period of public exhibition.

This was one of the fronts that provided a focus for what were referred to as the "urban social movements", which came to constitute a very valuable platform for understanding the future urban development situation of Barcelona in particular and Catalonia in general, as a direct criticism of the planning of the 1960s and 70s but also as a form of political opposition to the totalitarian system. One of the many examples was Plaça de Lesseps, which was destroyed by the construction of the First Beltway, giving rise to such widespread opposition that the project had to be continually modified.

Continuing in this field, the Vallbona-Torre Baró-Trinitat Plan for the very north of the city, a peripheral, self-built area, provoked a strong popular reaction that excited the solidarity of another six neighbouring districts and came to constitute a common front called "Nou barris", or Nine districts, later recognised as a city district in its own right.

Another paradigm project for its influence on the Barcelona of the future was the Ribera Plan, on the eastern coastal front. The initiative, begun in 1965, covered 225 hectares, of which 40 belonged to Renfe [Spanish railways]. With the publicity slogan "Barcelona, a city that can't go on living with its back to the sea", this project aimed to eradicate the population along the seafront from Barceloneta to the river Besòs. The large industries in the sector were relocating their plants outside Barcelona and wanted to achieve maximum capital gains on the old site. The industrial crisis affecting the Barcelona area was shared by various sectors, but it also happened that, on balance, capital gains on land counted for much more than capital gains on industrial products. This distortion often blames the crisis on the weakness of reinvestment, as surplus was directed into the stock exchange or real-estate operations.

The project of La Ribera S.A. was a plan for the "eastern seafront sector" and was met by the direct opposition of over 9,000 complaints. The neighbourhood and professional associations created a common front and even organised an ideas competition to challenge the official project.[32] The result of the competition brought

---

[31] Another variant of the ordinance allowed 40% more than permitted building levels to hotel use. Of the eight hotels that applied, only two were constructed. The ordinance was finally repealed as being contrary to law.

[32] The story of the competition and the winning project can be seen in M. de Solà-Morales, J. Busquets, M. Domingo, A. Font, J. L. Gómez-Ordóñez: *Barcelona: remodelación capitalista o desarrollo urbano*. Barcelona, 1974. The alternative discussion of the project sought to break with the ecological determinism that tended to use a remodelling plan as the official one, establishing a coherence that would allow for improvement of the sector, still maintaining the existing residential areas.

8.d The Ribera Plan and its Counter Plan.

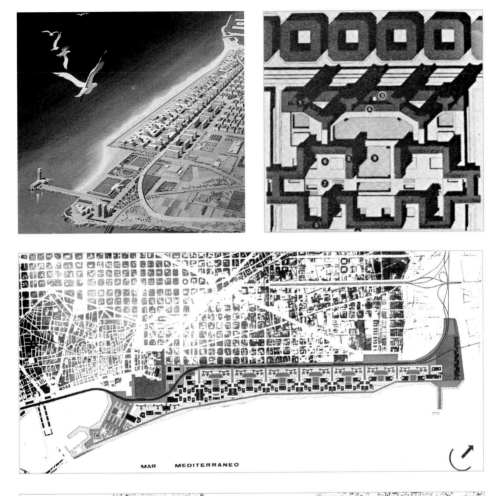

8.39
Repercussions of the debate
the daily press.

8.40
The coastal front in 1970.

remodelling efforts to a halt and the sector was redirected twenty years later by the projects to recover the city's beaches and Olympic development.

VIII.5 Crisis in the industrial sector

The restructuring of the industrial sector had started in the 1960s when it became apparent that the urban space occupied by former industrial plants had become central. To start with, major residential growth had sprung up in interstitial areas and the industrial installations themselves were obsolete. The relocation of industry outside the city in order to develop a technologically more advanced industrial process in turn had the incentive of the high value of the land on which the obsolete plant stood if it were put to use for housing or services; as explained above, this mechanism was behind the remodelling of large sectors of the city.

The industrial crisis of the early seventies then worsened in 1974, and the Barcelona area lost 18 per cent of its jobs in three years, when unemployment rose to 20 per cent.[33] This process has to be observed as part of an overall dynamic, because in this situation, a great deal of industry moved into the metropolitan area – even beyond the scope of the 1953 County Plan – and new activities were introduced to replace the industrial relocation. Principally tertiary and services began to emerge as a crucial sector in the municipal scope of

[33] See Joan Trullen: *Barcelona frente a la crisis*. Barcelona, 1988.

Barcelona: in the 1970s over 1,100,000 square metres of office space was constructed, practically doubling the existing area in use.

Nonetheless, the crisis in the traditional industrial sector was serious and it took a great impetus to recover it, as explained later. The urban situation of industrial centres worsened due to unemployment, adding to the difficulties caused by the urbanisation deficits that rapid pro-development growth had created. In turn, large industrial installations with only a minimum turnover appeared in the urban fabric, waiting for changes, which were to take very different forms.

VIII.6 The General Metropolitan Plan

Of the frenzied planning period of the 1960s there remained the 2000 Barcelona Plan, never approved as such, and Barcelona's Urban Development Commission continued its revision of the 1953 County Plan, which despite its fragility had provided the legal framework for a conurbation that doubled in population in 20 years.

Studies into this complex reality went on for five years, using the most modern techniques of analysis and urban planning evaluation. The territory was divided for reference into statistical units, using very advanced information processing systems: in this way, new categories were produced to explain the metropolitan process.[34] A simulation model was even applied, with automatic mapping systems that allowed the highly reliable reproduction of the behaviour of the different variables.[35] These innovations were key to understanding the conceptual and operative renovation that the future Plan introduced into Spanish urban design.

As part of this process, 1974 saw the creation of the Barcelona Metropolitan Corporation as a local authority[36] that embraced Barcelona and twenty-six other municipalities around it: the same area as the County Plan. This represented a major step forwards in administrative terms, but an end to the scope of the true Metropolitan Area that had been so insistently called for in the 1960s.

In this legal framework, public exhibition began of the first version of the General Metropolitan Plan in 1974. While the Plan's analytical instruments were very powerful, the proposal itself was a response to a highly complex

[34] This broad-based team was directed by Manuel de Solà-Morales and Joan Antoni Solans. Later, the former resigned and the Plan was finally directed by J. A. Solans and Albert Serratosa; the jurist Miquel Roca was responsible for the regulations.
[35] See LUB: *Modelo de simulación de la comarca de Barcelona*. Mímeo, Barcelona, 1972.
[36] Also called the Metropolitan Municipal Body in the terms of the 1975 Local Regime Act. In article one it is defined as a "specific body for the promotion, coordination, management, supervision and execution of urban planning and the provision of the relevant services to the metropolitan area as a whole". It covered an extension of 470 square kilometres and 3,100,000 inhabitants.

administrative situation. For example, the road structure of the General Municipal Plan was forced to literally follow the Barcelona Arterial Network drafted in 1962, with very heavy principles of road layout for a built city. This represented a great deal of remodelling: the designation of public property in suburban districts such as Gràcia and Sants, and in the old town itself, produced a whole host of complaints that still seem reasonable to us today.

The Plan also laid out very precise proposals for the reservation of empty or obsolete interstitial areas for facilities and open space that would, in the future, allow for improvement to the city's urban quality. In this case, local residents' opposition in the form of the period's urban social movements very precisely pinpointed the need for industrial wasteland or unused public or corporate property to be used for facilities and green areas, radically changing the restructuring trend of the sixties, when they were turned into intensive residential developments, such as the former Barcelona Football Club site in Les Corts, or the Elizalde development near Gràcia.

In this case too there were many objections to the Plan, but this time they came from the private sector, which feared a reduction in the expected capital gains to be made from speculation. However, it was necessary to stop the escalating build-up and the PGM was timely in its reaction.[37] The effect of the moment of crisis probably made it easier to endure a situation that was subject to very strong political pressure from the various groups in power.

In view of the 32,000 allegations made, the Plan was subjected to further study and the correction of the errors in drafting that are only to be expected in a planning project of this scope. Finally, the PGM was passed in 1976 after its second public exhibition. In the interim period, hundreds of cases of planning permission were applied for under the auspices of the 1953 County Plan, which unfortunately represented the loss of important sites for the future scheme.[38]

The new Land Act was also passed in 1975, adapting much of the technical and operative system used in the PGM and making it obligatory at state level. From this moment on, the PGM organised the territory on the basis of two concepts: systems or spaces set aside for public or communal use, and areas devoted to private use. New operating categories were introduced according to this distinct definition: firstly, facilities, as parts of systems, were specified as the reservation of land, but purpose and architecture could be decided at a later date; secondly, zoning was dissociated from use and building system, which had been the usual techniques, and replaced by

[37] There was some criticism of the fact that the PGM reserved untransformed sites and that it was these that bore the brunt of responsibility for consummated cases of speculation, which is true; however, it is necessary to understand that the planning context had no provision for redistribution and the limits of densification were dramatic.

[38] There has as yet been no in-depth study of this embarrassing period which was the last outlet for a markedly speculative form of procedure.

8.e The 1978 General Metropolitan Plan.

1
e road structure of the 1976
neral Metropolitan Plan
GM).

42
and uses proposed by the
GM.

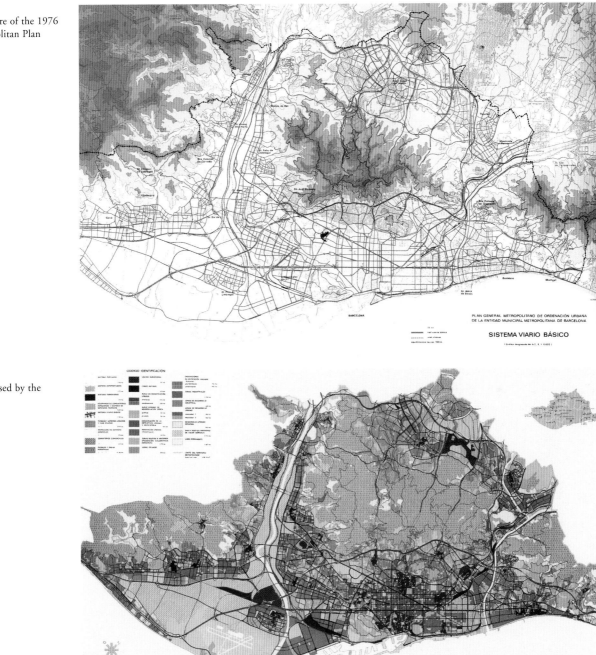

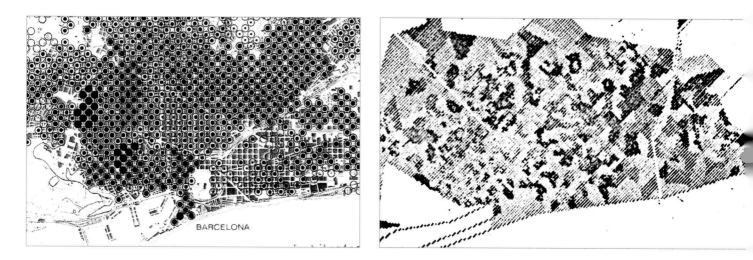

8.43, 8.44
Example of the type of analys
that accompanied the draftin
of the PGM. By way of
example, a further increase in
central density in 1970 and a
initial automatic representatic
of the Traffic Survey conducte
by SYMAP.

different "urban processes" such as densification, remodelling, etc., that were more in keeping with the dynamic of urban development, as detected in the preliminary analytical studies.

As a result, the General Metropolitan Plan represented a major attempt to build a critical social and political situation. Its fundamental contribution was the establishing of a more reasonable framework of reference in keeping with the general variables of the urban phenomenon of Barcelona.

Nonetheless, its main limitations lay in the controversial context in which it was produced: negotiations were at all times unequal and strained; establishing the limits of transformation was in itself a triumph. The general options of urban form necessarily remained in the background; without actually being denied, they were effectively masked, and the harsh impact of some of its road elements inside the city called for specific discussion. So the PGM went ahead and found platforms for development at both municipal and metropolitan level until the abolition of the Metropolitan Corporation in 1985. It was continually adapted as required by the construction or urban development interventions, this being the only way of making a draft plan compatible with previously unforeseeable strategies, as in the case of the Olympic areas, unthinkable during the drafting of the PGM.

There was, then, a good working relationship between the Plan, centring on interrelations and general strategies, and the Project, associated with the site of action. In the city's brilliant urban development trajectory there has always been an obvious need for both spaces of reflection and decision-making in order to overcome the bureaucracy that so often hampers planning offices and the incoherence of autonomous projects whose apparent short-term efficiency prevents overall coordination.

VIII.7 From opposition to democracy

While confrontations with the totalitarian political situation had been evident in Barcelona since the war, they merely intensified in the fifties with the strikes of 1951, 1956 and 1958, and the politicisation of the university as of this latter date. While this text cannot hope to summarise such a wide-ranging process, it is important to highlight firstly how protests at urban development gradually became a common platform for action against speculation, and secondly the marked Catalan involvement at the forefront of opposition;[39] throughout the Francoist period, the Catalan language was persecuted, and its teaching and diffusion actively prohibited.

It was hardly surprising that the combination of these two fronts was important when change began to make itself evident as the regime weakened and also in the transition period.

In political terms, the Assembly of Catalonia was constituted in 1971 as a common platform for the majority of democratic forces and was to play a crucial role in the country's normalisation, first in the opposition until Franco's death in 1975, then until the first parliamentary elections in 1977.

The Generalitat de Catalunya was restored provisionally in 1977 on the return of President Tarradellas[40] and Plaça de Sant Jaume once again became the seat of government of both Catalonia and Barcelona.

The city witnessed a situation of transition marked by the dual condition of the implementation of a recently passed Plan and the first attempts to turn the protests of the urban social movements into effective proposals.[41] This was a very exciting and dynamic moment when the most pressing urban problems were discussed with a view to finding solutions. The first movements on the part of the City Council set out to respond to the demands for the most requested facilities, including primary and secondary schools in the city's poorest working-class districts.[42] Social housing was also on the agenda, though public schemes still lacked structure. Investment had to be negotiated with the ministries in Madrid, which were under pressure from the various regions and most particularly from the Madrid city districts.[43]

The 1975-77 period also marked the opening of an unprecedented process of discussion in the form of the Congress of Catalan Culture, addressing the theme of the *Països catalans*, or Catalan-speaking regions, producing a broad-based body of reflection on 24 fields of culture, from language to architecture and from theatre to regional planning.[44]

Today we can appreciate the broad scope of many of those debates which channelled the critical force contained by so many years of opposition to gradually become the germ of policies for action on the part of

[39] For a summary of the "urban social movements" see Miguel Domingo and Maria Rosa Bonet: *Barcelona i els moviments socials urbans*. Fundació Jaume Bofill, Barcelona, 1998.

[40] The first elections in the Catalan Parliament were held in 1990, as a result of which Jordi Pujol was elected President.

[41] See the author's presentation: "A new look at old problems". University of Urbino 1979, published by ILAUD, Milan.

[42] At this time, the Urban Planning Councillor was the architect J. A. Solans. Information about the projects undertaken can be found in issues 28 and 29 of *Arquitecturas Bis*. Barcelona, 1979.

[43] This is explained by the fact that in the early eighties, the housing policy was mostly concentrated in Madrid's periphery, in compliance with the agreements signed by the Ministry of Housing of the Transition Government.

[44] Various authors: *Resolucions del Congrés de Cultura Catalana*. Barcelona, 1978.

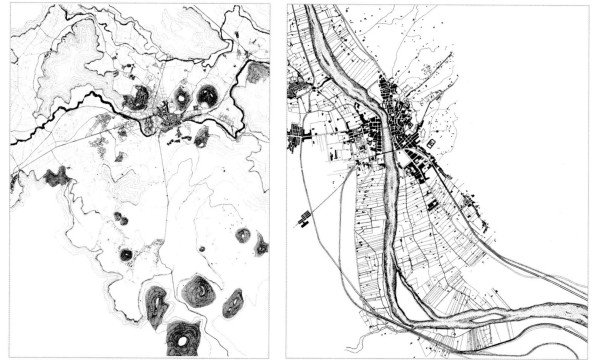

8.45, 8.46
Atlas comarcal del C.C.C.
Fragment showing Garrotxa
and Baix Ebre-Montsià. LUE
1977.

the new democratic bodies. Specifically, in Area VIII on territorial organisation, the many sessions served to reawaken the awareness of a rational discussion about the occupation and transformation of the territory. The bases of "regional planning" and the *comarques* of the thirties were now reconsidered; however, cities and towns, the territory and infrastructures by now called for other models or general referents.

In this context, and by way of a contribution to the closing session in Tortosa in 1977, a broad-based group of professionals, coordinated by the LUB, produced an atlas of Catalan counties, with a view to encouraging in-depth reflection on the current "identity" of the Catalan territory.[45]

Then, in 1979, with the advent of the new democratic councils and a restored Generalitat government, the revision of the urban development plans of most Catalan towns and municipalities came back to the forefront of attention.

While planning for Barcelona and its *Comarca* had been updated during the political changeover, most towns and cities had to wait for the new democratic situation. Only 50 plans in Catalonia had been updated by the new 1975 Act.

Now, at municipal level, each Catalan town and city staged a specific discussion with a view to passing from criticism to action. In many cases the administrative reshuffle coincided with a far-reaching urban planning discussion of the town or city's future.[46]

---

[45] See LUB: "ATLAS: identitat del territori català. Les Comarques". Barcelona, 1977. A summary can be found in the two monographic issues of *Quaderns* 1 and 2. Barcelona, 1980.
[46] See the author's article "La Escala Intermedia: nueve planes catalanes". *UR* 2, Barcelona, 1985.

In the eighties almost 500 municipal plans were drafted or subjected to a thorough revision, as a result of which no municipality of over 2,000 inhabitants, or fewer in the case of dynamic centres, was without its updated urban development regulations.[47]

Of course, although in some cases the Plan may have been invested with an excessive ruling force, this period has to be regarded as vital in the country's urban planning process: only a logic in keeping with each municipality and each valley could produce an ambitious strategy for Catalan territory. Reorganisation at a local scale had been the order of the day for two decades;[48] now it was the turn of more general urban structuring in successive phases.

[47] The planning programme was initially implemented with a half-and-half contribution on the part of the City Council and the Generalitat regional government. The programme was initially promoted by the architect Lluís Cantallops. In 1980, the architect Joan Antoni Solans took over the Directorate General of Urban Planning, until 2000, when he was replaced by Joan Llort, also an architect.

[48] Various authors: *10 Anys d'ajuntaments democràtics*. Barcelona, 1989. A broad-based work that takes stock of planning throughout Catalonia is Amador Ferrer and Joaquim Sabaté: *L'urbanisme municipal a Catalunya*. In the late 1990s, many of the new democratic government's plans were revised and in 2002 a new Urban Planning Act was passed which changed the procedures and systems for administering plans. Also, Ricard Pié: "Urbanistes, plans i problemes", *Quaderns* 165, Barcelona, 1985.

X . Barcelona's recovery in the eighties.
Urban development in the form of projects, programmes and strategies

IX.1 Urban relaunching under the new democratic City Council

Barcelona's urban relaunch programme was started up by the new democratic City Council in response to the strong social pressure that had been brought to bear on urban planning policies in the closing years of the old regime.[1]

The new democratic situation saw the arrival at City Hall of progressive forces that undertook the joint commitment to reform local government and improve the urban situation of a city that had been left to its own devices for several decades.

This long, broad-based operation of urban renovation involved a series of factors that we have already seen in other of the city's dynamic periods. Firstly, the commitment and political leadership expressed in this case by two mayors, Narcís Serra between 1979 and 1982, and Pasqual Maragall between 1982 and 1997, that gave material form and a tremendous boost to the relaunch.

It also involved a technical, theory-based capacity to direct a process of great administrative and operational complexity. There was the input of a series of outstanding professionals, of whom the architect Oriol Bohigas was initially the vital catalyst, comprising a whole host of young professionals who had trained in the critical years of the transition. At the School of Architecture, too, work groups such as the Laboratorio de Urbanismo, directed by Manuel de Solà-Morales, had put forward analysis and a methodological system for action in the city that could now be implemented.

Another factor was the favourable disposition of social and civic agents that were willing to take part in a large-scale undertaking, initially with a rather undefined outline, but which set out to transform the urban planning mediocrity that the city had been labouring under.[2]

The process started out with the innovative central idea of "recovering" the city. This involved a first phase of direct action expressed by urban improvements in the form of numerous small schemes for squares and parks, leading to a far more complex urban development programme.

In this way, various one-off *de facto* schemes gave way to mid-term interventions in various city districts. Later on, it was a series of overall strategies for certain critical sectors of the city, centring on obsolete or abandoned spaces, that would enable more ambitious operations to redress the balance. These different scales of action will be commented on individually.

Barcelona's nomination as Olympic host certainly acted as an important lever in this process of urban relaunch. However, the coherence of the project throughout the eighties provides an overall reading in which the Olympic programme must be seen as a singular stimulus within a broader strategy.

---

[1] The political profile of the municipal corporation after 1979 was progressive, with a higher participation of the Catalan socialist party in alliance with the Catalan Communist party. In the mid-nineties, the nationalist republican party was incorporated.
[2] Here, it is important to value the enormous value of the work carried out by specialist magazines such as *CAU*, *Quaderns* and *Novatecnia*, in the 1970s to establish a rigorous, critical discussion of Barcelona's urban problems, as noted in previous chapters.

9.01
Aerial view of the coastal front.

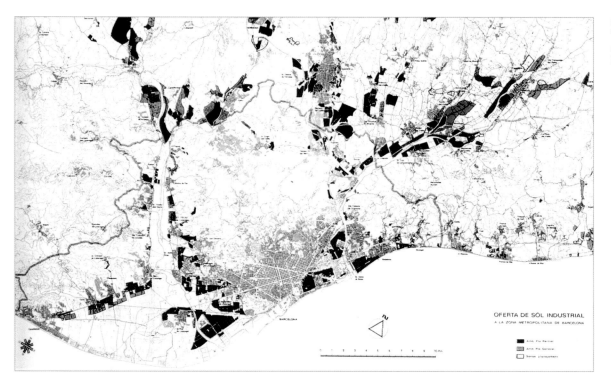

9.02
The industrial consolidation
of the 1980s took place in
Barcelona's area of influence.

IX.2 Restructuring of the industrial system in the Metropolitan Area

Once the process of urban rehabilitation had begun, it produced a degree of economic spin-off that led to a global restructuring of the industrial system.

The Metropolitan Area of Barcelona concentrated almost 60 per cent of Catalonia's total investment in the industrial recovery of the eighties. It thereby paved the way for a phase of mass industrialisation of the metropolitan ring that had previously hosted large industry back in the 1960s, but which now came to the fore. This process featured a series of specific characteristics.

a) Industrial development had a new profile in which R+D, or research and development, played a major role. This represented a qualitative leap from the manufacturing sectors that had hitherto been the protagonists of Catalan industrial development.

Much of the new industry was started up by the ZUR (urgent reindustrialisation area), converted into the "Plan for the industrial reindustrialisation of the centre of Barcelona" and applied to the perimeter of the Metropolitan Area.[3]

The activities promoted included electronics, information technology, auxiliary motor industries, plastics and the graphic arts as the sectors with the largest investment in technology. This represented the readaptation

---

[3] Modest Guinjoan + Joan M. Hernández: "Reindustrialització del cinturó industrial de Barcelona (1985-1988)", *Notes d'Economia 34*. Barcelona, 1989. The work studies two hundred projects approved by the ZUR scheme.

of existing companies (60 per cent), while the remaining 40 signified the creation of new companies with quite different profiles and sizes.

b) The Vallès corridor acquired a particular relevance in this development, joining the basins of the rivers Llobregat and Besòs to the other side of the Collserola range. The first developments took place in this corridor in the 1960s, on the basis of existing towns and cities, such as Sabadell and Terrassa, which had historically played an important industrial role. Sant Cugat had already given rise to a considerable residential complex on the other side of Tibidabo, thanks to the railways. The Autonomous University of Barcelona colonised this territory in the sixties, as did insurance companies and some education complexes. But most of all it was the B30 motorway that serves to interconnect a highly disjointed territory.

In the 1980s, a series of major installations marked new development in the sector.[4] The Vallès Technology Park also selected this location.[5] These sites were reinforced by the new Vallvidrera tunnel, opened in 1991, which directly connected the valley with the centre of Barcelona by means of Via Augusta, duplicating for private transport the trail blazed by the railway at the turn of the century.

c) These new developments meant a massive influx of foreign capital accompanied by a more general evolution of the Spanish economy. Of the investment made during this period, 43 per cent of capital came from abroad.[6] The basic sectors – transport and metallurgy – and those with larger technological investment – chemicals, information technology and plastics – were dominated by foreign capital.

d) This industrial restructuring also saw a change in the role of the city centre, which then began to function as the strategic centre of the modernised industrial system, with the development of a large service sector and a metropolitan whole whose subcentres – former county centres – were set to undergo a process of improvement to commerce and facilities.[7]

---

[4] Sites such as those of the Spanish Broadcasting Corporation, the High Performance Sports School, Baricentro, the General Hospital of Catalonia and the Catalan Motor Racing Circuit, opened in 1991, form the basic structure of the sector.

[5] Initiative of the Consortium of the Zona Franca and the Metropolitan Corporation to bring together high technology (R+D) installations in the sector, such as the National Microelectronics Centre or the General Testing and Research Laboratory of the Generalitat, and other firms.

[6] Joan Eugeni Sánchez: "Transformaciones en el espacio productivo de Barcelona y su Metropolitan Area, 1975-1990", *Papers* 6. Barcelona, 1991. According to the analyses conducted in this article which studies big companies with invoicing of over 2,600 million pesetas in 1988, 47 per cent of the these firms were in foreign hands. However, if real power is considered in terms of the capital indirectly controlled (by means of participation as shareholders), the percentage goes up to 56 per cent.

[7] A process of urban reclassification in metropolitan subcentres initially promoted by the CMB (Barcelona Metropolitan Corporation) in the form of parks and commercial installations and followed by industrial schemes in different municipalities. Various authors: *Projectar la ciutat metropolitana*. Barcelona, 1988.

A great deal of industrial land was promoted by the Barcelona Metropolitan Corporation in the form of the EPIs (axes of industrial promotion), that came to mobilise approximately 800 hectares of land in the Metropolitan Area. At the same time, the Generalitat regional government, by means of Incasol 56,[8] promoted 1,000 hectares, mostly outside the metropolitan area.

e) This process was accompanied by an appreciable change in the population dynamic of Barcelona and its Metropolitan Area. In fact, in the second half of the seventies Barcelona's population began to fall due to a drop in the birth rate and immigration. In the 1981-1985 period, Barcelona lost 50,000 inhabitants and its population pyramid underwent a substantial change. What was most significant was that the Metropolitan Area also began to decrease with a similar drop to that in the central city, indicating the far-reaching changes introduced by the crisis of the seventies.

These facts all serve to reflect the importance of immigration to the Catalan population, due to low biological reproduction and the sensitivity of immigration and, as a result, the overall population level to the general pace of the economy.

IX.3 New districts and the disappearance of the Metropolitan Area

The recovery of the city involved a series of urban development interventions that accompanied the administrative reorganisation of the municipality. The concern for greater operating efficiency on the part of municipal bureaucracy also involved a redistribution of the city territory into new municipal districts.

The new administrative limits signified new levels of competence and a degree of political decentralisation into 10 new districts. Their configuration recognised the different "parts" of the city, to a large extent reproducing the perimeters of the old municipalities that had been annexed in the late 19th century.[9]

The units defined in this way initially adopted this historical urban form and attempted to group together areas of approximately 200,000 inhabitants. By means of this strategy, the new districts would be of an entity and scale similar to that of other towns and cities in the Metropolitan Area, making the metropolitan region the sum

---

[8] This corresponds to the Catalan Land Institute, that promotes the residential and industrial schemes of the urban development policy of the Generalitat de Catalunya. The schemes nearest to Barcelona include the Can Graells estate near Rubí for the multinational Hewlett-Packard and an economic activity park of almost 280 hectares.

[9] Work on the municipal area, directed by the sociologist Jordi Borja, took place between 1983 and 1984 and was a political process approved by consensus.

...3
...e districts of Barcelona.

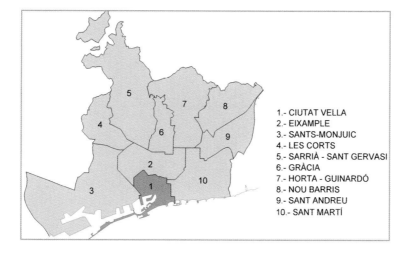

1.- CIUTAT VELLA
2.- EIXAMPLE
3.- SANTS-MONJUIC
4.- LES CORTS
5.- SARRIÀ - SANT GERVASI
6.- GRÀCIA
7.- HORTA - GUINARDÓ
8.- NOU BARRIS
9.- SANT ANDREU
10.- SANT MARTÍ

of 36 similarly-sized cities (26 municipalities and 10 districts) and thereby recover, duly brought up to date, the image of the great *Consell de Cent* as a new representative organisation of the big city.

This idea or project of the Maragall administration was however thwarted when in 1985 the Generalitat dissolved the territorial institution Barcelona Metropolitan Corporation, following the conservative practices of other countries.[10] The Barcelona Metropolitan Corporation had been constituted in 1974 and had carried out a series of important functions of planning control and deployment, as well as many schemes to redistribute investment among the various municipalities.[11]

The Metropolitan Corporation was substituted by a series of intermunicipal commissions or consortiums on the same scale set up to undertake highly specialised schemes associated principally with urban services such as water, drainage, transport and waste disposal.

Although this is not the place for a specific valuation,[12] it is important to highlight both the difficulties created by the body's dissolution – incoherence in council schemes, coordination difficulties – and the absence of technical analysis prior to decision-making, which would surely have prevented supposed incoherences and rationalised a body that despite having been created under the previous regime had allowed an extraordinary deployment of urban planning in the eighties.[13]

Despite these new imbalances, the municipal structure, organised in the form of consortiums or *mancomunitats*, and the Generalitat had to establish one or various frameworks for much needed political and administrative coordination.

[10] A well-known parallel is the dissolution of the GLC (Greater London Council) by the Thatcher government to reduce the protagonism of the institution which had played a central role in the development of post-war London. The results of this measure were disastrous and recent developments in the Docklands illustrate the difficulties attendant on a total abandonment of coordination and territorial redistribution in metropolitan regions.

[11] Its dissolution has been considered simply as a power struggle between the metropolitan space, in which Barcelona City Council was most representative, and the rest of Catalonia. However, this explication is simplistic given our awareness, after the country's experience, of how difficult institutional readjustments are, and we therefore have to understand that there is a latent, never explicit model that in part acts counter to Catalonia's urban planning history.

[12] See the author's article: "Algo más que un debate político", *La Vanguardia*. Barcelona, 1985.

[13] See the history of the "Metropolitan Area" explained in previous chapters.

IX.4 The different scales of urban recovery

The recovery of the city by means of urban development and economic relaunch paved the way for new experiences of urban intervention at European level, making for broader-based approaches.

In the face of the impasse produced by traditional planning and purely decorative urban design, new processes of urban transformation and new ideas for projecting the city began to emerge, and their application proved their conceptual and theoretical interest.

Therefore the idea of the "urban project"[14] took form as a way of overcoming the sterile dissociation between urban plan and architectural project that had relegated the former to the field of analysis and zoning and the latter to the one-off proposal. The concept of "urban piece"[15] comes to the fore in this discussion, pointing up the integrating capacity of the project that a stereotypical application of modern architecture had lost. There were calls for the "intermediate scale"[16] as a bridge between programmatic and structural decisions. The idea of "projects within the plan"[17] also emerged from the compromise between calls for the Plan as a necessary instrument to a form of social organisation that was to be increasingly equitable and the formulation of the central development themes of a city that required interim verification.

The complexity of the legal, spatial and decision-making mechanisms in the Western city is well known. All too frequently, urban planning mechanisms are seen as ends in themselves, becoming detached from their impact on the real city that they set out to enhance or project.

We can see paradigm examples of this situation in many urban plans that have represented a juggling of standards and a compromise with legality rather than an urban development proposal for the city. The existing regulatory framework of reference that established general magnitudes with regard to land rights and the structure of uses was necessary but insufficient. The Land Act was not the Plan; the city had specific disciplinary contents that were essential. Nonetheless, very often the standards of "acts" are confused with the "content" of planning. Likewise, the intervention project also tends to become automatic in relation to other urban variables that represent its condition and its existence. This context led to a crisis in planning and pro-development intervention in the most developed countries and redirected planning initiatives towards sectoral urban planning policies (traffic, housing, transport, urban utilities, etc.). These "sectors" became prime urban development agents in

[14] M. Solà-Morales: "El proyecto Urbano", *U.R.* 5 and 6. Barcelona, 1988.
[15] K. Garland: *Architecture and Urban Planning*. Section A. Montreal.
[16] J. Busquets: "La escala intermedia", *U.R.* 2. Barcelona, 1985.
[17] B. Secchi: "I progetti nel piano", *Casabella* 563. Milan, 1989.

4
cation of some specific
erventions in urban spaces
d green areas.

redirecting the transformation processes that the city needed. However, they were sectors that never considered the city as an object in itself and, therefore, as a subject for treatment in itself.

In all likelihood the keys to the Barcelona experience lay in work on different scales – sectoral and general – and in the urban integration – the interweaving of parts and sectors – that characterised its projects. The urban planning history of the city, as we have seen, contains excellent plans and projects with these selfsame conditions.

This, however, was precisely the problem. What should the new planning themes be? Where to find the principles for application? The mainstays of urban planning practice had been submitted to academic criticism in recent decades and were now considered obsolete. The schematic ideas of CIAM planning had been redirected to the residential district, and its spatial and formal proposals were criticised with regard to time scale or process: the dualism of centre and periphery existed and was well known. The planning imbalances of the development era were very familiar: the priority of private traffic, high-density residential units, the generalised lack of facilities in the periphery, etc.

Doubts began to emerge when the critical models were converted into real proposals: urban development in times of crisis is not necessarily all austerity. There was, then, a need to outline new theoretical topics in line with the urban development of the times. Here, the experience of Catalonia and Barcelona served as an "indicator" to evaluate whether the new interventions were merely a response to existing imbalances or how capable they were of generating a specific model for action.

This new attitude to planning represented a trend of deregulation or "anti-planning" which, on the basis of criticism of rigid traditional planning, sought a way through to the *laissez faire* of the last century which would allow case-by-case application, and particularly what "development" wanted. The idea here is not to discuss this approach which has had such dubious results in some European countries, but to understand that the objective difficulties of rigid planning have to be overcome without renouncing a more general urban coherence, and that this can only be achieved on the basis of overall interrelation which is the most important attribute of planning and the urban project.

The conditions of new urban planning development had to be extrapolated from experiences already under way. Different types of cities seemed to be advancing in specific directions. Southern European cities, like Barcelona, have a series of singular characteristics: the continuity of their urban fabric is categorical. A consultation of an aerial map reveals its historical events and still manifests the nature of its parts. It is a city without traumatic transformations such as the bombings of northern cities, yet it has a high degree of functional complexity: the buildings generally house many different activities and the residential base is spread out with a fairly high density. On the other hand, spatial segregation is perhaps less accused or more recent, with the powerful interruptions caused by heavy infrastructure and geographical relief, such as the railways or watercourses, etc.

Barcelona, as we have seen, responded to this profile with a very compact implantation around the old town and the Eixample, and recent development that segmented the east as a working class area with fewer services than the west of the city.

An urban reclassification programme had to address substantial improvements to infrastructures and define new central areas in order to redistribute levels of existing services and urbanism.

Although Western cities are subject to similar processes of transformation, alternative solutions may be applied according to the type of city in question. This is precisely the interest of working on the specific nature of the southern European city model instead of unquestioningly applying the patterns governing northern cities, which tend to be at more advanced stages of urban development.

Over two decades of new urban development experience in the city of Barcelona offer an important point of reference with regard to the scope and critical content of the various proposals. The form of planning implemented in Barcelona tended to side-step the old plan-project dualism, seeking instead to recompose a disciplinary field with a large overlap between architecture and urban development.

Because the Barcelona experience took the form of a change of scale, from the small scheme to the large intervention; an evolution from the simple, monographic project (a square, a park or a school) to the complex project (a street, building and green area with integrated management); from the public project to partnerships (cooperation), ensuring the involvement of private initiative in obviously public schemes;[18] from normal to exceptional planning, discovering common guidelines for the everyday regulation of the city and the major interventions for 1992.[19]

[18] In public project operations carried out by private bodies in accordance with conditions defined by the public sector, or by offering new fields of private insertion such as the restoration of listed and/or monumental buildings, and creating formulas for private sponsors of expensive urban maintenance work, such as the city's big fountains. The "Barcelona posa't guapa" programme was an obvious example.
[19] Think how exceptional events become the norm every 30-40 years in this and many other cities. In Barcelona, 1888, 1929 and 1953 signified a rate of renovation by medium-scope steps and a constant process of development and urban transformation that served to redress the balance.

9.a The construction of parks with facilities.

9.05, 9.06, 9.07, 9.08
Espanya Industrial Park,
using the land of an obsolete
industrial plant.

.09, 9.10
Park of El Clot.

9.11, 9.12
Pegaso Park.

These changes in scale, content, actor and scope were also the responses offered by the Plan to the change in dynamic of the context and the capacity of social and economic agents. In fact, the role of the public sector in this experience had shifted from that of a prime agent in reclassification work to that of rebalancing agent, seeking to intervene in the location of schemes and socialise the capital gains generated by the new urban dynamic.

"Urban reclassification", then, means bringing a new approach to the city on the basis of the city itself, with all its attributes and difficulties. We constantly see how, in Europe, cities turn back on themselves, seeking change and actualisation, renovating their old towns and coming up with modern answers to old problems. Barcelona was no exception to this process, and it concentrated its efforts on defining its seafront (port and coastline) as part of the old aspiration of a city that claimed its Mediterranean heritage yet had blocked off access to the sea and used empty, obsolete space as a way of drawing together working-class residential districts.

The Barcelona experience once again demonstrated the variety and wealth of its city planning and design instruments when appropriately adapted to the administrative, political and economic circumstances of the city in question.

It is interesting to note just how much the hypothesis of urban reclassification in Barcelona involved a great concern with the form of the city and the urban environment, using form as a synthetic element which could integrate urban processes and social agents. The effectiveness of this hypothesis was, to a large extent, gauged by its capacity to carry out proposals in the short or mid-term. Its capacity for innovation lies precisely in this approach: recognising the pragmatic nature of modern urban planning (applied in this case to the substantial improvement of the existing city), but without renouncing the referent of the scale of the Plan or the general idea of the city that was disseminated in big city planning in the early 20th century.

The specific case of Barcelona merely serves to ratify the need for in-depth theoretical work to formulate new hypotheses for city planning. Conventional "planning" theories, derived from other disciplines, come to a dead-end when analysis becomes proposal. Theories based on the social dimension of planning establish a cautious critique of the disproportionate plan. Procedural theories go no further than the implementation of standards and the observance of general norms. The only valid option, then, is to work on the definition of theoretical planning concepts that are appropriate and effective, which feed on advances in urban analysis with a view to formulating proposals for intervention, with a mid-term impact that can be previously estimated.

It seemed obvious that in this experimental phase, "practical knowledge"[20] was the fundamental resource for the reformulation of principles, and this wais the approach taken by Barcelona. Despite their contradictions,

[20] This is a conceptualisation of Foucault's that seems highly applicable to these disciplines. See Michel Foucault: *L'archéologie du savoir*, Gallimard. Paris, 1969.

9.b Squares and gardens.

13
aça Robacols: urban
abilitation schemes. The
oject sought a strategy to
prove the conditions of the
ban development context.

.14
aça Soller.

.15
aça Àngel Pestanya.

.16
aça de Sants.

plans and projects are capable of producing central ideas that are accepted and corrected by social agents, and serve to materialise the slogan of "urban reclassification". This principally took the form of city improvement by means of transformation and updating on the same site.

These overall ideas materialised by means of a working process that combined differing scales of approach and a strong commitment to the city's physical component and its real executive capacity.

More specifically, the different scales of work in Barcelona's process of urban development can be divided into three groups:

a) the first, urban rehabilitation, brought together smaller scale direct interventions under the heading of urban spaces and green areas, with the marked involvement of public management and investment. Sectoral plans were also presented, offering a more systematic way of reflecting on the city by parts with the engagement of schemes of varying scales.

b) the second group included urban restructuring, involving strategies of broader scope such as the reorganisation of the road network and areas of new centrality. This level of intervention highlighted a series of elements to relate or rebalance fragments and areas of the city, and was evidently reinforced by the 1992 Olympic programme. At the same time, as we will see, the scales can be seen as being interlinked, and these strategies could be approached from different links in the chain.

c) Finally, there were certain keys structuring the form of Barcelona that tabled some fundamental issues for the city's morphological organisation.

IX.5 Urban rehabilitation

I) Urban spaces and green areas

There are various reflections to be made on the structuring of the system of urban spaces and open spaces.

As Oriol Bohigas,[21] the man behind the idea, points out, the process was not the response not to a prior systematisation – the need for immediate action was an absolute priority. However, as the programme advanced, greater rationalisation was introduced into the process of intervention on green and open space.

The city sought to maximise its green structure throughout the entire urban fabric. From this we can deduce two hypotheses underlying intervention: firstly, it was necessary to work on the small empty gaps in the existing

[21] Oriol Bohigas: *La reconstrucció de Barcelona*. Edicions 62. Barcelona, 1985.

urban conglomerate, and secondly, the selection called for criteria of opportunity – which spaces were most available in relation to the adjacent residential fabric.

In this case, added to land management by purchase, there was also urban space that became available as a result of the Special Interior Reform Plans (PERI), which basically enabled singular management, compensation according to prior planning or, finally, expropriation.

Intervention centred on old industries that were now in disuse or facing serious crisis, and therefore interested in realising their assets, and the sites of old urban services, both municipal and state-wide, undergoing transformation. The former abattoir and land belonging to RENFE, the Spanish railway company, were spaces waiting to be converted into parks and squares.

With a view to establishing priorities for action among the sites available, the most central spaces in each urban fabric were chosen, so that every district or sector would be represented in successive waves of projects. This circumstantial condition of each project, which was specific as regards its size but also the surrounding urban context, was one of the most interesting dimensions of the projects for urban space in the Barcelona of the eighties.

Below is an outline of the location of the projects carried out between 1982 and 1990.[22] The selection was made pragmatically, including some categories of parks which, for their size and urban position, contribute an added degree of complexity to the types established by Rubió i Tudurí at the start of the century.

a) Urban parks, with an internal position – that is, set in the urban fabric, of a dimension of between 6 and 10 hectares, corresponding to the reuse of industrial and service precincts. Some obvious examples are the Escorxador (the former abattoir), Espanya Industrial, El Clot, Pegaso and RENFE-Meridiana.

In some cases, a singularity of situation was actually a hindrance to the project objective. This was, first and foremost, to restructure the "urban rear" that the walls of these precincts had historically created as permeable urban elements that could introduce a new service into the adjacent districts.

Furthermore, these parks were planned in spaces that were by no means the most suitable, often with high levels of land pollution, yet construction had to be rapid. The designers had to juggle vegetation, topography,

[22] J. Antonio Acebillo: "De la plaça Trilla a la Vila Olímpica", *Barcelona: la ciutat i el 92*. Olimpiada Cultural. Barcelona, 1990.

water and so forth in their endeavours to produce a park – in the same way that a building is designed – because the slow processes of plant life and the gradual adjustment of the traditional 19th-century parks were no longer possible. This was a development in a very important area.

b) Squares and gardens. These were small-format operations totally integrated into the city's different residential fabrics. The sheer number of schemes carried out (over 150) and their quality represented a thoroughgoing rehabilitation of Barcelona's urban space.[23]

Despite the smallness of their dimensions, their central positions in each district fragment produced a highly appreciable urbanising effect.

The squares responded to the clear functional need to systematise over-ground traffic and car parking and organise meeting places of varying kinds. Some occupied a more inner position and were designed almost as communal gardens: Salvador Allende, Baixa de Sant Pere, Sant Agustí Vell and La Mercè are just a few examples.

Most of the projects manifested an endeavour to retrieve the symbolic values of the square, incorporating elements of particular significance such as sculptures, which had hitherto disappeared due to excessive functionality of design.[24] The projects also had to overcome conditions of unfavourable context, as a result of which some squares were presented as works of "architecture of the void", seeking to establish an order of their own on conditions of constructed borders that were devoid of interest, principally in residential areas on the periphery that had been built during the speculative boom of the sixties. This is the case of Plaça Soller, Plaça de Robacols and many others which are spaces turned in on themselves and use the abstract order of their geometry to establish a new reading of the residential context.

In some cases, square design was addressed as a system of interconnected open spaces, as in the case of Gràcia's squares, the pedestrian precinct in Sant Andreu and some of the squares in Ciutat Vella. In the first case, it represented the integrated rehabilitation of a series of small 19th-century squares within the suburban development of the sector, and the second stringing together an itinerary of major facilities – market, district authority, church, station – which in this way came to function as a civic subcentre.

c) Gardens with facilities. This is a subtype of the previous heading and includes a series of former private estates that were given a new use as public spaces for the city. The old building was remodelled as a facility for the community. Some examples are Can Altamira, +Vil·la Cecília, Torre Groga and La Tamarita.

---

[23] There is a very extensive national and international bibliography on these projects. For a more comprehensive version, see Various authors: *Barcelona espais i escultures*. Ajuntament de Barcelona. Barcelona, 1987, and *Plans i Projectes 1981-82*. Ajuntament de Barcelona. Barcelona, 1983.

[24] Squares had frequently been designed according to commercial catalogues for urban furniture and children's play parks.

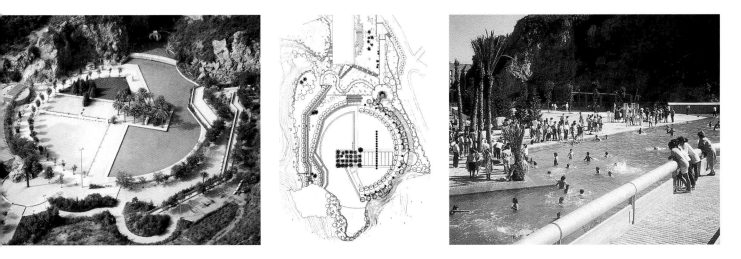

9, 9.20, 9.21
k of La Creueta del Coll.
abandoned quarry provides
ngular open space.

In their positions, they corresponded to an urban border or limit and most were located in the uptown part of the city, where these seigniorial estates had stood. Their purpose was to act as gardens with facilities or as gateways to the larger parks, mainly in the Collserola range.

In this case, the basic themes of the project were the adaptation of a garden, originally designed for private use, to new functional and urban needs. The case of +Vil·la Cecília is a clear example that combines the two situations with quite innovative compositional elements.

d) Urban axes. These were interventions to systematise the intermediate road network, increasing the protagonism of pedestrian space in principal elements of the urban form.

They were projects dominated by linear dimensions in which the most significant decisions turned on the design of the profile or cross section. The projects also gave rise to a lively dialogue with the general road and public transport system, in some cases introducing car parking and the most immediate private uses, principally ground floor business premises. It is easy to see how they might require a rather complex form of management.

This group includes Avinguda Gaudí, running diagonally across Cerdà's grid to join two large Modernista complexes, the Sagrada Família and the Hospital de Sant Pau; the introduction of this pedestrian precinct represented a remarkable improvement to the sector as a whole.[25] Another example is Avinguda Tarradellas, where the Eixample meets Les Corts, with the construction of an underground car park and increased pedestrian access; Carrer Tarragona, destined to become a space of bustle and animation; and the connection of the traditional Rambla with Rambla de Catalunya, finally connecting the Eixample and Ciutat Vella by means of a direct pedestrian route.

This category should also include the operation to rehabilitate large historical axes, such as Saló de Sant Joan and Avinguda Maria Cristina, entranceways to the monumental enclosures of 1888 and 1929, which were thereby reinstated as urban spaces of the first order.

[25] The Sagrada Família continues its construction amid controversy. Gaudí's very personal design process made it difficult to imagine that the monument now being built follows his architectural concept. This inspired architect would continually alter his designs on site and the final result may even devalue the original piece.

9.22, 9.23, 9.24, 9.25, 9.26, 9.27
Sculptures were incorporated into public spaces as one element more in their composition. Some examples by Miró, Tàpies, Lichtenstein, Gehry, Brossa and Chillida.

Via Júlia and Carrer de Prim were newly designed urban axes in Barcelona's periphery; their construction turned them from spaces lost among buildings to fully fledged civic axes that gave a new lease of life to Nou Barris and the Besòs, respectively. Later on they will be discussed further for their special position in the road system.

e) Large-scale parks corresponded to major interventions that changed Barcelona's overall system of green. They included the seafront, restructured as a great linear park with public beaches; the western slope of Montjuïc, descending into the Llobregat delta, where various Olympic sports amenities were installed; Vall d'Hebron in the north of the city, retrieving residential land for use as a large park with facilities in one of the densest sectors; and Diagonal Park, at this thoroughfare's western extreme, completing the city's large sports area.

The impetus to construct all of these parks in such a short period of time was provided by the 1992 Olympic programme; in some cases they covered more than a hundred hectares and made an effective impression on "internal space".

9.c The redevelopment of urban axes.

8, 9.29
nguda Gaudí between
rada Familia and Hospital
Sant Pau.

30, 9.31
inguda Tarradellas, before
d after redevelopment.

,32, 9.33
vinguda Mistral.

The project problems were specific in each sector. The Olympic component meant that some of them had to be designed with a dual use in mind, first for the Olympics and then "afterwards", to prevent a provisional need becoming a permanent constraint.

These large park operations often subordinated different executive projects to the more general logic of the open space envisaged. In some cases, the idea of park was based on the layout of various central elements and topography which allowed the park to continue growing and developing according to its own organic laws.

A general valuation of the various parks based on these five categories in relation to the green space that has existed since 1982 illustrates just how widespread the effects of these initial types was.

A reading of the city by levels with regard to green space is highly explanatory. The level below Gran Via was improved by the extension of the two large historic parks, in the form of Montjuïc's western slopes and the seafront.

The intermediate level corresponded to the most consolidated part of the city, where interventions took place between the borders of the Eixample and the traditional town centres. Another, more diffuse form of intervention also took place with the recovery of the inner patios of the Eixample, as we will go on to see.

On the higher topographic levels, the hillocks or *turons* of the city allowed greater access to green space.[26] Finally, the valleys among the foothills of Collserola accommodated "pre-park" interventions for a more intensive use of the gardens with facilities.

This interpretative model can also be applied to some extent on a metropolitan scale, where the recovery of large sectors as parks with facilities had also taken place in the early 1980s due to the impetus of the Metropolitan Corporation. Parks such as Torrerroja (Viladecans), Torreblanca (Sant Feliu) and Besòs (Sant Adrià) are good examples of this process.[27]

The metropolitan municipalities for their part also undertook small infill operations in the form of parks in the residential fabric, to a large extent as a response to the model being developed by the central city.

----

[26] In fact the central sector, known as *els tres turons* (the three hills), has its own strategy for increasing its green areas on the basis of the two existing parks, Güell Park and the recent addition, Creueta del Coll.

[27] See Various authors: *Projectar la ciutat metropolitana, op. cit.* Also Various authors: *La conurbació Barcelona: Realitzacions i Projectes.* Barcelona, 1993. Also Jaume Vendrell, *Realitzacions i propostes metropolitanes en els espais públics.* Barcelona, 1994.

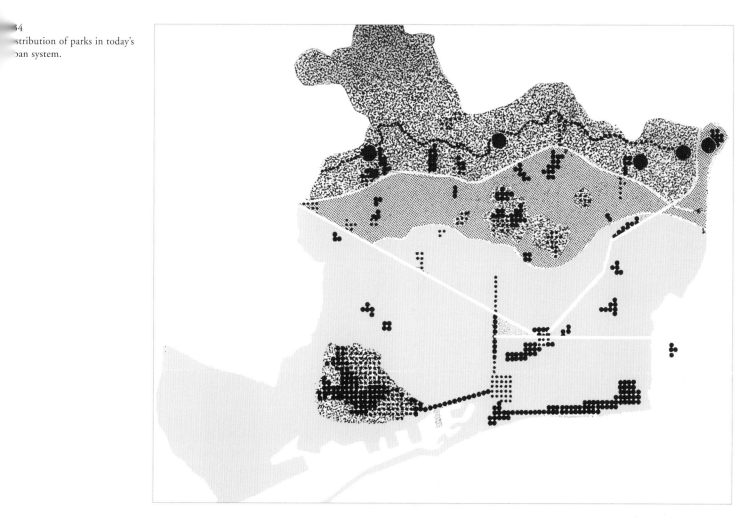

An initial evaluation of this experience has to highlight the enormous interest of a process whose basic criterion, despite responding to the general logic described, was a pragmatic, decisive first step. This is where the various projects had to compete: in the specific coordinates of each context, budget and functional requirements.

It seems only fair to recognise that a positive contribution was made to this process by many professionals employed by the authorities, but also from outside it.[28] Different lines of reflection on architecture and open space came together to find a proving ground. Common to most of them was the search for new answers

---

[28] A crucial element in this process was the creation of a specific municipal department, Urban Projects, which, under the direction of J. A. Acebillo until 1988 and later of R. Cáceres, promoted the development of many of these projects, with young architects working for the City Council as contracted civil servants or freelance professionals. See in particular *Barcelona: espacios y esculturas*, (*op. cit.*). The intervention of artists in this process was also important. Outstanding among the many sculptors to have taken part are Joan Miró, Antoni Tàpies, Xavier Corberó, Joan Brossa, Sergi Aguilar, Antoni Roselló, Eduardo Chillida, Roy Lichtenstein, Richard Serra, Bryan Hunt and Ellsworth Kelly. See Lluís Permanyar: *Barcelona, un museo de esculturas al aire libre*. Barcelona, 1991; also Various authors: *Barcelona Escultures*. Barcelona, 2001.

to the question "what is an urban space or a park today?", which is so vital when planning green space these days. They also shared a concern with the symbolism of urban space, which in many cases led to the collaboration of artists and sculptors in the overall discussion of the project and the physical execution of some of its parts.

II) The sectoral plans

Urban rehabilitation also called for more systematic complementary action to ensure its development in the mid-term. In this sense, Barcelona's urban planning process admitted the need to understand urban "differences" in order to find coherent forms of intervention that were most compatible with the existing fabrics.

In fact, Barcelona admits of an interpretation by parts corresponding to its traditional districts. The urban process of formation and transformation of the various parts was different in each case, though all the interventions shared the determination to free up space and design projects of high urban quality that would offer judicious guidelines for rehabilitation. They can be divided into three sections:

a) the recovery of Ciutat Vella, for example, was a nodal point in the city's new urban development policy. The forms of intervention in its various districts differed from other areas in the city as they involved particularly complex problems. It was impossible to ignore the dreadful housing conditions in some sectors of the Raval or Santa Caterina, or the high residential density of parts of the Barceloneta. These were problems that dated back to the densification of these historical sectors in the 19th century, aggravated by their abandonment by planning and real-estate sectors in the second half of the 20th century.

For this purpose, Ciutat Vella can be divided into three areas corresponding to the Raval, Santa Caterina and Barceloneta, each with their different hypotheses of intervention.

Though not identical in method, these were plans which shared a series of elements that gave them a general coherence. The variables at play were approached in great detail: the study of the structure of ownership, typological classification and sociological characteristics provided the departure point for each project in the Plan, which formed its own reading and interpretation.

Each Plan sought to minimise the designation of public property which was not subsequently developed, responsible to a large extent for the degradation of some of its parts. In turn, the search for alternative street layouts was based on the promotion of the idea of the precinct, concentrating traffic on the ring roads and existing thoroughfares within the fabric. The situated was rationalised by means of the construction of car parking and the resolution of specific points of conflict.

The modernisation of prominent buildings for communal and institutional uses was a recurrent theme for large architectural elements or "containers" of stylistic or morphological interest.

9.d The Special Interior Reform Plans (PERI) of Ciutat Vella.

35
ey included the walled town
d the Barceloneta.

36
rom the Liceu to the
minary", in the Raval, sought
etter use of large historical
ildings.

.37, 9.38
ambla del Raval, a large
ublic space that resolves the
ld constraints caused by the
venida García Morato Partial
lan.

9.e Rehabilitation and creation of public spaces in Ciutat Vella.

A)

B)

9.39, 9.40, 9.41, 9.42, 9.43, 9.44
9.45, 9.46
Various schemes to enhance public spaces in Ciutat Vella: a) reuse of existing space and b) creation of new spaces. Examples of a) are Carrer Montalegre, Plaça de la Catedral and Plaça de Sant Agustí and of b), Allada-Vermell and Plaça de la Mercè.

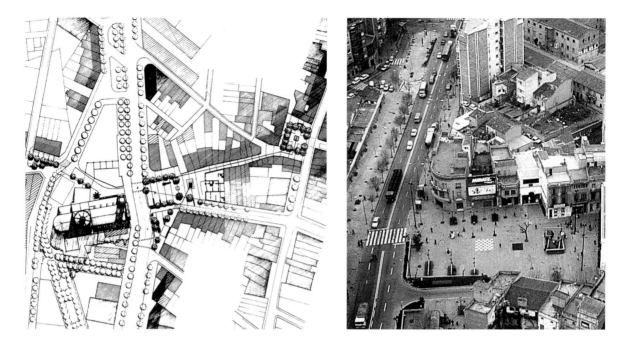

.47, 9.48
The pedestrian axis in Sant
Andreu recovers the continuity
between civic elements of the
old municipality, now a city
district.

Nonetheless, the idea of opening up the district was the prevailing trend in the case of Ciutat Vella. The strategy proposed by the GATCPAC back in the 1930s now involved the demolition of one or various entire street blocks in the Ribera or the Raval. Barcelona already had excellent examples with positive results, such as the recently created Plaça de la Mercè and Plaça George Orwell in the central fabric.

Once the Plan had been drawn up for the recovery of Ciutat Vella, a public company, Promoció Ciutat Vella, was set up to direct the intervention. The sector's housing difficulties called for major public investment with recourse to supralocal support to address the abandonment of so many years in the original heart of the city. The public beginnings of this process created a new threshold of recovery and gave rise to new forms of collaboration with other corporate and private operators.[29]

A look at the interventions carried out in 1988 and 2000 show that investment in Ciutat Vella, including the walled city and the Barceloneta, was in the order of 9,000 millions euros, with 50 per cent on facilities and infrastructure, 25 per cent on public space and the same again on housing. Major investment was concentrated mainly in the Raval, which received 60 per cent of the total, as it was one of the most deficient sectors.

This was a process of shock treatment that included: 1) both the process of improving public spaces and housing, including the maintenance of what was already there, and 2) giving rise to an appreciation of heritage by seeking to reactivate economic and cultural activity in this part of the city.[30]

[29] There is a monographic issue of the magazine *Barcelona Metròpoli Mediterrània* 1, May 1986, that presented rehabilitation projects in Ciutat Vella. More recently, issue 18 (1991) of the magazine offered an updated review. See also Various authors: *Ciutat Vella. Visions d'una passió*. Barcelona, 1995, and LUB: *Ciutat Vella de Barcelona. Un passat amb futur*. Barcelona, 2003.

[30] See section 5 of LUB. Joan Busquets *et al.: Ciutat Vella de Barcelona. Un passat amb futur (op. cit.*), describing schemes for public space, housing rehabilitation and new housing construction (over 2,000 publicly funded dwellings). In 2001 a new company was founded, Fomento de Ciutat Vella, that set out to continue the rehabilitation of the district with greater participation of private initiative.

9.f Restructuring residential buildings in the old town.

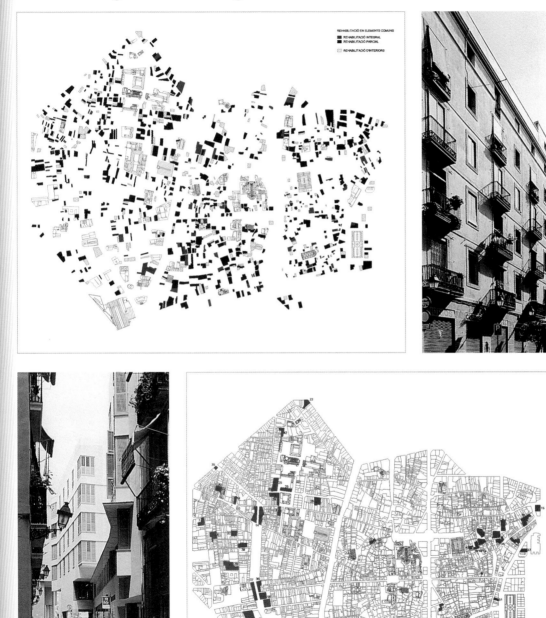

9.49, 9.50
CIVE: specific rehabilitation work carried out in the last 15 years.

9.51, 9.52
CIVE: new schemes to rehouse the local residents affected.

3
nversion of the vapor textile
l of Fabra i Coats in Sant
dreu into facilities for the
.

b) The plans for the traditional districts – the sectors defined here as suburban – had to verify the planning structure proposed by the 1976 Metropolitan Plan. The urban development coherence of these city parts required it: they were, as we have seen, districts consolidated in the 19th and the early decades of the 20th centuries, and the laws of the suburban formation of their streets, the typological structure of their houses, the distribution of their urban services and facilities called for specific recognition in each situation. These themes were taken as guidelines to produce important elements for their understanding which were vital in the replanning process.

For example, the concept of high street acquired new contents, but maintained a hierarchy of value in terms of its central and commercial uses, which made it seem appropriate to reduce the pressure of through traffic: the high streets of Gràcia, Sarrià and Sant Andreu, and the Rambla in Poblenou and El Carmel were all spaces in the district fabric with the capacity for enhancement. In addition, there were urban transformation operations that allowed improvement of the structure. This was the case of the substitution of old factories or disused spaces that could be turned into places of interest: the parks created are one example, and others followed suit: Fabra in Sant Andreu, Paperera in Poblenou, Vapor Vell in Sants and FECSA in Poble Sec all served to provide new facilities for these districts. The creation of central spaces with pedestrian areas gave them a whole new potential.

Another subject altogether was the rehabilitation of the residential districts constructed in the sixties, both mass housing estates and areas of self-construction. This theme called for extra investment as the rapid obsolescence – both architectural and planning – of these urban fabrics came to light.

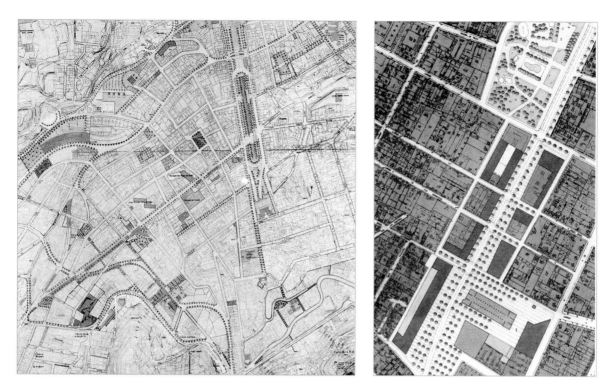

9.54, 9.55
PERI for El Carmel and Car
Joan Güell in Sants, example
of these schemes at district
level.

Particular mention should be made of the marginal neighbourhoods developed, due to the particular difficulties involved in their formation. Urban development was in general terms more costly than normal, sometimes requiring correction of poorly constructed parts. The legalisation process gave rise to specific problems at the start of the Plan. However, these were plans for intervention in consolidated realities which, when implemented, called for major public management.[31]

The instrument that provided a basis for rehabilitation by urban sector was the Special Internal Reform Plan (PERI), which generally struck a balance between the 1976 Metropolitan General Plan (PGM), urban reality and a possible dynamic for public and/or private intervention. These were "different" sectoral plans that established programmes of public intervention and forms of "agreement" with private intervention as and when possible. In order to implement these plans, the concept of Unit of Action or Integrated Intervention was defined as the field for the new project and urban management. These were schemes that integrated differential elements (a square and a residential building, a public car park and facilities, for example), presenting a highly stimulating challenge.

In turn, the city's new economic dynamic led once again to the rising concern of the government with the theme of the "affordable dwelling". Indeed, the pressure of demand for land and buildings meant that social or low-cost housing was essential. The Special Plans envisaged spaces for action, as did the sectors of major urban transformation, which could meet the need for this type of low-cost dwelling for the population in the lower income brackets.

[31] The types of plans can be seen in greater detail in J. Busquets *et al.*: *Plans cap al 92*. Ajuntament de Barcelona. Barcelona, 1987.

9.g Recovery of the courtyards inside Eixample street blocks.

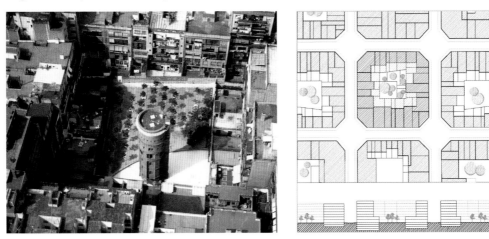

...6
...urtyard of the Water Tower.

...7
...orphology of courtyards
...ned into private open space.
...me are open to the public.

...58, 9.59, 9.60, 9.61
...he new ordinance set out to
...cover the courtyards inside
...eet blocks.

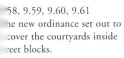

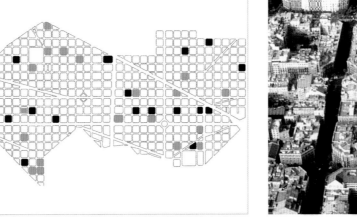

c) The Eixample required particular consideration due to its size and symbolic importance within the city.[32] It could be seen as a paradigm part that called for an integrated, unitary approach in the undertaking of operations to conserve and improve one of Europe's largest modern centres, where it still seemed possible to neutralise the functional specialisation towards which it was heading by promoting residential use to redress the balance.

The buildings in the Eixample were highly consolidated; few sites remained unoccupied, and there was a great deal of building of particular architectural and environmental importance. In this situation, it was a question of how to define more precise regulations to improve the buildings without having them listed, and how to facilitate the rehabilitation of buildings and ensure the judicious insertion of new constructions.

Another basic objective of the ordinance was to free up the patios inside the street blocks, a proposal retrieved from Cerdà's initial project that had never been carried out. The geometry and volume of the block required an inner space free of building to enhance the façade and internal space. The new ordinance stipulated that the centre of the block be left without building and, in the event of substitution or major transformation to the existing houses, it was to be landscaped. It opened a slow but increasingly positive means to the existence of green space inside the street block. Further, various courtyards were to be devoted to public use; they would be yards where it was possible to intervene with relative ease and maximum effect due to their position in relation to important axes and facilities. Work on a series of pilot courtyards was actually carried out. An outstanding example is one in Carrer Llúria, that turns the old water tower to use as an element in the new garden.[33]

IX.6 Urban restructuring

I) Reorganising the road system

Once work on the most pressing needs in terms of facilities and open space was under way, it was vital to address the urbanisation of road structures, due both to their capacity to redress the balance and their role in

---

[32] See J. Busquets + J. L. Gómez Ordóñez: *Estudi de l'Eixample* (*op. cit.*), which takes stock of the situation at the time and presents the types of urban planning schemes developed as it was formed. This reconnaissance study points up the present-day problems facing the Eixample (conflicting planning, systematic demolition of central buildings for conversion into sites, excessive traffic pressure creating difficulties for residence, etc.), but it also emphasises the key proposals of Ildefons Cerdà's project that still govern this vital part of Barcelona.

[33] "The Ordinance on Rehabilitation and Street Blocks in the Eixample", passed in 1986, stipulated that the inner courtyards of the almost 500 street blocks should be landscaped by means of the reconstruction or transformation of existing buildings, and envisaged that a dozen of them would be open to the public. See Various authors: *Rehabilitació de l'Eixample*. Barcelona, 1991.

configuring the image of a compact city. Here, there is a close correlation between areas with deficiently low levels of urbanisation and districts that required improved mobility.[34]

The road network schemes that consider traffic to be an autonomous element and overlook the urban implications behind their existence are surely doomed to failure. Traffic has all too frequently been addressed in too functionalist and one-dimensional a fashion, as though it were the most important variable in city design. This trend, rooted in the system design of the 1960s that established a hierarchy between well-defined functional variables has led to serious problems for most modern cities and introduced a discipline of road design and traffic functioning that has acted in excess and totally independently of other urban planning decisions in each city.[35]

An overview of the streets of Barcelona offered an image or real "graph" of the city showing the breakpoints and bottlenecks in the system that seriously distorted the general network and forced a very high volume of flow through the modern centre – the Eixample.[36] This meant that a journey between two sectors of the periphery would go right through the centre, and also that the centre became a mandatory crossroads, with a corresponding increase in the friction of traffic through it. In city use, the Eixample had become a place of passage and a turning point in urban itineraries, acting like a great turbine for journeys that began and ended elsewhere.

A stocktaking of this situation produced a dual valuation: the friction of traffic affecting some central districts was excessive, normally leading to a loss of residential quality and an increase in the number of buildings that were abandoned or reoccupied by a new tertiary activity; and there was a shortage of urbanisation in peripheral areas, which did not yet have a complete road structure despite a very high demand for mobility.

To this summarised diagnosis we have to add the potential for solutions and examples that any city has, and which in the case of Barcelona took the form of a whole list of streets and a fair repertory of junctions.

---

[34] Reworking of the article "De nuevo, la calle en el proyecto de ciudad: algunas reflexiones sobre el Plan de Vías de Barcelona", published in *Casabella* 553-4. Milan, 1989. The departure point is the need for integrated reflection on the project for the street system and the article summarises the work carried out in Barcelona with a view to establishing new bases for design in the form of projects for streets and urban highways. The discussion process began in 1984, with a seminar held in Sarrià organised by the Department of Municipal Urban Planning to debate the various professional attitudes and the bases for the street project. It gave rise to a publication, *Las vías de Barcelona*. Barcelona, 1984, and laid the foundations for an interesting common language and schemes.

[35] The seriousness of these problems in Barcelona could be similar to those of other European cities. However, traffic demands in the sixties went as far as prompting that Barcelona's exquisite Rambla should be turned into an expressway. Fortunately, the idea never got beyond the planning stage.

[36] J. Busquets *et al.*: *Estudi de l'Eixample* (*op. cit.*), pp. 15-18.

9.h The Streets Plan reorganised the entire urban structure.

9.62
The city streets in 1985.

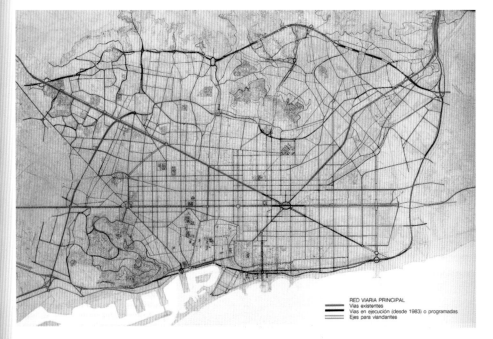

9.63
The proposed Streets Plan.

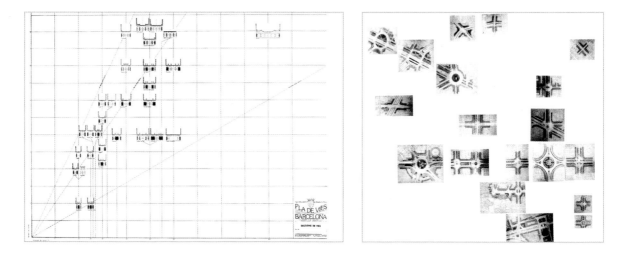

A catalogue of sections presented "twin" streets and thoroughfares of equivalent dimensions allowing their environmental condition and spatial quality to be measured and evaluated. Furthermore, there were good environmental results in streets whose section was divided equally between pedestrians and vehicles.

The repertory of junctions and squares also served as a referent to define new urban spaces that needed traffic efficiency. These elements in the "manual" of each city are crucial to directing an interdisciplinary discussion in each context and enriching the field of possible solutions. The road structure was conditioned by two general hypotheses.

a) It was necessary to adjust the differential nature of the various consolidated areas according to their specific road systems, at the same time seeking a general scheme to interconnect them.

b) Road connections between urban sectors took place on four levels:

1. The maxi-network or primary network, comprising the former Ronda beltways (along the coast and around the mountain), that functioned as prime distributors (later known as the Ronda ring roads) and linked up with the secondary network, facilitating the connection of areas with districts. Their purpose was to produce segregated traffic with little incidence in tangential areas and an urban road network to distribute traffic, preventing the formation of bottlenecks in built-up areas.[37]

2. The secondary network of main streets and/or boulevards whose fundamental value was to increase distribution to local streets. These were important elements in the organisation of public transport and tertiary and advertising activity. For their position and form, they acted as border elements (in an asymmetrical situation), as structuring axes (to order a sector) or as spaces with facilities (with a promenade or activities of their own).

3. The internal network, comprising the streets that formed the urban fabric. This corresponded to local streets whose grain and characteristics varied from one sector to another. At this level, the network was practically complete in built areas, and only in marginal districts was it still pending work.

4. Urban pedestrian spaces, including the elements set in consolidated areas that prioritised pedestrian and representative uses that sought to diversify this activity in the various traditional areas of the city, as the treatment of urban axes showed.

[37] The need for these great distributors or bypasses arose due to the very direct way in which the motorways "joined" Barcelona's system of major axes.

9.i The Ronda ring road strategy. Moll de la Fusta wharf.

9.66, 9.67, 9.68
Moll de la Fusta, a complex solution that combines through urban traffic, covering half the r to generate an axis that connects different urban sectors.

9.69, 9.70, 9.71, 9.72
Sections of the Ronda ring roads showing the different levels to conserve urban connectivity.

3, 9.74, 9.75, 9.76
structuring of Via Júlia in
u Barris, the development of
pace with difficult relief.

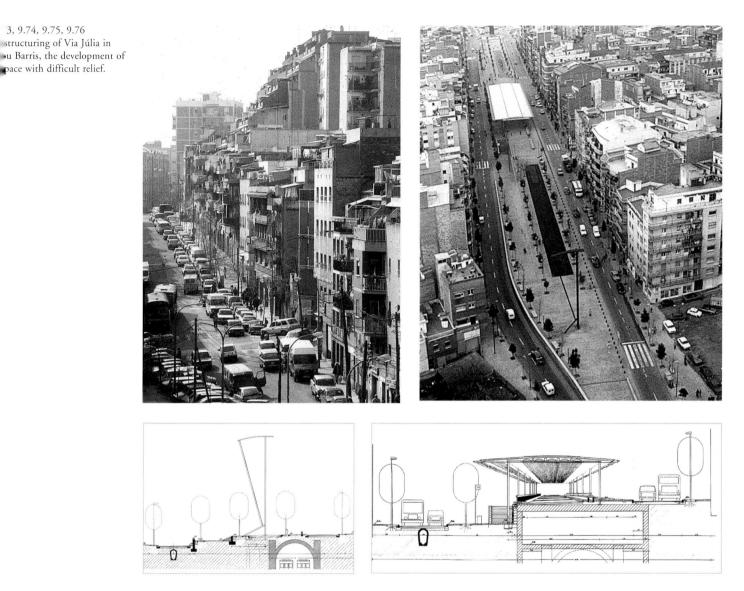

An intervention of this scope obviously had to be addressed in phases. The completion of each project or sector involved highly precise data in its executive definition.

This process also had to envisage two typical project situations, however:

a) The "active" project, that in itself lays out a "rule of urbanisation". The project provides the basis for future building and the cadence of spaces and activities.

Barcelona is a city with a history that includes excellent examples of "active" street projects, such as the main streets in the Eixample: Gran Via and Diagonal are excellent examples of streets that colonise and arrange the adjacent territory. This stance is more difficult in recent projects, since it is so frequently a question of urbanisation *a posteriori*.

The project for the Moll de la Fusta[38] is another example; what was supposedly a road intervention imposed overall order on the space between the old town and the port, thereby becoming an active project with regard to the renovation of the historic centre and the future development of the urban port. This attitude should serve as an excellent example for large infrastructures with levels of investment and impact that make them prime structures in the future city. Thanks to the meticulous project section, its route between Ciutat Vella and the port reconciled through traffic with urban surface traffic, devoting more space to pedestrians who, at last, once more had access to the waterfront.[39]

b) In the "passive" project, pre-existing conditions to a large extent shape the space and arrangement and, in general, limit the project's room for manoeuvre. This is a common situation in many of Barcelona's redevelopment schemes, though experience has proved that passive projects often have greater leeway for action, since imposed conditions often form an interesting field for design: from the formalisation of spaces to their influence on induced urban activities.

One such was the project for Via Júlia,[40] a high-quality urban axis in the northern periphery of Barcelona. Building in the sector took place before urbanisation and the gradient of the mountainside enforced a special cross section to prevent disrupting the houses that had already been built. A judicious choice of materials and the sequence of large palm trees are proof of the potential of the passive project today.

Barcelona's strategy as part of its Olympic programme was to construct the Ronda ring roads to form great urban distributors. Mention should be made here of the studied task of urban design to ensure the correct insertion of this new construction. Working on the hypothesis that the traffic in the principal network is, by nature, mixed – that is, its combines metropolitan movement and urban flows, it was possible to separate the two. It was estimated that between half and two-thirds corresponded to metropolitan traffic, which was to be segregated in a space of its own, either under ground or on the surface, provided that it did not interrupt urban traffic at normal city level. The highway constructed situated through traffic at a lower level, either under ground or uncovered, for two-thirds of the way. Meanwhile, urban traffic moved beside the Ronda, generally on service roads, like one street more in the district served. The study of each urban project (a dozen projects were involved

---

[38] The project can be seen in greater detail according to the plans and explanations of its author, Manuel de Solà-Morales, in *UR* 6, LUB. Barcelona, 1988.

[39] This is a very delicate project, judging by the difficulties so many cities are having as a result of addressing the issue too lightly, or by means of road schemes that are too weighty or orthopaedic. Genoa, Toronto, Boston and New York are all problematic cities. Genoa's *sopraelevata* is obstructing relations between the historic city and the port. Boston's J. Fitzgerald Expressway in the 1960s was built when the large-scale urban renovation of the city broke off its natural relation to the water. This viaduct is now being undergrounded at a cost of over ten billion dollars.

[40] A design of the Department of Urban Projects by B. Sola and J. M. Julià, on the outskirts of the city.

77
iagrams of different
terchanges.

.78, 9.79
he Nus de la Trinitat is an
xample of combining a major
oad interchange with a large
rban park.

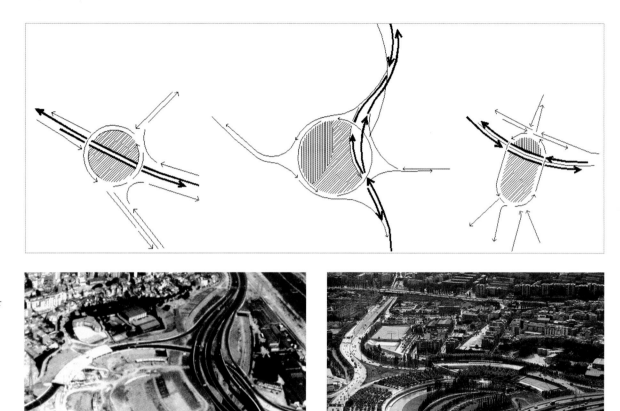

in all) provided a specific solution on the basis of model sections and took into account the fact that car drivers also had to be aware of their urban position and recognise the different parts of the city.

Another central theme was that of interchange with other networks. A strategic choice of where and how the junctions were constructed was therefore fundamental. These points required subsequent work on their urbanism, as the urban history of our cities has showed us that these great internal gateways can also be representative spaces with a degree of civic use. In some, public facilities can form meeting places, as in República Argentina, or large urban parks, as at the Trinitat junction, etc., and the leading lines of urban form generally emerge from city ground level.

This process was complemented by work on increasing urban connectivity, constructing streets or bridges to overcome bottlenecks in the general network, or introduce a more effective distribution of the main infrastructure.[41]

[41] The example of the Bac de Roda bridge is an emblematic one: the construction of a 200 metre long bridge brought into operation the first three-kilometre vertical axis in the east to connect the mountain and the sea. This bridge design by Santiago Calatrava just goes to prove the essential role of this former bottleneck, now a brilliant connection point.

9.80, 9.81
Transformation of Carrer del Prim, on Besòs estate, into a civic axis, Rambla del Prim, that structures the various par of this residential periphery.

A particular example is provided by the large streets in the periphery that were built to urbanise vacant land in districts with mass housing estates; in addition to increasing connectivity, they had the capacity and a strong enough image to structure and organise various parts of a disjointed residential periphery. The above-mentioned example of Carrer de Prim is particular illustrative.

Altogether, Barcelona's revision of the roads project was a difficult step on the way to an integrated project, in which the traffic component was an important variable that competed with environmental and spatial variables. In the modern history of the city, road schemes have always been a key indicator of the target level of urbanism at a given moment.

II) Areas of new centrality

The central spots of Barcelona gradually moved from the Portal del Mar, a symbol of institutional representation of the commercial city, to Plaça de Sant Jaume, at the heart of Ciutat Vella, before opening up to Plaça Catalunya and, in the course of the last century, identifying definitively with the Eixample, most particularly its central sector. The Rambla and Via Laietana now form the links between that great metropolitan centre and Ciutat Vella.

In recent decades, centrality in Barcelona has been based in the modern centre designed by Cerdà, like the CBD (Central Business District) of northern European and American cities. Nonetheless, the large surface area and the diversity of the specific initiatives created a model of a centre that was intense but fairly spread out, with a predominance of axes but a markedly heterogeneous functional distribution in which residence was firmly present.

The discussion of the future of the metropolitan centre or urban centres in Barcelona has often been confused with maximalist proposals of dual centres, outside the city, following the trend set by the discussion of French and Italian cities in the 1960s, and it was time to reconsider this body of reflection. It was a question that had been present at other times in the city's urban planning history, producing various attempts and incipient formulations.

This is the context in which the impact of the development of Plaça d'Espanya in 1929 for the Great Exhibition has to be understood, as an alternative to the initial idea of siting it in Glòries or Besòs Park. The reinforcement of Plaça d'Espanya took in the southward development and the consolidation of the axis connecting it to Castelldefels and the Zona Franca. Rubió i Tudurí himself referred to the square as an "active centre" of Barcelona in 1930.

Conversely, the geometric centre (Plaça de les Glòries) of the main axes structuring Barcelona is a rather indecisive spot in the city, bogged down by the road system. Cerdà and Jaussely both highlighted this potential focus, which is still an ongoing issue but will become a central spot in the mid-term.[42]

At the same time, the theme of the transformation of the urban port had been mooted by the GATCPAC's Macià Plan as the paradigm of a functional centre that never materialised.

These were images and ideas that the city had to reconsider from an up-to-date viewpoint, especially as the concept and content of central activity had changed. The borders between industrial activity and offices had blurred; the divisions in industrial production were perhaps no longer defined as much by specialised sectors as by functions, and automation and information processing were beginning to exert a decisive influence on the definition of new centrality.

These conditions had changed trends with regard to the size, location and content of the new centres. It is in this context that Barcelona's new centrality must be placed, and the strategies for its new implantation had to be set in the situation of new capitality occupied by Barcelona as the seat of the Catalan Government with the growing economic and representative importance that international events were giving it.

---

[42] The systematisation of an elliptical road ring forms the initial system, though visual continuities between the major roadways seem advisable.

In any case, Barcelona's capacity for restructuring lay in the city's primary resources of its districts and central areas, which were now coming to the fore.

Apart from the modern centre (the Eixample), small business activity was distributed throughout Ciutat Vella, where institutional functions also breathed representative, economic and cultural life into the old town of Barcelona. This characterisation had to be preserved to reactivate this important city sector. The commercial axes of the Rambla and Barnacentre had the potential to bring the old tertiary structure up to date.

Then traditional districts such as Gràcia, Sants, Les Corts, Sant Andreu and Poblenou all had highly diversified structures of personal and commercial services. The historical location of the municipal markets continued to be central to the city's districts. The new centrality was to take place in the interstices between neighbourhoods, not to negate the traditional structure but to reinforce it, with the distribution of activities to provide a complementary service.

A return to the discussion of strategic centres or new strategic activity throughout Europe saw in a change in attitude to the structural situation of 30 years previously, when strategic centres represented the paradigm of opulent urban development, in which the monumental tertiary sector was assigned a prime value in the functional city being planned. The very definition of the urban tertiary sector was vague and imprecise; now, however, the transformation of the industrial system was encouraging the reorganisation of the tertiary production cycle. The process of industrial decentralisation – like the location of companies in a rural environment – was accompanied by the growth of an emerging tertiary sector, including, for example, service companies, that had a centralised effect on the control of the fragmentation in the production process.

These issues led to the reappearance of the discussion of new centres in European cities. Now, however, the scale and position were very different: the enhancement of obsolete areas and the use of empty spaces were vital characteristics. Absolute confidence in the redeeming power of the tertiary sector was replaced by a determination to bring central uses up to date and ensure their judicious insertion into the urban fabric.

Furthermore, whereas the basis for centrality had been accessibility to major road and transport infrastructures, the new priority was access to quality urban spaces and well connected information systems.

Twelve Areas of New Centrality were defined; of these, four were Olympic areas that the City Council had undertaken to develop for the design year of 1992. The others required forms of cooperation with private initiative, under the direction of the public sector responsible for their promotion.[43]

---

[43] There is a special publication with several editions on the theme: *Áreas de Nueva Centralidad.* Ajuntament de Barcelona, and a summary "Varios corazones para una ciudad", published in the magazine *Barcelona Metròpoli Mediterrània* 8, 1988.

9.j Areas of New Centrality.

82
eas of New Centrality.
ctors with potential within
e urban fabric. The Olympic
ogramme included four such
ctors.

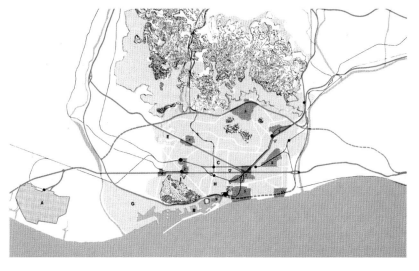

83
he Areas in the new urban
ructure.

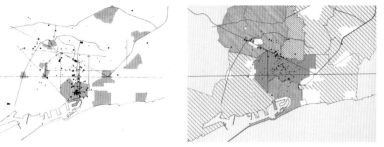

).84
Large shopping centres.

).85
Density of offices in 1985.

There were urban spaces that could become central places if they had activities to occupy them. The organisation and distribution of new centrality could offer improved services to neighbourhoods in Barcelona's urban fabric and, by according them centrality, diminish their dependence on the city's downtown, the Eixample. At the same time, the creation of space outside the Eixample would reduce pressure on it, avoiding the continual substitution of residence by offices. It also made sense to apply a policy of urban improvement in the Eixample to encourage its use as a residential space and to penalise or obstruct the indiscriminate installation of new offices.

An integrated strategy of this type would give specific form and a new dimension to the specialised or strategic centres envisaged by the 1976 PGM. At a time when the city was undertaking important projects to systematise the road system by means of the Ronda ring roads it was necessary to consider the differing revenues that could be created by open or undecided spaces. It was therefore necessary to establish a process of public initiative and control in order to guarantee the correct urban insertion of private or corporate schemes. It was not enough merely to anticipate the physical layout, though without it a programme of balanced activities would not be possible; it was also necessary to precisely evaluate the dimensions and the content of each central place. It is all too frequently thought that commerce is the only central activity, in the specific form of the shopping centre, forgetting that the centre has always been a combined place for tertiary and leisure activities, offices and open space, culture and residence.

The four Olympic areas pursued their own rhythm and will be commented on separately; the rest were implemented sequentially and could vary depending on the specific demands of their programmes.

The Diagonal-Sarrià area, situated above the axis of expansion of the CBD, was a tremendously attractive area for economic agents to develop hotel, commercial and strategic activities. The existence of specific projects suggested immediate interventions, with the fundamental backing of private initiative, involving recreational, commercial and hotel activities. One such was the project for the street block occupied by the former Hospital de Sant Joan de Déu, combining a major central development with the addition of public spaces and urban services of the first order, in such a way that public control would ensure the construction of a high quality urban part for the city.[44] It was to be called L'Illa.

The existence of important infrastructures and strategic facilities (Sants station, the Barcelona Fira trade fair complex, the relative proximity to the airport road, the existence of public interventions such as the Escorxador

[44] The project was completed in 1994 and was the work of the architects Manuel de Solà-Morales and Rafael Moneo after an international competition between five invited groups of architects.

and Espanya Industrial Parks) suggested Carrer Tarragona as an area for immediate urban redevelopment and a major lure for the location of hotels and offices.

In the case of RENFE-Meridiana, its situation at the northern gateway of Barcelona and a point of distribution of traffic from Vallès and the large population of local neighbourhoods made it a particularly attractive place for commercial and service activities, and, to a lesser extent, for hotels and offices. A large urban park would form the framework for the creation of a shopping and leisure centre with an enormous power of attraction. The importance of infrastructural works required the City Council to adopt a foremost role, initiating the process and defining the conditions for intervention of private investment, which was to undertake the development of the central spaces. This paved the way for spaces of collaboration between the public and private sectors, with overall control by the former of the contents and the final result.

The urban port was an area with excellent possibilities for the development of recreation and commercial activities and hotels, with the completion of the Moll de la Fusta wharf, the Ronda Litoral coastal ring road and

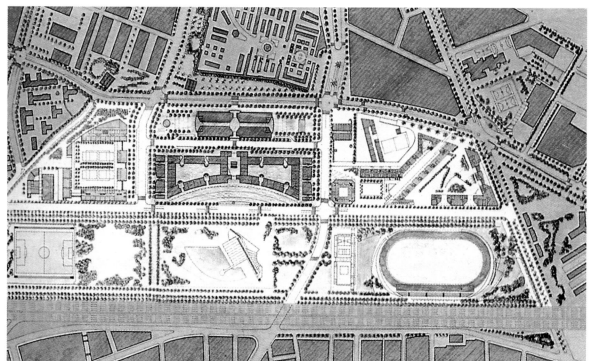

9.89
The RENFE-Meridiana secto
the initial proposal.

the revitalisation of Ciutat Vella. In fact it was probably the urban space with most potential for the city in the mid-term.

The Plaça de les Glòries, despite the enormous amount of work on infrastructure it required (traffic junction, creation of a large public park, undergrounding of the railway tracks, continuation of Diagonal as far as the sea), obviously had a great future in view of its size, prime location and future accessibility. Furthermore, public interventions in the form of strategic facilities (green spaces, the National Theatre of Catalonia, the Auditorium, bus station and a company hotel) would provide a driving force in an area where activities related to relaxation, culture, commerce and offices had an important role to play.[45]

The development of a programme of this type also called for a major change in the planning process and the way projects were carried out. Interstitial space was called upon to solve important problems of context. In turn, the content of these buildings was new and practically without precedent. These were complex programmes whose singular multiplicity of use and management could influence the project and its phases of implantation. As a result, work in these areas offered a whole range of forms of intervention: from the unitary project in sectors of concentrated action (e.g. Diagonal - Sant Joan de Déu) to interlinked fragments (e.g. RENFE - Meridiana), to lines of general composition that respected a degree of individuality in each pair of buildings (along Carrer Tarragona).

---

[45] The National Theatre was designed by Ricardo Bofill; the Auditorium by Rafael Moneo and the bus station, on the site of the old railway terminus, by Fargas and Tous.

0, 9.91
e L'Illa sector, the site of a
mer hospital converted into
trategic centre, park and
vices.

For each area there was a strategy with its own pace and a complex working process. The threshold of '92 was giving rise to prospects of centrality that needed to be canalised.[46]

The right location could multiply the enhancing effect of the four Olympic sectors. It was therefore necessary to promote the public sector to coordinate individual initiatives and ensure their correct insertion into the consolidated city.[47]

As opposed to this strategy, there was a centrifugal tendency of new central investment outside the city – though this might sound like a contradiction – which, without the functional requirements to justify it, rejected the urban condition that the city offered. The location outside the city of hospitals, shopping centres, offices, etc., had to be valued appropriately, since the selection of a cheap and easy plot could mean high social costs in terms of infrastructure and transport in the mid-term. There were activities that required development outside the city, though their incompatibility with insertion in urban fabric had to be evaluated.

Remember, for example, how in the 19th century markets made their way into the heart of our neighbourhoods, by demolishing convents or occupying squares, and thereby brought commerce and the urban fabric up to date.

[46] A prior diagnosis and a prognosis of central activity conducted by the CEP (Centre for Planning Studies) and directed by A. Soy and M. M. Isla defined the needs and potentials of offices, the tertiary sector and hotels.

[47] This was the case, for example, of the Hotels Plan drawn up by the City Council in 1988, in view of the need for hotel places for the forthcoming events detected by the CEP study. The Plan envisaged the proposal of bids for sites reserved for facilities that were neither being used nor had construction planned on them, according to which they would temporarily be used as hotels for up to 30 or 50 years, after which they would be returned to the city in a good state of conservation. In this way, 2,000 new hotel places were created.

This is a stimulating example of how we should work in cities: accepting innovation and seeking urban coherence with what is there.

We have to bear in mind that the city in itself represented the country's most important fixed capital. As a result, this urban logic had to be extended to include the participation of institutional and corporate operators in order to avoid the anti-urban autonomy to which investment in infrastructure had accustomed us.

IX.7 Other structural keys in the shaping of Barcelona

To the above-mentioned scales of intervention we have to add some keys to the underlying form of the city whose constancy or transformation had a major effect on the real or virtual image of the entire city. It is obvious that the Citadel, the Eixample, the peripheral neighbourhoods and large-scale urban layouts are keys to a present-day understanding of Barcelona. By way of example, below are four elements that despite their inclusion in the description of the general structure call for specific comment.

a) The Diagonal down to the sea

The Diagonal was a pending problem for Barcelona. It was the basic axis proposed by Cerdà in the mid-19th century: the city's 10 kilometre long avenue that crossed the Barcelona Plain from west to east, descending gradually from 100 metres to the sea.

Although these characteristics explain the significance of this axis to the general shape of Barcelona, it is important to remember how in the early 1950s this thoroughfare was configured and established the characteristic social use of the top third of the city.

The Diagonal once again represented a key episode in the urban restructuring of Barcelona. Its layout across the urban fabric and topography of the city gives its the masterful value of so many diagonal strokes in the history of painting.

However, the proposals for the western and eastern extremes of the Diagonal were absolutely diverse. In the west, in the uptown area, intervention was to be based on the infill of empty spaces, endeavouring to find the capacity to introduce more general readings than those of the built fabric. It was also one of the city sectors with highest land values, which meant that the authorities had to guarantee the urban quality of the projects selected and attempt to ensure that they offered higher levels of urbanisation than those established by general regulations, similar to the case of areas of new centrality.

Conversely, in the east the Diagonal desperately needed structure and identity. The continuity of layout involved slightly lowering the railway line running from the Estació de França station to Aragon. This intervention

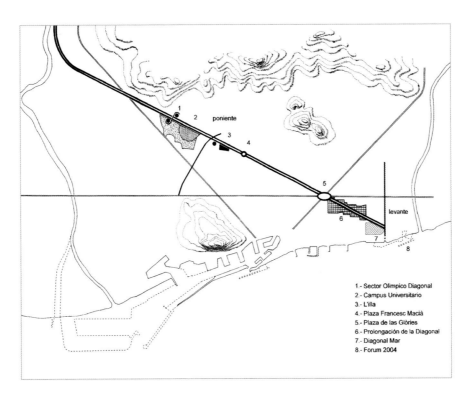

1.- Sector Olimpico Diagonal
2.- Campus Universitario
3.- L'illa
4.- Plaza Francesc Macià
5.- Plaza de las Glòries
6.- Prolongación de la Diagonal
7.- Diagonal Mar
8.- Forum 2004

ensured the continuity of the Diagonal and configured the Plaça de les Glòries as a meeting point for the three main urban axes.

    With this junction solved, the Diagonal could then run down to the sea, thereby conferring giving an urban nature to one of the city's unresolved sectors. The conflict between the division of farmland and the Eixample underlay the various phases of land use.[48] This project also signified a large contribution of central residential fabric for Barcelona in the short term. New forms of management were required if this project was to structure the eastern extreme and include popular housing sectors in its development,[49] thanks to the increase in value generated by this new scheme.

    The consolidation of this project led to the deployment of other ideas at the end of the Diagonal, as we will see later.

b) The city's big "containers": large-scale monographic uses

The appreciation of large, prominent monumental buildings was an important key to the Barcelona project. Large-scale monographic uses, such as culture or facilities, had great potential.

[48] This evolution can be seen in the work by the LUB: *Barcelona remodelación capitalista o desarrollo urbano* (*op. cit.*).

[49] The planning process was completed and was accompanied by the organisation in 1988 of an international competition by *Quaderns*, the magazine of the COAC, to design housing proposals in the Diagonal, in an attempt to revive the central housing project, which had recently been much devalued. A special agency called "Diagonal" was set up to organise its future management. The urban planning importance of the issue called for firm institutional cooperation to avoid the difficulties attendant on a new and uncertain situation. Later on, this was the site of proposals for new economic activity (22@) in the post-Olympic period.

The recovery of the historic centre called for representative, central uses that helped to highlight the area. An initial project dated 1982, "From the Liceu to the Seminary"[50] consolidated the cultural use of the Casa de la Caritat former workhouse and its surroundings with the MACBA. Similar enhancement schemes were the reuse of the National Palace on Montjuïc[51] and the systematisation of the Hospital de Sant Pau, seeking to rehabilitate Domènech i Muntaner's outstanding buildings and combine them with a modern extension of one of Barcelona's foremost hospitals.[52] There were also other important facilities in the city being put to new uses or envisaging transformation in the short term with valuable regenerative effects on the most immediate fabrics, including the installation of Pompeu Fabra University in the former barracks in Carrer Llull and the dismantling of the Model prison in Carrer Entença. The transformation of each of these large facilities extended beyond its specific context to structure a more ambitious functional system.

c) The role of Ciutat Vella in the metropolitan system

The recovery of the historic city gave rise to hopes that the old walled city would continue to be the seminal centre that organised the central metropolitan system.

As already explained, the morphological condition of the old town is highly singular. It has not been favoured by royal patronage like other big European cities, yet the configuration of its spaces and architectures is strong and close-knit.

It might be said that the charm of the former walled town of Barcelona lies in the coming together of very differing urban spaces, producing a spatial richness that is both pleasing and intriguing: the old roads, the squares that used to be devoted to food supplies, the colonnades, the regular spaces and the monumental squares all form itineraries that convey unique sensations as the most diverse, contradictory uses succeed one another.[53]

---

[50] Beginning with a proposal by Lluís Clotet and Oscar Tusquets in 1983, it led to the recovery of a series of buildings such as the Convent dels Àngels, with contributions by Clotet, Paricio, Cirici and Bassó, the siting there of Richard Meier's Museum of Contemporary Art and the launch of the CCCB (Barcelona Centre for Contemporary Culture) in the former Casa de Caritat workhouse building, remodelled by Viaplana and Piñón.

[51] A highly ambitious project that included the National Museum of Catalonia (MNAC), by a team headed by Gae Aulenti and Enric Steegman.

[52] This intervention responded to an attempt to rationalise the city's hospital system. See *Ordenació urbanística dels equipaments hospitalaris de Barcelona*. Barcelona, 1989.

[53] See chapter 7 of the book LUB: *Ciutat Vella de Barcelona: Un pasat amb futur* (*op. cit.*).

9.k Potential views of Ciutat Vella.

The city of districts

The city of commerce

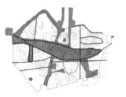 

The city of culture and leisure

The city of art

The city of representative spaces

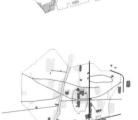 

The city of avenues

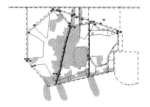 

Then the built systems, composed of monuments but also of a rich repertory of residential typologies, produce a dense and varied urban complex, in which the succession of houses becomes an almost indescribable sequence. Even today, this complex combination of conditions forms a fabric of commercial, residential and economic activities that constitutes intense, close-knit functional sectors.

Its centrality in relation to the metropolitan whole and easy access by public transport ensured its great potential for long-term use.

The strategies begun in the 1980s suggested various different functions of its spaces and buildings.

a) After the concentration of efforts on reinstating the protagonism of culture and teaching, perhaps this was the time to give a new lease of life to historic itineraries, thereby increasing their heritage value. As opposed to the museum city, the idea of a city of art would prevent negative specialisation.

b) The existing buildings suggested a more compact rehabilitation scheme that focused on Ciutat Vella as various series of "streets of houses", thereby highlighting its residential capacity.

c) The representative condition that it had maintained since its origins could be enhanced by the introduction of larger circuits to rationalise the presence of tourists, which perhaps concentrated excessively on monuments.

d) The richness and variety of its shops were grounds to strengthen its local and city-wide importance.

e) The attributes of its spaces, once freed from the indiscriminate use of the car, suggested the idea of a city for walking, to enjoy its continuity and morphological richness.

In short, the structural keys of the city once again hinted at a whole body of potential in Ciutat Vella that had been overridden during phases of frenetic development and abuse.

d) Barcelona's seafront

The reworking of Barcelona's urban form depended to a large extent on the forging of an open, well-defined relation with the sea. The pride of a city that had always aspired to be the capital of the north-western Mediterranean came into its own.[54]

The city's expansion beyond the town walls in the 19th century had moved inland, and the many qualities of Cerdà's Eixample did not include the development of the seafront. The city had therefore embarked on a process of installation of urban services, such as a cemetery and a gas works, and had continued with the construction of Spain's first railway line along the coast in 1849, forming a definitive rift. The Estació de França railway station

---

[54] Reworking of the article "Urban Transformations as Urban Project". *Lotus* 67. Milan, 1990.

9.I The new coastal front.

04
ae arrival of Cobi, the
ympic mascot, in Barcelona.

95, 9.96
raphs showing the situation
f infrastructures on the coastal
ont in 1987 and today. Public
vestment was concentrated
n undergrounding the railway
ne, improving drainage
nd providing vehicle access.
he coastline also had to
e stabilised to create new
eaches.

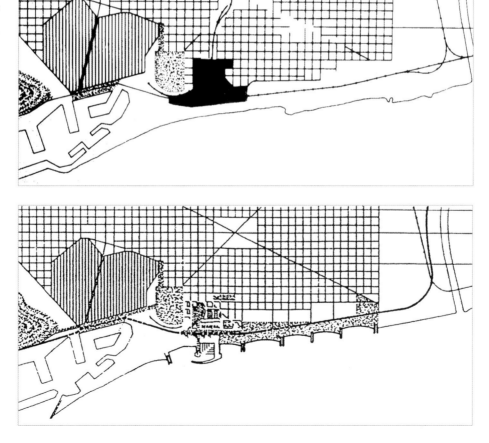

9.97
The coastal front in 1987.
with obsolete installations,
containers from the port on
beaches and sewerage draining
into the sea.

reached out to the port and Pla de Palau, the city's first strategic centre, and was located beside the old Citadel. Nor did any subsequent reconsiderations of the city firmly advocate the need to transform the seafront.

The last 30 years had shown a clear desire to open up the city to the sea; it is interesting to bear in mind that almost all major urban transformation projects include a meditated and sometimes tense undercurrent of discussion which too automatic an explanation may overlook.

The process of Barcelona's urban recovery cannot overlook the critical discussion of the 1970s that spoke out against speculative urban development projects such as the Ribera Plan, commented on elsewhere.

Above all, the major intervention projects were seen as a strategy to redress the balance. The Barcelona of the eighties was moving outwards in a centrifugal process common to many European cities, with particular attention to the western axis. Moving the city towards the sea meant in part transforming that process and changing public investment priorities. However, these were difficult processes because the inertia of cities and their users also played an important part: only quality in execution and persistence in action could offer effective results in the mid-term. In Barcelona, the creation of a new city-port link in the form of the project for the Moll de la Fusta wharf suggested the possibility of a more ambitious idea: new, clean beaches and new residential development (the Olympic Village), and even the transformation of the old harbour and the reclassification of the Barceloneta. This could lead to a large-scale process of restructuring of eastern Barcelona, which in the space of two decades was to completely recover its seafront, see the Diagonal extended as far as the sea and, in short, enhance the eastern sector of the city.

A central idea linking these projects was the 1992 Olympic Programme. Many different threads were involved: sport, security, advertising, and so forth, which could in themselves give rise to the urban development programme.

However, Barcelona brought together the requirements of the programme under the umbrella of a broader-based strategy: the Olympic Games would last a fortnight, but the city would be there forever. Therefore the existence of a specific programme would help to understand which requisites were essential, while the high public profile of the event would extend planning repercussions and, as a result, the possibilities for transformation and urban improvement.

Work began on the 1992 urban development programme in 1982, before the economic success of the 1984 Los Angeles Games was known, triggering off a burning desire to host the Olympics on the part of so many cities. The above-mentioned programme was drawn up before the summer of 1986, as the mayor, Pasqual Maragall, insisted that every aspect of the programme be under way or have the urban planning go-ahead, and that financing should be announced as guaranteed.

The '92 programme was approached as a major project for the urban restructuring of the city: within the urban continuum, seeking to interconnect empty interstitial areas, or by introducing breakpoints such as the triangle that was the Olympic Village to trigger off a process of larger scope.

Many other cities had adopted an external model: Munich, by justifying a large residential operation outside the city, and even Los Angeles by distributing installations throughout its vast region. The definition of alternatives outside the city was also considered in the face of the possible difficulties of time involved in all urban renovation, but was not required.

The Olympic Village became a prime referent in the process of Barcelona's urban development transformation due to its position as a step towards the city's waterfront.

However, taking Barcelona to the sea was no easy matter. The Citadel had cast a terrible shadow, but this circumstance also provided a unique opportunity to use centrally-positioned land with low commercial value which could therefore be used to redress the balance: this logic was revealed in the Counter Plan to the 1971 Ribera Plan[55] and granted great potential to the land on which the Olympic Village now stands in Poblenou. However, the lights that were to erase such a historical shadow had to be sure to conserve their own radiance.

The shadow of the Citadel had produced an "urban rear" and accumulated railway infrastructures that prevented access to the seafront; the new project was to transform all of these aspects.

After an initial evaluation of the Metropolitan Area's seafront carried out by the team of Lluis Cantallops, the project for the Olympic Village was begun in 1985 by a team made up of Martorell, Bohigas, Mackay and Puigdoménech.

The development of the project was interesting because it progressed alongside the weighty process of negotiating infrastructures: dismantling the coastline railway line and undergrounding the Glòries branch, ensuring the functional maintenance of the Estació de França railway station in the regional or national rail system; processing of wastewaters which were still partly evacuated into the sea; the creation and stabilisation of new beaches; and road and public transport access on a metropolitan scale.[56]

After just a few weeks of technical application, a general model was created so that the terms of each infrastructure could begin negotiation and be integrated as project data. This task was one of the Plan's great merits, being one of the most important aspects in raising the quality of the urban project. There was however very little experience of integrating very vital infrastructures, which tended to be designed by specialist engineering firms and therefore be marked by a detestable and all too frequent urban autonomy.

The project's urban structure was the product of a compromise between a slightly distorted Cerdà-grid style network of streets and the great historical layouts implanted before the city's expansion: Avinguda Icària, a broad boulevard that used to lead to the cemetery in the early 19th century, became an internal urban axis of great interest, engaging with Ciutadella Park and bordering the Moll de la Fusta wharf to Montjuïc; Avinguda Bogatell was a former overflow channel that cut diagonally through the orthogonal grid. Conversely, the layout of the undergrounded railway line suggested the enclosure of the original Citadel. The size of the intervention responded to the previously outlined residential needs and had sufficient critical mass to induce tangential transformation, without being large enough to change the general urban layout.

This structure was based on a great linear element of new infrastructures that extended along the coast which in fact guaranteed a positive transformation of Barcelona's east end: the new beaches, the seafront promenade,

---

[55] This reasoning is clearly expounded in the work of M. Solà-Morales, J. Busquets, M. Domingo, A. Font and J. L. Gómez O.: *Barcelona: remodelación capitalista o desarrollo urbano* (*op. cit.*).

[56] The complexity involved in each of these negotiations is illustrated by an anecdote telling how in late 1985, the first model for the Olympic Village was refused exhibition in the Arquería de la Castellana as being possibly in contradiction of the stipulations of another ministerial department.

9.m The Olympic Village in 1992.

9, 9.100
oject for the coastal front.
yout of the Olympic Village.
sidential sector with services
d two emblematic towers
rking the new Carles I axis
t joins the Eixample with
sea.

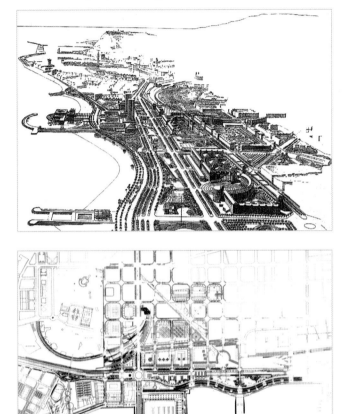

.101, 9.102
he new residential
eighbourhoods, ten years on.

the low-level coastal ring road and the avenue bordering the seafront all combined in a great open space to make up this project which, without having the large dimensions of Burle Marx's plans for Aterro do Flamengo in Rio, was responsible for offering the necessary signs of identity and innovation.

The street blocks produced by this grid were, then, irregular and varying in dimension. The general density of the area laid out by the General Plan for the city was moderately low in relation to the built fabric, producing for the first time an Eixample with reasonable building levels.

The building followed the dominant alignment of the street and respected the height of solid construction, two rules in keeping with those of Barcelona's Eixample. In turn, the lower density meant that the volume built along the street was shallower, a continuous block, 12-14 metres deep, allowing the possibility of the most varied typologies with good cross ventilation. This layout of buildings freed up the courtyard inside the street block for communal gardens or smaller-scale building.[57]

Although the dominant use was residential (approximately 2,000 dwellings), the project freely contemplated other compatible uses; the front area was occupied by hotels, offices and services.[58] This corroborated the determination to include residential use in the transformation of this central sector of Barcelona.

[57] The architectural project involved some twenty teams, corresponding to the creators of the FAD prizes of recent decades. See Various authors: *Barcelona. Arquitectura y ciudad.* Barcelona, 1990.
[58] On the vertical axis of the Olympic Village – the prolongation of Passeig de Carles I – two gigantic tower blocks were built, emerging high above the general ceiling to display the force of the event in the city skyline. The towers are occupied by offices and a hotel.

So far, the project seemed to grasp the opportunity of producing, at last, a city fragment that was well integrated in terms of urban development, architecturally innovative and socially diverse. But the development of the project led to doubts as to the maintenance of a progressive, innovative strategy for such an important urban fragment.

These were due to the fact that the project was begun and set under way quickly, adopting the most expeditious formulas to acquire land and institutional agreements for investment in large infrastructure. As explained above, the plan and the general project were drawn up in a year, at the same time as the process to negotiate the various infrastructures. During the planning procedure, the land was bought and expropriated. When the plan was approved, a public body was created (VOSA - Vil·la Olímpica Societat Anònima) with the statutes of a private firm. Once expropriation and eviction were negotiated, the executive projects for underground infrastructure went ahead: drainage, undergrounding the railway track, coastal and port defences. The various infrastructures were directed and controlled by the technical department of the new agency.

The demolition of old interstitial and residential buildings in 1987 was significant, showing the people of the city that the project was going ahead.

In this phase, project investment and initiative were totally public, and the investment was covered by the various administrations in the proportions negotiated for each infrastructure, at all times with the municipal authorities as the driving force. So far, the project and its application ensured the recovery (urban redevelopment and improvement) of obsolete industrial land; a great display of infrastructure broke the barriers and gave this operation centrality.

However, there are two important issues in the management of a sector of this size: 1) how to incorporate private initiative in a rather complex process; and 2) how to publicise and make housing available to future users and residents. These themes were of great importance in the urban and architectural development of the project.

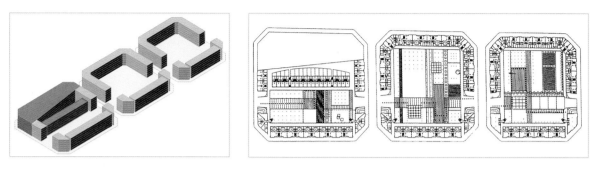

9.105, 9.106, 9.107
Street blocks in Carrer Llull
corresponding to one of the
complementary Olympic
Villages, with an interesting
morphological design.

An examination of the process suggests very strongly that there was an appreciable gap between the innovation of the urban development project and the traditional business management of it. This was significant because it could spoil positive dimensions of the general project for the city. Urban planning history reminds us how much the true scope and significance of projects can be measured and demonstrated in the management process.

To summarise, the 1986 urban development plan was capable of offering the city a socially diverse neighbourhood, avoiding the selection of pure market laws. This was not a utopian stance but low-cost expropriation and major investment in public infrastructure did make it possible to avoid speculative profit-making in this particular sector.

The context of rising house prices in big cities calls for elements to contain the situation. At no point was there any chance of extreme situations: handing the sector over totally to the open market or to social housing; Barcelona has excellent socially diverse city fragments.

It was therefore necessary to supervise the various stages in the management process to prevent the economic rent being appropriated by speculation and definitively conditioning the target or demand. Logically, before the entry of private investment capital, it was necessary to highlight the project's inherent values (e.g. publicity, exploitation of its uniqueness, etc.), and define the social and residential aims proposed.

However, in the summer of 1988, quite the opposite happened; the private sector became involved in development with shares equivalent to land values (in relation to residential surface area) that were apparently low, in no case advertising who the dwellings were intended for or what the final price would be. A new company, NISA, was set up for the construction of housing, with VOSA as a shareholder. This was not a felicitous step, because it accepted an unbounded market logic and, in an operation of this complexity and public orientation, could lead to problems. And indeed the alarm bells rang when in 1990, now backed by a large publicity and media campaign, the dwelling prototypes and sales prices were made public. They competed with free-market prices and, initially, did not have even the most basic of urban development strategies to address a socially diverse target.

Fortunately, the frenetic development of this new Barcelona had some interesting referents: two smaller Olympic villages, one in the adjacent blocks of Poblenou and another in Vall d'Hebron, were developed by private investors who accepted an agreement with the municipal authorities, in accordance with which a third of the dwellings were to have affordable prices, allowing their inclusion on special council programmes to provide housing for young people with moderate incomes who wanted to live centrally.

IX.8 The Olympic Games for 1992

As we have just seen, the process of urban recovery addressed different scales of intervention which, to some extent, followed one upon the last and superposed each other. The exceptional nature of the 1992 Olympic programme has been mentioned several times without receiving the full attention that its exclusiveness would merit in other descriptions. It seems fairer to realise that in this process, beginning in the early eighties, the programme for '92 came into being first as a general goal or objective, to then become an urban Plan or Programme in the form of a series of separate projects, each with a different content, but of great ambition and scope. These projects were very important for organisational deployment, financial scope and the fact that they had to be ready by a set date: they were to go into service in July 1992.

It seems reasonable to understand that the urban interrelation of the specifically Olympic projects would ensure a use and running that would make them fully-fledged urban pieces. Their sporting content, though highly specialised, allowed for a change in the use of these city facilities.[59]

[59] See the author's article: "L'esport en la formació urbana de Barcelona, 1900-1985", *L'Avenç* 92, Barcelona, 1986.

9.108, 9.109
The Vall d'Hebron provided new facilities for El Carmel and Nou Barris.

It is quite something else for the political and financial strategy adopted to endorse the suitability of the city's biggest projects having an Olympic label as of 1988. Because the first preliminary formulation dossiers dated from 1982, drawn up by the untiring Romà Cuyàs, during the mandate as mayor of Narcís Serra, who presented the candidature to the King.[60]

The candidature was a process of representation conducted by Jordi Serra and a small team. The urban development wheel began to roll with plans for the different sectors and the preliminary projects for major infrastructures in 1983-86.[61] The process was a highly complex one, as the plans presented a hypothesis that only Olympic nomination could ratify.

In any case, now that it is possible to establish the two hypotheses, the plans for 1992 seemed reasonable in scale, and some of the proposals may well have been carried out – with other timelines and probably another form of financing – even if the city had not been chosen. Barcelona was nominated in Lausanne on 17 October 1986, under the presidency of the COI (International Olympic Committee) of the Catalan Joan Antoni Samaranch. This saw a radical change in strategy, and the hypotheses contained in the plans and programmes became elements in a mechanism that had 1992 as its final output.

Barcelona's Olympic organisation was stepped up enormously; Josep-Miquel Abad was appointed representative director and a special urban development apparatus was created to promote work; first called the IMPU, it was later changed to HOLSA.[62]

The four sectors of the programme in Barcelona[63] were concentrated in the Olympic Ring, the Olympic Village (described above), Vall d'Hebron and the Diagonal Area. Other subsectors were defined in the metropolitan region, including those in Badalona, Sabadell, Granollers, Sant Sadurní and Castelldefels, and

---

[60] One of the early documents can be seen in Romà Cuyàs: "Projecte Jocs Olímpics Barcelona, 1992. Primeras aproximaciones". *Mímeo*. Oct. 1982.

[61] The detail of the various plans can be seen in Various authors: *Barcelona Plans cap el 92* (*op. cit.*).

[62] The IMPU was the Municipal Institute for Urban Development Promotion, set up in 1987, under the technical directorship of J. Antoni Acebillo. Later HOLSA (Holding Olímpico S.A.) was created to bring together the different operations created on the occasion of the Olympics.

[63] See the full description in Various authors: *Barcelona: la ciutat i el 92*. Olimpiada Cultural. Barcelona, 1990.

110
ne four Olympic areas.

some of the sporting events were to be held on Banyoles lake and in the environs of La Seu d'Urgell. In any case, the programme planned was a very compact one, as the four central precincts were located about four kilometres apart and were connected by the new ring road.

The Diagonal Area represented the systematisation of the surrounding spaces of the city's large private sports amenities (Barcelona FC stadium, Turó Tennis Club, the Polo Club, university sports facilities, etc.) and also incorporated open space.[64]

The Vall d'Hebron, in the north of the city, was to have a sports stadium and a series of open-air sports installations which, after the Olympics, could easily be turned into the largest park in the area.[65]

The Olympic Ring, on the upper slopes of Montjuïc, completed urbanisation work begun in 1929. The development of the mountain plateau took the form of four large sports buildings[66] constructed along a great east-west central axis. The Olympic stadium was a remodelling of the old building that was to have hosted the Peoples' Olympics in 1936, before the event was suddenly transferred to Berlin as a result of pressure from Hitler's government. Once again, the city chose to be faithful to its history and proposed to use the same stadium as a tribute to that thwarted event.

It also became evident that the 1992 project once more insisted on the issues that had been raised by earlier events: in 1888 with the Citadel and in 1929 with the conquest of Montjuïc. This time, the larger interventions once again concentrated on the other side of the Citadel (the Olympic Village), opening the city up to the sea, and on the western side of Montjuïc, opening the mountain up to the Llobregat delta and beginning a new urban redevelopment process that would erase the shadow that Montjuïc had cast on that sector.

[64] The general distribution was the work of the architects O. Clos and M. Rubert.
[65] The general distribution was the work of the architect Eduard Bru. The sports pavilion is by the J. Garcés + E. Soria team, and the tennis complex by E. Miralles + C. Pinós. Housing in the Olympic village is by C. Ferrater.
[66] The Olympic stadium was reconstructed respecting the original walls and formal layout by the team comprising V. Gregotti, F. Correa, A. Milà, J. Margarit and C. Buixadé. The Sant Jordi pavilion was designed by A. Isozaki to seek a good position halfway up the mountain. The INEF building is the work of Taller R. Bofill and the Picornell swimming pool was covered and remodelled by M. Gallego + F. Fernández.

9.111
In the Diagonal Sector, many
existing installations were
recycled and given a new
structure.

The volume of economic investment in the Games was evaluated in 1990 at half a billion pesetas – approximately 3,000 million euros – of public investment, with half as much again in private investment, which gives an idea of the magnitude of the event, not counting the induced impact of a similar overall sum. The most representative sectors in this investment were evidently construction, with 58 per cent, and electronics, telecommunications and information technology, with 22 per cent.[67]

These magnitudes give an idea of the major investment mobilised, but also of their profiles. The process of reclassification of Barcelona and the 1992 years probably served to adapt the city's urban infrastructures to the new international production situation, as we will go on to see.

[67] See Lluís Serra: "Gestión y Financiación", *Barcelona Olímpica. La ciudad renovada*. Barcelona, 1992. His article lists the investment figures and the role of HOLSA in the management process.

9.n The Olympic ring completed Montjuïc.

12
e Olympic ring sector
Montjuïc completed
banisation of the mountain,
gun with the 1929 Great
hibition.

113, 9.114
ections of the Stadium and
he Sports Centre.

.115
lan of the mountain,
ntegrating the two great 1929
nd 1992 projects.

This called for substantial improvements in the urban development standards of the city in the form of its communication, drainage and transport infrastructures, particularly the railways and the airport, and the sport and leisure infrastructures[68] most closely linked to the Olympic programme, and a more dynamic approach to strategic hotel and company services.

But it also required improvements to telecommunication infrastructures, which were to have great importance in the mid-term with the location of central and/or strategic activity. The great power and scope of Olympic broadcasts to the entire world served as to update the telecommunications of the area around the city: the Collserola communications tower[69] and other projects included in the BIT 92 programme[70] made this possible.

---

[68] Olympic installations obviously have to meet the standards of elite sports men and women, which are quite different to their normal urban use. To enable their everyday functioning, the city created a special agency to supervise the running of the installations.

[69] A tower designed by Norman Foster's team after a restricted project competition organised in 1988. The force of this project set in a really difficult enclave made it a true symbol of the Barcelona of '92.

[70] BIT stands for Barcelona Information Technology and Telecommunication, and covered a whole series of telecommunication projects as part of the Telephony Campaign that was so important in the centralisation of these services at metropolitan level: the tower on Montjuïc designed by S. Calatrava formed part of the same initiative.

IX.9 A look at the "special" projects

In the framework of this experience, a new body of reflection on urban organisation in the form of special projects seemed to emerge.[71] Plans for cities must exist and must be implemented on the basis of thorough knowledge of a given reality and commitment to resolve the specific urban issues of each city and each historical context. However, important actions seem to be based on "special projects" with the power to integrate the infrastructural contents of each urban part with a more general urban planning vision.

The great profusion of special urban planning projects in the last two decades in Europe should perhaps be seen through the filter of the relative impasse of municipal plans and the scant results produced by state urban programmes (for housing, facilities, etc.).

The idea of the special or monographic project had played its part in the past, providing the driving force behind major plans for some cities; examples in the USA include Burnham or Olmsted's grand proposals for Chicago, San Francisco, Boston or New York. New housing was also the umbrella slogan for large-scale plans for Berlin, Frankfurt, Hamburg and Vienna.

In the case of Barcelona, there were specific circumstances forming a spatial context for these projects:

1. Many European cities undertake a process of urban redevelopment by means of which the traditional city once again becomes the centre for new urban activities and even some forms of residence. While this interpretation highlighted the difficulties of the "deurbanising" process of the seventies and pointed out the consolidation of a major transformation of the economic system with the powerful growth of the service sector, it was important to avoid an excessive determinism which would make these variables a precedent for an urban dynamic.

2. This return to the centre was possible due to the existence of many apparent or concealed "opportunities" in numerous cities that were beginning to mobilise themselves.

The 1980s and 1990s were the decades of consolidation of new areas of transformation in the existing city: **a)** old city-centre ports, become obsolete due to the increase in ship size, changes in unloading systems and the protagonism of containerisation (the big ports of London, Antwerp and Rotterdam are good examples); **b)** railway stations, which require a periodic overhaul, normally every 20-25 years, with the addition of new uses (Paris brought a dozen stations up to date in a decade, London ten or so); **c)** the change in hierarchy of stations with the possibilities introduced by the high-speed train, along with the dismantling of large railway spaces, now without a train service (Lille and its new TGV station is a paradigm case); **d)** large industrial sectors that change

---

[71] Reworking of the article by J. Busquets: "Villages and Cities". Lotus International. Milan, 1991.

9.0 The "special" projects on Europe

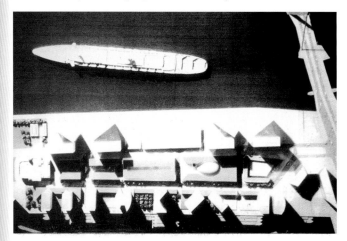

9.118
Kop van Zuid, Rotterdam.

9.119
Expo '98 in Lisbon.

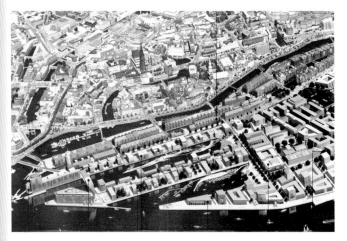

9.120
Hafencity, Hamburg.

their main use (such as the well-known Bicocca in Milan, Lingotto in Turin, Billancourt in Paris, and many more), and **e)** the development of experimental neighbourhoods with specific programmes, whether residential or service-oriented; for example, the German IBA schemes are a prime reference.

3. These opportunities however were mostly occupied by the new innovative activities generated or promoted by changes in the economic system. New services, big shopping centres, intelligent offices, representative spaces, well endowed residence, etc., were the dominant uses in special projects.

In these transformations, the spatial evolution of cities found its central explanation, as confirmed by recent studies of the dynamic of advanced tertiary activity in Paris, where it has been installed in western sectors.

4. But above all these processes are frequently the result of labels that give rise to the special aspect of the operation. For example, the Barcelona Olympic Games, as we have seen, justified work on infrastructure that the city had been needing since the sixties and on opening it up to the sea. London's Docklands found a new use for Europe's largest port area after a twenty-year standstill due to doubts as to the plan's content; with its conversion into Europe's great international office centre, it formed part of the Millennium slogan. Expo '92 modernised Seville in the form of the urban development of the island of La Cartuja and the regularisation of the river's passage through the city. With Expo '98 Lisbon was looking for an excuse to establish its first urban façade over the river Tagus.

In other cases, however, a local objective is used to simulate the same energy that these cities applied to the special event. This was the case of Munich and its new airport to the north, which gave it the opportunity of undertaking an ambitious urban scheme, with big offices, a new trade fair precinct, housing and services on the land reclaimed from the former airport to the east of the city, etc. By undergrounding its railway, Rotterdam sought to define the first north-south urban axis in a strategy to restructure its old port as a residential enclave, a little Manhattan in the Kop van Zuid.

The desire to establish a time limit for the operation is plain, and the idea of marketing is part and parcel of its definition: cities seem to be sure that in addition to convincing their citizens, they have to persuade other operators to buy or develop these excellent opportunities.

These general characteristics have a definitive influence on how the new urban development dynamic of big cities takes place and is managed. The following aspects should be highlighted:

1. The urban development process no longer follows the pattern of general plan, partial plan, architectural project; instead it comprises schemes and/or projects with executive capacity which together are capable of setting the city or a large city sector in motion. They therefore have a force of their own, but also a large capacity for induction.

This idea of schemes and central projects had a tradition in urban planning history, though it had been abandoned in favour of more bureaucratic forms that identified urban development as the administrative management of the city, which, though important, should not be regarded as exclusive. These schemes had to be set in the context of a general strategy – a programme or the content of a fully-fledged urban plan – to prevent them being mutually restrictive; otherwise they could limit or even cancel each other out. These experiences were to lead to changes in traditional urban planning and management in keeping with the need for agility and commitment to action.

2. Once again, however, the commitment to the form of the city came to the fore. Special projects were used to address difficult, delicate parts of the city, urban rears and abandoned areas, for use as first-rate urban spaces. This gave rise to very sophisticated design strategies and highly committed processes of defining urban form and intervention.

These experience also involved an unprecedented renovation of urban design instruments. The "urban project" was recovered and urban composition was once again a priority. Such an intense renovation of instruments had not been seen since the post-war years, and it was certainly indebted to the methodological and theoretical experience of the seventies, which had sound analytical and critical baggage.

In any case, the integration of various functions, infrastructure and building were plausible endeavours on the part of these special projects that led to the redesign of urban form, overcoming the fatal dualism between infrastructure and architecture that had been instated by a mistaken interpretation of the modern movement.

3. Relations between the public and private sectors in urban development also changed radically. The apparent segregation of interests and competences was smoothed over. Terms such as partnership came right to the fore. There were difficult cases to justify, such as the extreme deregulation implemented in London's Docklands in the early eighties, leading to a serious impasse before ten years had passed due to a lack of urban planning control and the highly speculative regime of some of its property developments. Will it serve as a lesson or be an easy option to adopt?

But partnership also had brilliant precedents in public-private cooperation, which proved the need in each set of circumstances to clearly and adequately define the role of the two sectors and establish guidelines for interaction.

As in all cities, there were obvious precedents in Barcelona of cases of partnership, such as the New Town Commissions that made possible the development of the Eixample in the 19th century, with the participation of property owners and councillors.

4. The commitment to schemes and projects, and new collaboration agreements between the public and private sectors gave rise to new ways of managing and implementing urban development. The creation of special public and/or mixed bodies was the order of the day. Improved efficiency and the organisation of *ad hoc* task forces were the main benefits.

These structures did however involve the risk of duplicating administrative and/or political missions. It was vital to clearly outline tasks and relations with the institutional or corporate "centre". It was also necessary to ensure that the general urban and city aims were satisfied by the relevant control mechanisms to avoid management efficiency "justifying" the absolute privatisation of more ambitious social tasks.

However, these general attributes were countered by questions raised by a superficial application of these processes. There is an increasing tendency for marketing to be converted into propaganda, and irrelevant or partial projects to be sold as great urban planning ideas. The importance of the media is evident in new urban development, as is the competition between cities disputing the space of innovation and attraction in an attempt to win the prize of recognition and example. However, this calls for a more detailed discussion of the why, how and where of these projects in each city.

a) The **why** calls for a more in-depth valuation of the "anything goes" attitude to investment of some desperate cities at this time. The hinterlands and economic capacities of cities have proved themselves to be rather more powerful than expected in these critical circumstances. Special projects have to offer the chance to redress the balance in the existing city, promoting sectors that have been forgotten in the ecological model of each city. The eastern sector is critical in many cases, such as Barcelona's recovery programme, Paris and its East with the Bercy project, Rome and its Levant, among others. The idea of counterweight rather than balance can serve to reduce problems of segregation between the different parts of the city.

b) The **how** requires guarantees that reduce to a minimum the private appropriation of capital gains in any urban transformation scheme. This calls for joint management, with transparent income statements.

It also requires a process of flexible, advanced design. Because the contribution of this period may lie in the capacity to activate large areas with the intervention of various operators. At last, complex city ideas can be implemented with a richness and diversity of design.

c) The **where** obliges the selection of strategic points in the city that can generate change and innovation. In fact many cities have "pending issues", which can in this way be addressed and in which it is relatively simple to reach a consensus as to transformation ideas. Old ports tend to fall into this category, as in the cases of Antwerp, Rotterdam, Genoa, Hamburg, Marseilles and Trieste, among others.

In any case, the critical aspects of this special situation have to be explored to enable them to have a far-reaching effect on the renovation of the disciplinary corpus of urban architecture and development, which have stagnated in administrative and bureaucratic backwaters. Only in this way can full advantage be made of what may be a period of contradiction and change, but which has all the potential of new possibilities for action in the existing city.

In short, we can optimistically imagine that the door is open to further-reaching reflection about forms of intervention in the city, and we can be quite sure that this is the only way that our cities have a chance of winning the prize for this new dynamic that they so desperately seek.

Barcelona, a European city.
Another change of scale?

X.1 Post-Olympic Barcelona

The city emerged successfully from the great Olympic event[1] and Barcelona received a great deal of international recognition that was to continue to exert its influence in following years. Fortunately, this time there were none of the "lunatics" of 1888 or the insipidness of 1929.

However, the pace and euphoria of both economic and cultural development in the late eighties and early nineties began to slow.[2]

Many of the services developed for the Olympic Games led to the constant flows of foreign visitors, promoting hotels, business and services. The representative value of Barcelona as a capital was much boosted. The singular nature of the city was fostered by many of the large cultural infrastructures under construction in 1992, such as the Casa de la Caritat arts centre, the MACBA, the Auditorium, the National Palace, the Liceu opera house, etc., which were only the beginning of institutional endeavours.

Now, the deployment of the European single market changed the scope of markets and production organisation in general. Barcelona's new role in Europe lay in the judicious orientation of the city's intrinsic capacities, including its urban planning and geographical qualities.

[1] Joan Antoni Samaranch created a byword when, on officially closing the Games, he referred to them as "the best Olympic Games of the new era", in line with the general enthusiasm of the time. What does seem to be true is that Barcelona's urban development model for the Olympics was a landmark in the planning of these major events. In the previous case of Los Angeles 1988, the motivations of private developments and sponsorship had a blatant effect on the evolution of urban development. For example, Lisbon with Expo 98 and Sydney 2000 adopted Barcelona's approach and also developed dual cycle projects, thinking about "afterwards", to justify investment in the big event.

[2] From the mid-1980s onwards, essays and works about the city, its history and its current projects abounded. In the local sphere, mention should be made of *La ciudad de los prodigios*, by Eduardo Mendoza, Barcelona, 1985, translated into many languages, which simulates the process of major past events. The city that was taking off at such a rate was condemned by Felix de Azúa in the late seventies, using the metaphor of the *Titanic*, due to its scant cultural content.

In the field of architecture and urban planning, the burgeoning of these new projects has been explained in dozens of articles and special publications all over Europe. In the face of the generalised impasse in urban interventions, Barcelona has been seen as the advance party of an incipient resurgence of urban development. Perhaps as a result of this feeling, the city of Barcelona was awarded the Prince of Wales Prize in Urban Design 1990. *The Urban Public Spaces of Barcelona 1981-87*. Cambridge, 1991. In 1996 Barcelona hosted the congress of the UIA (International Union of Architects) which attracted ten thousand architects and corroborated the attraction of the city's urban planning processes. See Various authors: *Present i futurs. Arquitectura a les ciutats*. UIA, Barcelona, 1996. Later on, in 1998, the RIBA of London awarded the city its Gold Medal in recognition of its urban development endeavours.

10.01
New infrastructures being built.

10.a New urban cultural spaces.

10.02, 10.03
MACBA and the Casa de la Cari[...]
CCCB.

10.04
Auditorium and National Theatre
of Catalonia beside Les Glòries.

10.05, 10.06
The reconstructed Liceu on the
Rambla.

10.07
Can Casarramona, the new La
Caixa Forum.

X.2 New spatial dynamics

Urban redevelopment schemes led to the creation of the service sector that promoted an increasing internationalisation of the production base.

The possibility of an economic model, set in the new post-industrial context, was drawn out behind the urban transformation of the city and its area of influence. It is true that the majority of industry had moved to further outlying rings and that most work in the centre basically involved the tertiary and service sectors. In this change of location, industrial sectors were gradually incorporating more refined technological systems with a view to achieving higher productivity.

Here, the mature towns and cities – those with sustained industrial development over the last one hundred years – had also joined a new production phase, albeit different to the first industrialisation process. The former industrial city, with its political dominance based on a domestic market and protectionism, had become an open structure that formed part of international flows of services, production factors and goods.

Trullén highlights the leading role of the knowledge economy in our advanced cities and detects a strong transformation in this direction.[3] Furthermore, his study of the different territories and their connections leads him to detect networking systems of cities – in the metropolitan region – that acted as subsystems within the whole. These groups of cities were arranged along eight radial axes that took Barcelona as their centre.

This new spatial organisation was evident above all in the mobility of people within the wider metropolitan system, forming well tensed subsystems, as described above.[4] This represented an increase in the total number of journeys using different means of transport, but it was private mobility that increased most, mainly in the metropolitan context.[5]

In this way, the last decade of the century witnessed an increase in the dispersion of the metropolitan system towards the inner rings. Since the eighties, the old Metropolitan Area, comprising Barcelona and its 27 most immediate municipalities, had started to be overtaken by the growing dynamic of the metropolitan "region", which emerged as a *de facto* reality with regard to everyday housing, work and service relations.[6]

---

[3] See Joan Trullén: *El territori de Barcelona, cap una economia del coneixement.* Barcelona, 2001.

[4] See Salvador Giner *et al.*: *Enquesta de la regió de Barcelona 2000: primers resultats.* Barcelona, 2002. Also Various authors: *Mobilitat urbana i modes de transport.* Papers 24. Barcelona, 1995, particularly the articles by O. Nel·lo, Manuel Villalante and Joaquim Clusa.

[5] Mobility in Barcelona municipality has a modal layout (private-public-pedestrian transport system in percentages) of 42-35-19, whereas overall figures for the metropolitan region are 55-19-21.

[6] In terms of population, Barcelona municipality lost 6 per cent of its population in the last two decades, without reducing the overall number of jobs, but the population of the old Metropolitan Area also fell (by 0.4 per cent) though its working capacity increased. The new metropolitan region in itself, however, gained over 12 per cent in population and also in employment.

10.08
Flow chart showing growth i
regional mobility.

10.09
New phenomena in the
transformation of coastal and
prelittoral space.

Overall, the population of the Barcelona region was relatively stable with a slight increase.[7] But land consumption continued to grow at a constant rate of rather more than 600 hectares a year.[8]

The spatial distribution of this new urban land began to obey a different model, according to a recent study carried out by Antonio Font's team,[9] which points in metropolitan formation to the development after the mid-eighties of a system of growth by polarisation as opposed to growth by aggregation or by dispersion in the sixties and seventies, respectively.

At the same time, the coastline along the great triangular block of Catalonia began to form a growing attraction.[10] In fact the littoral and prelittoral space concentrated the strongest growth dynamic and underwent a major evolution in its forms of urban growth. Whereas the industrial model led the field until the late seventies, forms associated with leisure, second homes, tourism and services began to come to the fore in the new urban dynamic.

This was, then, a situation of major land consumption unaccompanied by population growth, with the appearance of new models of spatial distribution that went beyond municipal logic and the manifestation, in both Catalonia and the entire western Mediterranean, of the powerful attraction of the coastline as a place of settlement for new urban activities, both residential and to a large extent economic.

[7] The stability of the population is due to the reduction in the number of births in conjunction with its progressive ageing due to an increase in life expectancy, the final result being a drastic reduction in natural growth. See, among others, Carme Trilla *et al.*: *Estudi de les necessitats d'habitatge a la provincia de Barcelona.* Barcelona, 2002.
[8] See Joan Antoni Solans: *L'ocupació de sòl en el sistema metropolità central durant el periode 1980-1998.* Barcelona, 2002. During major expansion in the seventies, this figure was higher than 1,880 ha/year.
[9] See Antonio Font, Carles Llop and Josep M. Vilanova: *La construcció del territori metropolità.* Barcelona, 1999. Although the period covered ends in 1994, the tendency remained the same.
[10] See J. B. *et al.*: *Coast Wise Europe.* NAI, Rotterdam, 1994. Chapter on Catalonia. Also *Las formas urbanas de la costa catalana.* Diputació de Barelona, 2003.

X.3 The various scales of new urban development projects

3.1 Barcelona after 1993

The main urban development schemes of this period had their origins in earlier programmes or projects and were marked by a predominance of private initiative. It was logical that the public sector should change its rate of investment and concentrate its efforts on stabilising and recovering a situation of debt. Nonetheless, the improvement of urban space at district level continued and became established as a common practice in Barcelona's urban management which was also adopted in many municipalities in the metropolitan region and other Catalan cities. This generated a qualitative change in public space with the reformulation of Mediterranean city values of appreciation and respect for communal space.

The major changes of this period can be grouped into three blocks:

a) **Redefinition of the road system**

The implementation of the Ronda ring roads as a big urban development project promoted by the Olympic Games led to a radical change in volumes of through traffic in the city centre.[11]

However, Barcelona also discovered that while an increase in the network capacity improved distribution, it could easily induce an increase in traffic. As a result, major urban axes such as Meridiana and Gran Via, among others, changed their section in order to reduce their road capacity and recover space for pedestrians, cyclists and vegetation.

As we have already seen, a discussion of traffic cannot be taken apart from mobility in general and it is therefore in this aspect that changes have to be brought about in user behaviour by attempting to avoid the unnecessary use of private vehicles. The only way of dealing with this important issue in our cities[12] is to modulate private mobility, parking and collective transport on the basic of an integrated logic; the major contributions of the Infrastructures Master Plan (PDI) are described below. In any case, the interconnection of modes of transport suggests hybrid forms rather than the classical confrontation between public and private transport.

Alongside this general discussion, it is important to highlight some issues generated by the new road network.

---

[11] See Carme Miralles: *Transport i ciutat*, Barcelona, 1997, and Pere Riera: *Rentabilidad social de las infraestructuras: las Rondas de Barcelona. Un análisis coste-beneficio.* Madrid, 1993.

[12] This issue is generating a large bibliography and a great deal of discussion. Interesting examples are Brian Richards: *Future Transport in Cities.* London, 2001; Robert Cervero: *The Transit Metropolis: A Global Inquiry.* Washington, 1998; John Pucher and Christian Lefèvre: *The Urban Transport Crisis in Europe and North America.* London, 1996; Simon Guy *et al.*: *Urban Infrastructure in Transition.* London, 2001; David Banister *et al., European Transport Policy and Sustainable Mobility.* London, 2000.

10.b Projects to redefine the road system.

10.10, 10.11
Flow diagram before and after the Ronda ring roads.

10.12, 10.13
Redevelopment of the "empty" spaces between the new Ronda and existing neighbourhoods.

.14, 10.15, 10.16
ansformation of the environs
Plaça de Cerdà to ensure
proved urban continuity.

).17, 10.18, 10.19
vinguda Carles III changed its
en section for an improved
sponse to the excessive
esidential densities constructed
the decades of development.

Firstly, the central value being acquired by the spaces adjacent to the new Ronda ring roads; rather than closing in the city, they were actually inducing new activities.[13] This gave rise to efforts to re-develop these residual spaces once the infrastructures were complete. Then the new pressure on these spaces called for the incorporation of forms of collective transport to prevent the relegation to suburbs of the new functions, served only by cars.

[13] This tendency was seen in other European cities that had previously carried out this systematisation: for example, Munich, Frankfurt and Paris. By way of reference, see Tomato: *Paris: La ville du Peripherique*, Baume-les-Dames, 2003.

10.20
L'Illa Diagonal seen from the Diagonal.

This improvement of major internal roads also led to the enhancement of spaces and avenues that had been created in accordance with an exclusively car-centred logic. This was the case of the transformation of Plaça Cerdà, finally restructured as an urban space rather than a road intersection; Via Carles III, now Avinguda Brasil; and even Gran Via in eastern and western directions. For example, Carles III was converted from an uncovered, low-level thoroughfare to a long, costly tunnel of over two kilometres, giving rise to a new discussion as to the appropriateness of such complex restructuring, which ultimately once again specialised traffic by completely segregating its function. Wouldn't it be preferable to modulate internal traffic in order to reduce the need for such dramatic specialisation?

The car in the city obviously involves specific urban conditions such as speed and noise, etc., and therefore "orthopaedic" solutions for key points should perhaps be reserved, integrating this form of mobility to the environmental conditions that are acceptable at any given time. This is, however, a very basic approach to an ongoing discussion.

b) The culmination of some areas of new centrality

One area to merit particular attention is L'Illa, completed in 1994, which became a reference for shopping centres that form a fully-fledged urban part of the city: the integration of various uses within a macroblock turned the Diagonal into an interesting point of transition between the compact and the open city.

Also completed was Port Vell, a major leisure, shopping and service operation on the Moll d'Espanya wharf. The main attribute of this initiative of the Port Authority was the construction of a large free-time complex with quality open spaces and a footbridge that directed flows of pedestrians from the Rambla towards the port. A later phase of the Barcelona wharf set out to rationalise the terminuses and other arrival spaces for passenger

ships, mainly from the Balearic Islands, and introduce a large office complex which, though intended as back-up infrastructure for port activity, was excessive bearing in mind the delicate position of the wharf and its impact on vistas from Ciutat Vella.

The Carrer Tarragona axis, which incorporated new tower blocks in keeping with the general composition and singularity of the location, could have found more ambitious architectural responses. In any case, this spacious promenade establishes good relations between the streets of Sants and the Eixample fabric.

The former La Maquinista industrial sector in Sant Andreu gave rise to a large shopping centre, with a residential district made up of street blocks that stepped over to the other side of the railway tracks. The new dynamic developed by these projects can be seen as the vanguard of the major impact to be produced by the power of induction of the future Sagrera station. The RENFE-Meridiana sector is advancing at a slower pace but is gradually filling in the spaces between Sant Andreu and Nou Barris. Various service activities, such as the Can Dragó leisure centre, are now joining the facilities and parks constructed in the eighties.

c) New large urban axes

Barcelona's Fira trade fair complex also finally began to develop a new show precinct on the Pedrosa estate near Zona Franca in the municipality of L'Hospitalet, making the most of the proximity of the historic area of Montjuïc and the advantages offered by Gran Via as an airport approach road. The first installation, opened in 1994, consisted of two pavilions with modern entrances and technology that were soon extended further. The purpose was to provide complementary functions – that is, the more urban shows were to be held in the old precinct and the more modern, service-intensive ones in the new sector. An unresolved issue was an efficient public transport connection between the two precincts, which are 2.5 kilometres apart. The construction of this trade fair focus in Zona Franca marked the start of a series of future transformations, enhancing urban spaces such as Plaça Cerdà (completed in 2000) or involving a change in use of old factories in the area, such as Phillips or SEAT, which was moved to Martorell-Abrera. These were signs of further changes in the country's largest industrial estate to a new economic and productive role.

Furthermore, the continuation of the Diagonal finally materialised and this singular layout designed by Cerdà was completed with the construction of the final kilometre needed to connect Glòries to the sea.[14] This involved the construction of the promenade with a central boulevard and the accompanying residential buildings. But a new dimension of this project was later to appear with the proposal of restructuring the sector's former industrial function. The introduction of tertiary industrial zoning in associated with the "new economy" in Poblenou, christened 22@, aspired to reactivate production activity in the city. This programme was backed up by the promotion of building levels and improved technological services, so necessary for this type of use. The centrality of this part of the city may be of great utility in achieving objectives that are not at all straightforward, such as influencing the location of activities which, by definition, seek non-specific sites.

The seafront of Poblenou, too, was the site of the construction of five blocks that share a common volumetric form, though with different architectural designs.[15] Each block combines residential and tertiary uses and comprises one-third assisted housing.

This period was also marked by growing difficulties in institutional relations between local (City Council) and autonomous (Generalitat) authorities with regard to the type of schemes described here; the Olympic process and the very tight timeline had tended to force the rate of decision-making, perhaps facilitating agreement. After 1993, this was a dominant factor underlying both large-scale urban development issues and major infrastructures such as the AVE (the high-speed train line), the airport, and so forth. Meanwhile, as we have seen, projects to recover squares and small urban spaces continued to be one of Barcelona's most effective programmes. In this scenario, the rehabilitation of Ciutat Vella reached an appreciable level of effectiveness, forming one of the main keys to the city's urban development process.[16] Whole new horizons of opportunities were opening up to the old town as its potential developed.

---

[14] See Various authors: *Barcelona. La segona renovació*. Barcelona, 1996. Also, Various authors: *1999. Urbanisme a Barcelona*. Barcelona, 1999.

[15] The urban project is by Carlos Ferrater after an ideas competition. The alternatives are summarised in *Barcelona. La segona renovació, op. cit.*, 1996.

[16] See LUB, *Ciutat Vella a Barcelona. Present i futur*. Barcelona, 2003, mainly chapters 5 and 6. They describe the rehabilitation work begun by the public sector which has helped to change the negative content of this Barcelona district. This strategy gives grounds for hopes for the recovery of other problematic sectors in the metropolitan context.

10.c The metropolitan approaches. Between Gran Via and the river Llobregat.

.24, 10.25,
.26, 10.27, 10.28
ran Via as a new
etropolitan approach is
tracting new activities,
ch as Fira 2, the law court
mplex and new shopping
ntres, calling for strict spatial
ordination to prevent the
nstruction of a disjointed
ty.

10.d The Diagonal in Poblenou.

10.29, 10.30
The continuation of the Diagonal as an urban connection with Poblenou.

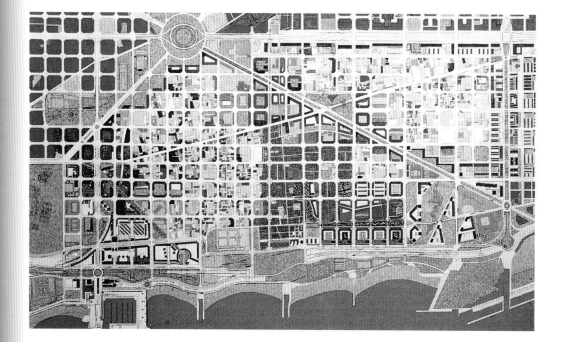

10.31
Various transformations under way: the construction of the Diagonal, the 22@ sector and coastal projects.

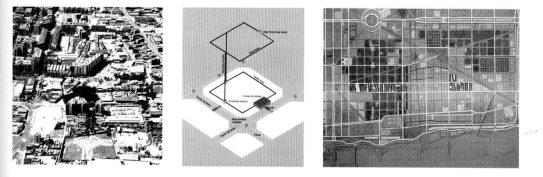

10.32, 10.33, 10.34
Transformation and proposals.

10.e The intermediate scale. Internal transformation and interstitial public spaces.

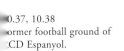
.35
. Maquinista dwellings.

.36
ve street blocks in Poblenou.

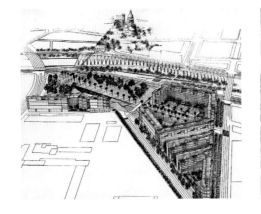

0.37, 10.38
ormer football ground of
CD Espanyol.

0.39
Botanical gardens.

0.40
Diagonal Mar Park.

10.41
Passeig Joan de Borbó.

10.42
Passeig de la Barceloneta.

3.2 Major pluri-municipal projects of the turn of the century

The late nineties saw a return to major projects, linked this time to the updating of the city's main infrastructures, particularly the extension of the airport, the high-speed train network and the public transport plan. Joan Clos began his mandate as mayor in 1997. On the basis of his experience with the renovation of Ciutat Vella, he undertook responsibility for the city.

While preparation for 1992 had tabled some of these issues, it was not until this time that the restructuring of major infrastructures and their interaction really came to the fore.

These infrastructures were metropolitan and/or regional in character, and the central city therefore found itself promoting schemes such as the airport, which was physically situated in another municipality. This pluri-municipal or metropolitan condition constituted the fundamental characteristic of the time. The non-existence of an integrated metropolitan body was to be a source of difficulties for these initiatives, the most important of which were: the Llobregat Delta Plan,[17] involving a series of major infrastructural interventions, including the diversion of the last five kilometres of the river and the construction of a water treatment plant; the extension of the airport with a third runway running parallel to the main one beside the coast, and a new terminal;[18] the extension of the port by about 600 hectares, doubling its current capacity, on land regained from the river and the sea, to create a logistic platform, and the arrival of the AVE branch line and the Llobregat expressway.

This was a scheme that strongly advocated interchange,[19] principally of goods, between the different means of transport in a very central area of the metropolitan system, in a place where the environment was of prime importance. It is important to bear in mind the growing role of the logistics sector, due to the increase in goods mobility created by new transport techniques and computerised management.[20]

The Llobregat delta has always had a high-profile presence in the various episodes of the formation of Barcelona, if only as an unoccupied spot with prime topographical conditions and a fragile natural structure. Hence the dramatic importance of these projects, calling for the utmost attention to compatibility with the delta's territorial system. With its marked vocation as a space for entry and services, as suggested by Rubió i Tudurí's proposals in the 1930s, it now comprises a strong system of towns around the delta, with a powerful

[17] See the monographic issue of *Papers*: "El Baix Llobregat: Planejament urbanístic i problemática territorial". Barcelona, 1994.

[18] The airport terminal was opened in 1991 and the passenger figures for 1993 were ten million, rising to over 21 million in 2002.

[19] See the notebooks *El Plan Delta I, II* and *III*, by J. Trullén, Ezequiel Baró and Joan Alemany. Barcelona, 1995.

[20] This logic sought to maximise cargo flows with a view to producing an ideal model, in which storage approached zero level. See Alfonso Rodríguez Bayraguet: "La logística i la circulació de mercaderies a la regió metropolitana de Barcelona". *Papers* 10. Barcelona, 1992.

10.f Rationalisation and new uses of the port.

.43
ew of the port in 1996.

0.44
roject for the Llobregat
elta: diversion of the final
ilometres of the river,
onstruction of a water
reatment plant, and extension
f the airport and the sea port
Logistic Activity Area) on land
eclaimed from the sea.

10.45
Future structure of the port in
the mid-term.

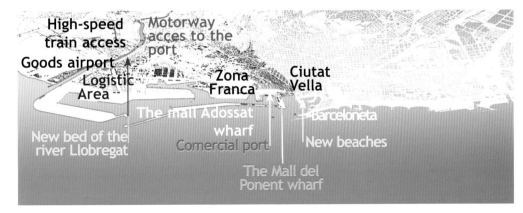

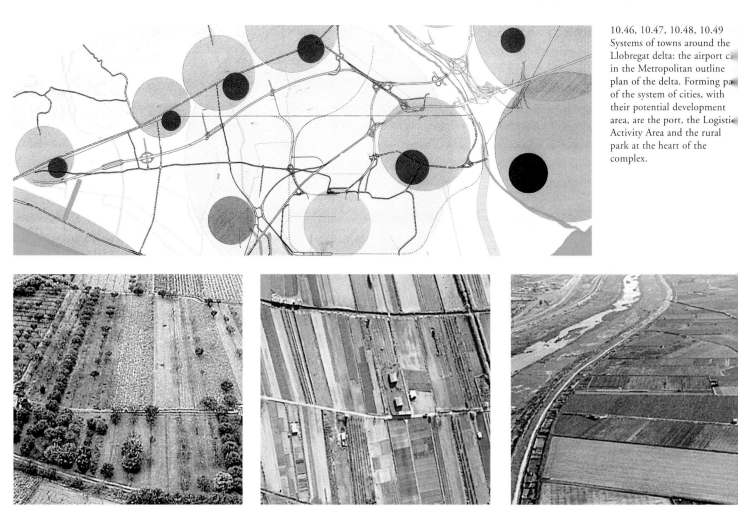

10.46, 10.47, 10.48, 10.49
Systems of towns around the Llobregat delta: the airport ci[...] in the Metropolitan outline plan of the delta. Forming pa[...] of the system of cities, with their potential development area, are the port, the Logisti[...] Activity Area and the rural park at the heart of the complex.

economic and demographic dynamic due to the prospects created by its new condition as a centre for logistics and interchange. What is important is to ensure that this dual condition does not contradict the maintenance of the delta's attributes, duly brought up to date. This is surely one of the city's biggest challenges if it is to make the existence of this great green lung to its west compatible with interchange infrastructures at a national level. The delta must be actively preserved to prevent its progressive deterioration under the classification of farmland, given the inability of this activity to continue to guarantee its permanence.[21]

Meanwhile, in the harbour, the port was completing the transformation of Port Vell and the new opening bridge was built in the Moll de Ponent dock, providing access for heavy goods vehicles without passing through

---

[21] Perhaps the best option would be a classification or a "positive" treatment to ensure the condition of open space used for farming, like so many large urban parks in central European cities. Along these lines, see the work of Joaquim Sabaté: "El Parc Agrari del Baix Llobregat", *Barcelona 1979-2004*. Barcelona, 1999. The discussion as to the compatibility of heavy infrastructures and the delta was addressed in the 1970s. LUB, *Jano*, issue 80, *op. cit.* Barcelona, 1976.

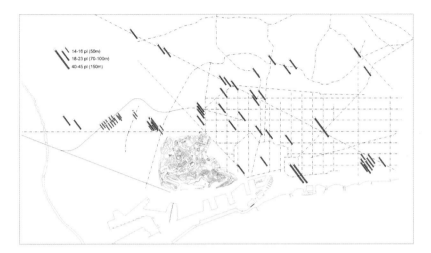

14-16 pl (50m)
18-23 pl (70-100m)
40-45 pl (150m)

the city. The layout was completed with the opening of a new entrance beside the Barceloneta in mid-2003, providing access for fishing and recreational boats. This operation involved the construction of a high-rise hotel which was justified to support the financing of infrastructure works. This was one more example of the growing trend to build new skyscrapers to provide individual solutions without too much heed to historical morphology and the precise composition of the resulting urban landscape.

The AVE is planned to connect Barcelona, Madrid and Seville in around 2007, followed by immediate connection with the French network. The dream of our forefathers from the early 20th century will then become reality: fast and efficient European rail transport.

The central station will be built in Sagrera, to provide a complement in the north to the existing station of Sants. The rational nature of this decision could have saved many alternative hypotheses suggested by sterile discussions, such as Sant Cugat, which will find its place in the mid-term but not yet, or Sants, already overcrowded, involving a great deal of unreasoned discussion and turning the executive phase into an unnecessary marathon.

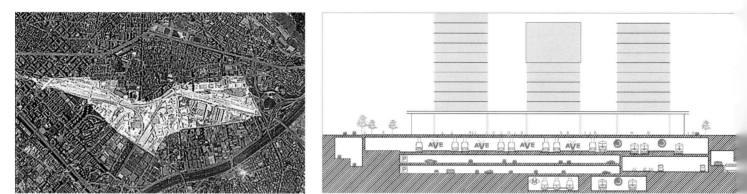

10.52, 10.53
La Sagrera: an intermodal station where various public transport infrastructure system converge.

The location of the new intermodal station including the underground train and suburban network will lead to the development of a service and activity complex that will give the Sagrera and Clot sectors a new lease of life.

In turn, the new PDI (Infrastructures Master Plan) sought to strengthen the distribution of public transport in the real metropolitan region.[22] The Metro network was given particular priority with the extension of some existing lines.[23] A new line, L-9, has also been built; rather than following a central route, it aims to form a clear connection with some of the new metropolitan economic focuses, such as Badalona, Santa Coloma, Sagrera, the Fira trade fair complex, El Prat and the airport, among others, forming an upper ring of 40 kilometres.

As in so many European cities, the tram is regaining a place in the metropolitan system, with the planning of a line from Diagonal, specifically Plaça Francesc Macià, to Baix Llobregat, initially as far as Sant Feliu with the Tram-Baix project.

The city's interest in being an international point of reference led the City Council to plan the project of the Universal Forum of Cultures for 2004 in the Besòs area – once again on Barcelona territory, but again shared with another metropolitan municipality, in this case Sant Adrià.[24] The aim this time is to create a new type of event, under the auspices of the UNESCO, based on cultural diversity, the conditions of peace and the sustainable city. For five months, it will host a whole programme of debates and exhibitions to express the world's cultural diversity.

The urban development project is located at the end of the Diagonal, where it reaches the sea, extending towards the Besòs and creating a 200 hectare space in a very low-quality residential and environmental area, with the aim of recovering it.[25] This is a large open space for mass use that will later be used as a convention centre, the new zoo and other aquatic activities on the seafront. This large-scale development project is to complete Barcelona's seafront, relaunching the initiative of the Diagonal-Mar project, including a series of residential buildings and a large park to finish off the layout of the Diagonal.[26]

[22] Collective public transport is undergoing a degree of growth due to an integrated ticket system. The number of passengers to use the Metro and buses rose from 691 million in 1997 to 800 million in 2001; the RENFE and Ferrocarrils de la Generalitat railways increased from 114 million to 138 million in the same period.
[23] See Josep Parcerisa and Maria Rubert de Ventós: *Metro*. UPC. Barcelona, 2002.
[24] See Various authors: *Barcelona 1979-2004*. Barcelona, 1999. Also *Barcelona: una ciudad abierta a la nueva economia*. Barcelona, 2000.
[25] The operation is concentrated in large buildings designed by Herzog and De Meuron, José Luís Mateo, Elías Torres and J. Antonio Lapeña, among others, representing the high profile of the event.
[26] A layout of vertical blocks designed by Óscar Tusquets' team around a large park which is the work of the sorely missed young architect Enric Miralles. The complex also includes a large shopping centre which is very introverted in relation to the new context created.

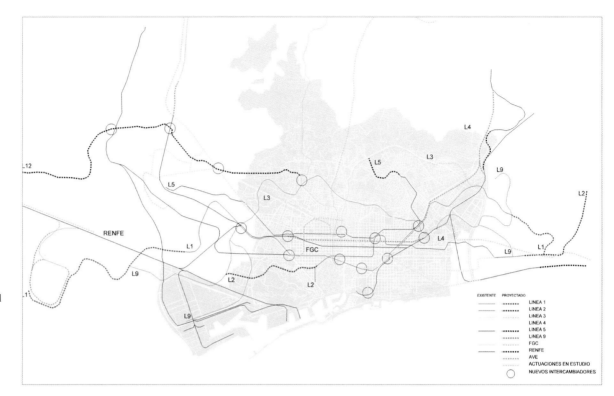

.54
xtension of Metro lines.

.55
he Trambaix, simulating
s route through Sant Just
eside the Walden 7 residential
uilding.

X.4 Big cities in Europe

On the new map of Europe, the creation of a large market place led to high-level competition between cities. Specifically, big cities with their hinterlands and regions were offering unwonted competition. This new movement has been compared with the situation in the Renaissance period, leading cities to represent the production, trade and culture of vast territories.[27]

In this new definition of space, both the Barcelona and the Catalan political authorities set out to strengthen their positions in the European market.[28] Barcelona became central on the European map; from being a city on the outskirts of Spain, it became the Pyrenean gateway to Europe, as well as a natural port linking Europe with the Mediterranean and further afield. This vocation had already been prefigured by the motorway layout, but in the new political and administrative organisation, it came into its own.

[27] Ch. Jensen-Butler *et al.*: *European Cities in Competition.* Aldershot, 1997.
[28] From the viewpoint of the city, Barcelona is forming a lobby with the group of nearest, most important cities (Saragossa, Valencia, Palma de Mallorca, Montpelier and Toulouse) to define a more solid, complementary bid. It also promotes the Eurocities platform, including cities such as Rotterdam, Lyon and Munich which, despite not being formal capitals, have economic and urban planning dynamics that set them apart as main movers on the new European stage. The Generalitat Catalan regional government also promotes close relations between Catalonia and three European regions (Lombardy, Rhône-Alpes and Baden-Württemberg), called Four Motors in Europe, with a view to gaining credibility in the European market.

10.g The Diagonal embraces the river Besòs. Forum 2004.

10.56, 10.57
Forum building and aerial view of the prolongation of t Diagonal.

10.58
Forum building and aerial view of the mouth of the rive Besòs.

The result was a completely new situation. Even the European Union, with its policies for sectors such as industry, farming and major infrastructures had no specific policy for big cities to balance out the processes of urban transformation that were taking place.

It became increasingly necessary in view of cities' major economic and social role to consider them as specific, active subjects of the general policies of the EU, which could therefore cease to be the passive objects receiving the direct consequences of other sectoral policies that almost never took into account the urban impact that they produced.

This situation was reminiscent of the urban difficulties caused by a certain type of industrial or farming restructuring policies, which in most cases were "helped out" by policies of aids – for unemployment, for example, or new industrial investment – though never associated with the type of city or the specific problem of a given urban system.

The important social and economic role of cities also made them the cause and the driving force of economic development in some periods, as studies of historical evolution show, as well as proving themselves to be absolutely crucial in times of recession or crisis.[29]

As a result, there were a growing number of supporters of the hypotheses that accorded European cities not just a central role in territorial structure, but also saw them as the best potential basis for a coherent transformation of the changing economic system.

Basic studies already existed on the classification of cities and urban categories,[30] and it was time to highlight the need for further discussion in the field of intervention policies and urban problems or imbalances.

Particular mention should be made of Brunet's study, conducted for the Datar in Paris in 1989, offering a general summarised interpretation with a view to understanding the future of urban development problems. It

[29] "The city is one of the most powerful machines of production that humanity has invented". Andreu Mas-Colell: "L'economia de les ciutats", *Barcelona económica*. Barcelona, 1993.
[30] Particularly P. Hall + D. Hay: *Growth Centres in European Urban System*. London, 1980; D. Burtenshaw *et al.*: *The City in West Europe*. New York, 1981; P. Cheshire + D. Hay: *Urban Problems in Western Europe: An Economic Analysis*. London, 1989; R. Brunet: *Les villes européennes*. Datar. Paris, 1989. Other studies seek a worldwide reference and their analyses therefore lose the specificity of the macro region. See for example Saskia Sassen: *The Global City*. Princeton, 1991.

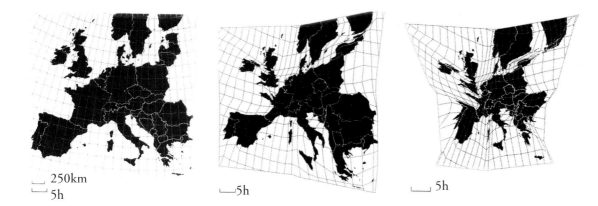

10.61
Map of Europe in which rea[l]
distances seem shorter thank[s]
to the high-speed train.

established, for example, the "banana" model which connected London, Paris, Frankfurt and Milan and drew out a central European space in the style of the structuralist hypotheses of the sixties.[31]

Without wishing to deny its interpretative value, it is important to remember that it goes some way to explaining the phenomenon; furthermore, the new processes of transformation were far more subtle. With regard to some variables, space is evidently much more discontinuous than before. It is important to remember that despite these macrolevel interpretations, the true transformation operations take very different forms, in some cases with a great potential for compatibility with existing urban structures, in others with highly innovative urban models.

On this subject, the Kunzmann and Wegener report[32] detects a series of spatial tendencies in Western European cities and voices the foremost problems. It confirms the significant role of the European city in the economic and social development of the continent and endorses its indispensable value in the mid-term. The report highlights the urban inequalities which, though based on the history of each country, may tend to increase as a result of the growing internationalisation of the economy furthered by the European single market.

At the same time, in most European cities a series of general urban development tendencies could be detected, as we have in broad terms seen in Barcelona.

The population of big cities was ageing due to the fall in the birth rate and a decrease in major waves of immigration. There were, however, important movements of population within the metropolitan regions in keeping with the changing phases of the urban development process. The size of the family unit was falling, gradually lessening the densification of existing urban fabrics. Women were increasingly joining the labour market and new lifestyles emerged to affect both housing and working patterns. In general, the length of the working week tended to decrease with a subsequent increase in free time and, therefore, new demands on leisure, up until then a little-developed urban planning sector.

Urban economic activities underwent a far-reaching reorganisation in production and distribution: there was a polarisation in the size of companies and the presence of "abnormal" means of production in the form of the

---

[31] When the phenomenon of urban development was explained on the basis of large-scale formal models such as those by Lloyd Rodwin or Jean Gottmann for the American city. The impact of this report when it was published by *Le Monde* was evident, as was the interest of cities close to the axis in feeling a part of it.

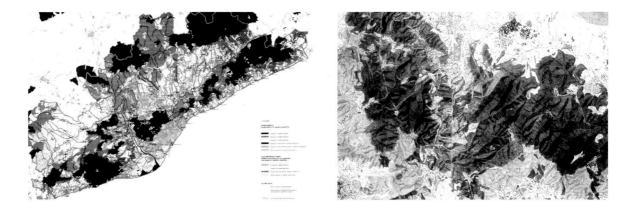

black economy that had arisen in response to the crisis in the seventies and then continued. The keynotes marking the economic sector were liberalisation, deregulation, privatisation and internationalisation.[33]

In turn, technological changes in communication and transport systems stimulated the mobility of persons and goods: road transport came to the fore and the high-speed train emerged as an element of regional structuring. There was an appreciable increase in the volume of air transport and the use of telecommunication systems, as a result of which environmental problems began to be regarded in a more serious light, and related aims in the city became more of a priority.

These were the general tendencies that could be observed in big European cities which, at the same time, were undergoing changing rates of development. To refer to Leo Klaasen's classification,[34] cities that were physically close to each other were undergoing different phases of urban development. The four phases detected by the study, and presented sequentially, were:

a) Traditional urbanisation: when urban growth occurs in the central space.

b) Suburbanisation: suburbs grow faster than the centre. The development of central residence decreases and new residence moves outwards, whereas work remains in the centre. The centre may therefore lose population and centrally-located jobs may decrease in a later phase.

c) Deurbanisation or contra-urbanisation: when jobs follow residence and the centre therefore loses population and employment. In contrast to the advantages of low-density systems so desirable to the population, particularly the middle classes, deurbanisation gives rise to serious problems for cities without high levels of infrastructure: better distributed work and services create a higher demand for transport and increase energy consumption. There is a slight increase in land consumption.

d) Re-urbanisation: this is the fourth phase in the process and is characterised by a return to the centre of both new economic activities and a degree of residence. This phase, which characterised the rebirth of European urban centres with a positive increase in commercial use and tourism, has also led to an increase in speculative pressure on the central city.

32 Klaus Kunzmann + Michael Wegener: *The Pattern of Urbanisation in Western Europe 1960-90*. Dortmund University, 1991.
33 See Jordi Borja: *Barcelona y el sistema urbano europeo*. Eurociudad 91, Barcelona, 1990.
34 L. Klaasen *et al.*: *Urban Europe: A study of growth and decline*. Oxford, 1982. Also Leo van den Berg *et al.*: *Governing Metropolitan Regions*. Aldershot, 1993. A summarised description of Western cities can be found in Stephen Ward: *Planning the Twentieth-Century City*. West Sussex, 2002.

This classification is useful for understanding the overall dimension of these processes and their influence on the demands for infrastructure, the evolution of the property market and the use of the built city. However, it has been detected that the phases are superposed in many cities and the interplay of interests may delay or advance their succession or overlapping.[35] Above all, it is evident that infrastructures – physical and non-physical – enable a more open use of the territory, in some cases promoting forms of occupation or transformation, without the relative spatial continuity of traditional models. This leads to a generalised phenomenon of scattered growth requiring new forms of interpretation[36] that explain it within the overall system of spatial transformation.

The European context reinforces the dominance of big cities in economic and social development in the mid-term with a series of new characteristics. One was the apparent increase in competition between cities to offer appropriate spaces for the new location requirements of industry and services. Apparently too this competitiveness attracted public investment back to an urban context with a view to improving relative position. The big city could continue to represent the centre of a more extensive hinterland organised around it. Then regional polarisation increased on the basis of the structuring axes of communication and transport, with a priority role for "high speed", airports, teleports, and so forth.

X.5 Opportunities and weaknesses

In the new European framework, Barcelona and Catalonia emerged with improved prospects to those in a similar situation in the seventies. However, their opportunities and weaknesses must also be assessed in a more open playing field than in the past.

This gives particular interest to attempts to evaluate and correct the weaknesses of the Barcelona area such as those undertaken in the form of the Barcelona Strategic Plan as of 1988,[37] which set out to define weak points

---

[35] See Oliver Gillham: *The Limitless City: A Primer on the Urban Sprawl Debate*. Washington, 2002. Also Thierry Paquot *et al.*: *La ville et l'urbain, l'état des savoirs*. Paris, 2000.

[36] See, for example, the study by Stafano Boeri *et al.*: *Il territorio che cambia*, Milan, 1993.

[37] See, in other works, Manuel de Forn: *Evolución de la planificación y programación y de las administraciones locales*. Barcelona, 1980. Also Francesc Santacana, Joan Campreciós: "La planificació estratègica, un métode d'anàlisi per a les ciutats?", *Revista Econòmica de Catalunya* 10, Barcelona, 1989. For the most recent version see: Francesc Raventós *et al.*: *Els grans temes del III Pla Estratègic*. Barcelona, 2002.

.64
esent-day metropolitan
lity.

and study ways of reducing their impact on the profile of Barcelona's bid. The Strategic Plan involved a high level of corporate and institutional participation, indicating that civil society in general took part in the process or to a large extent agreed with the discourse established by the documents in question. The Plan has since been updated, and is now in its third version.

The difficulties involved in extending the strategies laid out in these plans to the territory did not detract from the force of this discourse, which opened very useful channels of institutional and corporate work.[38]

In present-day circumstances it is difficult to imagine that a Territorial Plan for Catalonia[39] could or should produce a physical "design" of the territory as it did in the 1930s. Perhaps the study and design of innovative urban patterns (for residence, work, open space or mixed systems) produce a greater understanding of territorial needs in the mid-term, thereby establishing guidelines for regulation or incentive.[40]

[38] This seems to be the main difficulty in previously drafted Strategic Plans, such as those for San Francisco or Rotterdam. See for example Various authors: *Vernieuwing van Rotterdam*. Rotterdam, 1987. More recent experiences such as those of Lisbon, Rome or Toronto set out to create a clear sequential and/or simultaneous link between strategic plan and physical plan. See, for example, Various authors: *Plan Estratégico de Lisboa*. Lisbon, 1991. Also INU: "Il nuovo Piano di Roma", *Urbanística 116*. Rome, 2001; and Paul Bedford: *Toronto Official Plan*. Toronto, 2002.

[39] The General Territorial Plan of Catalonia had to be drafted according to the 1989 Territorial Act of the Catalan Parliament. The document was drawn up after much delay and, judging by information revealed, it did not seem to fit in with the conceptual and operative components expected of a plan of this scope in the present-day context, especially bearing in mind the interesting planning experience on various scales that Barcelona and Catalonia have accumulated in the last one hundred years.

[40] See Alexandre Tarroja: "L'Estratègia Territorial Europea, un referent per al canvi de cultura en les polítiques territorials a Catalunya", Various authors: *Estrategia territorial europea*. IERM. Barcelona, 2002.

The modification of prevailing Urban Development Plans also imposed the need for updates. The example of the evolution of the PGM (General Metropolitan Plan) of Barcelona demonstrated the restrictions of variation when unsupported by a change in methodological structure.[41]

The drafting of a Catalan territorial model in a European context should perhaps involve an interpretation of the process of condensation produced in the capital, as being capable of generating a new overview of Catalan space in the mid-term, with essential formal components. The lack of a specific approach could lead once again to territorial break-up as a result of the temporary pressure of the growing European market.[42]

On the one hand, there is the city's geographical potential in the form of its situation and climate: heavily urbanised regions of the Mediterranean shores are seen in the European context as potential areas for tourism and new residence. Also, efficient cities in this system can aspire to attract high-technology industry or specialised services whose workforce appreciates the quality of urban space and the temperate climate.[43]

On the other, there may be changes in the population due to the evolution of the demography of Catalonia and Barcelona in particular, and the demand for labour produced by these new developments.[44] This necessarily calls for a reference to an increase in immigration as a variable that compensates for the drop in the birth rate and the subsequent fall in the size of families that have marked recent decades.

This new demographic condition made itself felt in an increased housing demand and the reuse of parts of the city, mainly in the old neighbourhoods, for new residents. This is a field requiring judicious strategies to prevent the overcrowding and substandard housing described during the pro-development period.

[41] See the monographic issue of *Papers 28*, "Els 20 anys del Pla General Metropolità de Barcelona". Barcelona, 1997.

[42] Manuel Ludevid: "Barcelona en el mercat europeu. Punts forts i punts febles de l'Area Econòmica de Barcelona", *Revista Econòmica de Catalunya* 10, Barcelona 1989. Study conducted by the Development Agency of the Zona Franca Consortium. According to this study, the major weak points were in the field of infrastructures (telecommunications and industrial land), training (vocational training, research, company organisation, etc.) and administration (bureaucracy, legal insecurity). The strong points were its economic and market potential and its industrial and business tradition. Added to this precise definition of the "economic area" are other characteristics and weaknesses of the urban development profile of Barcelona in the foreseeable panorama of the nineties.

[43] Many parallels have been drawn with the take-off of developments in the sunbelts of the American West as opposed to the winter cities in the north-east. See Larry Sawers and William Tabb: *Sunbelt/Snowbelt: Urban Development and Regional Restructuring*. New York, 1984.

[44] See the article by Anna Cabré: "Algunes reflexions sobre el futur de població de Barcelona", *Papers 6*. Barcelona 1991. The article is a brilliant summary of the evolution of Barcelona's population. Within the falling tendency of the city's population, she presents the relative "age increase" of the population and the need both to fix, by means of policies such as affordable housing, the young population, and to bear in mind that immigration of both cheap and qualified labour will be needed in the transformation of the industrial and service sector. Also the work by M. Antonia Monés and Josep M. Carrera: *La regió metropolitana de Barcelona. Els propers vint anys. Prospectiva del mercat de treball, demografia i habitatge*. Barcelona, 2003. Facsímil.

.65
rious reinterpretations of the
stern sector of the Eixample:
Clot de la Mel, 2. Llull
reet blocks, 3. Vila Olímpica,
Bac de Roda, 5. Five street
ocks on the coastal front, 6.
iagonal Mar.

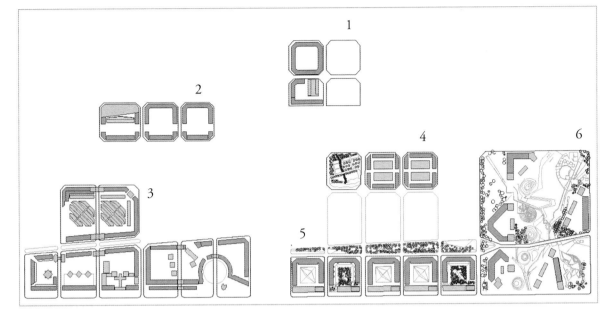

However, in addition to calling for central space, these forms of development also required new spaces in the metropolitan region. We have seen how the urban structures of Barcelona and its hinterland are marked by a major impedance: the natural corridors that condition their development. We have also seen the importance of major territorial axes: infrastructures such as the high-speed train, motorways, etc. These are elements that can change the distribution of regional and metropolitan accessibility and constitute new nodes or points of centrality. In turn, evolution towards a more technologically developed urban society shaped a social system organised more on the basis of networks of relations (communication and interchange) than on the continuities of the traditional system. In these scenarios, the network of cities has to provide a specific response and appropriate forms of action.[45] In this system, the advantages of location of certain innovative activities – new industry and services – over other urban centres can be considerable.

In fact the change-over to the so-called system of post-industrial or post-Fordist production was influencing the way in which the metropolitan region was organised.[46] It exerted particular influence on the interconnection of the territory produced by new mobility and also on the way in which urban pieces or fragments were produced. There was however still a need for rigorous studies to understand how the existing city was transformed in keeping with the new demands of the social and production system, and how other parts simply evolved thanks

[45] See Joan Eugeni Sánchez: "Avenços tècnics i efectes territorials a l'Àrea de Barcelona, 1975-1995", *La formació del cinturó industrial*, Barcelona, 1997.
[46] New demands involve above all flexibility in the organisation of production, seeking another scale in the definition of industrial districts or sectors. However, recent studies of these phenomena reveal the need of large economies for agglomeration, the importance of face-to-face transactions, the power of geographic conditions to establish networking organisations, factors of urbanism that metropolitan systems can activate more easily than other deurbanised options. See, for example, Marco Cenzatti: "Leaping into the Abyss. Planning Theory and Postmodernism", *Critical Planning*, Vol. 7, 2000.

to the adaptability of certain urban morphologies and urban planning projects. One example of the latter was the continuing reinterpretation of the Eixample, across Poblenou, over the last 20 years.[47] Urban systems also adapt by means of a new understanding of pre-existing structures that are modified, as shown in earlier periods. It is however important to pay attention to innovative phenomena that can contribute better environmental conditions than the traditional industrial processes. Once again, the project and the scheme find their respective niches for development.

In this respect, Barcelona capital with its cultural and institutional services was instrumental in hosting the strategic functions of the new production system. In the future characterisation of this capital role, the historical and cultural dimension of the city and its people was the principal attribute for promotion. Its wide and varied content, its contrasts and minor faults, its cosmopolitanism and its everydayness were all fundamental values.

At the same time, the impact of foreign investment could be a limitation, though this would depend to a large extent on whether it acted as a focus for production or also provided a strategic space and other kinds of services. Foreign investment could be a predator or give a new lease of life to the local production sector, as occurred at the turn of the century with the consolidation of Catalan industry. The Catalan industrial and business sectors could play a vital role in getting foreign investment to take root.

From this viewpoint, the correction of existing problems and a grasp of those approaching had to be regarded as a priority. On the one hand, the weaknesses introduced in our urban fabric during the pro-development era were patent: blatantly inadequate residential districts and urban structures that still require further investment and improvement work today. On the other, the prognoses of the European market suggested that the advantages of new industrial development could also lead to further imbalances in existing urban systems: environmental problems and an increased transport demand were some of the most evident,[48] along with an increase in urban poverty as the result of a very unbalanced labour market.[49]

Once again, the excessive protagonism that the property market continued to have in our urban systems called for measures to control the capital gains of speculation, which to a large extent were compromising the

---

[47] For example the seminar held in Vienna with the title: "Conceiving Urban Form in the Post-Fordist Networked Economy", comparing these new phenomena in such far-flung cities as Vienna, Paris, Barcelona and Los Angeles. See Eve Blau and Renate Banik-Schweitzer Ed.: *New Urban Forms*. Vienna, 2003. My own presentation dealt with the great adaptability of the urban structures designed by Cerdà, with an appreciation of the adaptability of new functional programmes to the original idea of the street block.

[48] See Kunznann *et al.*: *op. cit.*, pp. 53-62.

[49] World Bank: *World Development Report. Poverty*. Oxford, 1990.

10.h The urban restructuring of metropolitan cities.
Examples of urban development projects in metropolitan cities.

10.66
stems of mature towns that
nction as a network within
e metropolitan region.

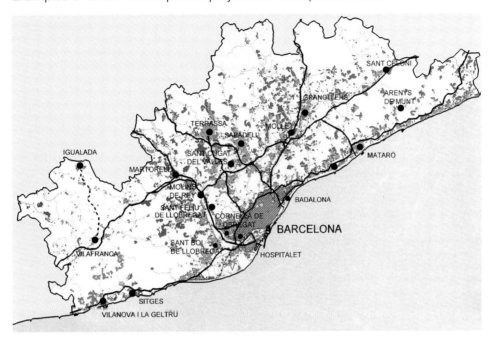

10.67
Badalona's new port.

10.68
Eixample de Mar, Vilanova i
la Geltrú.

10.69
Macià Axis, Sabadell.

10.70
The Railway Axis, Vilafranca.

10.71
Project for the area of Les
Casernes, Girona.

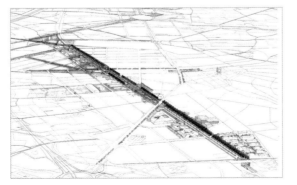

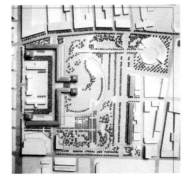

achievements of urban rehabilitation.[50] The improved interconnection of the territory at both administrative and operative levels would perhaps allow greater efficiency in public sector policies.[51] In any case, the development of the potential and the correction of these weaknesses called for a well defined field of action in the city and its urban region, allowing the combination of transformation and rehabilitation projects. There were obvious targets for action in interstitial sectors of the traditional Metropolitan Area and in the city itself. The seafront took off with the Olympic Village and the major coastal infrastructure, but there was still room for the development of residence, services and central space, and along the metropolitan seafront stretching towards Maresme and the river Llobregat and Garraf, too. The big cities in the metropolitan system, as well as other of Catalonia's mature towns and cities, were undergoing restructuring processes of great interest.

Projects such as the Macià Axis in Sabadell, Can Mulà in Mollet, Badalona port, La Pirelli in Vilanova i la Geltrú, the Railway axis in Vilafranca del Penedès and the Campus in Terrassa were just some of the many examples under way that indicated this potential for incipient transformation.[52]

This is surely the way forwards – recognition of a larger scope of action, such as the space of the metropolitan region. Experience has shown major decentralisation processes in residence, but also in work, and at the same time we have to avoid the excessive compacting or vertical expansion of the central city, which is worryingly incipient in Barcelona and other European cities.[53]

[50] While the functioning of the land market is a representative ingredient in the economic take-off of a city, the inflation of prices due to speculative retention in a monopolistic market is a real threat to urban development, as seen in the late 1980s in London, Paris, Munich, Madrid, Barcelona and many other cities, where the profit outlook placed any kind of housing operation beyond the reach of the working classes. In Barcelona city, for example, while the price of construction doubled between 1983 and 1989, the price of land multiplied by three. While the difficulties of operating in a free-market capitalist system are obvious, it is also generally accepted that in a "special" segment of the market (that of affordable housing) there are experiences of planning and action that have given excellent results in Central European countries.

[51] The disappearance of the Metropolitan Area of Barcelona, as in many other European cities, has limited the political and administrative capacity of municipalities to really deal with this kind of problem. In Europe there is a growing feeling that a new form of interconnection is needed; in Holland, large municipalities set themselves up as urban conurbations in 2000; London re-established the Metropolitan Authority in 2001. Perhaps this issue will find a more rational context at European level that will enable its development in keeping with the idiosyncrasy of each country and the different urban systems.

[52] See by way of example the compendium, Various authors: *Transformaciones urbanas*, COAC. Barcelona, 1997. Also issue 39 of *Papers*, "Estratègies territorials a les regions catalanes", Institut d'Estudis Regionals i Metropolitans de Barcelona. Barcelona, 2003.

[53] The European urban tradition has incorporated the skyscraper into city morphology as in an element to distinguish outstanding or strategic points in the city, avoiding the banal logic of the land market: "the more you pay, the higher you can build". This decision is central today in cities such as Vienna or Amsterdam, which aspire to escape the difficulties caused by more relaxed regulations such as those in Frankfurt, which had a negative effect on the old town.

.72
ew of the seafront.

X.6 Barcelona, a city with a future

The closing paragraphs of a book like this provide the opportunity for some open reflections that are invited by the very nature of this summary and perhaps express a veiled desire to offer some suggestions for the future of our city. This is in part the result of the open urban development process of recent decades, representing a forward-looking challenge in which the improvement of the quality of spaces and buildings can be seen as a catalyst for a larger-scale process.

Also because the recovery of Barcelona has proved the enormous strength of its existing urban structure and the social and civic bodies operating within the metropolitan system.

For this reason, despite an optimistic view of our city and its potential, this seems like a good point to put forward a few points for reflection about the conditions that should guide urban planning approaches.

a) Diversity versus homogeneity. As we have seen, Barcelona's evolution is proof of the diversity of its urban pieces that still maintain a strong identity. The "Barcelonas", to quote the writer Manuel Vázquez Montalbán, can still provide some very useful guidelines. But this alternative, if generalised to the metropolitan region, calls for decisive projects or schemes to avoid the sameness of many sectoral policies or property market developments that push for more homogeneous space to which they can apply their capital gains.

b) Innovation and tradition. The city today can be viewed from both of these contrasting but coherent viewpoints. The high capacity for transformation of our present-day culture and our means of urban construction have to lead to new projects with the permanent innovation that characterises Barcelona, but also with attention to the insertion into the urban fabric of markets, theatres and the many other episodes that have marked the urban history still reflected in Ciutat Vella.

c) An increase in size of schemes and coordination. The progressive internationalisation of urban interventions has positive aspects to contribute provided they are in keeping with the scale that the city requires. As we have seen, Barcelona is a city with highly specific forms on the basis of which it can operate very efficiently. Cooperation between institutions at administrative level is vital to guarantee the compatibility of large urban projects.

d) The compact city and its evolution. The model of the southern European city has been referred to as the compact city, regarded as having major advantages in terms of historical evolution and sustainability.[54] However, this calls for a discussion of the evolutive models of the compact city. It is necessary to avoid direct associations between compactness and systematic densification, or between compactness and territorial continuity. This requires a new conceptualisation of emerging urban development problems with a view to creating referents or models for discussion to direct subsequent development in the mid-term.[55]

e) Redefinition of the relations between urban planning and action. Barcelona tradition in the modern age has presented a sequence of general-scale plans or projects every 20-25 years. Their effective capacity has varied a great deal according to the political framework, but they still offer reflections on the city and introduce important new urban issues.

The city continues to be a truly complex organism in its definition and administration – urban development is increasing in scope, the actual management of "the urban phenomenon" is increasing in importance. This calls for a reformulation of the concept and content of plans and projects. It does not seem to be the case that the project cancels out the plan to become the omnipresent method. It is however patent that the contents of the project – those forward-looking aspects – have to feed all levels of urban planning formulation to prevent them becoming mere bureaucracy.[56]

---

[54] See, for example, Mike Jenks *et al.*: *The Compact City. A Sustainable Urban Form?*. Oxford, 1996; Katie Williams *et al.*: *Achieving Sustainable Urban Form*. London, 2000, and Hildebrand Frey: *Designing the City*. London, 1999. Of numerous recent publications in support of the necessary sustainability of interventions in the territory, for the case of the Barcelona region, see the very complete *Atles ambiental de l'Àrea de Barcelona*, by J. A. Acebillo and R. Folch, published in 2000 by Ariel Ciencia, Barcelona. In a broader context, see Herbert Girardet: *New directions for sustainable urban living*. London, 1992; *Creating sustainable cities*. Bristol, 1999; Andrew Scott *et al.*: *Dimensions of sustainability*. London, 1998; Joe Ravetz: *City Region 2020: Integrated Planning for a Sustainable Environment*. London, 2000.

[55] Richard Rogers *et al.*: *Towards an Urban Renaissance. Final Report of the Urban Task Force*, London, 1999. A series of works for the urban development restructuring of the United Kingdom, including some criteria already tried and tested in Barcelona, seeking above all to produce a structural interpretation of new urban phenomena.

[56] See by way of reference the work of J. B.: "Urbanism at the turn of the century", *The fifth Van Esteeren lecture*. Bn/SP. Amsterdam, 2000. The strong field of action of the urban development project is being discovered in most European cities. It is therefore vital to understand how, in Barcelona but also in other Spanish and Western cities, these practices can rearm research and methodological definition in the disciplinary field of urban planning, as we celebrate a century of social and administrative recognition. Otherwise, we will reproduce the critical situation of our cities and territories.

73
erview of the Eixample
lay.

f) Urban space and the integration of programmes. Nor must we forget, in our urban experience, how much new projects have to take into account both the existing city and the various social agents that produce proposals. Infrastructure and city, and public, collective and private space have to be analysed and proposed in an integrated approach, as some superb elements of Barcelona have shown. And today's greater complexity or our greater executive capacity must not be used as an excuse for further urban offences such as those that just a few decades ago inundated our cities. In Europe we have seen how the rehabilitation of urban space is a real driving force in the recovery of our cities.[57]

In short, the city will continue to incubate new forms of urban life and provide the foundations for the most advanced of economic activities which, in turn, will ensure its future. My commitment to and affection for the

---

[57] See, among others, Jan Gehl and Lars Gemzoe: *New City Spaces.* Copenhagen, 2001. Also Various authors: *Projets urbains en France,* Paris, 2002.

city in which I have worked for so long may have distorted the orientation of this work; I can only hope that it may be justified by its contribution to Barcelona's being seen in the mid-term as a "city of the future", without visionary philosophising, but simply as a city that continues to be able to create for itself spaces that ensure its enhancement and continuance. In this undertaking, one book can merely contribute to the hope that this is possible.

10.74
Aerial view of Barcelona in th
context of Catalonia.

Maps of the city

Monographic illustrations of the city of Barcelona, its area of influence and/or relevant parts that provide complementary information.

11.1 Ciutat Vella. Built systems, 2000.

11.2 Open and monumental spaces in Ciutat Vella.

11.3 Waterfront development. Infrastructure and phasing. 1985-2004.

11.4 Building in the Eixample, 1983.

11.5 Photomap of Barcelona on four sheets, 2003.

11.6 Outline map of the metropolitan area.

11.7 Outline map of the urban axes of Barcelona.

11.8 The metropolitan region. Uses and forms of building. 2000.

11.9 The metropolitan region. Growth in land occupation. 2000.

11.10, 11.11 The Catalan coastline. Illustration of urban and territorial systems, 1995.

11.12 Landsat-5 satellite image, 2003.

11.1
Ciutat Vella. Built systems,
2000.

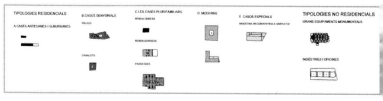

11.2
Open and monumental spaces
in Ciutat Vella.

Squares with
monuments

Squares produced by demolition

Regular spaces

Irregular spaces

Spaces around
the town walls

Gardens

Paths

Newly created streets

Unitarian layouts

Integrated projects

Passages

Street widening and
extension

11.3 Waterfront development. Infrastructure and phasing. 1985-2004.

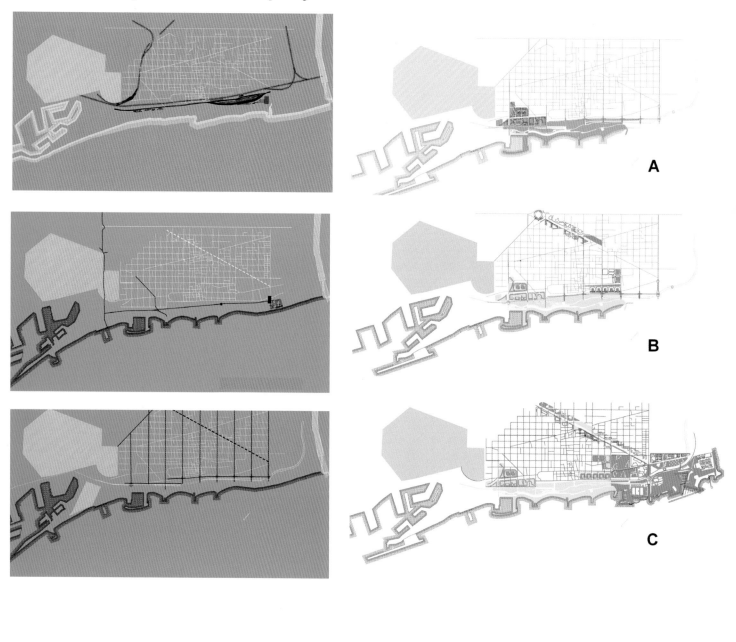

A

B

C

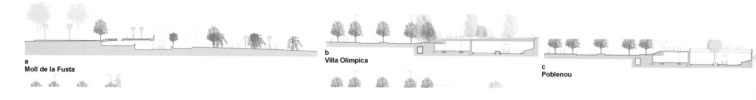

a
Moll de la Fusta

b
Villa Olimpica

c
Poblenou

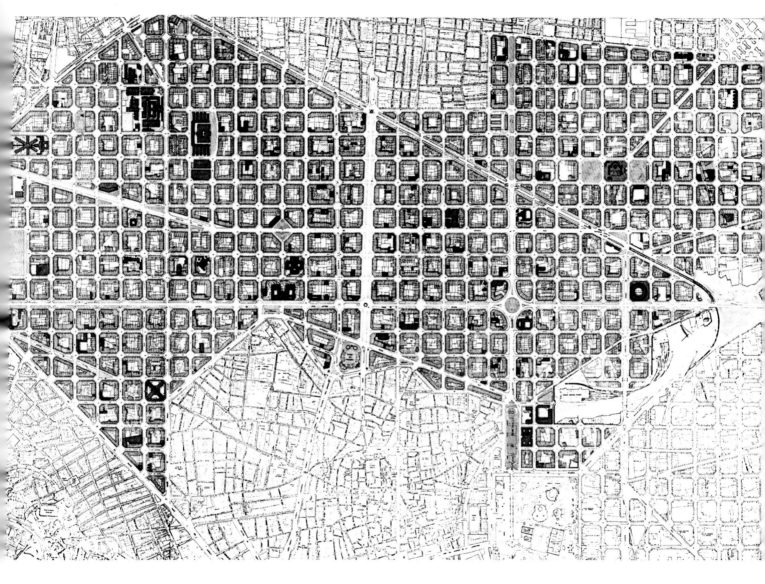

0   800

11.4
Building in the Eixample,
1983.

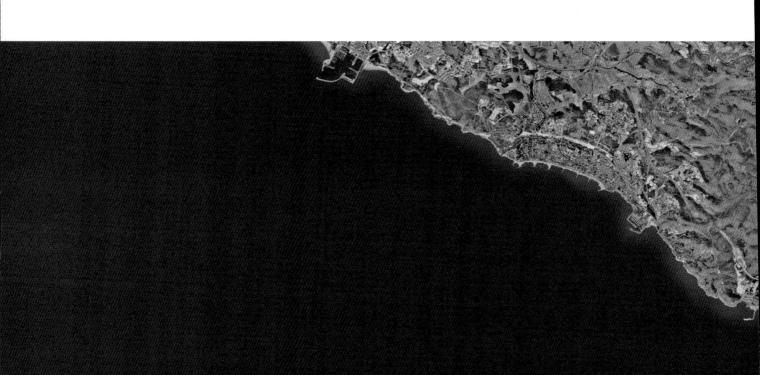

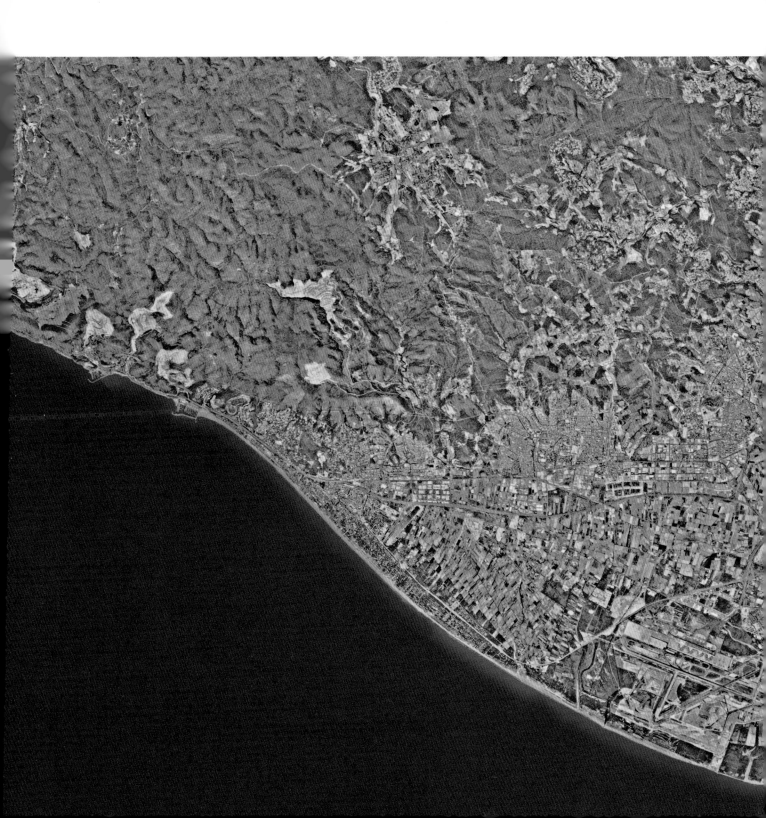

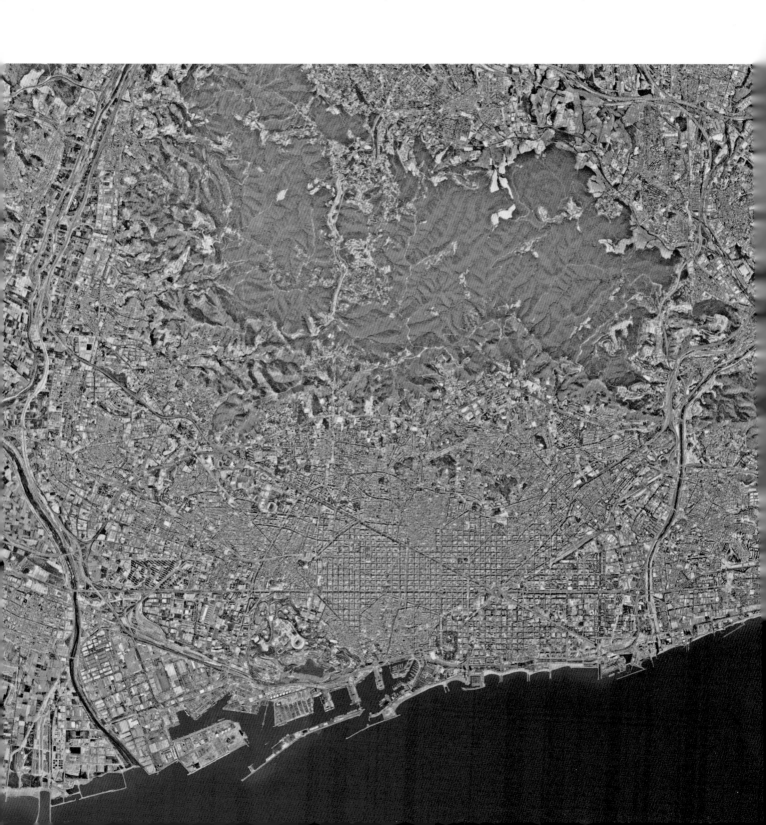

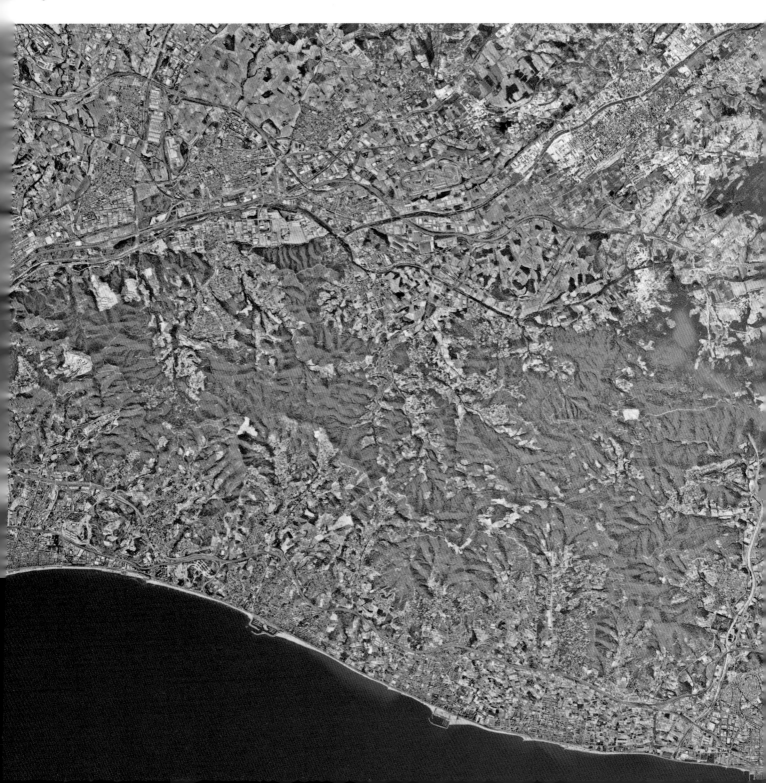

11.9
Outline map of the metropolitan area.

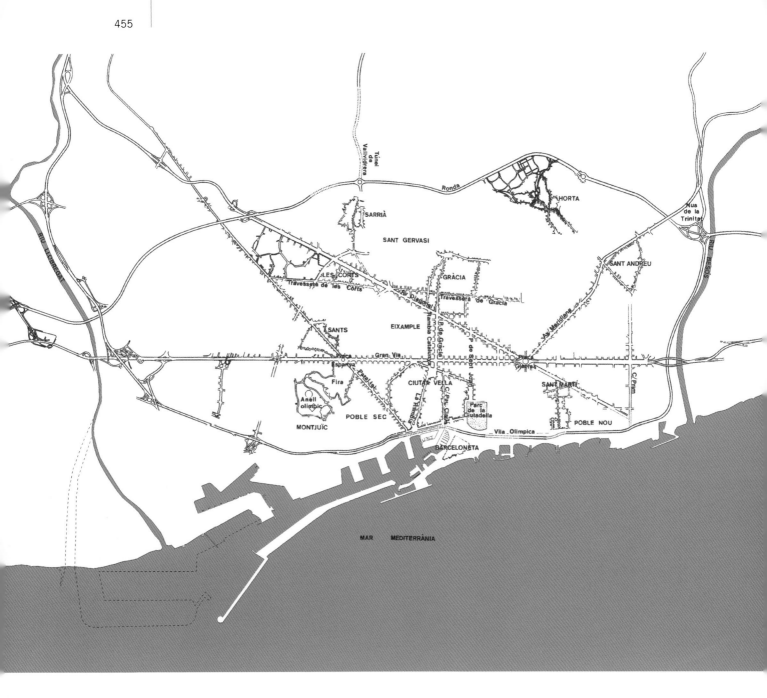

11.10
Outline map of the urban axes of Barcelona.

11.11
The metropolitan region. Uses and forms of building. 2000.

COMUNICACION   EDIFICACION   SUELO

0 1 2 3 4 5   10 Km

N

11.12
The metropolitan region. Growth in land occupation. 2000.

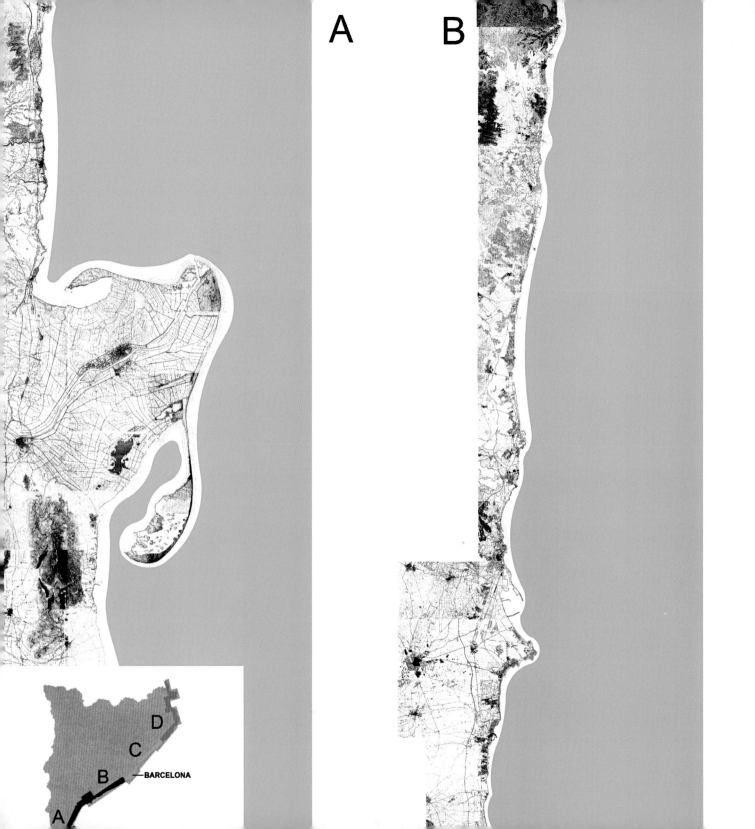

A

B

D

C

—BARCELONA

B

A

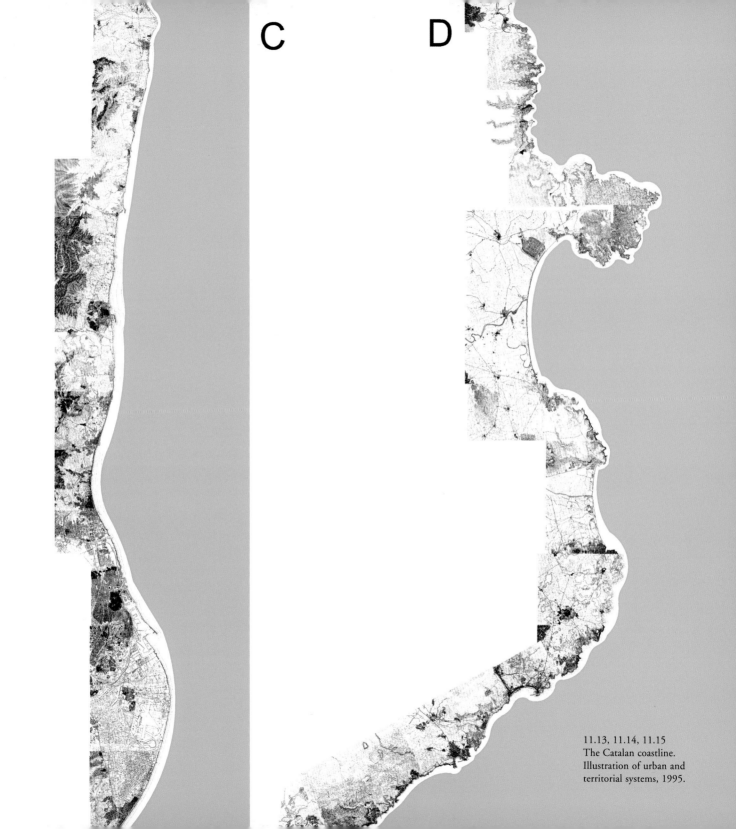

C

D

11.13, 11.14, 11.15
The Catalan coastline.
Illustration of urban and
territorial systems, 1995.

Bibliography

This book includes several hundred footnotes throughout the text with references for further reading about the various episodes. However, listed below are the books that might be considered to be classics in the history of the city.

CARRERAS CANDI, Francesc: 'La ciutat de Barcelona' in *Geografia General de Catalunya*. Barcelona, 1914. An excellent geographical description of the situation of the city in the context of turn-of-the-century Catalonia.

CIRICI, Alexandre: *Barcelona pam a pam*. Barcelona, 1970. An interesting guide to the city organised by walks, with lots of drawings of the buildings and a complete explanation of the episodes in its planning history.

DURAN I SANPERE, Agustí: *Barcelona i la seva història* (3 vol.). Barcelona, 1973. A comprehensive work that brings together dozens of works about the city written between 1917 and 1970, organised in three volumes: the first is devoted to the formation of the big city, the second to the social structure and the third to art and culture.

DURAN I SANPERE, Agustí *et al.*: *Història de Barcelona*. Vol. I 'De la Prehistòria al segle XVI'. Barcelona, 1975. A collective work offering a historical explanation of the various phases of the formation of the city.

GALERA, Montserrat; ROCA, Francesc; TARRAGÓ, Salvador: *Atlas de Barcelona (siglos XVI-XX)*. Barcelona, 1982. Reproduction in a good format of the most important planimetric documentation of the city over a long period.

HERNÁNDEZ CROS, Josep E.; MORA, Gabriel; POUPLANA, Xavier: *Guía de Arquitectura de Barcelona*. Barcelona, 1973. An interesting summary of the city's evolution from the early 18th century, with good graphic documentation.

HUERTAS, Josep Maria: *Els barris de Barcelona* (4 vol.). Barcelona, 1999.

SOBREQUÉS, Jaume *et al.*: *Història de Barcelona* (8 vol.). Barcelona, 1994-98.

VILA, Pau; CASASSAS, Lluís: *Barcelona i la seva rodalia al llarg del temps*. Barcelona, 1974. A comprehensive explanation of the formation and transformation of Barcelona and its most immediate counties.

VILA, Pau: *Barcelona i el seu pla*. Barcelona, 1981. A compilation of works about Barcelona and its most immediate surroundings by the distinguished Catalan geographer.

VILAR, Pierre: *Catalunya dins l'Espanya moderna* (4 vol.) Barcelona, 1966. A vital work of research to understand the geographical and socioeconomic structure of Catalonia and Barcelona's role in the process.

We also recommend other, more specialised books that are referred to in the text:

ACEBILLO, Josep; FOLCH, Ramon: *Atles ambiental de l'Area de Barcelona*, Barcelona, 2000.

ALEMANY, Joan: *El Port de Barcelona. Història i actualitat.* Barcelona, 1984. A comprehensive explanation of the evolution of Barcelona's port, from its origins up until the early 1980s.

ALEMANY, Joan; MESTRE, Jesús: *Els Transports a l'àrea de Barcelona: Diligències, tramvies, autobusos i metro.* Barcelona, 1986. An illustrated summary of public means of transport in the city.

VARIOUS AUTHORS. *Barcelona, la ciutat i el 92.* Barcelona, 1990. Summary of the projects carried out for 1992.

– *Plans cap al 1992.* Barcelona, 1987. A compendium of maps on different scales, drawn for the restructuring of Barcelona.

– *Homenatge a Barcelona. La ciutat i les seves arts 1888-1936.* Barcelona, 1987. A book by various authors, centring on different social and cultural aspects of this dynamic period of the city. It was published as a catalogue to accompany the exhibition that took place in London and Barcelona.

– *AC/GATEPAC. 1931-37.* Barcelona, 1975. Facsimile reproduction of the 25 issues of *AC* magazine, representing an excellent summary of the work of the GATCPAC.

– *Barcelona. La segona renovació.* Barcelona, 1996. Catalogue of the urban planning projects under way since 1992.

– *Barcelona 1979-2004: del desenvolupament a la ciutat de qualitat.* Barcelona, 1999. Catalogue of an exhibition coordinated by Josep Maria Montaner about the most recent urban planning experiences and their immediate prospects.

– *1999. Urbanisme a Barcelona.* Barcelona, 1999. A summary of projects under way at the turn of the century.

BOHIGAS, Oriol. *Reconstrucció de Barcelona.* Barcelona, 1985. A book about the city's urban rehabilitation strategy in the first half of the 1980s.

FABRÉ, Jaume; HUERTAS, Josep Maria: *Tots els barris de Barcelona* (7 vol.) Barcelona, 1976. A series of volumes describing the different neighbourhoods that make up the amalgam of urban fabrics that are Barcelona.

FONT, Antonio; LLOP, Carles; VILANOVA, Josep Maria: *La construcció del territori metropolità*, Barcelona, 1999.

GARCÍA ESPUCHE, Albert; GUÀRDIA, Manuel: *Espai i societat a la Barcelona pre-industrial.* Barcelona, 1986. A comprehensive explanation of the periods of formation of the walled city of Barcelona.

GARCÍA ESPUCHE, Albert; NAVAS, Teresa: *Retrat de Barcelona.* (2 vol.) Barcelona, 1995. The catalogue of an exhibition at the CCCB that presented the changing representations of the city.

GONZÁLEZ, Antoni; LACUESTA, Raquel: *Barcelona. Guía de arquitectura 1929-2000.* Barcelona, 2000. A summary of the main landmarks in Barcelona's architecture since the 1930s.

HEREU, Pere *et al.*: *Arquitectura i Ciutat a l'Exposició Universal de Barcelona 1888.* Barcelona, 1988. A summary of articles about the background and development of the 1888 Great Exhibition.

LABORATORI D'URBANISME: *Treballs sobre Cerdà i Barcelona.* Barcelona, 1992. A collection of articles about the history and development of the excellent project for Barcelona's Eixample.

MARTORELL, Vicente *et al.*: *Historia del Urbanismo en Barcelona. Del Plan Cerdà al Área Metropolitana.* Barcelona, 1970. The evolution of plans for modern Barcelona, particularly from the turn of the century to the 1953 County Plan.

NADAL Jordi; MALUQUER, Jordi: *Catalunya, la fàbrica d'Espanya 1833-1936.* Barcelona, 1985. An excellent summary of a dynamic century in Catalan industrialisation. This was the catalogue of an exhibition held in the Born.

SOLÀ-MORALES, Ignasi de: *L'Exposició Internacional de Barcelona; 1914-1929: Arquitectura i Ciutat.* Barcelona, 1985. A synthetic work about the long process of development and organisation of the 1929 Great Exhibition.

SOLÀ-MORALES, Manuel de: *Les formes del creixement urbà.* LUB-UPC. Barcelona, 1983. A methodological introduction to forms of residential growth, with many references to the case of Barcelona. The 'Architecture Collection' of the Laboratorio de Urbanismo (LUB) includes other books about metropolitan formation.

TORRES, Manuel *et al.*: *Inicis de la Urbanística Municipal de Barcelona. 1750-1930.* Barcelona, 1985. A compendium of documents about the urban planning carried out by the City Council of this period.

– *La formació de la urbanística metropolitana de Barcelona.* Barcelona, 1999. A study of the city's planning proposals since 1930.

VÁZQUEZ MONTALBÁN, Manuel: *Barcelones.* Ed. Empúries. Barcelona, 1987. A synthetic work about the city's historical development up until the 1980s.

On the Barcelona website, produced by the City Council, you will find comprehensive information about urbanism and new projects in the city:
www.bcn.es/urbanisme

Illustration credits

The illustrations of the author and his team are not credited.

P. Frigerio: Antichi Instrumenti Technichi. Como, 1933: 1.04

Museu Arqueològic de Barcelona: 1.09

Biblioteca de Catalunya: 1.10, 2.36

Arxiu Històric de la Ciutat – Institut Municipal d'Història: 1.11, 1.13, 1.24, 1.40, 1.43, 2.02, 2.06, 2.09, 2.13, 2.14, 2.17, 2.20, 2.21, 2.25, 2.32, 2.35, 3.04, 3.06, 3.10, 3.11, 3.12, 3.14, 3.15, 3.18, 3.22, 3.26, 3.33, 3.34, 3.35, 3.41, 3.43, 3.45, 3.46, 3.54, 3.55, 3.71, 3.74, 3.82, 4.01, 4.02, 4.06, 4.07, 4.08, 4.15, 4.43, 4.46, 4.47, 4.48, 4.49. 4.50, 4.55, 5.11, 5.13, 5.14, 5.16, 5.17, 5.40, 5.46, 5.48, 5.69, 5.70, 5.71, 5.73, 5.75, 6.02, 6.17, 7.43, 7.80, 9.37

AHC - Private collection of Ramón Manent: 1.20, 1.21, 4.18, 4.36, 4.37, 4.42, 5.08, 5.45, 6.04, 6.12, 6.14

AHC – Photography Archives: 1.44, 1.45, 4.41, 4.51, 4.52, 4.54, 5.04, 5.05, 5.06, 5.07, 6.03, 5.72, 7.14

AHC – Cerdà Holdings: 3.47, 3.48, 3.49, 3.50, 3.51, 3.52, 3.53, 3.56, 3.57, 3.58, 3.59, 3.60, 3.61, 3.62, 3.63, 3.64, 3.66, 3.68, 3.73, 4.38, 4.39

Bibliothèque nationale de France, Paris: 1.22, 2.16, 3.16

A. Durán i Sanpere: Barcelona i la seva història (3 vol.). Barcelona, 1973: 1.23, 7.02, 7.06

F. Carreras Candi: Les Drassanes Barcelonines. Barcelona, 1928: 1.25, 1.42

F. Carreras Candi: La Ciutat de Barcelona. Barcelona 1914: 1.26

Museu d'Història de la Ciutat: 1.27, 1.28, 1.29, 2.04, 2.05, 2.22, 2.26, 2.31, 3.02, 3.13, 3.21, 3.24, 3.29 ,3.67, 5.01, 7.84

Museu Marítim: 1.37

A. García Espuche, T. Navas: Retrat de Barcelona (2 vol.). Barcelona, 1995: 1.38, 5.10, 5.26, 6,08

A. Cirici i Pellicer: Barcelona pam a pam. Barcelona, 1970: 1.39

MAS Archives, Barcelona: 1.41, 3.05, 5.58, 10.54

S. Vila: La Ciudad de Eiximenis. Valencia, 1984: 1.48

G. Alomar: Urbanismo Regional en la Edad Media: Las 'ordinacions' de Jaume II (1300) en el Reino de Mallorca. Barcelona, 1976: 1.19, 1.49, 1.50

Reial Acadèmia Catalana de Belles Artes de Sant Jordı: 2.03

Historic Archives of Urbanism, Architecture and Design. Col·legi d'Arquitectes de Catalunya: 2.10, 2.18, 5.38, 5.39

P. Figuerola, J. M. Martí: La Rambla. Els seus convents. La seva història. Barcelona, 1995: 2.12

M. Roig, X. Miserachs. Barcelona a vol d'ocell. Barcelona, 1987: 2.15, 5.47, 5.49

Arxiu Històric de l'Hospitalet de Llobregat: 2.19, 10.27

Musée du Louvre, Paris: 2.23

Pusey Map Collection, Cambridge, Mass: 2.24

Museu Militar de Montjuïc: 2.28

S. Sanpere i Miquel: Història de Barcelona, Vol. I: 'De la Prehistòria al segle XVI'. Barcelona, 1975: 2.29

Ajuntament de Barcelona: Plans i Projectes per a Barcelona 1981-1982. Barcelona, 1983: 2.37, 2.38, 9.41, 9.47, 9.68, 9.76

AB: Barcelona, Memoria desde el cielo. Barcelona, 2002: 3.20, 7.07, 9.10, 9.38, 9.44, 9.56, 9.79, 10.14, 10.15, 10.26, 10.38

AB: 'El Parc de la Ciutadella', L'Avenç. Barcelona, 1984: 4.03

Ajuntament de Barcelona, various municipal departments and divisions:4.04, 7.18, 7.26, 7.54, 7.63, 7.87, 8.03, 8.04, 8.06, 8.07, 8.09, 8.11, 9.01, 9.05, 9.06, 9.07, 9.08, 9.09, 9.13, 9.14, 9.16, 9.15, 9.17, 9.19, 9.21, 9.22, 9.23, 9.24, 9.25, 9.26, 9.27, 9.30, 9.40, 9.48, 9.54, 9.55, 9.67, 9.73, 9.74, 9.75, 9.78, 9.80, 9.81, 9.82, 9.83, 9.86, 9.87, 9.89, 9.90, 9.91, 9.97, 9.98, 9.99, 9.103, 9.104, 9.105, 9.109, 9.112, 9.117, 10.01, 10.04, 10.06, 10.10, 10.11 10.12, 10.13, 10.21, 10.23, 10.25, 10.29, 10.30, 10.31, 10.32, 10.33, 10.34, 10.36, 10.39, 10.41, 10.42, 10.43, 10.44, 10.49, 10.52, 10.56, 10.57, 10.58

AB: Pla Especial de l'Equipament Comercial Alimentari de la Ciutat de Barcelona. Barcelona, 1988: 4.33

AB: Retrobar Barcelona. Lunwerg, Barcelona, 1986: 4.40

AB: Les Construccions Escolars de Barcelona. Barcelona, 1923: 5.36, 5.37

AB: Barcelona Espai Públic. Barcelona, 1991: 7.53, 9.11, 9.12, 9.29

AB: Estudi de L'Eixample. Barcelona, 1986: 7.64, 7.65, 7.67, 7.68, 9.59, 9.61

AB, Planning Archives: 8,08

AB: Barcelona, Metròpolis Mediterrània. Barcelona, 2003: 8.24, 8.25, 9.36, 9.115

AB: La Gaceta Ilustrada. Barcelona: 8.30, 8.31, 8.32

AB: Barcelona, Espais i Escultures 1982-1986. Barcelona, 1987: 9,20

AB: Urbanisme a Barcelona. Barcelona, 1999: 9,33, 10.62

AB: Ciutat Vella, Área de Rehabilitación Integrada. Mimeograph, 1989: 9,35

AB: Les Vies de Barcelona, Materials del Seminari. Barcelona, 1984: 9.62, 9.63, 9.64, 9.65, 9.66

AB: Barcelona 1979-2004: Del desenvolupament a la ciutat de qualitat. Barcelona, 1999: 9.70

AB: Àrees de Nova Centralitat. Barcelona, 1985: 9.84, 9.85

AB: 'Barcelona en Joc', CAU. Barcelona, 1986: 9.110, 9.113, 9.114

AB: Barcelona i els jocs olimpics de 1992. Barcelona, 1992: 9,111

Gaspar: Barcelona desde el aire. Barcelona, 1929: 2.37, 2.40, 3.76, 4.44, 5.42

Biblioteca de la Prefectura d'Enginyers: 3.01

ATP Collection, Sant Feliu de Codines: 3.03

Collection of Manufacturas Villadomiu, SA, Barcelona: 3.07

J. Bacardit i Sagüer: Tres Itineraris per la Terrassa Industrial. Museu de la Ciència i de la Tècnica de Catalunya, Terrassa, 1984: 3.08

La Expresión, May 1887: 3.09

A. García Espuche: El Quadrat d'Or. Centre de la Barcelona Modernista. Barcelona, 1990: 3.36,

W. Wolfang: Barcelona 1923-1928. Barcelona, 1993: 3.37, 3.38, 5.34, 5.35, 7.71, 7.72

R. Maristany: Un siglo de Ferrocarril en Catalunya. Barcelona, 1992: 3.40, 3.42, 5.33

Mataró private collection: 3.44

Arxiu Municipal Administratiu de Barcelona: 3.65

Laboratori d'Urbanisme de Barcelona: 3.75, 3.80, 3.81, 3.83, 3.84, 3.85, 6.15, 6.16, 7.01, 7.09, 7.10, 7.11, 7.17, 7.21, 7.22, 7.23, 7.24, 7.25, 7.28, 7.29, 7.30, 7.31, 7.32, 7.33, 7.34, 7.35, 7.37, 7.38, 7.39, 7.40, 7.41, 7.45, 7.46, 7.47, 7.48, 7.49, 7.50, 7.55, 7.56, 7.58, 7.66, 7.76, 7.77, 7.81, 7.82, 7.83, 8.35, 8.38, 8.39, 8.43, 8.44, 8.45, 8.46

Centre de Cultura Contemporània de Barcelona: 3.86, 5.15,

J. Alemany, J. Mestre: Els Transports a l'Area de Barcelona. Barcelona, 1986: 4.09, 4.53, 5.44, 7.13

P. Hereu: Arquitectura i Ciutat a l'Exposició Universal de Barcelona. Barcelona, 1988: 4.10, 4.11, 4.12, 4.13, 4.14, 4.16, 5.19

O. Tusquets: Palau de la Música. Barcelona, 2000: 4.19, 4.20, 4.21, 4.22

Ll. Doménech i Montaner: Hospitales de la Santa Cruz y de San Pablo. Barcelona, 1903: 4.23

C. Martinell: Gaudí. Barcelona, 1967: 4.24, 4.25, 4.26, 4.27, 4.30, 4.31, 5.52, 5.53

J. Roher, I. de Solà Morales: Puig i Cadafalch. Barcelona, 1989: 4.32, 5.24, 5.25,

Museu d'Art Modern: 4.35

Museu Gaudí: 4.28, 4.29, 4.45, 5.50, 5.54

PROCIVESA: 5.02, 10.02

Museu Picasso de Barcelona: 5.09

Diputació de Barcelona: 5.18

Private collection of Joan Prats: 5.27

D. Giralt-Miracle: Avantguardes a Catalunya, 1906-1939. Barcelona, 1992: 5.28, 5.29, 5.30, 5.31, 6.06, 6.41, 6.43

Archives of S.A. El Tibidabo: 5.41

Joan Villoro: Guia dels espais verds de Barcelona. COAC, Barcelona, 1984: 5.55, 5.56

C. Soldevila: Guía de Barcelona. Ed. Destino, 1951: 5.57

I. Solà Morales: L'Exposició Universal de Barcelona; 1914-29. Arquitectura i Ciutat. Barcelona, 1985: 5.59, 5.60, 5.61, 5.64, 5.67, 5.74, 5.76

E. Roca: Montjuïc, La Muntanya de la Ciutat. Barcelona, 1984: 5.62

MOMA Archives: 5.63, 5.65

M. Galera et al.: Atlas de Barcelona. COACB, Barcelona, 1972: 5.68

N. Rubió i Tudurí: La Barcelona Futura. Barcelona, 1930: 5.77

GATCPAC Archives: 6.01, 6.22, 6.23, 6.24, 6.30, 6.31, 6.33, 6.34, 6.35, 6.36, 6.37, 8.12, 8.13, 8.14

Private collection of J. Suñol: 6.05, 6.07

Generalitat de Catalunya: El Pla de Distribució en Zones del Territori Català ('Regional Planning'). Barcelona, 1932: 6.09, 6.10, 6.11

Fondation Le Corbusier, Paris: 6.18, 6.19, 6.20, 6.21, 6.26, 6.27, 6.28, 6.29

Museo Nacional Reina Sofía, Madrid: 6.38, 6.39, 6.40, 6.42

Quaderns, Col·legi d'Arquitectes de Catalunya: 7.04, 7.15, 7.27, 7.36, 8.15

Comissió d'Urbanisme de Barcelona, Corporacio Metropolitana de Barcelona: 7.05, 8.01, 8.05, 8.10, 8.26, 8.27, 8.28, 8.29, 8.41, 8.42, 9.02, 10.28, 10.47, 10.48, 10.63

M. Andreu, J. M. Huertas: La Ciudad Transportada. Barcelona, 1997: 7.19

Private collection of J. A. Solsona: 7.20

CAU magazine, Barcelona. Col·legi d'Arquitectes Tècnics de Catalunya: ⁻.52, 8.33, 8.34

F. Terán: Planeamiento Urbano en la España Contemporánea. Barcelona, 1978: 8.02

Wigley Mark, Wite de With: Constant's New Babylon, The Hyper Architecture of Derive. Rotterdam, 1998: 8.23

Various authors: Antonio Bonet. Barcelona, 1996: 8.36, 8.37, 8.40

I. de Solà-Morales, Ll. Dilme, X. Fabré: L'Arquitectura del Liceu. UPC, Barcelona, 2000: 10.05

Papers 24. Barcelona, 1995: 10.08

J. B. et al.: Coast Wise Europe. Rotterdam, 1994: 10.09

Archives of La Vanguardia, Barcelona: 10.37

Novetats Catalunya no. 2: 10.55, 10.67

Ch. Jensen Butler et al.: European Cities in Competition. Aldershot, 1997: 10.59

J. Acebillo, R. Folch: Atles Ambiental de l'Àrea de Barcelona. Barcelona, 2003: 10.60, 10.64

M. Echenique, A. Saint: Cities for the New Millennium. London, 2001: 10.61

Various authors: Transformacions Urbanes. COAC, Barcelona, 1997: 10.69, 10.71

Institut Cartogràfic de Catalunya, Landstad 5: 10.74, 11.5, 11.12, Book cover.

A, Font, C. Llop, J. M. Vilanova: La Construcció del Territori Metropolità. Barcelona, 1998 (drawings updated in 2000): 11.11 11.12

Various authors: Les formes urbanes del litoral català. Diputació de Barcelona, 2003: 11.13, 11.14

Printed in May 2006
by Litografia Stella, Rovereto (Tn) - Italy